FINANCIAL CLAIMS AND DERIVATIVES

DAVID N. KING

Department of Economics,
University of Stirling, Stirling FK9 4LA

INTERNATIONAL THOMSON BUSINESS PRESS
I ⓉP® An International Thomson Publishing Company

London • Bonn • Johannesburg • Madrid • Melbourne • Mexico City • New York • Paris
Singapore • Tokyo • Toronto • Albany, NY • Belmont, CA • Cincinnati, OH • Detroit, MI

Financial Claims and Derivatives

British Library Cataloguing-in Publication Data
A catalogue record for this book is available from the British Library

First edition published 1999

Typeset by The Florence Group, Stoodleigh, Devon
Printed in the UK by The Alden Press, Osney Mead, Oxford

ISBN 1-86152-448-X

International Thomson Business Press
Berkshire House
168–173 High Holborn
London WC1V 7AA
UK

http://www.itpb.com

To my students in finance, especially
Ioannis Gatzoflias and Lorraine O'Neill,
whose questions caused this book to be written.

CONTENTS

7 FACTORS AFFECTING OPTION PRICES

8 MODELS FOR ESTIMATING OPTION PRICES

9 SWAPS

INDEX

PREFACE

In recent years there have been many developments in the variety and use of financial instruments. The chief aim of this book is to explain the main instruments that are in use in the United Kingdom today. In explaining these instruments, I have tried to follow four principles:

- to use a clear, straightforward and jargon-free approach;
- to assume no prior knowledge of economics or finance;
- to use numerous examples, many of them simple hypothetical ones, to aid understanding;
- to illustrate the text with numerous examples of information published in the press.

My examples of published information cover virtually all the types of information that appear in the financial press or on the television text pages.

Financial instruments may usefully be divided into financial claims and financial derivatives. The book begins with two chapters on claims and ends with six chapters on derivatives; in between, there is a chapter on the returns from securities and portfolios.

Chapter 1 looks at financial claims in general while Chapter 2 looks more closely at securities which form a very important type of claim. Chapter 3 looks at the returns from securities and at portfolios of securities; its treatment is relatively brief and is intended to enable some references to be made to the theory in other chapters rather than as a full introduction to portfolio theory and practice.

The six chapters on derivatives are Chapter 4, which considers forwards, Chapter 5, which considers futures, Chapters 6, 7 and 8, which all consider options, and Chapter 9, which considers swaps. These six chapters focus chiefly on financial derivatives, which are contracts that concern financial claims, but they also look at commodity derivatives which are contracts that concern commodities.

I am very grateful to Simon King for reading a preliminary version of the text, and to Ioannis Gatzoflias for reading the draft of this version; both of them made many invaluable comments. I also wish to thank Laurence Copeland, Eric Levin, Lorraine O'Neill and Robin Ruffell for kindly discussing numerous points with me, as well as Roger Hurst of LIFFE, Keith White of LME, and several members of the Bank of Scotland's Treasury, for answering a number of very tedious queries. Finally, I am grateful to my wife Susan, and my editor Maggie Smith, for patiently tolerating my repeated hopes that 'the book should be finished next week' over a period of several months.

David King
Stirling, May 1998

1 FINANCIAL CLAIMS

1.1 WHAT ARE FINANCIAL CLAIMS?

From time to time, everyone wants to spend at a level beyond their income. Each year, this situation confronts many households and companies, and it also usually confronts the central government and many local governments. The households, companies and governments concerned are called **deficit units**. To solve their financial problems, they have to obtain funds from other households, companies or governments which want to spend at a level below their income. These other units are called **surplus units**. Most financial claims arise when funds pass from surplus units to deficit units, for the surplus units then acquire some sort of claim on the deficit units.

This passing of funds is of great importance, chiefly because it enables deficit units to make purchases which otherwise they could not afford. For example, it helps them to acquire items such as homes and cars, factories and shops, and hospitals and schools. The passing of funds also enables surplus units to earn a financial return on their savings. Because financial claims lie at the heart of this important passing of funds, they are themselves of considerable significance.

Topics covered in this chapter

Section 1.2 explains the relationship between financial claims and balance sheets. Section 1.3 looks briefly at financial intermediaries, which are businesses that are involved with many financial claims. Section 1.4 looks at the units or parties who hold financial claims, and at the relationship between their financial claims and their wealth. Sections 1.5 to 1.8 look at the main types of financial claim. They do this by taking in turn the claims that are held against different types of unit or party. So Section 1.5 looks at the claims that are held against households, Section 1.6 at the claims that are held against central and local governments, Section 1.7 at the claims that are held against companies (other than those which are financial intermediaries) and Section 1.8 at the claims that are held against financial intermediaries. Section 1.9 explains why the interest rates on some financial claims vary according to the period of time covered by the claim. Finally, Section 1.10 explains what is meant by the prefix Euro which occurs on some financial claims.

1.2 FINANCIAL CLAIMS AND BALANCE SHEETS

To understand the nature of financial claims, it is helpful to begin by looking at a **balance sheet**. Table 1.1 gives as an example the balance sheet for a hypothetical company, LML plc. The balance sheet was drawn up on 30 June 1998. It uses typical terminology, but it is a little simpler than many published balance sheets. Also, it is shown without the extensive notes that accompany published balance sheets to give further details of each entry.

The main sections of a balance sheet

LML's balance sheet has nine sections. The first two sections show the items which were owned by LML on 30 June 1998. These are its **assets**, and they fall into two groups.

The first group of assets, **fixed assets**, comprises items that LML generally expects to keep for over a year. The main examples are **tangible assets** which include land and buildings, plant and machinery, tools and vehicles, and fixtures and fittings. LML also has some **intangible assets** such as patents, trade-marks and brand names, all of which help it to sell its products; but these items appear on its balance sheet only if LML bought them from other firms. In addition, LML has some **fixed-asset investments**, which include the value of any subsidiary businesses it owns.

The second group of assets, **current assets**, contains items which usually have a high rate of turnover. First, there are **stocks**, which include stocks of raw materials and finished goods together with the value of any work in progress on unfinished products. Secondly, there are **debtors**, an item which covers any money that is owed to LML. Some of this owed money may be accounted for by loans that LML has made, for the borrowers must pay LML back at some future date, but probably most of this owed money is accounted for by trade debt and accrued income. **Trade debt** arises when LML has supplied some of its customers with products but has not yet been paid by them because they have not yet attended to its invoices; in some cases this may be because LML has agreed that payment need not be made at once. **Accrued income** arises when LML is owed any other income: this will include the interest due shortly on any loans that it has made, together with any money due from customers who have accounts with LML and who have received products from LML

Table 1.1 Balance sheet for LML plc as at 30 June 1998

Item	(£m)	Financial asset or financial liability?
1 Fixed assets		
Tangible assets	600	
Intangible assets	10	
Fixed-asset investments	70	
	680	
2 Current assets		
Stocks	50	
Debtors	150	Financial asset
Short-term investments	100	Financial asset
Cash at bank and in hand	20	Financial asset
	320	
3 Current liabilities – amounts due within one year		
Short-term borrowings	(150)	Financial liability
Other current creditors	(50)	Financial liability
	(200)	
4 Net current assets (= 2 – 3)	120	
5 Total assets less current liabilities (= 1 + 4)	800	
6 Non-current liabilities – amounts due after more than one year		
Medium- and long-term borrowings	45	Financial liability
Other non-current creditors	5	Financial liability
	50	
7 Provisions for liabilities and charges	5	
	5	
8 Capital and reserves		
Called-up share capital	100	Financial liability[1]
Share premium account	150	Financial liability[1]
Profit and loss account	470	
Revaluation reserve	25	
Total shareholders' funds	745	
9 = 6 + 7 + 8	**800**	

[1]LML does not have to repay these sums, but they are regarded here as financial liabilities because they are also financial assets to other parties.

but who have not yet been invoiced by LML. Thirdly, there are **short-term investments**, which include the value of any securities which LML might own. Securities are discussed at length in Chapter 2; one example would be shares in other companies. Fourthly, there is the value of LML's **cash at bank and in hand**, which covers its bank deposits and any notes and coins it holds.

The total value of LML's assets is £680m plus £320m, or £1,000m in all. However, this figure gives a generous view of what LML is worth because LML also owes some money to other people. The balance sheet allows for this partly in section 3, called **current liabilities**. These liabilities show the money which

LML owes to others and which it must pay within the next year. This money falls into two groups. First, there are **short-term borrowings,** which cover loans that must be repaid within one year. These loans might include money borrowed from the bank along with money borrowed by issuing certain types of security which have to be repaid within one year. Secondly, there are **other current creditors,** which cover any money owed to other businesses as trade credit and accruals together with any money owed to the government. **Trade credit** arises when LML has been supplied with products but has not yet paid for them because it has not yet attended to the invoices; in some cases the suppliers may have agreed that payment need not be made at once. **Accruals** arise when LML owes other sums within the next year. For example, it may have to pay some interest on loans that have been made to it, and it may have accounts for items such as electricity and telephone calls, so that it owes money for items that have been already used even though the invoices have not yet arrived. As for the central government, LML doubtless owes some national insurance contributions, which it has to pay on behalf of its employees, and it doubtless owes some value added tax and some corporation tax, which is a tax on company profits.

The values of LML's current liabilities are printed in brackets to show that they should be deducted from the value of its assets to give a better view of its worth. The way this deduction is done is to deduct the total value of current liabilities, £200m, from the total value of current assets, £320m, and so produce a figure of £120m which is shown in section 4 as **net current assets**. This £120m is then added to the £680m for fixed assets to give a figure of £800m, which is shown in section 5 as **total assets less current liabilities**. Essentially, sections 6, 7 and 8 show how this worth of £800m was financed, a point confirmed in section 9 which shows these three sections totalling £800m.

Section 6 covers **non-current liabilities**. These are the sums that LML owes to others but need not pay to them for at least one year. They mostly comprise **medium- and long-term borrowings** which cover all loans due for repayment after one year, including any types of security that must be repaid after one year. Non-current liabilities also cover **other non-current creditors** which would include, for example, any trade credit or tax payments due after one year.

LML has also obtained funds by retaining some of the profits it has made in its lifetime. It will have been unable to retain all its profits because some will have been paid as dividends to its shareholders and some will have been paid as corporation tax to the government. One small part of the profits that it has retained is shown in section 7 as **provisions for liabilities and charges**. This covers sums set aside for specific purposes such as, perhaps, restructuring costs or redundancy payments.

Section 8, called **capital and reserves**, shows the other sources of funds available to LML. £250m has been raised by selling securities called shares to LML's owners, but this £250m is divided into **called-up share capital** and **share premium account**. Suppose that LML initially raised £50m by selling 50 million shares at £1 each, calling them naturally enough '£1 shares'. And suppose that many years later, when these shares were being traded on the stock exchange at £4, LML raised a further £200m by selling 50 million more shares at £4 each. LML doubtless decreed that the new shares would be given identical dividends to the old ones, so it still called them '£1 shares'. The total face value of LML's shares is £100m, for it has sold 100m £1 shares. This figure is shown as the called-up share capital. But LML has actually raised £250m by selling shares, and the remaining £150m of this sum is shown by the item share premium account. The next item, **profit and loss account**, covers all LML's retained profits except the £5m shown in section 7. Finally, there is a **revaluation reserve** which is simply a bookkeeping item. Suppose LML finds that some of its assets, such as its land and buildings, have recently risen in value, and suppose it wants to include the new value in item 1 of the balance sheet. Then the total value of item 5 will also rise. This means that the value of item 9 will be less than the value of item 5 unless some other change is made. So LML will raise the value of the revaluation reserve by just enough to ensure that item 9 now equals the new item 5. Finally, note that the total value of section 8 is called **total shareholders' funds**.

Financial assets, financial liabilities and financial claims

The final column of Table 1.1, which would not appear in a published balance sheet, shows that some of LML's assets can be regarded as **financial assets**. The crucial characteristic of these assets is that, unlike the other assets, they also show up as liabilities in someone else's balance sheet, where they are regarded as **financial liabilities**. Table 1.1 shows that LML has some financial liabilities of its own, and these will show up as financial assets in someone else's balance sheet.

To explore this further, consider LML's financial assets. The loans covered by the term debtors will show up as liabilities in sections 3 and 6 of the balance sheets of those who owe money to LML, just as any money owed by LML is included as liabilities in sections 3 and 6 of its balance sheet. Also, LML's current asset investments, which take the form of securities, will show up as liabilities in sections 3, 6 and 8 of the balance sheets of those who issued the securities, just as any securities issued by LML are included as liabilities in sections 3, 6 and 8 of its balance sheet. LML's bank deposit is a liability to the bank where it is held, for LML could demand its repayment by the bank. Finally, LML's cash in the form of notes are liabilities to the Bank of England or any Scottish or Northern Irish bank whose notes it holds, while its coins add to the Bank of England's liabilities.

Financial claims and financial instruments

As anything which is a financial asset to one party is also a financial liability to another party, it can be misleading to call it simply a financial asset *or* a financial liability, for each of these terms covers only part of its nature. Consequently, the more general term **financial claim** is often used instead.

Financial claims form an important group of items called **financial instruments**. There is a second group of financial instruments called **financial**

derivatives. These differ from financial claims in two ways. First, and most critically, financial derivatives are contracts that concern, or derive from, financial claims: so while it would be possible to have a world with financial claims but no financial derivatives, it would not be possible to have a world with financial derivatives but no financial claims. Secondly, while a party's financial claims should all show up on its balance sheet, a party's financial derivatives rarely do, so they are often called **off balance sheet items**. The chief reason that derivatives make little appearance on balance sheets is that they are usually agreements to make purchases or sales in future and are therefore simply promises. Chapters 4–9 look at financial derivatives, and they also look at the only other sorts of derivatives which concern commodities.

1.3 FINANCIAL INTERMEDIATION

Financial intermediaries

Most financial claims arise when funds pass to an individual deficit unit, that is a household, company or government which is short of funds, from a surplus unit which has funds to spare. Sometimes surplus units transfer funds directly to deficit units, and sometimes they place their funds with a financial intermediary; then the financial intermediary transfers the funds to deficit units, either directly or through one or more other financial intermediaries.

The **financial intermediaries** which undertake this **financial intermediation** are frequently divided into **banks** and **non-bank financial intermediaries** (NBFIs). There are many types of NBFI including the following:

1. **Building societies.** These resemble banks except that their lending is chiefly confined to people who wish to buy or improve homes.
2. **Discount houses.** These mostly borrow short-term loans from other financial intermediaries, and then buy securities and make loans of their own.
3. **Finance houses.** These borrow from other financial intermediaries and then make loans to companies and households.
4. **Investment trusts.** These are companies which raise money from shareholders and then, instead of using it to buy fixed assets with which they will themselves produce products, they use it to buy securities. They are discussed further in Section 2.6.
5. **Life insurance companies.** These usually handle both life insurance policies and pension funds. They use the funds they receive to buy securities and make loans.
6. **Unit trusts.** These closely resemble investment trusts except that they secure funds by selling units rather than shares.

The advantages of financial intermediation

Financial intermediaries make profits by paying lower rates of return to surplus units than the rates they want from deficit units. This raises the question of why surplus units do not pass their funds directly to deficit units, for all units would gain if they cut out the intermediaries and agreed a rate in between those applied by the intermediaries. In fact, funds do sometimes pass directly from surplus units to deficit units, for example when companies and governments offer securities to the public. But financial intermediation is very common and it occurs because it offers three major advantages.

First, surplus units often wish to lend short while deficit units often wish to borrow long. These requirements can be met by using financial intermediaries. A classic example is a building society, which borrows money by taking deposits that can be withdrawn on demand and yet lends money to home-buyers for periods of many years. The society transforms short-term loans from depositors into long-term loans to home-buyers. This advantage of intermediation is called **maturity transformation**.

Secondly, many surplus units have only small sums to lend, whereas many deficit units wish to borrow large sums. It would be tedious for deficit units to seek out many individual surplus units. Instead, deficit units may prefer to approach one financial intermediary which can pool the resources of many small lenders. This advantage of intermediation is called **aggregation**.

Thirdly, a surplus unit with modest funds may be reluctant to transfer them all to one deficit unit which might default. It would be safer for a surplus unit to spread its funds among a number of different deficit units, and so spread out the risk, but it would require a lot of effort for an individual surplus unit to seek out numerous deficit units, check their credit-worthiness, and then pass them each tiny funds. By placing its funds with a financial intermediary which spreads them among many deficit units, individuals effectively spread their risks among those many deficit units. Also, the intermediary can check the credit-worthiness of each one on behalf of all the people who place funds with it. A few deficit units will still default, but the effects on the individual surplus unit who places funds with the intermediary will be negligible. This advantage of intermediation is called **risk transformation**.

Risk transformation has two important implications. First, by making it safer for surplus units to save, intermediaries encourage them to save more, which means that more funds become available to deficit units. Secondly, intermediaries can afford to make a few very risky loans which individual lenders might never make, so they may support projects that might otherwise not receive finance.

Some key bank interest rates

Banks are very important financial intermediaries. Banks receive deposits, which are essentially short-term loans to them, and then make longer-term loans to borrowers. It is useful to note some key interest rates which are applied by the banks. The best known are **base rates**. Many bank deposit rates are linked to their base rates, though the deposit rates are lower; and many bank loan rates are linked to their base rates, though the loan rates are higher. Banks change their base rates infrequently. They are most likely to change them when they feel that interest rates generally will move slightly higher or lower for some time to come.

Banks do not link all their interest rates to their base rates. For example, the interest rates on some large bank deposits, and also the interest rates on many large bank loans, are instead linked to the **interbank interest rates** which banks offer on deposits from other banks and which they charge on loans to other banks. Banks often do pass funds between themselves, in what is called the **interbank market**, for often some banks have surplus funds while others are short of funds. Table 1.2 gives some examples of the interest rates that applied to sterling on the London interbank market at the close of business on 21 May 1998. The figures cover loans of different lengths, and there is a pair of interest rates for each length.

Table 1.2 Examples of interbank interest rates (end of 21 May 1998)

	Overnight	Seven days	One month	Three months	Six months	One year
Interbank (£)	8⅜–7	7½–7⅛	7⁷⁄₁₆–7⁵⁄₁₆	7¹⁷⁄₃₂–7¹³⁄₃₂	7¹⁷⁄₃₂–7¹³⁄₃₂	7¹⁷⁄₃₂–7¹³⁄₃₂

Except for overnight loans, the higher rates in the pairs shown in Table 1.2 are the rates which London banks charged on various length large loans to other London banks that wanted to borrow from them at the close of business on 21 May. These are the **London interbank offered rates** (LIBOR). There is a usually a slightly different LIBOR for each length loan, but people often use the term LIBOR on its own to refer to the three-month rate or the six-month rate. Also, except for overnight loans, the lower rates in the pairs are those which London banks paid on various length large deposits placed at the end of the day by other London banks. These are the **London interbank bid rates** (LIBID). LIBID rates are usually about ⅛% below the LIBOR rates, which means there is usually **bid-offer spread** of about ⅛%. This spread is very narrow. Banks charge higher rates on virtually all the other loans they make that are linked to LIBOR rates, and they pay lower rates on many of the deposits whose rates are linked to LIBID rates. The table implies that there is a much wider spread of 1⅜% on overnight loans. In fact, overnight loans do usually have a wider spread, but most of the apparently wide spread in the table is due to the fact that the overnight figures there record the highest and lowest rates of the day, not the closing figures.

Unlike base rates, LIBOR and LIBID rates change hourly. Suppose a bank borrowed £10m for 12 months at the close of business on 21 May when the relevant LIBOR was 7¹⁷⁄₃₂%. It would have agreed to pay £753,125 interest at the end of the year. But if it had borrowed an hour earlier, then it might have found that the 12-month LIBOR was only 7½%. In that case, it could have borrowed at that rate and would have to pay only £750,000 in interest at the end of the year.

1.4 PARTIES WITH FINANCIAL CLAIMS AND THEIR WEALTH

Parties who may hold financial claims

Anyone can hold a financial claim or have a claim held against themselves. For example, even a toddler might have a little cash in hand, and he might owe his mother some money which she has lent him against next week's pocket money. It is useful to divide the parties who may hold claims, or who may have claims held against them, into households, governments, companies and financial intermediaries. Any one party can hold claims against other members of the same group as well as against members of other groups. Thus an individual company can hold claims against other companies as well as against households, governments and financial intermediaries.

Financial claims and wealth

To estimate the **wealth** of any unit, such as a household, a government, a company or a financial intermediary, it is necessary to add up the current value of its assets and then deduct the current value of its financial liabilities. In the case of a government, for example, the assets would include fixed assets such as buildings and computers, along with financial assets such as bank deposits and cash in hand. Against these assets must be deducted the current value of any financial liabilities, such as loans made to the government and any securities that it has issued. For governments, and indeed for other units, balance sheets would be useful in listing the assets and financial liabilities to include. Unfortunately, however, balance sheets would rarely give the correct current values, for balance sheets seek chiefly to show what has been done with the money that units have had at their disposal in the past. So they often record the purchase costs of assets rather than current values.

Nevertheless, there are official statistics which estimate the current values of the assets and the financial liabilities for the four groups of units. The figures for 31 December 1996 are summarised in Table 1.3. The figures apply to each group as a whole. This means, for example, that the figures for households exclude any financial claims that are held by some households against other households. Unfortunately, these official statistics are not quite complete because some types of wealth are omitted. For example, the figures for households omit the value of their consumer durables such as cars and furniture, the figures for governments omit military hardware such as warships and tanks, and the figures for companies omit the value of subsoil deposits such as oil and natural gas (for further details, see HMSO, 1987).

It will be seen that households as a whole have financial assets whose value, £2,126.1bn, far exceeds the £583.3bn value of their financial liabilities. This gives them a positive **net financial wealth** of £1,542.8bn which is actually worth more than their non-financial assets. The fact that households have a positive net financial wealth implies that they are typically surplus units. On the other hand, governments as a whole, and companies as a whole, have financial assets whose values are well below the values of their financial liabilities.

Table 1.3 United Kingdom net wealth, 31 December 1996

	Sector				
	Households	Governments – central and local	Companies – except financial intermediaries	Financial inter- mediaries	Total for United Kingdom
Item	(£bn)	(£bn)	(£bn)	(£bn)	(£bn)
Non-financial assets	1,448.9	345.8	889.1	109.9	2,793.6
Financial assets	2,126.1	159.5	509.4	4,017.5	1,665.8
Financial liabilities	−583.3	−485.4	−1,621.2	−4,119.6	−1,662.7
Net financial wealth	1,542.8	−325.8	−1,111.8	−102.1	3.1
Net wealth	2,991.7	20.0	−222.7	7.8	2,796.7

Source: *United Kingdom National Accounts – the Blue Book – 1997 edition* (London: HMSO), 137–47.

So they have a negative net financial wealth, which implies that they are typically deficit units. For financial intermediaries, the values of financial assets and financial liabilities are very comparable.

The final column of Table 1.3 shows figures for the United Kingdom as a whole. However, this column ignores all financial claims which are held by one United Kingdom unit against another, so that it covers only those claims that are held by United Kingdom units against the rest of the world, and vice versa. It can be seen that the value of the United Kingdom's final **net wealth** is very little higher than the value of its non-financial assets. This is because most of the financial assets belonging to any units in the United Kingdom are also financial liabilities to other units in the United Kingdom. The only reason that the United Kingdom has any net financial wealth at all is that its units have between them more financial assets than financial liabilities, which implies that the converse must be true for the rest of the world as a whole.

If a table like Table 1.3 was prepared for the whole world, then its final column would show that the total net financial wealth of the entire world was zero. In other words, the value of the world's wealth exactly equals the value of its non-financial assets and is not increased by one pennyworth through the addition of financial assets. This is because every financial asset that adds to one unit's wealth is simultaneously a financial liability that reduces another unit's wealth. This result may make it seem that financial claims are unimportant, but this is not so. Without using financial claims, households, companies and governments would find it very hard to finance their purchases of fixed assets. In turn, they would find it very hard to create wealth.

Listing the main types of financial claim

The following four sections outline the main types of financial claim. They do so by taking in turn households, governments, companies and financial intermediaries and looking at the financial claims that may be held against the parties concerned. Only two types of claim mentioned in these sections are **marketable claims**, which means that they can be traded on established second-hand markets. These types are securities and certificates of deposit (CDs). Securities are discussed at greater length in Chapter 2.

1.5 THE MAIN CLAIMS HELD AGAINST HOUSEHOLDS

The main types of claim that can be held against households fall into six groups.

Bank advances

First, there are **bank advances**. These come in three main forms: overdrafts, personal loans and mortgages. An **overdraft** is a loan whose amount is just sufficient to prevent the borrower's deposit from going below zero. The sum borrowed rises and falls as and when the borrower debits or credits the deposit concerned, and interest is due on the fluctuating amount borrowed. The interest rates that banks charge on overdrafts are related to their current base rate but are always well above their base rate. In principle, they add different amounts to their base rate for different customers according to their perceived credit-worthiness, but in practice they apply a standard amount for most personal customers. However, they do charge much higher rates for any depositors who run up overdrafts without prior agreement. Banks change their base rates fairly infrequently, but because their base rates often change over the life of an overdraft, overdrafts are said to be charged interest at a **floating rate**.

With a **personal loan**, a bank customer agrees to borrow a fixed sum, say £1,200, and also agrees a repayment schedule which might, for example, involve repaying £100 a month over the next year. Some personal loans are made for as long as 10 years. Interest is charged at a **fixed rate** that is agreed in advance. The rate on a personal loan is linked to the base rate at the time when the loan is made, but it is always higher than the base rate. The addition is measured in terms of **basis points**. For example, if the addition in the case of one borrower is 800 basis points, then that borrower will pay a rate that is 8% above base rate, each basis point adding 0.01%. The number of basis points on a loan may depend a little on the length of the loan and on the amount borrowed, but it will depend chiefly on the credit-worthiness of the borrower. The stated interest rates on personal loans often look deceptively low because they may not be the actual interest rates. This arises because the stated rates are sometimes expressed by working out the interest payments as a percentage of the initial loan, which would be £1,200 in the example given here, even though the average amount borrowed over the period of the loan is considerably lower.

A **mortgage** is a loan that is made for a long period to help someone buy or improve a home. Bank mortgages are made at floating rates and closely resemble building society mortgages. However, the latter are far more common, and they are discussed below.

Card loans

The second type of claim held against households is **card loans** which arise on cards of various sorts. One sort, known as **credit cards**, are issued by banks, so the loans associated with these cards could, arguably, be seen as another form of bank advance. Credit card holders can charge purchases to their credit card accounts, and they receive monthly statements. If they pay the full amount shown on their monthly statements fairly promptly, then no interest is due. If they do not, then interest is due on the outstanding amount at a relatively high and floating rate. There are individually agreed limits on the total amount that people can charge to their card accounts.

Charge cards are similar to credit cards except that full payments must be made promptly so that extended borrowing is not allowed. The main examples are *American Express* and *Diners Club*.

Some credit cards and charge cards are called **gold cards**. These offer higher credit limits and, if they are credit cards, usually offer slightly lower interest rates. However, they usually involve also the payment of a significant annual fee, perhaps up to £50.

There are also **store cards** which are run by stores, usually well-known high-street retailers. They take different forms, but they usually closely resemble credit cards, charge cards or gold cards except that they can be used only in the relevant stores.

Building society loans

Thirdly, there are **building society loans.** Most of these loans are mortgages which, like bank mortgages, are made specifically for buying or improving homes. Building society mortgages are usually made on a long-term basis, often up to 25 years, but many of them are paid off within that time as people rarely stay in one home so long. Of course, when people move, they may want a new mortgage to help purchase their new home. Mortgages are typically made on a floating rate basis. Some mortgages are made on the understanding that borrowers will pay them off steadily over the period of the loan, while others are made on the understanding that the borrowers will pay them off at the end in a single instalment.

Hire-purchase loans

Fourthly, there are **hire-purchase loans** from finance houses. Many households buy items such as cars, televisions and furniture on a hire-purchase basis. They will usually arrange the loan with the retailer who supplies the products, but the money will actually be lent to them by a finance house. Strictly, the product belongs to the finance house until the loan is fully paid off, so the household has to pay a hire charge to use it as well as paying interest and paying off the loan. The interest is typically charged at a fixed rate.

Trade credit and accruals

Fifthly, households enjoy some trade credit and accruals. For example, trade credit would arise if a furniture shop promoted sales by allowing people to take deliveries of furniture and pay nothing for three months. Accruals can arise when households have a monthly account with a shop or a garage, and also when they make telephone calls, or use electricity, or receive newspapers, before they pay for them. In effect, the suppliers lend money to the households until payment is received. There is usually no interest on this sort of claim.

Other loans

Sixthly, households may have other loans. For example, many students borrow from the Student Loans Company, many people with life insurance policies also borrow money from the companies with whom they have the policies, many employees negotiate loans from their employers, and, of course, many members of households negotiate private loans from members of the same household or from members of other households.

1.6 THE MAIN CLAIMS HELD AGAINST GOVERNMENTS

The main types of claim that can be held against governments also fall into six groups.

Securities

First, there are securities. The central government and local authorities issue two types of security called bills and bonds, though central government bonds are often referred to simply as gilts. These securities are discussed in Chapter 2.

National Savings Bank deposits

Secondly, there are **National Savings Bank deposits**. The National Savings Bank belongs to the central government and operates through post offices where depositors may place or withdraw deposits. These deposits represent loans to the central government and earn interest at a floating rate. They can be divided into **ordinary accounts**, where limited amounts may be withdrawn on demand, and **investment accounts**, which attract higher interest rates but where a month's notice is required before a withdrawal can be made.

National Savings certificates and bonds

Thirdly, there are National Savings certificates, National Savings bonds, and National Savings premium saving bonds. The central government sells all of these, and the people who buy them are effectively lending money to it. There are several different types of **National Savings certificates** and **National**

Savings bonds. The certificates earn interest which is tax-free. The bonds earn interest on various terms, though it is taxable except for **children's bonds** which may be held only by people under 16. Some bonds, known as **pensioners' bonds** or **granny bonds**, have relatively high interest rates, but these are available only to people aged 60 or over. Premium savings bonds, or, more simply, **premium bonds**, earn no interest. Instead, their holders have a chance of winning a prize of up to £1m in the weekly prize draws.

The holders of the bonds and certificates can sell them back to the government when they want their money back, but some notice, such as a month, is usually required. In many cases, the returns are higher for people who hold them for at least five years. Usually the holders are repaid the original cost-price, but some certificates and bonds are **index-linked**, which means that their values rise in line with inflation, as measured by the retail prices index (RPI).

Local authority deposits

Fourthly, there are **local authority deposits**. These are loans made to local governments. Most of them are made for periods between two days and a week, but some are longer, occasionally up to a year. From the lenders' point of view, these loans are effectively an alternative to bank deposits. The minimum amounts involved are usually around £25,000. The interest rate is fixed when the deposit is made.

Inter-government loans

Fifthly, there are **inter-government loans**. These claims are usually held against local authorities by the central government which often lends to them.

Trade credit and accruals

Sixthly, there are trade credit and accruals which arise when governments take deliveries before paying for them. These items represent loans which are usually interest-free.

1.7 THE MAIN CLAIMS HELD AGAINST COMPANIES

This section covers the five main types of claim that are held against companies, other than those which are financial intermediaries.

Securities

First, there are securities. Companies issue an even wider variety of securities than governments. They are discussed in Chapter 2.

Bank advances

Secondly, there are bank advances. Like households, companies may borrow floating rate overdrafts and fixed rate bank loans. Loans under about £500,000 are made like personal loans at fixed rates that are so many basis points above the bank's base rate. The number of points depends partly on the sum borrowed and the length of the loan, but it depends chiefly on the credit-worthiness of the borrower. Small companies might have credit ratings as high as 300 to 500 basis points, while large ones might have ratings as low as 100 to 200 points.

For companies taking out large loans, perhaps £500,000 or more, the interest rates used are often linked to LIBOR instead of base rates. As already seen in Table 1.2, the banks have a number of different LIBOR rates for different periods. Suppose a company wishes to borrow £10m for one year. It might agree to borrow at so many basis points above the 12-month LIBOR, but it might instead agree to take out a succession of four three-month loans, each at so many basis points above the three-month LIBOR at the start of the relevant three-month period. In the latter case, it would have a floating rate loan; however, the rate would be liable to change only every three months, even though LIBOR rates are subject to continuous change. Long-term company loans are usually agreed as a succession of loans at so many basis points above the three-month or six-month LIBOR. As many long-term loans are not made for an exact number of three-month or six-month periods, but might be for, say, two years and three weeks, so special arrangements are made for determining the interest rate due on the final period, which in this case is three weeks.

Hire-purchase loans

Thirdly, there are hire-purchase loans from finance houses. Like households, companies may borrow from finance houses to buy assets on hire-purchase terms. This means the finance house buys the asset and hires it to the company while the company pays off the loan. The interest rates are usually fixed.

Inter-company loans

Fourthly, there are **inter-company loans**. These are usually made between about the largest 500 companies. The most usual lengths for these loans are between three months and five years, and the sums involved are usually £100,000 or more. The appeal of these loans is that they cut out financial intermediaries who charge higher rates to borrowers than they pay lenders. Of course, it is necessary for surplus companies to get in touch with deficit companies which have complementary requirements, and vice versa. So the companies concerned often approach a **money broker**, that is a firm which will put parties with complementary borrowing and lending requirements in touch and will negotiate the terms. The broker will want a fee in return, but this should be less than the rewards that financial intermediaries would seek.

Trade credit and accruals

Fifthly, there are trade credit and accruals which arise when companies take deliveries before paying for them. These items represent loans which are usually interest-free.

1.8 THE MAIN CLAIMS HELD AGAINST FINANCIAL INTERMEDIARIES

There are more types of claim held against financial intermediaries than against households, governments or companies. Many financial intermediaries are companies and, like other companies, they issue a wide variety of securities, as discussed in Chapter 2. Financial intermediaries may also enjoy some trade credit and accruals. Otherwise, virtually all the claims held against financial intermediaries come in forms that are unique to them. These are outlined below.

Bank and building society deposits

There are three main types of **bank deposit** and **building society deposit**. First, there are **sight deposits**. These are defined as deposits which may be withdrawn on demand without limit or penalty. Most of them earn interest, usually at a floating rate which moves in step with the occasional changes in bank or building society base rates. The rates on deposits are generally well below base rates. Sight deposits can be withdrawn through cash dispensers or by cheque and are often called **current accounts**.

Secondly, there are **time deposits** which always earn interest. The name time deposit arises because, in principle, these deposits may not usually be withdrawn without notice. The notice will be agreed between the bank and the depositor when the deposit is first opened. However, there is one group of time deposits called **instant savings accounts** where limited withdrawals may be made without any notice being formally required.

For modest time deposits, like those held by many households, periods of a week or a month are most common, and these deposits are often called **deposit accounts**. In practice, these small deposits can often be withdrawn without notice, but in that case there is a penalty in the form of some loss of interest. The interest rates on these small deposits are usually floating rates, and they are usually 2–5% below the banks' current base rates. However, higher fixed rates are available on some deposits, notably many long-term building society deposits called bonds. For sums of, say, £500 or more, households can use **fixed-term deposits** whose terms range from a few days up to perhaps five years. These deposits earn higher interest rates, which may be fixed or floating, but no withdrawals are allowed until the term has ended.

People can earn limited amounts of tax-free interest from special time deposits called **tax-exempt special savings accounts** (TESSAs). In 1999, these will be replaced by personal funds called **individual savings accounts** (ISAs). ISAs will also allow people to earn some tax-free income from securities.

On very large fixed-term deposits of perhaps £100,000 or more, which would generally be placed only by companies, banks tend to offer even higher interest rates. These rates are usually linked to their LIBID rates rather than to their base rates. With a deposit of, say, £5m, a company might secure the full LIBID rate, but with anything less it would probably be offered a slightly lower rate. Most deposits like these are made on the basis that the rate will be changed every three or six months in line with the current three or six-month LIBID rate.

Thirdly, there are **certificates of deposit** (CDs). These are large deposits, usually over £100,000, that cannot be withdrawn until an agreed **maturity date**. This date is usually between one month and one year after the deposit is placed, but it may be up to five years later. CDs always earn interest, almost always at a fixed rate, and the interest is paid at maturity except on CDs lasting over a year, when it is paid annually. CD rates are not tied to base rates or LIBID rates, but, like LIBID rates, they change frequently. Although CDs cannot be withdrawn, they can be marketed, that is sold, at any time. This means that CDs are more flexible than fixed-term deposits, so banks and building societies can offer slightly lower interest rates on them.

CDs are traded in the **money market**. This means that people who wish to buy or sell CDs will usually either approach a money broker or a bank. All banks actually hold some CDs – which means they are effectively holding deposits at other banks – and they are usually willing to trade in CDs. They quote a **bid price** for the CDs which they buy and a slightly higher **ask price** for those which they sell; thus they have a **bid ask spread**. Money brokers do not generally hold CDs, but they put parties who wish to trade CDs in touch with each other. The parties may trade at a price in between the bid and ask prices offered by the banks, and this means the buyer will secure a slightly lower price and the seller a slightly higher price than would be secured by trading with banks; but these gains may well be offset by the commission fees which the broker will charge.

Table 1.4 gives some examples of interest rates on sterling CDs. The figures are those applying at the close of business on 21 May 1998, and they cover CDs with four different periods to maturity. There are two rates for each period. In each case, these rates determined the bid and ask prices at which banks bought and sold CDs at the end of 21 May. For example, suppose that a year earlier X bought a two-year £100,000 CD, and suppose that the interest rate then offered on two-year CDs was 7% a year. Suppose that a year later, on 21 May 1998, X collected his first interest payment of £7,000 and then decided to sell the CD to a bank. Interest rates then were higher: Table 1.4 shows that the rate being offered on new one-year CDs was 7¹⁄₁₆%, while the rate which fixed the price which banks paid for existing CDs with a year to maturity was 7⅜%. If a bank bought X's CD, then it would receive £107,000 one year later when it withdrew the deposit of £100,000 and received £7,000 interest. If the bank bought this CD at the rate of 7⅜%, that is 7.375% or 0.07375, then it would pay £107,000/(1 + 0.07375), that is £99,651, and so gain £7,349 over the year, that is £107,000 – £99,651. This gain of £7,349 equals 7⅜% of the purchase price of £99,651.

Table 1.4 Examples of CD interest rates (end of 17 January 1997)

	One month	Three months	Six months	One year
Sterling CDs	7⅜–7⁵⁄₁₆	7¹³⁄₃₂–7¹¹⁄₃₂	7¹³⁄₃₂–7¹¹⁄₃₂	7⅜–7⁵⁄₁₆

Cash

Cash comprises coins and notes, neither of which earns interest. **Coins** are made by the Royal Mint which sells them at face value to the Bank of England. The Bank then supplies them to the other banks which in turn supply them to the public. The Mint holds its bank deposit at the Bank of England. Consequently, when the Bank buys new coins, the value of its deposits rises by an equal amount, and hence the value of its liabilities also rises by an equal amount.

Notes are mostly printed for the Bank of England; it issues them to the other banks which in turn supply them to the public. Notes may also be printed by the Scottish and Northern Irish banks and then issued directly by them to the public, although these banks are generally allowed to issue their own notes only if they possess Bank of England notes which they could supply instead. Notes are liabilities to the banks that issue them.

Money market loans

Money market loans are large loans, usually made for less than a year, that are borrowed by financial intermediaries. Frequently the lender is another financial intermediary. These loans are often called deposits because their holders see them as an alternative to time deposits at banks and building societies. The interest rates are fixed when the deposits are made. The main examples are discount house deposits, finance house deposits and interbank deposits.

Discount house deposits are loans made to the discount houses, most frequently by banks. Most of these loans take the form of **money-at-call** and **money at short notice**. Money-at-call comprises loans that are repayable 'at call', which in practice means by noon on the next business day, while money at short notice comprises loans where the notice required for repayment is within fourteen days. **Finance house deposits** are loans made to finance houses, mostly by banks, discount houses and companies. The most usual terms for these deposits are from one to six months. **Interbank deposits** are loans between banks, and here the terms commonly range from overnight to a year. The sums involved are usually £250,000 or more. As noted in Section 1.3, a London bank will offer a LIBID rate on any large deposit, say £5m or more, that is placed with it by another London bank.

Life insurance policies and pension funds

Life insurance policies and pension funds are quite distinct types of financial claim. However, they are taken together here because the companies which handle one type usually also handle the other.

Life insurance policies may be bought either with regular periodic premiums or with lump-sums. There are many types, but the most common are probably whole-life insurance policies, term insurance policies, endowment policies and annuities. A **whole-life policy** usually involves paying regular premiums for life in return for a benefit payable on death. A **term policy** usually involves paying regular premiums over an agreed period in return for a benefit that will arise only if death occurs during that period. An **endowment policy** usually involves paying regular premiums over an agreed period in return for a minimum guaranteed benefit which will be paid at the end of the period if the insured person is still alive, or on death if the insured person dies earlier. An **annuity** usually involves paying a lump-sum and in return being given a fixed annual income for the rest of the insured person's life.

Pension funds are claims held by households against the companies which operate pension schemes. People who pay money into pension schemes acquire thereby claims which they cannot usually exercise until they reach retirement age. However, most pension schemes include extra clauses under which they would make payments before normal retirement age was reached, but only in certain circumstances, such as if the holder of the claim retired early on grounds of ill-health or died before retiring and left a dependent relative.

Unit trust units

Unit trusts are financial intermediaries from whom people can buy units. Usually, the unit holders can sell their units back to the trusts at any time. However, many unit trusts are run by life insurance companies so that the people who pay premiums actually buy units, and here there are sometimes restrictions over selling the units back. Unit trusts invest the funds they raise, usually by buying securities. Many trusts reinvest most or all of the income they acquire from their securities, so they pay little or no income to the unit holders. However, they are required by law to change their unit prices daily to reflect changes in the value of their investments. They actually quote two prices for each unit: an offer price which they charge people who buy units, and a slightly lower bid price which they pay people who sell them back. The companies who own unit trusts often run many different ones. Some of these may invest in selected geographical areas, such as the United Kingdom, or Europe or the far east, while others may invest in specific types of asset, such as property, or companies that are thought very safe, or companies that have had a poor time and are thought likely to recover.

Table 1.5 gives examples of two unit trusts. The figures are those applying at the close of business on 21 May 1998. Both trusts are owned by Hill Samuel Life Assurance Ltd, but the UK Emerging Companies Trust pays some income while the US Smaller Companies Trust pays none. The table shows the bid or **selling prices**, at which holders could sell units back to Hill Samuel, and it also shows the ask, **offer** or **buying prices**, at which people could buy units from Hill Samuel. Thus on 21 May people could buy UK Emerging Companies units at 171.65p and sell them back for 163.93p. The price rose by 1.11p that day. These units had a **gross yield** of 0.75% which means the latest declared

Table 1.5   Examples of unit trusts (end of 21 May 1998)

	Selling price	Buying price	Change	Gross yield (%)
Hill Samuel UK Emerging Companies	163.93	171.65	+1.11	0.75
Hill Samuel US Smaller Companies	205.49	215.18	−0.30	—

level of annual income payment was equal to 0.75% of the average of the closing buying and selling prices on 21 May.

1.9 TIME PERIODS AND INTEREST RATES

Tables 1.2 and 1.4 showed that on 21 May 1998 the longer-term CDs and the longer-term interbank loans had similar interest rates to the shorter term ones. The figures for long-term rates are usually above the short-term rates, but are sometimes similar to, or even below, the short-term rates.

The relationship between long-term and short-term interest rates depends chiefly on current interest rates and **expected interest rates** for the future. If interest rates are generally expected to rise, then lenders will be less willing than normal to lend long-term and commit their funds for some time, for they will think that they could soon lend for a higher rate; so people wishing to borrow long-term will have to offer lenders a margin above short-term rates. In contrast, if interest rates are generally expected to fall, then people who wish to borrow for long terms will prefer to borrow one short-term loan followed by another at, hopefully, a lower rate. So the demand for short-term borrowing will rise and short-term loans will have higher rates than long-term ones.

This argument implies that, if interest rates are expected to be constant, then long-term deposits will have identical rates to short-term ones, say 7.82% per year. However, even if deposits of different lengths do all have rates that are equivalent to 7.82% per year, only the 12-month rate would be expressed as 7.82%. The expressed rates on shorter-term deposits would be lower. To see why, compare X, who decides to lend £100 in a 12-month deposit, and Y, who decides to lend £100 in two consecutive six-month deposits. X secures his interest at the end of the twelve months at the published 12-month rate of 7.82%, so he ends up with £107.82. However, Y receives some interest after six months, and she could lend this as well as her £100 for the remaining six months. To end up with £107.82, the published six-month rate faced by Y must be lower than 7.82% and must in fact be expressed as 7.67% per year. For in that case, Y would get interest at half of that rate, that is 3.835%, after six months. So after six months she would get her £100 back plus £3.83½ interest. She could lend all of this £103.83½ for another six months, again at 3.835%, and this would secure her about £107.82 at the end of the second six months.

In general, the rate that must be expressed on a loan lasting T years, r_T, to make it equivalent to an annual rate, r, is given by $r_T = [(1 + r)^T - 1]/T$. In the present example for Y, where $T = 0.5$, the six-month rate equivalent to 7.82%

is $[(1.0782^{0.5} - 1)/0.50]$, which is 0.767, or 7.67%. Likewise the three-month rate, where $T = 0.25$, would be expressed as $[(1.0782^{0.25} - 1)/0.25]$, which is 0.0760, or 7.60%.

It follows that if interest rates are expected to be stable, and the true long-term rates are the same as the short-term ones, then the published rates on longer-term deposits will be slightly higher than those on shorter-term deposits. If interest rates are expected to rise, then the true long-term rates will be higher than the short-term ones, so the gap in the published rates will be even wider. But if interest rates are expected to fall, then the true rates on longer-term deposits will be below those on short-term deposits, so the gap in the published rates will be narrower; indeed, the published rate on long-term deposits could even be below that on short-term ones. Assuming that people expect rises and falls with equal frequency, and sometimes expect no change, the published long-term rates would more often than not exceed the published short-term rates.

In practice, there may be another factor which affects relative long- and short-term rates. It could be that borrowers generally want to borrow for rather longer than lenders generally want to lend. In this case, longer-term loans would have to be rewarded with slightly higher rates of interest to reward lenders for tying up their funds for longer than they would wish and hence losing liquidity. An asset is a fully **liquid asset** if it can be spent at once for a certain amount. Fixed-term bank deposits, such as interbank deposits, cannot be withdrawn early so they cannot be spent at once, and although CDs can be sold quickly, the amount that will be raised is never certain until the moment of sale. As this extra return on long-term deposits is a return for losing liquidity, it is usually called a **liquidity premium**, though it is sometimes called a risk premium. But it is hard to say how much liquidity premium is involved in longer-term deposits, for even these usually last a year at most. If there is a significant liquidity premium, then it would accentuate the tendency for the published rates on long-term deposits to exceed those on short-term deposits when interest rates are expected to be stable or rise, and it would make it harder for the rates on long-term deposits to go below those on short-term deposits when interest rates are expected to fall.

1.10 EUROCLAIMS

Many financial claims have the prefix Euro. For example, some claims are called **Eurocurrencies**. These are deposits which are held in currencies other than the national currency of the country where they are held. The most important Eurocurrencies are **Eurodollars**, **Euromarks** and **Eurosterling** which are dollars, marks and pounds that are respectively held in deposits outside the United States, Germany or the United Kingdom. Other important Euro-currencies include **Eurolira**, **Euroswiss francs** and **Euroyen**. The prefix Euro is used because the first examples, Eurodollars, were dollars held in Europe. Originally, most Eurodollars were held in branches of United States banks that were located outside the United States. However, Eurodollars can be held in banks of any nationality, as can any other Eurocurrencies. The prefix Euro is rather misleading because, for example, a deposit of Japanese yen held in a branch of an Australian bank in Brazil would still be regarded as Euroyen simply because it is held outside Japan.

Banks naturally pay interest on Eurocurrency deposits, and they charge interest on Eurocurrency loans, that is to say loans in currencies other than the one used in their own country. Table 1.6 gives some examples of the Eurocurrency interest rates that applied in London at the close of business on 21 May 1998. The rates relate to various length deposits and loans that might be made between banks in London using Canadian dollars and Italian lira. There is a pair of interest rates for each length. As in Table 1.2, the higher rate is the one at which banks would lend large sums to other banks while the lower rate is that one which they would offer on large deposits placed by other banks. There would be higher lending rates and lower deposit rates for most non-bank customers.

The London rates would be identical to those applying on interbank loans in Canada and Italy. To see why, suppose that rates in Canada were higher than in London. Then a British bank could borrow Canadian dollars from a bank in London at one rate and lend them to a bank in Canada at a higher rate and so make a virtually riskless profit. Seeking riskless profits is called **arbitrage**. In the circumstances considered here, arbitrage would drive the two rates together as the rates on loans borrowed in London would rise while the rates on loans lent in Canada would fall. The table shows that the interest rates on long-term Canadian dollar loans and deposits were above the short-term rates, and this suggests that Canadian interest rates were generally expected to rise. In contrast, the interest rates on long-term lira loans and deposits were below the short-term term rates, and this suggests that Italian interest rates were generally expected to fall.

Table 1.6   Examples of Eurocurrency interest rates (end of 21 May 1998)

	Two days	Seven days	One month	Three months	Six months	One year
Canadian dollar	$4\frac{3}{4}$–$4\frac{5}{8}$	$4\frac{7}{8}$–$4\frac{11}{16}$	$4\frac{7}{8}$–$4\frac{5}{8}$	5–$4\frac{3}{4}$	$5\frac{3}{32}$–$4\frac{27}{32}$	$5\frac{1}{4}$–5
Italian lira	$5\frac{3}{4}$–$5\frac{1}{2}$	$5\frac{5}{8}$–$5\frac{17}{32}$	$5\frac{15}{32}$–$5\frac{3}{8}$	$5\frac{3}{32}$–5	$4\frac{3}{4}$–$4\frac{11}{16}$	$4\frac{1}{2}$–$4\frac{13}{32}$

Related to Eurocurrencies are deposits of **European Currency Units** (ECUs) which are effectively deposits – that may be held in any country – which contain a mixture of all 15 EU currencies in proportions specified by the EU. Finally, **Eurobonds** and **Euroequities** are securities, specifically bonds and equities, that are initially sold for a currency that is not the national currency of the country where they are sold. Thus a Japanese company selling equities in Taiwan for yen or in Japan for United States dollars is selling Euroequities.

SUMMARY

1.1 Most financial claims arise when funds pass from surplus units to deficit units.

1.2 Any given financial claim appears as an asset on one party's balance sheets and as a liability on another party's balance sheet. Like financial derivatives, financial claims are financial instruments. Certificates of deposit (CDs) and securities are the only marketable financial claims.

1.3 Many financial claims arise when surplus units transfer funds to deficit units via financial intermediaries which comprise banks and non-bank financial intermediaries. Financial intermediation offers the advantages of maturity transformation, aggregation and risk transformation.

1.4 Financial claims may be held by, and held against, households, governments, companies and financial intermediaries. Financial claims add nothing to the wealth of the world, but they allow deficit units to acquire funds with which they can acquire assets that do add to wealth.

1.5 The main financial claims held against households are bank advances, card loans, building society loans, hire-purchase loans, trade credit and accruals, and other loans.

1.6 The main financial claims held against governments are securities, National Savings Bank deposits, National Savings bonds and certificates, local authority deposits, inter-government loans and trade credit and accruals.

1.7 The main financial claims held against most companies are securities, bank advances, hire-purchase loans, inter-company loans, and trade credit and accruals.

1.8 The main financial claims held against financial intermediaries are securities, bank and building society deposits, which fall into sight deposits, time deposits and CDs, cash, which comprises notes and coins, money market loans between financial intermediaries, life insurance policies and pension funds, and unit trust units.

1.9 Published interest rates on longer-term loans are usually higher than those on shorter-term loans, but they may be lower if interest rates are expected to fall significantly.

1.10 Euroclaims comprise bank deposits that are held outside the country which uses the currency in which they are denominated, together with securities which are first sold for a currency that is not the currency of the country where they are sold.

QUESTIONS

1. To what extent, if any, do financial claims add to wealth? Are they relevant to wealth?

2. Explain briefly five types of financial intermediary.

3. Explain briefly sight deposits, time deposits and CDs. Why will people accept lower rates on sight deposits than on CDs?

4. Look at a recent newspaper and find the interest rates for CDs. Calculate the price which banks would pay at the close of business on the previous day for a CD which would mature in six months for £100,000 and which would also entitle the holder to an interest payment of £5,000 at the same time.

5. Look at a recent newspaper and find the section on unit trusts. Is the proportion that offer income payments (a) under a quarter, (b) between a quarter and a half, (c) between one half and three-quarters, or (d) over three-quarters? Take a sample of five unit trusts and work out by what percentage, on average, the ask price exceeds the bid price.

6. Look at the Eurocurrency interest rates in a recent newspaper. Are there any countries where rises in interest rates seem widely expected? Are there any countries where falls in interest rates seem widely expected?

REFERENCE

HMSO (1987) 'National and sector balance sheets 1957–85', *Economic Trends*, **403** (May), 92–119.

2 SECURITIES

2.1 WHAT ARE SECURITIES?

The term **securities** is not always used in the same way. Often it is used to cover all marketable financial claims except certificates of deposit, and this usage is adopted here. All the marketable claims concerned are issued by governments and companies, and they issue many different types. Some of these types have lives of a year or less, and sometimes the word securities is used in a narrower sense than that adopted here by excluding these very short-term types.

One reason why these marketable claims are called securities is that the parties who issue them to borrow funds thereby issue formal documents which make the holders' position more secure. This usage dates back at least as far as 1576. Another reason is that a holder may subsequently find it easier to borrow money from, say, a bank. This is because the claim can be placed with the bank and retained by it if the holder defaults. This meaning can be traced back only as far as 1690.

Each security represents either **debt** or **equity**. Securities which represent debt represent loans by their holders to the government or company that issued them. These securities can be divided into those which pay no interest to their owners, those which pay fixed interest, and those which pay variable interest. Naturally, the holders of securities which earn no interest expect some other form of reward. Securities which represent equity are issued only by companies, and then only to their owners. These securities, or equities, represent the owners' stakes in the company. The owners get no interest, but hope each year to receive part of the company's profit in the form of dividends.

Topics covered in this chapter

Sections 2.2 to 2.5 look more closely at the main types of security by dividing them into four groups. Section 2.2 looks at those securities which earn no interest; the term zero-interest securities will be used for these. Section 2.3 looks at fixed-interest securities, Section 2.4 looks at variable-interest securities and Section 2.5 looks at equities. These four sections also cover some of the arrangements whereby securities are issued and traded. Section 2.6 looks briefly at investment trusts and at some of the more unusual securities that are issued by them. As equities are by far the most important securities in terms of total value, Section 2.7 looks at indices of equity prices. Finally, Section 2.8 explores the impact of interest rate changes on security prices and explains why this impact depends on the duration of security, which is a measure of its remaining lifespan.

The chapter often refers to the returns that investors obtain or want from different securities. Investors usually require higher returns on securities with long lives than on securities with short lives. The reasons for this are related to those noted in Section 1.9 in connection with bank deposits, where a similar tendency arises. The main reason is probably that borrowers generally wish to borrow for longer than lenders wish to lend, so that there is a liquidity premium on longer-term loans. This issue is explored further in Section 3.10.

2.2 ZERO-INTEREST SECURITIES

When people buy **zero-interest securities**, they are making loans to the government or to the company that issues them, so these securities represent debt to the issuers. The loans are usually short-term, and their repayment dates are called their **maturity** or **redemption** dates. The buyers are not paid any interest. Instead, they get a reward because they buy the securities for less than their face value or **par**, yet they are repaid the full face value at maturity. In other words, they buy the bills at a **discount**, and they end up making **capital gains**.

There are five main types of zero-interest security, and they are listed in Table 2.1. It will be seen that they are issued by the central government, local authorities and companies. The first three types are all called bills. The best-known bills are the central government's **Treasury bills** which always mature after 91 days. There is rather more variety of maturity date with **local government bills** and companies' **commercial bills**. By law, any funds that companies borrow by issuing commercial bills must be used to buy raw materials or goods for resale, so that the loans will be **secured loans**.

Companies issue two other types of zero-interest security: **promissory notes** and **zero-coupon bonds**. These differ from commercial bills in that there are no rules over the use of the funds raised by issuing them. However, promissory notes may be issued only by companies whose assets exceed £50 million. Zero-coupon bonds are distinctive in that maturity occurs after some years rather than after some months. This means that their holders have to wait a

Table 2.1   The main types of zero-interest security

Type	Issued by	Issued at	Redemption
Treasury bills	Central government	Discount	91 days at par
Local government bills	Local authorities	Discount	2–6 months at par
Commercial bills *or*			
Bills of exchange	Companies	Discount	1–6 months at par
Promissory notes *or*			
Commercial paper	Companies	Discount	1–52 weeks at par
Zero-coupon bonds	Companies	Deep discount	Long-term at par

long time for their capital gains, so they want high returns which they secure by buying the bonds at deep discounts.

How zero-interest securities work

As noted above, anyone who buys a zero-interest security obtains a reward by buying it at a discount off its face value. The face value is often called the maturity value as it is also the sum which will be paid at maturity. Suppose that X pays £990 for a 91-day bill with a maturity value of £1,000, so he gets a return of £10 after three months. He might buy four similar bills over a year and so get a total return of £40 over the year. As £40 is 4% of the face values of the bills, X would be said to be getting a return at a rate of 4%; this rate is called the **discount rate**. However, X's true rate of return is rather higher. One reason for this is that his annual gain of £40 is 4.04% of his initial outlay of £990. Another reason is that, during the year, he could in principle lend the first gain of £10 for the remaining nine months, the second gain of £10 for six months and the third gain of £10 for three months; if he lent each gain at equivalent rates of return to those earned by the bills, then it could be shown – and is shown shortly – that the total return on his £990 would be 4.10%.

How zero-interest securities are issued and traded

New zero-interest securities are often sold by auction. For example, the Bank of England holds weekly auctions for new Treasury bills which it issues on behalf of the central government. Each week's Treasury bill issue has two parts. One part, called the **tap issue**, is *not* an auction. Instead, it consists of the Bank selling a few bills privately to foreign central banks and to government departments with temporary surpluses of funds. However, the other more important part, called the **tender issue**, *is* an auction. Here, new bills are auctioned to the discount houses and to the banks, who bid both on their own behalf and on behalf of their clients. Bids, or tenders, are made to the Bank which allocates the bills to whoever makes the highest tenders. Individual buyers pay the individual prices which they bid, so the bills are sold at a variety of prices. If there are too few bids to take up all the new Treasury bills, then the Bank sells all the remaining ones to the discount houses at a special favourable price. This ensures that all the new bills are in fact bought.

Local authorities and companies may auction their own zero-interest securities, or they may get a financial intermediary to do so on their behalf. When a financial intermediary is involved, a company pays it a fee to **endorse** the bills, which means that the intermediary will guarantee redemption if the company defaults. The intermediaries concerned here may either be specialists called **accepting houses** or ordinary banks, but in both cases an endorsed bill is called a **bank bill**. Commercial bills which are not endorsed in this way are called **trade bills**.

Existing short-term zero-interest securities are traded on the money market. This does not mean that they are traded in a special place. It simply means that banks and other money brokers may put buyers and sellers in touch with each other, or else buy and sell the securities themselves. Existing zero-coupon bonds are traded on stock exchanges like equities, as discussed in Section 2.5.

Factors that affect the prices paid for zero-interest securities

The price that a buyer will offer for a zero-interest security with a given face value and maturity date depends on three factors:

1. The risk that the borrower might **default** on the payment at maturity. Treasury bills are risk-free in this respect because the government can always raise taxes to honour its obligations. Consequently, its bills secure the highest prices and so have the lowest or **finest** discount rates. Company securities are the riskiest, so they secure the lowest prices and hence have the highest discount rates. The prices paid for company securities vary. For example, bank bills have higher prices, and hence finer discount rates, than trade bills. Also, the trade bills issued by the riskiest companies have the lowest prices and the highest discount rates.

2. Current interest rates. The interest rates which lenders could get elsewhere on loans with comparable risks of default will affect the discount rates they want from zero-interest securities.

3. The time left to maturity. If the holder of a zero-interest security sells it before maturity, then the price will typically be higher if maturity is due soon than if it is some time away. The reason is that when maturity is close, the buyer has less time to wait to secure a return.

Figure 2.1 illustrates the impact of interest rates and the time to maturity on the price of a 91-day bill with a face value of £1,000. Suppose, first, that the returns on comparable loans are just over 4% so that buyers require a discount rate of 4% on this bill. When it is issued, they will offer £990 for it and so gain £10 after three months. They could make four similar gains in a year to gain £40 in all, which is 4% of the face value of the bills. If interest rates had been higher and they had wanted discount rates of, say, 8% or 12%, then the initial price would have been £980 or £970, allowing them to make gains of £20 or £30 after three months and £80 or £120 over a year, that is 8% or 12% of the face value of the bill. The three sloping lines on Fig. 2.1 begin with the initial values that the bill would have at discount rates of 4%, 8% and 12%

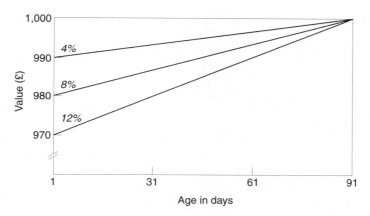

Figure 2.1   The effect of time and discount rates on the price of a 91-day £1,000 bill.

respectively, and then they show how its price would rise as maturity neared because there would be less time to wait for a capital gain.

The three lines in Fig. 2.1 also show the effect on the bill's price of any change in interest rates that causes the required discount rate to move between 4%, 8% and 12%. The impact on the bill's price of a change in interest rates diminishes as maturity approaches. For example, suppose that interest rates are initially such that the discount rate required on the bill is 4%, so that it is initially sold for £990. If interest rates doubled immediately after it was issued, then its value would immediately fall by about 1% to £980. But suppose that interest rates instead doubled on day 31. At the beginning of the day, the bill would be worth about £993, as shown by the top sloping line, but immediately after interest rates doubled its price would fall by about 0.6% to £987. If, instead, interest rates had doubled on day 90, then its value would fall by a negligible amount.

Present values and a formula for the prices of zero-interest securities

The three lines in Fig. 2.1 have been drawn straight. In fact, there are two reasons why the price lines for a zero-interest security need not be quite straight, though any likely curvature would be extremely slight. To see these two reasons, it is useful to develop a formula for the price of a zero-interest security. To understand this formula, it is necessary to understand the concept of present values. And to illustrate this concept, it is helpful to imagine that each year a hypothetical company, LML, issues some two-year zero-coupon bonds.

More specifically, suppose that LML today issues some two-year zero-coupon bonds with a face value of £100. Suppose also that some existing two-year LML zero-coupon bonds with exactly one year left to maturity are available second-hand. The prices that investors will offer for both of these bonds depend on the rates of return they require from them. These rates depend on the remaining life of the bonds, chiefly because lenders typically want higher returns on longer-term loans.

Suppose that lenders require a return of 10%, or 0.1, on one-year loans to LML. So if an investor X lent LML £1 for one year, then in one year X would want £0.10 in interest plus £1 repayment, making a total of £1.10 or £1(1 + 0.1). This figure can be expressed as £1(1 + r_1), where r_1 is the rate required on a one-year loan. It is said that £1 is the **present value** of £1(1 + r_1) in one year's time, at an interest rate r_1, because the loan means that £1 today will be worth £1(1 + r_1) in one year's time. It is often useful to work out the present value of other sums in one year's time. For example, the present value of £1 in one year's time is less than £1 and is £1/(1 + r_1); so if r_1 = 0.1, that is 10%, then the present value of £1 in one year's time is £1/1.10, which is about £0.91, for a loan of £0.91 will secure interest of about 9p in one year and so be worth £1. Also, the present value of £100 in one year's time is £100/(1 + r_1); so if r_1 = 0.1, then the present value of £100 in one year's time is £100/1.10, or £90.91. This figure shows the amount that people like X will lend to LML for one year if they are repaid £100 at the end of the year. So it also gives the price that X would pay now for a £100 zero-coupon bond that matures in one year. By paying £90.91, X would make a gain £9.09 when he was repaid the face value of £100, and this gain equals 10% of the loan of £90.91.

Suppose that lenders require a return equivalent to 11% a year, or 0.11, for two-year loans to LML. So if X lent LML £1 for two years on a loan where no interest would be paid until the two years were over, then he would work out the repayment he would want as follows. He would begin by reckoning that after one year he was entitled to 11p in interest. He would not actually be given any interest in one year, but he would feel that for the second year he should be seen as lending LML £1.11, or £1(1 + 0.11), and he will want interest at 11% on this sum. So the total payment he will want after two years is £1(1 + 0.11) (1 + 0.11), or £1(1 + 0.11)^2, which is £1.23. £1(1 + 0.11)^2 can be expressed as £1(1 + r_2)^2, where r_2 is the annual return required on a two-year loan. It follows that the present value of £1(1 + r_2)^2 in two years' time, at an interest rate of r_2, is £1. The present value of £1 in two years' time is less than £1 and is £1/(1 + r_2)^2, while the present value of £100 in two years' time is £100/(1 + r_2)^2. As LML's two-year bonds have a face value of £100, and hence will be worth £100 in two years' time, their present value or price is £100/(1 + r_2)^2. As r_2 = 0.11, that is 11%, the price that investors like X will pay now is £100/1.11^2, or £81.16.

The figure of £81.16 can readily be checked. If someone lent £81.16 at 11% for one year on a conventional loan, then after one year they would receive £8.93 interest and a repayment of £81.16, making £90.09 in all. If they lent that sum for the next year at 11%, then after the second year they would receive £9.91 interest and a repayment of £90.09, making £100 in all.

A more general formula for the present value or price of a zero-interest security, P_{ZIS}, with a maturity value M and a life of N years, is:

$$P_{ZIS} = M/(1 + r_N)^N \qquad\qquad (2.1)$$

where r_N is the annual return required on a security issued by the issuer concerned with N years to maturity. With bills, N is often less than one year.

Suppose that Y thought of buying a three-month bill, so that $N = 0.25$, with a redemption value of £1,000. If the rate of return thought appropriate for three months was equivalent to an annual rate of 4.10%, or 0.041, then Y would pay £1,000/$(1.041)^{0.25}$ which is £990. So the equivalent annual rate of return on a £1,000 91-day bill that is bought for £990, and hence at a discount rate of 4%, is 4.10%; this figure was noted earlier.

It is now possible to see the two reasons why the lines on Fig. 2.1 need not be quite straight. To see the first reason, suppose that people would be happy to accept the same rate of interest, 4.10%, on loans of one month, two months or three months to the borrower, so that people would not want a higher return for longer-term loans. Then, as just noted, they would pay £990 for a new three-month bill. A straight line on the figure implies that this bill's value will be exactly £995 after one-and-a-half months when there are one-and-a-half more months to go. But (2.1) shows that the price would be given by $P_{ZIS} = M/(1 + r_N)^N$, where $M = £1,000$, $r_N = 0.041$ and $N = 0.125$; N is 0.125 because this is one-eighth, and one-and-a-half months are an eighth of a year. Thus the price would be 1,000/$(1.041)^{0.125}$, which is £994.99. The difference between this and £995 is trivial, but on, say, a £100,000 bill the difference would be £1 rather than 1p.

To see the second reason why the lines need not be quite straight, suppose that investors do want higher rates on longer-term loans. Thus they might want a rate of 4.10% on loans or bills with three months to maturity, but they might be willing to accept a rate of only 4.05%, or 0.0405, on bills with one-and-a-half months left to maturity. In this case, the price of a bill with one-and-a-half months left would be given by $P_{ZIS} = M/(1 + r_N)^N$ where $M = £1,000$, $r_N = 0.0405$ and $N = 0.125$. Thus the price would be 1,000/$(1.0405)^{0.125}$ which is £995.05. This is slightly above the £995 that would be predicted by a straight line path.

Examples of zero-interest securities

Table 2.2 gives some examples of discount rates on Treasury bills with different periods to maturity. The rates shown determined the prices at which Treasury bills were bought and sold on the money market at the close of business on 21 May 1998. Treasury bills are available with various face values between £5,000 and £1m. If a dealer sold Y a £100,000 bill with two months to run for the discount rate shown of 7⅛%, then he would charge her £98,812.50. For at this price, Y would gain £1,187.50 over the two months; and if she made similar gains on six bills over a year, then her total gain would be £7,125, which is 7⅛%, or 7.125%, of £100,000. However, Y's true rate of return is over 7.125%. This rate can be found from (2.1), which shows that the bill's present value, £98,812.50, equals £100,000/$(1 + r)^{1/6}$. This can be solved to show that r is 7.43%.

Table 2.2 shows that, on 21 May 1998, the longer term bills had similar discount rates to the shorter-term ones. Usually, long-term bills have higher rates. The reasons are the same as those discussed in Section 1.9 in the context of different length bank deposits. One reason is that people who lend short-term soon get a return which can also be lent, so they can accept a lower rate of return while still actually making an equivalent return over the year as a whole. Another reason is that people who lend long-term usually want a higher

Table 2.2   Examples of bills (end of 21 May 1998)

	One month	Two months	Three months
Treasury bills	7¼–7⅛	7¼–7⅛	7¼–7⅛

rate of return as a result of a liquidity premium. Long-term zero-interest securities will secure even higher relative rates if interest rates are expected to rise, but they will have lower relative rates, and possibly lower absolute rates, if interest rates are expected to fall.

2.3 FIXED-INTEREST SECURITIES

As with zero-interest securities, people who buy **fixed-interest securities** are making loans to the government or company that issues them, so these securities represent debt to the issuers. The loans concerned are usually long-term. Indeed, some fixed-interest securities are called **perpetuities** because they represent loans where no promise of repayment or redemption has been made. Those securities which represent loans that will be repaid are called **longs** if they have over 15 years left to maturity, **mediums** if they have from five to 15 years left, and **shorts** if they have under five years left. So a security that is issued with a maturity date in 20 years' time will initially be a long, and will then become in turn a medium and a short as maturity gets closer.

The holder of a fixed-interest security essentially buys it by paying the full face value or par which is often £100. If the security is redeemed, then the holder will be repaid the face value. To tempt people to buy these securities, they earn interest. Each security has a fixed-interest rate called the **coupon rate** or, simply, the **coupon**. Each year the holders are given a fixed-interest payment, or **coupon payment**, which equals the face value times the coupon. So if a security has a face value of £100 and a coupon of 8%, then the holder will be paid £8 a year in interest. This would often be paid in two half-yearly instalments of £4.

The main types of fixed-interest security are listed in Table 2.3. Many are called bonds. The central government's bonds are called **gilts**, or **gilt-edged securities**, because there is no risk that the central government will be unable to honour the obligations for interest and repayment as it can always raise money through taxes; gilts are discussed at length by Phillips (1996). Most gilts are called **Treasury stock**, but some are called **Exchequer stock**, usually to help distinguish between two issues with similar coupons and maturity dates. A few issues are called **conversion stock**: the holders of these can convert them on pre-determined terms into other gilts with more distant maturity dates. Some gilts are double-dated and have two maturity dates, such as 2003–07. The government can redeem these on any anniversary of their issue between the two dates. It may hope that in at least one of those years it will have a surplus of tax revenue over spending which it can use to repay them. However, if it seems unlikely to run a surplus at any time, then it will have to issue some new gilts to raise the funds needed to pay off the old ones. In this case, it will try to choose a year when interest rates are low so that it can offer a low coupon on the replacements and thereby minimise its interest obligations on them.

The government has also issued some undated gilts called **consols**, though it has not issued any since the 1920s. The word consol is short for consolidated and arises because the oldest consols were issued in 1752 as a consolidation of earlier issues. The government has the right to redeem its consols, but they have very low coupons, so it would prefer to repay virtually all its other debt first.

Local authorities issue two types of fixed-interest security. These are **local government bonds** and **local government stocks**. They differ chiefly in their maturity terms.

Table 2.3 divides the fixed-interest securities issued by companies into **corporate bonds** and **preference shares**. The main distinction between them is that each year a company must pay the full interest on its bonds before it pays any interest on its preference shares. The priority claims of bondholders over preference shareholders extend also to what happens in the event of closure or **liquidation**, for then the proceeds from asset sales must be used to repay bondholders in full before anything is paid to preference shareholders. In law, preference shareholders are regarded as a special group of part-owners of a company rather than creditors, so their income payments are called dividends rather than interest. Strictly, therefore, the conventional approach adopted in Table 2.3 of placing preference shares under fixed-interest securities is incorrect, and they should instead be placed in a separate category called fixed dividend securities, but the conventional approach is useful in drawing attention to the fact that preference shares resemble fixed-interest securities in every respect except the term used for their income payments.

Corporate bonds may be subdivided into **debentures** and **loan stocks**. One distinction is that debenture holders have prior claims over loan stock holders. Another distinction is that, by law, debentures must represent secured loans, so that a company must own specific assets which it could sell off to repay its debenture holders in full in the event of liquidation. Loan stocks are rarely secured and are often explicitly called **unsecured loan stock**. Some debentures and loan stocks are **convertible bonds** which means that they may be

Table 2.3 The main types of fixed-interest security

Type	Issued by	Income	Redemption at par
Most central government bonds or 'gilts'	Central government	Interest	Usually within 20 years
Consols or undated 'gilts'	Central government	Interest	Never
Local government bonds	Local government	Interest	1–10 years
Local government stocks	Local government	Interest	2–20 years
Corporate bonds	Companies	Interest	Usually 10–40 years
Preference shares	Companies	Dividend	Long-term at par or never
Permanent interest-bearing shares (PIBSs)	Building societies	Interest	Never

converted on a set date into other securities, usually equities; but most deben-tures and loan stocks are non-convertible or **straight bonds**.

Finally, **permanent interest-bearing shares** (PIBSs) are issued only by building societies. PIBSs are really rather like fixed rate building society CDs. The main difference is that PIBSs are undated.

How fixed-interest securities are issued and traded

The markets where securities other than bills are traded are called **capital markets**. These markets can be divided into **primary markets** for new issues and **secondary markets** for existing securities. However, the term market does not always imply a special market building or exchange.

Issues of new gilts are handled by the Bank of England which usually sells them by **auction**. It sets a coupon which it thinks makes the bonds worth about their face value of £100, and it then invites bids in which buyers say what price they will offer and how many gilts they will buy at that price. The Bank gener-ally accepts the highest bids that are sufficient to sell all the bonds. Thus it might have to accept some bids as low as £98 to sell them all. In that case, every-one who bid more than £98 will get some gilts, but they will all pay the price which they bid, so some people might pay, say, £101 while others are paying only £98. However, the Bank might decide to reject any bids under, say, £99, which means that some gilts will remain unsold. In this case, it would sell off the remaining gilts in small amounts on later dates at current market prices.

Existing gilts are mainly traded by using **gilt-edged market makers** (GEMMs) who operate on the London Stock Exchange as dealers in gilts. They can be contacted directly by anyone with a large holding, but private individuals would normally deal with them via a stockbroker.

The arrangements for the issue and trading of local authority and company fixed-interest securities largely resemble those that are used for equities. As equities are of far greater importance in value terms, these arrangements are discussed in Section 2.5.

There is one feature of trading in fixed-interest securities that does not arise with equities, and this is the creation of **stripped securities** whereby owners sell part of their rights. For example, X may own some debentures and sell the rights to the interest but not to the repayment, while Y may own some gilts and sell the rights to the repayment but not to the interest. These part-sales are handled by financial intermediaries.

How fixed-interest security prices are quoted

When a fixed-interest security changes hands, the price actually paid is called the **total price** or, sometimes, the **dirty price**. This total price may fluctuate in response to external factors such as changes in interest rates. Aside from external factors, it tends to rise between each coupon payment and then fall when the payment is paid, for people will pay a little more the nearer the next coupon payment is. Take a £100 bond with an 8% coupon and a £4 coupon payment every six months, that is about every 182 days. Its total price will drop by £4 just after each coupon payment is made. In between, its total price will tend to rise by about 2.2p a day, that is £4/182.

The prices for bonds which are quoted in the press are *not* their total prices. Instead, the press quotes adjusted figures called **market prices** or **clean prices**. These adjusted figures are defined in a way that removes the tendency for the total price to rise by a small amount each day between coupon payments and then plummet on those days. The clean price is set equal to the total price on each coupon payment day, just after the total price has plummeted. On the next day, the total price will rise by about 2.2p as the next coupon payment is closer, but this rise is eliminated in the clean price by setting it 2.2p below the total price. The total price will rise by another 2.2p the next day, so on that day the clean price is set 4.4p below the total price. The clean price is set an additional 2.2p below the total price for every day that passes, so that by the time of the next coupon payment it is £4 below the total price. Then the payment is made and the total price falls £4, so that it once again equals the clean price. Aside from this cumulative 2.2p-a-day difference, movements in the clean price match all movements in the total price.

In practice, although the clean price and total price are set equal on each coupon payment day, there is one additional complication. Suppose, for simplicity, that the clean price and the total price both equal £100 one coupon payment day and that there are no subsequent fluctuations in the total price aside from those caused by the next coupon payment getting closer. Then the total price will rise by about 2.2p every day, while the clean price is set progressively further below the total price to keep the clean price at £100. But the total price will not rise by 2.2p every day until the next coupon payment day because it will fall by £4 some weeks *before* that payment day. It will fall by £4 when the security goes **ex-dividend**, which means that the next income payment will be paid to the existing owner, even if the security is sold first, so that a new buyer will not get the next payment. This arrangement enables the income payments to be prepared well before the day when they are made. Say the ex-dividend day is 28 days before the coupon payment is made. On that day, the total price will have reached only £103.38, not £104, and it will fall by £4 to £99.38 and so be 62p below the clean price. It will at once start to rise by 2.2p again to reach £100 by the next coupon payment day, but until that payment day the total price will actually be below the clean price.

The upshot is that a clean price ignores that part of the total price that arises because the next coupon payment is not exactly six months away. As a clean price ignores the tendency for the total price to rise because a coupon payment is due within six months, it shows what the total price would be if a coupon payment had just been made, so that the next one was just six months away.

Examples of fixed-interest securities

Table 2.4 gives two examples of fixed-interest securities. The figures are those which applied at the close of business on 21 May 1998. They concern two gilts which each have a £100 face value. The first gilt is the Treasury 6¼%

Table 2.4 Examples of fixed-interest securities (end of 21 May 1998)

High – 52 week – Low		Stock	Price (£)	+/–	Int yld (%)	Red yld (%)
104½	99⁷⁄₁₆	Treasury 6¼% 2010	103¹⁷⁄₃₂xd	+⅜	6.04	5.84
42¹⁵⁄₃₂	38½	Treasury 2½%	41¹¹⁄₃₂	+⁵⁄₃₂	6.05	–

2010 bond. These bonds have a 6¼% coupon, so their owners will receive £6.25 interest each year until maturity in 2010. Their price at the end of 21 May was quoted as £103¹⁷⁄₃₂*xd*. This price is the market price, or clean price, not the total price which is the amount of money that would have changed hands on a deal at the close of business that day. The *xd* means it is an ex-dividend price. The clean price rose £⅜ on 21 May, having moved between £99⁷⁄₁₆ and £104½ over the previous year. The **interest yield** shows the annual interest payments as a percentage of the clean price, that is £6.25 as a percentage of the £103¹⁷⁄₃₂ price which is 6.04%. This is a fair indication of the return in the form of interest, because the market price shows what the security would be worth if the next interest payment was due in exactly six months and ignores any effect caused by the fact that the payment might not be due then. Because the interest yield is worked out using the clean price, it alters whenever that price changes, which means that it alters whenever the total price alters for any reason other than the next coupon payment getting closer.

Anyone who actually bought one of these securities on 21 May 1998 and held it until 2010 would get a lower return than the 6.04% from the interest. They would also suffer a capital loss at maturity equal to the £100 maturity value less the total price they paid. The **redemption yield** – which is sometimes called the gross redemption yield – is an estimate of the average annual return in each year up to 2010 allowing for both the capital loss and the interest; it is 5.84% of the clean price. The way in which it is estimated is discussed below.

The second gilt in Table 2.4 is an undated 2½% consol. The figures for it are analogous to those for the dated gilt except that no redemption yield is shown, for consols need never be redeemed.

The prices of fixed-interest securities

The price paid for a fixed-interest security with a given coupon rate, face value and, where relevant, maturity date, depends on two main factors:

1. How likely the borrower is to default on the annual interest payments and at maturity. Central government securities are risk-free in these respects and so, other things being equal, sell for the highest prices. In contrast, risky companies are regarded with most caution, so their securities sell for the lowest prices.
2. The interest rates which lenders could get on other loans with comparable risks of default. These interest rates determine the returns that investors want from fixed-interest securities and therefore affect the prices which they will pay for them.

To see the effect of these factors, it is useful to derive formulae for the prices of dated securities and perpetuities. To see how the formula for a dated security works, recall X who considered buying some zero-coupon bonds issued by LML with a face value of £100. Suppose X wants a return of 10% on one-year loans to LML and an annual return of 11% on two-year loans. Using equation (2.1) for the price of a zero-interest security, $M/(1 + r_N)^N$, it was shown earlier that X would pay £100/1.10 for a one-year bond, that is £90.91, and that he would pay £100/(1.11)^2 for a two-year bond, that is £81.16. Suppose, next, that X considered buying one one-year bond and 11 two-year ones. His total payment would be £983.67, that is £90.91 plus 11 times £81.16. In return, he would receive £100 in one year's time when the one-year bond matured and £1,100 in two years' time when the two-year bonds matured.

Next, suppose that X considers buying ten 10% LML debentures with a face value of £100 and two years to maturity, and suppose that interest is paid in one instalment at the end of each year. Then after one year, X will receive £10 in interest on each debenture, which makes £100 in all. After two years, he will receive for each debenture £10 in interest plus a redemption sum of £100, which makes a total of £110 on each debenture and £1,100 in all. As X's payoff is identical to that in the last paragraph, he would be willing to pay an identical amount for the ten debentures, that is £983.67 in all or £98.37 each. So the present value, or price, of each debenture is given by 10/(1.10) + 110/(1.11)^2 or £9.09 + £89.28, that is £98.37.

More generally, the present value or price of a dated fixed-interest security, P_{DFIS}, with an annual coupon payment, C, a maturity value, M, and N years to maturity, is given by:

$$P_{DFIS} = C/(1 + r_1) + C/(1 + r_2)^2 + \ \ldots \ C/(1 + r_N)^N + M/(1 + r_N)^N \qquad (2.2)$$

Here, r_1, r_2 and r_N are the annual rates of return required on loans of one, two and N years to the security issuer. For simplicity, (2.2) assumes that the next coupon payment is exactly one year away. This means that the last coupon payment must have just been paid, so that the total price and the clean price will be the same.

It can be seen from (2.2) that the price will be sensitive to the required rates of return. Suppose that interest rates generally double. Suppose, in turn, that the rates of return required by lenders who buy fixed-interest securities also double. Then X might now want a 20% return on a one-year loan to LML and 22% a year on a two-year loan. In that case, (2.2) can be used to show that the price of a two-year debenture with an annual coupon payment of £10 and a face value of £100 will be 10(1.20) + 10/(1.22)^2 + 100/(1/22)^2, which is £82.24.

Often interest is paid in half-yearly instalments. In this case, (2.2) needs replacing by (2.3):

$$P_{DFIS} = c/(1 + r_{0.5})^{0.5} + c/(1 + r_1) + c/(1 + r_{1.5})^{1.5} + c/(1 + r_2)^2$$
$$+ \ldots \ c/(1 + r_N)^N + M/(1 + r_N)^N \qquad (2.3)$$

which assumes that the next coupon payment is due in just six months. To understand the differences between (2.3) and (2.2), note first that all the terms shown in (2.2) reappear in (2.3) to cover the end-of-year coupon payments and the maturity value. In (2.3), however, the end-of-year coupon payments will be half the value of the full yearly payment, so, as a reminder of this, each coupon payment is shown by c rather than C. Also, (2.3) has extra terms for the extra payments of c that are paid after half a year, 18 months and so on. (2.3) shows that these payments have to be divided by expressions that include values such as $r_{0.5}$, and $r_{1.5}$ which are the interest rates required on loans of six months and 18 months to the issuer, expressed as annual rates.

Some examples will be used to show how these interest rates can be calculated. Suppose that Y requires a 5% return on a six-month loan to the security issuer. This means that if £100 was lent, then Y would want £105 repaid after six months; if this £105 was subsequently re-lent at the same rate for, say, another six months, then Y would secure £105(1.05) or £110.25 after one year. Thus the 5% return required on six-month loans can be expressed as 10.25% per year. It is this figure, or more precisely 0.1025, which would be used for $r_{0.5}$. Suppose, also, that Y requires a return of 16% on an 18-month loan to the security issuer. This means that if £100 was lent, then Y would want a repayment of £116 after 18 months; if this £116 was subsequently re-lent at the same rate for, say, another 18 months, then Y would secure £116(1.16) or £134.56 after three years. This sum of £134.56 would also be secured by someone who made a loan of £100 for three years at an annual rate of 10.40%, for they would secure £110.40 after one year, £110.40(1.104) or £121.88 after two years, and £121.88(1.104) or £134.56 after three years. So the return of 16% required by Y over 18 months is equivalent to an annual figure for $r_{1.5}$ of 10.4%, that is 0.104.

It may seem that the formulae for the price of a perpetuity, or undated fixed-interest security, P_{UFIS}, should resemble (2.2) and (2.3), except that the last term would be omitted as redemption never occurs. However, such formulae would have an infinite number of terms which used an infinite number of different possible required rates of return for an infinite number of different possible length loans to the borrower. Not surprisingly, a simpler approach is used. First, buyers of undated securities tend to think only of a single annual rate, r, which they require on a loan to the borrower that will never be repaid. Then the buyers can be seen as slotting this rate into every term in the formulae. This still leaves an infinite number of terms. However, it can easily be shown mathematically that, if there is only one interest payment a year and if the next payment is due in exactly one year, then the total value of that infinite number of terms, which gives P_{UFIS}, is given by this simple formula:

$$P_{\text{UFIS}} = C/r \qquad\qquad (2.4)$$

For example, suppose Y wants an annual return of 12%, or 0.12, from a perpetuity that pays £12 a year. She would clearly pay £100 for it to get a 12% return, and this can be found from (2.4) as £12/0.12 which is £100. The price of a perpetuity is very sensitive to the required rate of return. For example, suppose that interest rates doubled so that Y would now want twice the rate of return from the perpetuity, that is 24%. Then (2.4) shows that Y would now pay just 12/0.24, which is £50. Thus with perpetuities, a doubling of interest rates causes a dramatic halving of price.

If the perpetuity offered two equal half-yearly coupons, c, of £6, then its price would be given by the following modified formula, assuming that the next payment was exactly six months away:

$$P_{\text{UFIS}} = c/[(1 + r)^{0.5} - 1] \tag{2.5}$$

In the present example, this would give £6/[$(1.12)^{0.5} - 1$] which is £102.92. A buyer like Y would offer a little more here than for the perpetuity offering £12 once a year because the existence of two coupons a year means that the returns come a little quicker.

Redemption yields

It has been seen that an investor should use (2.2) or (2.3) to estimate the price that should be offered for a fixed-interest security when the rates of return required on different-length loans are known. Suppose that all these rates were the same. Then (2.2) and (2.3) would simplify to:

$$P_{\text{DFIS}} = C/(1 + r) + C/(1 + r)^2 + \ldots C/(1 + r)^N + M/(1 + r)^N \tag{2.6}$$

and

$$P_{\text{DFIS}} = c/(1 + r)^{0.5} + c/(1 + r) + c/(1 + r)^{1.5} + c/(1 + r)^2 \\ + \ldots c/(1 + r)^N + M/(1 + r)^N \tag{2.7}$$

in which r is the annual rate of return required on loans of any length to the issuer. (2.6) and (2.7) are actually used to calculate the redemption yields on fixed-interest securities with annual and twice-yearly coupon payments. As noted above, the redemption yield on a fixed-interest security is the average annual rate of return that will be earned by a buyer who pays the current market price and holds it until maturity. This return allows for the interest, and for any capital gain or loss that will arise at maturity. (2.6) and (2.7) assume that a coupon payment has just been paid. So the next payment is one year or six months away, and the clean price equals the total price. So either price can be used for P_{DFIS} in (2.6) and (2.7). Then they can be solved to find r which is the redemption yield. If the next payments are not so neatly timed, then (2.6) and (2.7) must be slightly modified and the total price must be used.

Solving equations like these is best left to computers, but one example will be given. This will use the 10% LML debentures considered earlier where there was only one coupon payment a year and two years to maturity. It was explained that X would be willing to pay £98.37 for one of these. In terms of (2.6), P_{DFIS} is £98.37, C is £10 and M is £100, so 98.37 = 10/(1 + r) + 110/(1 + r)^2. This can be solved to show that r, the redemption yield, is 10.95%. This is a just under the 11% that X requires on two-year loans to LML. This difference stems from the fact, shown earlier, that buying a two-year debenture is equivalent to making a small one-year loan and a larger two-year loan. As X in the example requires a lower return on one-year loans than two-year ones, so he accepts a lower average return on the two-year debenture than he would require on a two-year zero-coupon bond which is a wholly two-year loan. If X had wanted a higher return on one-year loans than on two-year loans, then the redemption yield would have exceeded his required return on two-year loans like the two-year zero-coupon bond.

The results found here can be generalised a little. Suppose, as is normally the case, that investors want higher returns on long-term loans than short-term ones. Then redemption yields will tend to be highest on those securities that have the longest time to maturity. It might also be thought that the redemption yield would always be the same on securities with the same time left, at least if they were issued by the same borrower. But this is not always so. To see why, suppose that in addition to the 10% LML debentures with a face value of £100 and two years to run, investors can also buy 15% LML debentures with a face value of £100 and two years to run. It must be supposed that these two debenture stocks were issued at different times when interest rates, and hence the coupon rates that LML had to offer, were quite different. However, they both mature in two years. It has already been seen that the 10% debentures will have a price of £98.37 and a redemption yield of 10.95%.

The 15% debenture will secure for its holder £15 in one year, in the form of interest, and £115 in two years in the form of a repayment plus interest. Allowing that investors want returns of respectively 10% and 11% on one-year and two-year loans to LML, (2.2) gives the price of this debenture as $15/(1.10)$ + $115/(1.11)^2$, which is £13.64 + £93.34 or £106.97. So (2.6) here becomes $106.97 = 15/(1 + r) + 115/(1 + r)^2$ Solving this for r gives 10.93%. This is lower than the 10.95% figure on the 10% debenture. The reason is that the 10% debenture gives returns of £10 and £110, while the 15% one gives returns of £15 and £115. A lower proportion of the 15% debenture's returns arise after two years, so the average rate required on this is lower. The average rate would be higher if investors wanted a higher return on one-year loans than on two-year loans.

In practice, the situation is complicated by tax considerations which have so far been ignored. Over the two years, the 10% debenture will give the buyer £20 in income plus a capital gain of £(100 – 98.37) or £1.63. In contrast, the 15% debenture will give the buyer £30 in income and a capital loss of £(106.97 – 100) or £6.97. As capital gains and income have different treatments for tax purposes, with capital gains generally being favourably treated, investors might prefer bonds where part of the return comes in a capital gain. So the 10% debenture might attract a slightly higher price than the £98.37 calculated above when tax considerations were ignored. This would reduce its redemption yield and might even push it below that of the 15% debenture.

2.4 VARIABLE-INTEREST SECURITIES

Variable-interest securities resemble fixed-interest securities except that either the coupon rate or the face value is variable. They are issued by the central government and companies to secure long-term loans. They are issued and traded in similar ways to fixed-interest securities, and their quoted prices are clean prices. The four main types of variable-interest security are listed in Table 2.5. The first two types are issued by the central government and the other two by companies.

Table 2.5   The main types of variable-interest security

Type	Issued by	Income	Redemption
Index-linked central government bonds (index-linked gilts)	Central government	Fixed interest in real terms	Long-term at par in real terms
Floating rate central government bonds (floating rate gilts)	Central government	Variable interest	Short-term at par
Variable-rate bonds *or* floating rate notes (FRNs)	Companies	Variable interest	Long-term at par
Perpetual floating rate notes (Perpetual FRNs)	Companies	Variable interest	Never

The central government's **index-linked gilts** have a fixed coupon rate and an initial £100 face value. Before every interest payment, and also before redemption, they are given new face values. Each new face value is set as follows: if the retail prices index (RPI) rose by, say, 30% between eight months before the bond was issued and eight months before the next interest payment or redemption, then the new face value is £130. Each interest payment is based on the coupon and the latest face value, while the redemption payment equals the final face value. Ignoring any problems caused by the eight-month lag, the interest payments are all the same in real terms, that is after allowing for inflation, and the maturity value is the same in real terms as the original £100. The lag arises because the RPI on the dates when interest payments and redemption are made is not actually known on those dates. Still less is it known some weeks earlier when the payments are prepared.

The government's **floating rate bonds** have been issued only since 1994. So far, their redemption dates have been set at five years after issue, so that the bonds became shorts immediately after being issued. Coupon payments on these bonds are made every three months. At each payment time, the coupon rate is set as the current three-month LIBID rate minus ⅛%.

Floating rate notes (FRNs) are issued by companies. They mature after 7–15 years and have fixed face values. Their coupon rates float in line with another rate, usually LIBOR. One variant, which is called **drop-lock bonds**, incorporates a minimum floor value for the coupon. FRNs appeared in the 1970s when large changes in interest rates made lenders wary of fixed-coupon bonds. Many FRNs are issued by banks and are, in effect, long-term time deposits. **Perpetual floating rate notes** (perpetual FRNs) are simply undated FRNs and are relatively rare.

Prices of variable-interest securities

If a variable-interest security has a face value that moves in line with inflation, then its price will usually rise when the face value rises, for the higher face value will lead to higher future coupon payments and a higher repayment at maturity. The price will also change if interest rates change. For example, if interest rates rise, then people will want higher returns from the security, and buyers can secure a higher return by paying a lower price.

In contrast, if a variable-interest security has a variable coupon, then its price will be relatively stable. It is true that if interest rates generally rise or fall, then people will want higher or lower returns from these securities, just as they do from any other securities. But whereas with other securities, buyers can secure the higher or lower returns they require only by paying lower or higher prices, here the returns alter automatically, so there is no need for a change in price.

Examples of variable-interest securities

Table 2.6 gives two examples of variable-interest securities. The figures are those which applied at the close of business on 21 May 1998. The first example is an index-linked (IL) gilt with a 2½% coupon and maturity in 2009. At the close of business on 21 May, it was trading at a total price which, when adjusted to allow for any interest due in less than six months, gave a clean price of £194½₂. The price change column shows that the price rose by £¹⁵⁄₁₆ from the end of the previous day. It had varied between £187¹⁄₁₆ and £194½₂ over the previous year. The table also gives two illustrative **real redemption rates** which relate to two different future inflation scenarios.

Table 2.6   Examples of variable-interest securities (end of 21 May 1998)

High – 52 week – Low	Stock	Price (£)	+/–	Real redemption rate %	
194½₂	187¹⁄₁₆ Treasury (IL) 2½% 2009	194½₂xd	+ ¹⁵⁄₁₆	2.85 at 5%	2.96 at 3%
100⁵⁄₃₂	100⁵⁄₃₂ Treasury floating rate 1999 100³⁄₁₆		+ ½₂	–	–

To understand real redemption rates, suppose first that this gilt was not index-linked. Then it would earn £2.50 a year and be redeemed for £100. Suppose, too, that its total price was under £100. Then its redemption yield or rate would be over 2.50%. However, if retail prices subsequently rose, then the *real* value of its coupon payments and its redemption payment would fall. Now allow that it is index-linked, and suppose that changes in its face value kept up with the RPI *with no lag*. Also, suppose prices have doubled since it was issued. Then, if its total price was under £200, a buyer would secure a *real* redemption rate over 2.50%, for the first year's income of £5.00 would be over 2.50% of its price, and its future payments and its redemption value would keep up with the RPI. In practice, there *is* a lag between changes in the RPI and changes in its face value. So, if inflation speeds up, then its returns will not quite keep up with the RPI, and its real redemption rate will fall. Published figures, like those shown in Table 2.6, give real redemption rates for two illustrative inflation scenarios. For a buyer who paid the 21 May total price, the rate would be 2.85% if inflation sped up to 5% that day and stayed at 3% until maturity, but it would be 2.96% if inflation instead slowed to 3% that day and stayed at 3% until maturity.

The second example in Table 2.6 is a floating rate gilt which matures in 1999. These gilts have a face value of £100. They also have very stable prices because their coupon rates vary when other interest rates vary. The published clean prices are especially stable because they ignore that component of the total price which is accounted for by any coupon payment that is due within the next three months. It will be seen that in the previous 52 weeks, the clean price had never departed far from £100. Although these gilts have stable prices, it is impossible to calculate redemption yields or redemption rates for them because their future coupon payments are unknown.

2.5 EQUITIES OR ORDINARY SHARES

Equities or **ordinary shares** are issued only by companies and are held by their owners. Equities never mature as they represent ownership or equity, not debt. Because a company's ordinary shareholders own it, they have some powers. For example, they elect the directors and authorise any new share issues.

The face value of an equity is its original purchase price which is often 25p or £1. Instead of receiving interest payments, shareholders get **dividends** that are paid out of company profits. The shareholders do not receive all the profits as some must be paid to the government in **corporation tax**, that is a tax on company profits, and some are usually retained by the company to finance expansion. Also, companies often save some profits in good years to help maintain dividends in future bad years. The uncertainty about the future dividends on equities means their prices settle so that their expected returns exceed those on other company securities and on government securities.

Because a company's ordinary shareholders are its owners, they have the lowest priority in a bad year. So interest must be paid in full to holders of fixed- and variable-interest securities before any dividends are paid to ordinary shareholders. Also, in the event of liquidation, the proceeds of asset sales must be used to repay in full all other security holders before any money is paid to shareholders. However, the shareholders of companies do have one privilege, and this is **limited liability**. This means that if the asset sales realise too little to repay the company's debts, then that is unfortunate for the creditors, for the owners will not have to dip into their private savings or sell off their private assets such as houses and other investments. This privilege is not enjoyed by the owners of partnerships and sole proprietorships, who would have to do precisely that. Companies have to draw attention to the fact that their owners' liability is limited to the value of the company's assets by putting 'plc' or 'Ltd' after their name. '**Plc**' means public limited company and is used by **public companies**, that is companies whose shares are available to the general public and whose shares have a total face value over a level specified by the government. '**Ltd**' is used by other companies which are called **private companies**.

Each year, people may place limited amounts of shares in so-called **personal equity plans** (PEPs). Any dividends and capital gains made by these shares are tax-free. From 1999, PEPs will be replaced by ISAs which, as noted in Chapter 1.8, will also cover some deposits with tax-free interest.

How equities are issued

When a new private company is established, its new equities are usually bought by a few members of a family and their friends. If it later becomes a public company, then it may simply be given an **introduction**, which means that it is introduced to a stock exchange so that its existing shares can in future be traded there. However, when private companies go public, they often take the chance to issue some extra new shares to the public, or else their existing shareholders sell some of their existing shares to the public; thus they **float** some new or existing shares to the public. Of course, when a new public company is established, then it has to float its new shares to the public.

There are four ways in which a company can have a **flotation**, and so float shares for the first time. In each case a financial intermediary is usually involved and acts as an **issuing house** or **sponsor**.

1. **An offer for sale.** Here a company gets the sponsor to sell the shares to the public on its behalf. The sponsor advertises the shares by writing a prospectus that quotes their price and gives details of the company. If the sponsor receives more applications than there are shares, then it rations them out. If it receives fewer applications than there are shares, then it usually agrees to buy for itself those that are left over. This means that the sponsor **underwrites** the issue.
2. **A public issue.** This resembles an offer for sale except that the company plays a larger role and the sponsor plays a smaller role. In particular, the shares are bought directly from the company, and unsold shares are not taken up by the sponsor.
3. **A placing.** Here, the new shares are sold to selected stockbrokers and market makers who deal in equities. These purchasers then sell them in due course to their clients, or other people, at whatever price they can then get. This method is very common for new small companies.
4. **A tender.** Here the sponsor invites people to make bids, and then it sets a uniform price which is the highest price that allows all the shares to be sold. It is a rare method but an appropriate one when it is hard to assess in advance the price that the public will pay.

When an existing public company wishes to float additional new shares, then it can again use one of these four methods. However, there are five other methods which it could use instead, as noted below, although only the first three of these alternatives can be seen as significant sources of funds.

1. **Rights issues.** Here, a company offers new shares to its existing shareholders for less than the current market price. All the shareholders are offered a number of shares in proportion to their existing holdings, say 1 to 5. So, if they all took up their rights, then they would each own the same fraction of the company as before. If some shareholders do not take up their rights, then the company sells their allocations for them on a stock exchange. Rights issues are frequently used.
2. **Warrants.** Companies sometimes give warrants to people who purchase securities other than equities. The warrants entitle these purchasers to

buy equities, or occasionally other types of security, at a fixed price on one or more specified later dates. The share price fixed in the warrants is below the price which the company expects to apply on the relevant date or dates. In this way, the company hopes to tempt the warrant holders to buy shares when the time comes. Warrants are explored a little further in Section 6.9.

3. **Scrip dividends.** Many companies offer to give shareholders extra shares instead of dividends. The value of the shares offered equals the value of the dividend due. Strictly speaking, scrip dividends do not raise extra funds for companies. However, they have an identical effect because companies pay out less money in dividends when offers of scrip dividends are taken up.

4. **Scrip issues.** Here a company simply gives new shares to existing shareholders so that the company raises no money at all. Say LML has a one-for-four scrip issue. Then its future profits must be shared among 25% more shares, so the dividend per share drops. The share price will probably drop so that five shares are now worth what four used to be worth. Most scrip issues are made to reduce high share prices, for lower prices may make shares a little easier to trade.

5. **Share option schemes.** Many companies offer share option schemes to senior executives, and perhaps to some other employees, and perhaps even to their families. A typical arrangement is to offer them the chance to buy a certain number of shares on a specified future date at the share price applying when the scheme is introduced. This gives the employees an incentive to make the company prosper and send its share price up, for they will then be able to buy shares at a large discount off the future price and, if they wish, at once sell their shares for a profit. These schemes should not be confused with the equity options discussed in Chapters 6 to 8, which may be held by people who have nothing to do with the companies concerned.

How equities are traded

Existing shares in private companies are often traded privately. In many cases, the directors may have to give permission before a sale can take place. Also, the directors may be allowed to vet potential new shareholders.

Existing shares in public companies are almost always traded on a **stock exchange**. Until the late 1980s, it was possible to by-pass a stock exchange by using the so-called **over-the-counter market**. Here, licensed dealers in securities would either agree to buy and sell shares in selected companies, or they would put buyers and sellers into direct contact. These dealers were given little supervision. Their position became very difficult after the 1986 Financial Services Act came into force. Their share of the market was always small.

The main stock exchange in the United Kingdom is the London Stock Exchange (LSE) in London. The LSE also runs six small exchanges outside London but plans to close them in 1998. Most large United Kingdom companies are on the LSE's *Stock Exchange Daily Official List*, which means that their shares are officially accepted by the LSE for quotation and trading. For its shares to be **listed securities**, which means being included on this list, a company must meet stringent requirements of financial behaviour and financial reporting. The principal benefit to a company of being listed is to prove that it has passed these tests. This increases confidence in the company and so makes its shares acceptable to more people. Consequently, the company should find it easier to float additional shares. The official list includes many foreign companies as well as United Kingdom companies. And, indeed, many United Kingdom companies are also listed on foreign stock exchanges.

The LSE also runs an **alternative investment market (AIM)**. The requirements for companies seeking recognition in AIM are a little less stringent than those for full listing. AIM is chiefly a market for shares in new and small companies. Although AIM covers many companies, their total value is trivial compared to the value of the companies on the official list.

The key players in a stock exchange are **market makers** who buy and sell the shares of many companies. At the LSE, there are between two and twelve competing market makers for the shares of most listed companies. These market makers quote their bid and ask prices throughout the day on a computer network called the **Stock Exchange automated quoting system (SEAQ)**. People who wish to buy and sell shares contact a stockbroker who does a deal on their behalf with the market maker offering the most favourable terms. Some market makers also act as stockbrokers, but the LSE requires them not to buy and sell to their own clients unless their prices are the most favourable.

In 1997, the LSE began moving to a new computerised **Stock Exchange electronic trading system (SETS)**. Here, stockbrokers also signal their bids and offers on behalf of their clients, and these are automatically matched with those of the most favourable market makers. Thus SETS effectively fixes trades, whereas SEAQ merely provides brokers with price information.

For smaller listed companies there is only one market maker, and for AIM companies there are usually only one or two. These market makers use a network called **SEATS PLUS**; SEATS stands for **Stock Exchange alternative trading service**.

The prices of equities

The market prices of equities fluctuate greatly. There are two major factors that affect share prices as a whole. The first is the level of interest rates. For example, if interest rates on loans rise, then investors become less keen to buy shares, so the demand for shares falls and their prices fall. As shares are perpetuities, their prices are very sensitive to interest rate changes. The second factor is the future outlook for the economy. Thus any news which suggests that the economy will prosper, so that profits and dividends should rise, leads to a widespread rise in share prices, and vice versa.

The price of the shares in any given company, such as LML, is also affected by news about the company itself. Sometimes news causes a large change in the share price but leads to little turnover in shares. For example, LML might announce a new discovery which suggests that its dividends will rise. In this case, market makers will raise the price of LML shares so that few people will buy them. Alternatively, there may be bad publicity about LML's products which suggests that its dividends will fall. In this case, market makers will reduce the price of LML shares so that few existing holders will sell them. At other times, news causes little change in the share price but leads to a large turnover. For example, LML may announce that it is licensing a rival to make some of its patented products. Some people may think that this will lead to higher dividends as a result of the licence revenue, so they will want to buy LML shares, but some existing shareholders may think that the rival will reduce LML's own sales and thus reduce its dividends, so they will want to sell their LML shares. So there may be many buyers and sellers but little change in the price.

The price of an equity can be related by a formula to its expected future dividends. The formula can be derived from (2.2) which related the price of a dated fixed-interest security to its future coupon payments and its redemption value. (2.2) assumes that only one coupon payment is made each year and that one has just been paid. It is repeated here:

$$P_{\text{DFIS}} = C/(1 + r_1) + C/(1 + r_2)^2 + \ldots C/(1 + r_N)^N + M/(1 + r_N)^N$$

This formula needs to be modified in four ways to get an equivalent formula for equities. First, equities secure dividends, not coupon, payments, so the annual incomes should be shown with a D, not a C. Secondly, the dividends may all be different, so they should be called D_1, D_2, and so on. Thirdly, an equity never matures, so there should be an infinite number of terms, although the last term in (2.2) should disappear as it allows for the value of the redemption payment. Finally, as with perpetuities, investors usually refer to a single average annual return required on each equity, r, rather than use different annual rates for the period up to each dividend. So the formula becomes:

$$P_{\text{EQUITY}} = D_1/(1 + r) + D_2/(1 + r)^2 + \ldots D_\infty /(1 + r)^\infty \qquad (2.8)$$

As (2.8) has an infinite number of terms, it looks intractable. A common way of making it tractable is to assume that dividends will grow at a constant rate, g. Call the dividend that has just been paid D_0. Then $D_1 = D_0(1 + g)$, $D_2 = D_0(1 + g)^2$, and so on. For example, suppose that LML has just paid a dividend of 3p and that its dividends are expected to grow by 5% a year, so that g is 0.05. Then its dividend at the end of the present year, D_1, will be 3(1.05) or 3.15, and D_2 will be 3(1.05)^2, or 3.31. Substituting $D_1 = D_0(1 + g)$, $D_2 = D_0(1 + g)^2$, and so on in (2.8) gives:

$$P_{\text{EQUITY}} = D_0(1 + g)/(1 + r) + D_0(1 + g)^2/(1 + r)^2 + \ldots D_0(1 + r)^\infty /1 + g)^\infty \qquad (2.9)$$

This can be further simplified. To see how, define w as $(1 + g)/(1 + r)$. Then (2.9) becomes:

$$P_{\text{EQUITY}} = D_0 w + D_0 w^2 + \ldots D_0 w^\infty \qquad (2.10)$$

Dividing each side of (2.10) by w produces:

$$P_{\text{EQUITY}}/w = D_0 + D_0 w + \ldots D_0 w^{\infty\ -1} \qquad (2.11)$$

and subtracting (2.11) from (2.10) gives:

$$P_{\text{EQUITY}} - (P_{\text{EQUITY}}/w) = D_0 w^\infty - D_0 \qquad (2.12)$$

Recall that $w = (1 + g)/(1 + r)$. If $g < r$, then $w^\infty = 0$, so (2.12) can be simplified to $P_{\text{EQUITY}}(1 - 1/w) = D_0$. This can be rearranged to give $P_{\text{EQUITY}} = D_0 w/(w - 1)$, and this in turn can be re-expressed as:

$$P_{\text{EQUITY}} = D_1/(r - g) \qquad (2.13)$$

For example, if the required return from LML shares, r, is 12% or 0.12, while g is 0.05 and D_0 is 3p, so that $D_1 = 3.15$, then the price of LML shares, P_{EQUITY}, will be 3.15/(0.12 – 0.05), which is 3.15/0.07 or 45p.

Examples of equities

Table 2.7 gives two examples of equities. The examples are Pilkington, the glass makers, and Tate & Lyle, the sugar refiners. The figures shown are those applying at the close of business on 21 May 1998. For example, at the end of that day, Pilkingon shares had a **mid-point price**, P, of £1.36; this is actually the mid-point of the closing bid and ask prices set by market makers. P rose 2p that day having moved between £1.03½ and £1.39 over the past year. The **market capitalisation** of £1,417m is the total value of all issued Pilkington shares at £1.36 each. The figures for Tate & Lyle have identical meanings with xd indicating that the price is ex-dividend.

Table 2.7   Examples of equities (end of 21 May 1998)

High – 52 weeks – Low		Company	Price	+/–	Mkt cap. (£m)	Yield (%)	P/E
139	103½	Pilkington	136	+2	1,417	4.3	17.4
583	440½	Tate & Lyle	485*xd*	–13	2,180	3.5	10.9

The **yield**, or **dividend yield**, figures give the latest annual dividend per share, D, as a percentage of P. The yield figures of 4.3% and 3.5% show, for example, that an investor with £1,000 to invest could buy Pilkington shares and get dividends worth £43, that is 4.3% of £1,000, or buy Tate & Lyle shares and get dividends worth £35. So it may be wondered why any investors would buy Tate & Lyle shares. Part of the answer is that investors also care about future dividends, as implied in (2.8). For although Tate & Lyle has less D in relation to P, it actually has more **earnings**, that is more profit after paying corporation tax, and it may well be using much of its earnings to finance expansion.

To find the companies' earnings per share, E, as a percentage of P, it would be helpful if figures for E/P were published. But published figures always concern P/E. These **price–earnings ratios** show the price in pence that must be spent on shares to secure 1p worth of earnings. As Tate & Lyle has a lower P/E, it has a higher E/P, so that it is earning more in relation to P than Pilkington. It is possible to work out each company's E as a percentage P. This is given by $100/(P/E)$, which is (100/17.4) or 5.7% for Pilkington and (100/10.9) or 9.2% for Tate & Lyle. So, for each £1,000 worth of shares, Pilkington earns £57, while Tate & Lyle earns £92. This means that Pilkington has little earnings left over, after paying its dividends of £43, to finance expansion. In contrast, Tate & Lyle has plenty of its earnings left over, after paying its dividends of £35, to finance expansion. Indeed, it may now be wondered why anyone would buy Pilkington shares. But, again, people think ahead. They may expect Pilkington's earnings to rise more than Tate & Lyle's in the next few years. For as the economy moves out of recession, glass makers should see more profits growth than sugar refiners.

2.6 INVESTMENT TRUSTS

Most equities are issued by companies which spend the funds they raise on fixed assets that are used to produce goods and services. But, as noted in Section 1.3, there are some companies called investment trusts which spend the funds raised on securities. These trusts are financial intermediaries which in many ways resemble the unit trusts discussed in Section 1.8, but there are two differences between unit trusts and investment trusts. First, existing unit trust units can only be sold back to the trust which issued them whereas existing investment trust shares are traded on stock exchanges. Secondly, unit trusts are required by law to buy back their units at prices which reflect the value of the securities they own, whereas the prices of investment trust shares are fixed by supply and demand. The share prices for investment trust shares often reflect large discounts on the value of the underlying securities which the trusts own. This is probably because the trusts' managers take a slice of the income from those securities as a payment for their services, so that their shareholders get lower returns than they would get if they bought the securities directly.

As investment trust shareholders get lower returns than they would get if they bought the underlying securities directly, it may seem surprising that people ever buy investment trust shares. Some people buy them hoping that the managers will invest their money more effectively than they could do themselves, though the efficient markets hypothesis discussed in Section 3.9 casts some doubt on how successful the managers could hope to be. Other people buy them because some trusts specialise in holding certain types of security, such as equities in Pacific rim countries, and it may be difficult for private investors to buy these themselves. Yet other people buy trust shares because the trusts effectively spread their funds among far more companies than private investors could do themselves economically, once dealing costs are allowed for.

Examples of investment trust securities

Table 2.8 shows the prices of the securities issued by two investment trusts. The figures applied at the close of business on 21 May 1998 when the shares in the first trust, Fleming Overseas, were trading at £4.30½. This share price was up 4p from the close on the previous day, and it had ranged over the

Table 2.8   Examples of investment trusts (end of 21 May 1998)

High – 52 week – Low		Trust	Price	+/–	Gross yld (%)	NAV (£m)	Dis or Pm (–)
431	350½	Fleming Overseas	430½	+4	1.3	487.3	11.7
287½	202½	Jos Holdings Capital	287	+½	—	444.4	35.4
78	68	Income	73	...	25.6	—	—
181¾	177¾	Zero div. pref.	181	...	—	—	—

previous year between £3.50½ and £4.31. The trust's latest annual dividend was a mere 1.3% of the value of its shares. For, like many trusts, it spends most of its income on extra securities. This means that the value of its assets should rise quite quickly, and the price of its own shares should rise to reflect this; thus its shareholders should make high capital gains to offset their low dividends. The trust's **net asset value** (NAV), that is the value of its assets minus any sums it has borrowed through normal loans or by issuing fixed-interest securities, was £487.3m, but the market value of its shares was £11.7m less, as shown by the **discount** or 'Dis' of £11.7m. Very occasionally trust shares sell at a **premium** which would be shown by a negative 'Pm' figure in the final column. This could occur if, for example, the trust managers invested in small companies where private investors would have difficulty in finding information and sellers of shares.

As investment trust shares typically trade at prices that reflect a discount off the value of the trusts' underlying securities, the trusts are vulnerable to **takeovers**. For example, suppose a trust has issued 500 million shares which are currently trading at 100p and so have a value of £500m, and suppose the trust's assets are worth £570m. Then a takeover company might offer the trust's shareholders 110p for their shares. If the shareholders agreed, then they would be given £550m in all. But the takeover company could raise £570m by selling the trust's assets and so gain £20m for itself.

To deter such activities, many investment trusts are established with limited lifespans. At the **winding-up date**, when they terminate, their entire value is credited to the shareholders. This helps reduce any enthusiasm the shareholders might have to accept takeover bids. The usual way of fixing the lifespan is to set up a **split-capital trust**, or **split-level trust**, with at least two different sorts of share. Investment trust shares have a wide range of names and characteristics.

Jos Holdings, shown in Table 2.8, is a split-level trust and will wind up in 2003. It has issued three sorts of securities called capital shares, income shares and zero-dividend preference shares. The trust's constitution provides that the holders of the **zero-dividend preference shares** will receive nothing until 2003 when they will have first call on the trust's assets at up to 248p per share. These shares were naturally selling at a deep discount on 21 May 1998, when their price was 181p. The holders of the **income shares** will have the second call on the trust's assets in 2003 at a mere 1p per share; meanwhile, however, they will receive a high income. Thus in 1998 their dividend yield was 25.6%, but, of course, anyone who owns these shares and holds them until 2003 will receive a mere 1p back for each share. The holders of the **capital shares** will receive nothing until 2003. Then, after the zero-dividend preference shareholders have received their 248p and the income share holders their 1p, they will divide anything that is left over between themselves. On 21 May 1998, these shares were selling at a deep discount off their likely value in 2003. Indeed, their market value represented a discount of £35.4m off the amount which their holders would have received that day if the other shareholders had been paid their due amounts that day.

Income shares appeal to people who want a high income for a short period and yet who are not worried about losing their capital in the long term. Some elderly people might fall into this category. Capital shares appeal to people who want capital gains, for capital gains tend to get favourable tax treatment. Holders of capital shares need not wait for maturity to make some gains. For their shares are zero-income securities whose prices, therefore, should rise as maturity gets closer, as shown in Fig. 2.1. So they should be able to sell their shares at any time for more than they paid, unless interest rates rose sharply meanwhile. Some investment trusts also issue various other types of share such as conventional preference shares and **stepped preference shares** where either the coupon rate rises each year or the redemption value is way above the original face value.

2.7 SHARE INDICES

The Financial Times Industrial Ordinary Share Index

The *Financial Times* (FT) produces several indices to indicate trends in equity prices. Its oldest index is the **FT Industrial Ordinary Share Index** or **FT 30 Share Index** which was introduced in 1935 with a starting value or **base value** of 100. It is updated every minute to give virtually current information, which means that it is a **real-time** index. It is based on the average price of the shares of 30 leading companies. The constituent companies are reviewed periodically and are chosen to represent a variety of industries. The average price used is a geometric mean, so that the 30 share prices are multiplied together and the 30th root taken. To see how this works, suppose for simplicity that the index involves only four companies and that the fourth root is taken. Suppose, also for simplicity, that on 1 July 1935 when the index was launched, the four share prices were all four shillings, or 20p. The geometric mean of these four prices is $\sqrt[4]{(20 \times 20 \times 20 \times 20)}$, which is $\sqrt[4]{(160,000)}$, or 20. This figure would be multiplied by five to give the index a base value of 100.

Suppose that a month later, three of the four share prices were the same while the other had risen to 30p. Then the new geometric mean would be $\sqrt[4]{(20 \times 20 \times 20 \times 30)}$, which is $\sqrt[4]{(240,000)}$, or 22.13. This figure would also be multiplied by five to obtain that day's index, which would therefore be 110.65. The index would be 110.65 irrespective of whether the company whose price had risen was large or small, for this index makes no allowance for company size. This index is now rarely quoted, but it is interesting for long-term comparisons. Its lowest recorded value was 49.4 on 26 June 1940, and its highest value up to 21 May 1998 was 3,920.3 on 11 May 1998.

The main FTSE indices

Since 1984, several new indexes have been introduced which are worked out in similar ways to each other but in a quite different way from the older index. These *Financial Times* stock exchange indices are usually called **FTSE®** (or **Footsie®**) **Indices**; ® indicates that FTSE and Footsie are registered trade marks. Most of these indices follow rules set by the FTSE Actuaries Share Indices Steering Committee and are thus sometimes called FTSE-Actuaries or FTSE-A indices. The eight main FTSE indices are listed below. Three of these are shown as real-time indices; these are calculated at least once every minute of the official index period, 0900 to 1630, with further estimates calculated during the period from 0830 to 0900 when some trading takes place. The other indices are calculated only at the end of each business day. The constituent companies in the first five indices are reviewed every three months.

1. The **FTSE 100 Index** (real-time). This was introduced on 31 December 1983 with a base value of 1,000. It covers the 100 largest United Kingdom companies in terms of the value of their issued shares. These companies account for about 75% of the value of all listed equities.
2. The **FTSE 350 Index** (real-time). This was introduced on 12 October 1992, but it has been calculated back to a base date of 31 December 1985 when its base value was 682.94. It covers the 350 largest United Kingdom companies and about 94% of the value of all listed equities.
3. The **FTSE 350 Higher Yield Index**. This has the same base date and base value as the FTSE 350 index. It covers the companies in the FTSE 350 Index with the highest dividend yields. Specifically, the 350 companies are arranged in order of their dividend yields, and then enough of the higher yielding ones are selected for inclusion in the FTSE 350 Higher Yield Index to make the total value of their shares equal to about half the total value of the shares of all the 350 companies.
4. The **FTSE 350 Lower Yield Index**. This also has the same base date and base value as the FTSE 350 Index. It covers the companies in the FTSE 350 Index which are not in the FTSE 350 Higher Yield Index and which thus have the lowest dividend yields of the 350 companies.
5. The **FTSE 250 Index** (real-time). This was introduced on 12 October 1992, but it has been calculated back to a base date of 31 December 1985 when its base value was 1412.60. It covers the 250 companies in the FTSE 350 Index which are not in the FTSE 100 Index.
6. The **FTSE All-Share Index**. This was introduced on 10 April 1962 with a base value of 100. It is even wider than the FTSE 350 index, but, despite its name, it does not seek to include all listed companies. Instead, it seeks to include enough companies to cover 98–99% of the total value of all listed equities, which means including over 900 companies in all.

7. The **FTSE SmallCap Index**. This was introduced on 31 December 1992 with a base value of 1,363.79. It covers the companies in the FTSE All-Share Index which are not in the FTSE 350 Index.
8. The **FTSE Fledgling Index**. This was introduced on 31 December 1994 with a base value of 1,000. It covers all the listed shares that are excluded from the FTSE All-Share Index.

The *Financial Times* publishes several other indices related to these. For example, there are indices equivalent to the FTSE 250, FTSE SmallCap and FTSE Fledgling Indices except that they exclude any constituent companies which are investment trusts. The argument for omitting investment trusts is that they own shares in other companies so that their share prices merely reflect what is happening to other companies. There are also **industry basket** indices which each cover the shares of companies in a particular industry. Each day the *Financial Times* publishes figures for about 40 baskets, that is about 40 industries, using the relevant companies in the FTSE All-Share Index. It also gives figures for a few baskets that use only the relevant companies in the FTSE 350 Index.

To see how these FTSE indices are worked out, imagine for simplicity a similar index that involves only four companies, Aco, Bco, Cco and Dco, and suppose this index was launched on 31 December 1983 with a base value of 1,000. Suppose that on that day the issued shares of the four companies were worth respectively £1,000m, £500m, £300m and £200m, so their total value was £2,000m. This value would then be divided by £2m to get the base value for the index at 1,000. If, one week later, the prices of the first three companies' shares were the same but the price of Dco's shares had risen by 20%, then the value of Dco's shares would have risen by 20%, or £40m, so that the total value of the four companies' shares would be £2,040m. Dividing this by £2m gives an index for that day of (£2,040m/£2m), which is 1020. If, instead, Aco's shares had risen by 20%, then the value of its shares would have risen by £200m so that the total value of the four companies' shares would have been £2,200m and the index would have been (£2,200m/£2m), which is 1100. Thus indices like these are affected by both the price of each company's shares and the size of each company.

Some foreign indices

There are some broadly similar indices in many other countries. Two of the oldest and best known foreign indices are based on the arithmetical means, or simple averages, of the prices of some leading companies' shares, with no weighting for size. Thus the **Dow Jones Industrial Average Index** is based on one 30th of the total price of the shares of the 30 largest industrial companies in the United States, and the **Nikkei Stock Average** index is based on one 225th of the total price of the shares of 225 leading Japanese companies. Another well-known index, which shares the FTSE index method, is **Standard and Poor's 500 Index** (or **S&P 500**). This covers 500 United States companies over a range of industries. In 1987, the *Financial Times* and S&P introduced a **FT/S&P World Share Index** that is based on over 2,400 shares from about 30 countries. The financial press also quote indices from many other individual countries, and even individual exchanges, most notably in the United States where the three main stock markets are the New York Stock Exchange (NYSE), NASDAQ (the National Association of Securities Dealers Automated Quotation System) and the American Stock Exchange (Amex).

The *Financial Times* also publishes some European indices. The **FTSE Eurotop 300 Index** covers the 300 largest companies in Europe. The **FTSE Eurotop 100 Index** covers 100 representative leading companies in Europe. The **FTSE Ebloc 100 Index** covers 100 representative companies in those EU countries which will use the euro when it is introduced in 1999.

Examples of indices

Table 2.9 gives examples of the FTSE 100 Index, the FTSE 350 Index and the FTSE All-Share Index for the close of business, that is 1630, on 21 May 1998. The first column of figures gives the index values at that time; these values reflect the various base dates and base values. The day's changes in percentages allow the changes since the close on 20 May to be compared directly, but the indices for 20 May and a year ago reflect the varying base dates and values once again.

Dividend cover

To understand the next three columns in Table 2.9, it is helpful to focus on one index, say the FTSE 100 Index, and to imagine that on 21 May 1998 an investor, X, owned £10,000 worth of shares in a portfolio that exactly mirrored the current composition of the FTSE 100 Index. The gross yield figure shows that the total declared dividends in the previous year for this portfolio were 2.77% of the portfolio's current value, which for X is 2.77% of £10,000 or £277. The *P/E* figure shows that the price–earnings ratio in the previous year was 22.29, which means that the most recent level of earnings on X's portfolio was £10,000/22.29 or £449. The **net cover** or **dividend cover**, figure shows that, on average, the 100 companies could afford to pay their recent dividends 2.03 times over out of their earnings. This may seem surprising as the total earnings for a portfolio like X's are £449, while the total dividends are £277. The explanation lies in the way in which dividends are taxed.

To see this, consider one company, LML. Suppose its total 1997 profit was £100m, and suppose it has issued 100 million shares. Then the profit per share was 100p. LML was liable to corporation tax at the 1997 rate of 31%, so it had to pay £31m or 31p per share. So its earnings, or profits after corporation tax,

Table 2.9 Examples of share indices (end of 21 May 1998)

Index	21 May	Day's change (%)	20 May	Year ago	Gross yld (%)	Net cover	*P/E*	Xd adj. ytd	Total return
FTSE 100	5,935.6	+0.5	5,907.4	4,651.8	2.77	2.03	22.29	67.23	2,592.43
FTSE 350	2,885.5	+0.5	2,871.6	2,253.3	2.78	2.03	22.18	31.65	2,574.63
FTSE All-Share	2,821.98	+0.5	2,808.79	2,212.70	2.78	2.00	22.48	30.44	2,555.24

were £69m, and its earnings per share, E, were 69p. Broadly speaking, the government aimed to ensure that the tax liability on LML, or, strictly, on its owners, was £31m, no matter whether LML paid all of its £69m earnings in dividends, or paid none of it in dividends, or paid any intermediate amount in dividends. The easiest way of ensuring this might seem to be to make LML pay £31m in corporation tax and do what it wants with its £69m earnings. However, dividends are taxable as personal income, so if the government adopted this strategy, then LML's shareholders would lose just the £31m in corporation tax if there was no dividend, but they would lose the £31m in corporation tax *plus* the income tax on their dividends if any dividend was paid.

To sort this out, the government made LML remove 20% from any dividends that it paid, 20% being the lowest rate of personal income tax. Then LML had to pay this removed money to the government as a contribution towards its corporation tax. This contribution is called **advance corporation tax**. LML also had to pay the balance of the £31m that it owed in corporation tax. As a result, it paid a total of £31m in corporation tax, yet its dividends were regarded as having being taxed for personal income tax at 20%. If LML did pay a dividend, then the only extra income tax liability for its shareholders would fall on those who were liable to higher rates of income tax than 20%, and they would each individually pay the excess. Conversely, any shareholders exempt from income tax could claim back the 20% tax that was removed from their dividends.

The upshot of this arrangement was that LML could pay a dividend *in excess of* £69m, even though its profit was £100m and it was liable for corporation tax of £31m. It could actually pay a dividend of £86.25m, leaving £13.75m in profit left over. If it paid such a dividend, then it would have to pay advance corporation tax of 20% of £86.25m, which is £17.25m, and this would leave its shareholders with £69m. This £17.25m in advance corporation tax would be set against its total corporation tax liability of £31m to leave it another £13.75m to pay, which it could just manage from that part of its profit that was not paid in dividend. So the maximum dividend that LML could pay out of its 1997 profit was £86.25m, with shareholders actually receiving £69m. If LML did pay a gross dividend of £86.25m, leaving shareholders with £69m, then its dividend cover would be said to be just 1.00, for it could only just cover this.

Suppose LML actually paid half as much in dividend, or £43.125m, so that its dividend per share, D, was 43.125p. Then its dividend cover was 2.00 because it could have paid twice as much. LML would have removed 20% of its dividend in advance corporation tax to leave its shareholders with £34.5m, or 34.5p per share. So its dividend cover was *not* the earnings per share, E, divided by the dividend per share, D, which is 69p/43.125p, or 1.60. It was, in fact, $[E/(0.8D)]$ which is 69p/34.5p, or 2.00. For the companies in the FTSE 100 Index, X's portfolio shows that the ratio of E to D was 449/277, or 1.62, but the dividend cover, or net cover, was $[449/0.8(277)]$, or 2.03.

Ex-dividend adjustment and total return

Table 2.9 shows the day's change figure for each index. Each day, X can look at the day's change figure for the FTSE 100 Index and work out how much the value of his shares has risen or fallen. But the rise or fall in the value of his shares does not tell him the total return that he gets from his portfolio, for it ignores the fact that he gets dividends from his shares. This means that if the FTSE 100 Index rises, then X will enjoy more reward than the rise in the value of his shares because he will get dividends as well. Conversely, if the index falls, then X will not lose as much as the fall implies because he will have dividends to offset against the fall. The figure for the **ex-dividend adjustment year to date (Xd adj. ytd)** helps X work out the value of his dividends.

To see how the ex-dividend adjustment for one day is calculated, consider the example given earlier which involved a share index launched on 31 December 1983. This index covered only four companies, Aco, Bco, Cco and Dco. Suppose that the total value of their issued shares on 31 December 1983 was £2,000m and that the index base value was set at 1000 by dividing this by £2m. Imagine that on, say, 30 June 1998, Bco and Cco each pay a dividend, and suppose that the total value of their dividends is £20m. This can also be divided by £2m to give a figure of 10. That figure is the value of the dividends paid that day in terms of the index. The *Financial Times* does not actually publish the ex-dividend adjustment for each day. Instead, it publishes a cumulative figure for the year to date. The cumulative figure is zero at the start of the year, when no dividends have been paid, and rises to about 200 by the end of the year. Table 2.9 shows it was 67.23 on 21 May.

Table 2.9 also gives figures for **total return indices**. These were introduced by the *Financial Times* on 31 December 1992 with base values of 1,000. They show what would happen to the value of people's wealth if they invested it in the shares covered by the related FTSE index, and if they immediately used any dividends they received to buy more of those shares. The closing figure on 21 May 1998 for the total return on the FTSE 100 Index is shown as 2,592.43. This means, for example, that if Y had invested £100,000 in the 100 companies covered by the FTSE 100 Index on the base date for the total return index, that is 31 December 1992, and had reinvested all her subsequent dividends, then her portfolio would be worth £259,243 on 21 May 1998.

2.8 DURATION

Earlier sections have argued that if interest rates change, then the returns that investors require from securities change likewise. And they have shown that changes in required returns lead to changes in security prices. This section shows how the effect on a security's price of a change in the required return depends on its remaining lifetime. It begins by recalling what has been seen so far.

In the case of bills, it was seen in Fig. 2.1 that if the discount rates that people required doubled, say from 4% to 8%, then the price of a bill with 91 days to maturity would fall by only about 1% from £990 to £980, while the price of a bill that was about to mature would be insignificantly affected. In the fixed-interest securities, it is clear from Section 2.3 that if the required yields rose, then the effects on security prices would tend to be greatest on those securities with longest to run. For example, Section 2.3 considered a two-year debenture with a face value of £100 and a 10% coupon, and it showed that if investors required returns of 10% on one-year loans to the issuer and 11% on two-year loans, then its price would be £98.37, but if the required returns doubled, then its price would fall to £82.24, that is a fall of over 16%. Yet Section 2.3 also showed that if the required rates of return doubled for a perpetuity, then its price would fall by half, that is by 50%.

These examples show that security prices tend to be more sensitive to changes in the required returns when there is longer to maturity. Assuming that security prices adjust so that the actual returns or yields on securities equal the required returns, it follows that security prices tend to be more sensitive to changes in actual yields when there is longer to maturity. However, the effect of a change in the yield does not depend precisely on the time to maturity, but depends instead on a closely related measure called **duration** which was put forward by Macaulay (1938). This section shows what is meant by duration and it shows how it can be measured. It also explains how, when a security's duration is known, the sensitivity of its price to changes in its yield can be measured.

The meaning and calculation of duration

It may seem odd that there could be any measure of a security's remaining life other than the length of time left to maturity. However, Section 2.3 showed, for example, that a two-year fixed-interest bond could be seen as combining a small one-year loan with a large two-year loan on which no interest was due until the end of the two years. It follows that a two-year fixed-interest bond is not precisely equivalent to a two-year zero-coupon bond, even though it has the same time to maturity, for the latter is a *wholly* two-year loan on which no return is paid until maturity in two years.

The way in which duration is calculated is shown in Table 2.10. This considers three bonds issued by LML. These include a two-year zero-coupon bond and a two-year fixed-interest bond, to see how they differ, and they include a three-year fixed-interest bond to show the effect of a longer time to maturity. Each security has a face value of £100, and the two fixed-interest bonds have 10% coupons.

The table has three parts, one for each security. The first line in each part shows the payments to the holder at the end of each of the next three years. Part (a) shows the holder of a two-year zero-coupon bond securing just one payment of £100 after two years when the bond matures. Part (b) shows the holder of a two-year 10% bond securing £10 interest at the end of year 1 and £110 at the end of year 2, when the holder receives £10 interest plus £100 repayment. Part (c) shows the holder of a three-year 10% bond securing £10 interest at the end of both years 1 and 2, and securing £110 at the end of year 3, when the holder receives £10 interest plus £100 repayment.

The second line in each part of the table gives the present values (PV) of all these payments, and it adds these values up to give the current prices of the securities, which are termed P_0. These present values and prices are derived from formulae given earlier to relate security prices and yields. For simplicity, it is supposed here that investors want and secure an annual yield of 10% on the two-year zero-coupon LML bond and that they also want and secure 10%

Table 2.10 Duration and security price changes

Security	Variable	End of year 1	End of year 2	End of year 3	Totals	Showing that $-D^*\Delta r = \Delta P/P$
(a) Two-year zero-coupon bond	Payments (£)	0	100	–		
	PV at 10% (£)	0	82.645	–	$P_0 = 82.645$	$D^* = 1.818$
						$\Delta r = -0.001$
	Weight	1	2	–		$-D^*\Delta r = 0.0018$
	Weighted PV (£)	0	165.290	–		
	Weighted PV/P_0	0.000	2.000	–	$D = 2.000$	$\Delta P = 0.15$
						$\Delta P/P_0 = 0.0018$
	PV at 9.9% (£)	0	82.795	–	$P_1 = 82.795$	
(b) Two-year 10% bond	Payments (£)	10	110	–		
	PV at 10% (£)	9.091	90.909	–	$P_0 = 100.00$	$D^* = 1.735$
						$\Delta r = -0.001$
	Weight	1	2	–		$-D^*\Delta r = 0.0017$
	Weighted PV (£)	9.091	181.818	–		
	Weighted PV/P_0	0.091	1.818	–	$D = 1.909$	$\Delta P = 0.17$
						$\Delta P/P_0 = 0.0017$
	PV at 9.9% (£)	9.099	91.075	–	$P_1 = 100.17$	
(c) Three year 10% bond	Payments (£)	10	10	110		
	PV at 10% (£)	9.091	8.264	82.645	$P_0 = 100.00$	$D^* = 2.486$
						$\Delta r = -0.001$
	Weight	1	2	3		$-D^*\Delta r = 0.0025$
	Weighted PV (£)	9.091	16.529	247.934		
	Weighted PV/P_0	0.091	0.165	2.479	$D = 2.735$	$\Delta P = 0.25$
						$\Delta P/P_0 = 0.0025$
	PV at 9.9% (£)	9.099	8.280	82.870	$P_1 = 100.25$	

redemption yields on both the two-year and the three-year 10% LML bonds. This simplifying assumption actually implies that investors want annual 10% returns on one-year loans, two-year loans and three-year loans to LML.

The zero-coupon bond has only one payment. The present value of this payment, and the bond's price, are derived from (2.1). With a return or yield of 10%, or 0.1, (2.1) gives the present value of the payment, and the bond's price, P_0, as £100/(1.10)^2 which is £82.645. For the two fixed-interest bonds, the present values of the payments and the prices are derived from (2.6) which relates a bond's price to its returns and its redemption yield. In the context of (2.6), the present value of a year 1 payment is found by dividing it by (1 + 0.10), the present value of a year 2 payment is found by dividing it by (1 + 0.10)^2, and the present value of the year 3 payment is found by dividing it by (1 + 0.10)^3. Thus the present values of the two payments with the two-year 10% bond are £10/(1 + 0.10) and £110/(1 + 0.10)^2, which are £9.091 and £90.909; these can be summed to give this bond's price, P_0, which is £100.00. The present values of the three payments with the three-year 10% bond are £10/(1 + 0.10) and £10/(1 + 0.10)^2, and £110/(1 + 0.10)^3, which are £9.091, £8.264 and £82.645. These can be summed to give this bond's price, P_0, which is also £100.00.

The next three lines in each part show how the durations are calculated. First, each year is given a weight. Year 1 has a weight of one, year 2 has a weight of two, and year 3 has a weight of three. Then all the present values of the payments are multiplied by the relevant weights, to get what are termed weighted PVs. Thus the year 1 payments are multiplied by one, the year 2 payments by two and the year 3 payments by three. Then each of these weighted PVs is divided by the relevant P_0, which is £82.645 for the zero-coupon bond and £100.00 for the others. Finally, these values are added up to give the durations, D. It will be seen that D is exactly two years for the two-year zero-coupon bond, but it is a little less than two years for the two-year 10% bond, for it is 1.909 years. It is naturally longer for the three-year 10% bond, but it is 2.735 years rather than three years.

The general formula for the duration of a security with N years to maturity is:

$$D = (PV_1 w_1/P_0) + (PV_2 w_2/P_0) + ...(PV_N . w_N/P_0) \qquad (2.14)$$

where PV_1, PV_2 and PV_N are the present values of the payments in years 1, 2 and N, and where w_1, w_2 and w_N are the weights for years 1, 2 and N.

Modified duration and price changes

It is now possible to relate the change in a security's price to a change in its yield. In formulae, changes are indicated by the Greek letter delta, or Δ, so the change in a security's yield is Δr and the change in its price is ΔP. The relationship between ΔP and Δr can be expressed in a fairly simple formula that uses the duration, D, as one of its terms. But the relationship can be expressed in an even simpler formula that instead uses a **modified duration** denoted D^*. D^* is defined as $D/(1 + r)$, where r is the initial yield. The formula relates the proportional change in a security's price, $\Delta P/P_0$, to Δr as follows:

$$\Delta P/P_0 = -D^* \Delta r \qquad (2.15)$$

The final column of Table 2.10 demonstrates this result by considering the effect of a change in r from 10% to 9.9%, that is from 0.100 to 0.099, so that Δr is −0.001. As r is initially 0.100, $D^* = D/(1 + 0.100)$ in each case. The final column begins by giving D^*, Δr and $-D^* \Delta r$ for each security. To estimate each ΔP, it is first necessary to estimate the new price, P_1, and this is done in the middle part of the table by using the same present value procedure as before, but with r equal to 0.099 instead of 0.10. Thus P_1 for the zero-coupon bond is £100/(1.099)^2, or £82.795. This is £0.15 above the original P_0, £82.645, so ΔP is 0.15. P_1 for the other securities is £100.17 and £100.25 respectively, so their ΔP values are respectively 0.17 and 0.25. The final column shows each ΔP value and then works out each $\Delta P/P_0$. In each case, this does indeed equal $-D^* \Delta r$.

If both sides of (2.15) are multiplied by P_0, then it can be re-expressed to show the absolute change in a security's price in relation to a change in the yield, as follows:

$$\Delta P = -P_0 D^* \Delta r \qquad (2.16)$$

In each case in Table 2.10, the yield changed from 10% to 9.9%, that is by one-tenth of a percent. Equivalently, it changed by ten-hundredths of a percent, which is 10 basis points. The change in a security's price in response to a rise

of one basis point in its yield is called its **basis point value** (BPV). Slotting 0.0001 in place of Δr in (2.16) gives the following formula for BPV:

$$\text{BPV} = -0.0001P_0D^* \tag{2.17}$$

It can readily be shown that the BPVs of the bonds in Table 4 are –£0.015, –£0.017 and –£0.025, that is one-tenth of the size of the price changes caused by the 10-basis-point fall in the yield that are shown in the last column of the table. One use of BPVs is noted in Section 5.8.

This section explored securities which pay interest once a year. Most securities pay it twice yearly. With them, it is necessary to work in periods of 6 months. Suppose a bond with a 9% coupon matures in exactly 5 years, and that its required yield, r, is 6%, per year. Its remaining life is 10 periods and its required yield per period is taken as $r/2$, or r', or 3%. The present value of each remaining payment is found by dividing it by (1.03) to the appropriate power from 1 to 10. So the next payment has a present value of 4.5/(1.03) and the final one has one of $104.5/(1.03)^{10}$. The total present value or price, P, is £112.80. Weighting the 10 present values by appropriate weights from 1 to 10 gives a total weighted present value of £945.87. Dividing this by the price gives the duration, D, of 8.39 periods. D^* is $D/(1+r')$ which is 8.39/1.03 or 8.15. The effect of a change in r of, say, –0.001 to 6.1%, is given by a modified form of (2.16), $\Delta P = -P_0D^*\Delta r'$. So ΔP = –£112.80(8.15)0.0005, or –£0.46, and the price falls to £112.34.

SUMMARY

2.1   All marketable financial claims other than certificates of deposit can be seen as securities. Some securities may represent debt, that is a loan by the holder to the company or government which issued it, while others represent equity, which means the holder is a part-owner of the company that issued it.

2.2   Zero-interest securities usually represent short-term loans. They are bought at a discount off their face values, or par, and are redeemed at maturity at par. So the holder makes a capital gain. The discount rate on them is calculated by comparing the capital gain with the face value, but this is not the true rate of return. The price of a zero-income security is given by:

$$P_{ZIS} = M/1(1 + r_N)^N \tag{2.1}$$

where M is the maturity or par value, N is the time to maturity in years (or as a fraction of a year), and r_N is the annual rate of return required on a loan of N years to the issuer concerned.

2.3   Most fixed-interest securities are dated and are redeemed at maturity for their face values. Their holders are given a fixed annual income equal to the face value multiplied by a fixed-interest rate called the coupon rate. The price of a dated fixed-interest security, P_{DFIS}, with an annual income or coupon payment, C, and a maturity value, M, is given by:

$$P_{DFIS} = C/(1 + r_1) + C/(1 + r_2)^2 + \ldots C/(1 + r_N)^N + M/(1 + r_N)^N \qquad (2.2)$$

where r_1, r_2 and r_N are the required annual returns on loans of one, two and N years to the security issuer. If the interest is paid in two half-yearly instalments, then the price is given by:

$$P_{DFIS} = c/(1 + r_{0.5})^{0.5} + c/(1 + r_1) + c/(1 + r_{1.5})^{1.5} + c/(1 + r_2)^2$$
$$+ \ldots c/(1 + r_N)^N + M/(1 + r_N)^N \qquad (2.3)$$

where c is the half-yearly coupon payment and $r_{0.5}$ and $r_{1.5}$ are the required returns on loans of six months and 18 months to the issuer expressed as annual rates. The price of an undated fixed-interest security, P_{UFIS}, is given by:

$$P_{UFIS} = C/r \qquad (2.4)$$

if there is only one coupon payment, C, each year, and by:

$$P_{UFIS} = c/[(1 + r)^{0.5} - 1] \qquad (2.5)$$

if there are two semi-annual coupon payments each worth c. In each case r is the annual rate required on undated loans to the issuer.

2.4 Variable-interest-rate securities resemble fixed-interest securities except that either the face value or the interest rate is variable. If the face value is variable, then it rises in line with prices. If the coupon rate is variable, then it floats in line with another rate such as three-month LIBOR.

2.5 Equities are issued to the owners of companies. They get an income in the form of dividends, though the dividends are apt to vary in line with the company's profits. If the dividend is paid annually and is expected to grow at a rate g, then the price of an equity is given by:

$$P_{EQUITY} = D_1/(r - g) \qquad (2.13)$$

where r is the annual rate of return required on the equities of the company concerned and D_1 is the dividend at the end of the first year after purchase.

2.6 Investment trusts are companies which use the money raised from selling securities to buy other securities. They often issue a wide variety of securities, largely to try and avoid takeover bids, for the value of their issued securities tends to be less than the value of their assets.

2.7 There are many FTSE share price indices which each relate the current total value of the shares of a group of companies to the total value of those shares on the base date for the index. Total return indices show what would happen to a portfolio of shares reflecting the shares in the index concerned if all dividends were at once used to buy more of those shares.

2.8 Duration is a measure of the remaining lifespan of a dated security, allowing for the timing and value of its interest payments as well as its redemption date. The higher a security's duration, the more responsive is its price to changes in its yield or actual return, and hence also to changes in its required return and so to changes in interest rates.

QUESTIONS

1. What are the main factors which determine the prices that people will offer for: (a) a bill and (b) a dated fixed-interest security?

2. Distinguish between the following pairs: (a) a long and a short; (b) a dated security and a perpetuity; (c) a preference share and a corporate bond; (d) a debenture and a loan stock; (e) a total price and a clean price; and (f) a floating rate bond and an index-linked bond.

3. Look at a recent newspaper and find the figures for Treasury bill prices. What discount rate was used to determine the prices at which one-month and three-month bills were bought and sold on the money market? What annual rates of interest are these discount rates equivalent to?

4. Suppose that a fixed-interest security will earn coupon payments of £5 in exactly six months, 12 months, 18 months and 24 months, and will then be redeemed for £100. What is the annual coupon on this security? A lender want annual rates of interest of 5.25% on six-month loans to the issuer, 5.5% on 12-month loans, 5.75% on 18-month loans and 6% on 24-month loans. Show that the lender will pay £107.77 for this security. Show also that the redemption yield on this security is 5.97%.

5. Suppose that a fixed-interest perpetuity has a face value of £100 and a coupon payment of £5 every six months. A coupon payment has just been made. Lenders want a return of 6% per year on indefinite loans to the issuer. What is the value of the perpetuity?

6. Suppose that a company has just paid a dividend of 10p, and suppose that its dividends are expected to grow by 7% a year. What is the expected dividend for the end of the present year? Assume that the return required on this company's shares is 15%. What is the price of the company's shares? Suppose that in the year just ended, the earnings per share were 16p. What was the dividend cover in that year if corporation tax is levied at 33%?

7. Consider a bond with a 12% coupon that has three years until maturity. Suppose that it pays interest once a year and that a payment has just been made. What remaining payments will be made? Suppose that it has a redemption yield of 10%. Use (2.6) to work out the present values of the remaining payments from this bond. What is its duration? What is its modified duration? How much will its price change if the yield changes by 0.1%?

REFERENCES

Macaulay, F. (1938) *Some Theoretical Problems Suggested by the Movements of Interest Rates, Bond Prices and Stock Prices in the United States Since 1856* (New York: National Bureau for Economic Research).

Phillips, P. (1996) *The Merrill Lynch Guide to the Gilt-Edged and Sterling Bond Markets* (Sussex: the Book Guild).

3 RETURNS AND PORTFOLIOS

3.1 WHY ARE RETURNS AND PORTFOLIOS RELATED?

Almost all financial claims offer returns. For example, Chapter 1 showed that CDs earn interest, annuities earn an annual income, and premium bonds may win prizes. And Chapter 2 showed that securities offer interest or dividends or capital gains. One apparent exception is trade debt, but even here, firms which give customers some time to pay may well charge higher prices than they would charge if they demanded instant payment, so they may actually secure a return.

The only financial claim that never offers returns to its holders is cash. Despite the lack of a return, people hold some of their wealth in cash because it is a fully liquid asset: that is, it has a precisely certain value and can be used immediately for spending. It is especially convenient for small transactions. Sight deposits are also fully liquid, and they are convenient for large transactions, so people would willingly hold some of their wealth in them, even if they offered no interest. Indeed, people *did* hold sight deposits in the days when no interest was paid on them, which is to say before computer technology allowed the interest due on rapidly fluctuating deposits to be calculated. All claims other than cash and sight deposits are less liquid, either because their values can fluctuate, as with CDs, or because it may take some time to sell them and spend the wealth that is tied up in them, as with premium bonds, or because both factors apply, as with equities. People require returns for holding these less liquid claims, and, on average, these returns must be sufficient to tempt surplus units to run large surpluses so that they can then help deficit units finance their usually large deficits.

However, people require different returns on different claims. It might be thought that the main factor which would determine the required return on any given claim would be the overall risk or uncertainty attached to its future value and its annual return. But this is not so. The reason is that most people spread their risks by acquiring portfolios that contain many different claims, so what matters to them in the case of an individual claim is not the risk on that claim as such, but rather how it affects the riskiness of their portfolio as a whole. So it is not possible to discuss the returns that investors require on individual claims without looking also at how they select their portfolios.

Topics covered in this chapter

Section 3.2 looks at precisely what is meant by the returns on financial claims and at the various risks they entail. Section 3.3 explains the terms variance and standard deviation which are used to measure some types of risk, and Section 3.4 applies these terms to individual securities and to portfolios. Section 3.5 shows how different investors might react to risk. Section 3.6 shows how different investors might select their portfolios, and Section 3.7 builds on this analysis to consider the capital asset pricing model (CAPM) which is a hypothesis about how individual assets are priced or, equivalently, about how their required returns are determined. Section 3.8 looks at the arbitrage pricing theory (APT) which is a more recent hypothesis about portfolio choice, asset prices and required returns. Section 3.9 looks briefly at the issue of market efficiency to see whether it is possible for 'smart' investors to devise portfolios that will perform better than the portfolios of other investors who take the same overall degree of risk.

Sections 3.2 to 3.9 focus on equities as they account for the bulk of most portfolios, but the final section, 3.10, looks at the term structure of interest rates on fixed-interest securities to see why people want varying returns on the various fixed-interest securities that might be issued by one borrower such as the government. For simplicity, the chapter assumes that each security receives only one interest or dividend payment per year.

3.2 RETURNS AND RISK

The meaning of returns

Required **returns** are usually expressed in percentages per year. So investors might be said to want a return of 7% next year on a two-year gilt and a return of 12% next year on a particular share. It might be thought that investors would calculate the returns on these securities over the next year by dividing the expected income over that year by the price that they pay for them now. So if the gilt was due a coupon payment of £6.50 in one year's time, and if X wanted to buy it and hold it for one year, then it might seem that he would offer about £93 for it, as £6.50 is about 7% of £93. Also, if the share promised a dividend of 60p in one year's time, and if Y wanted to buy it and hold it for one year, then it might seem that she would offer £5 for it, as 60p is 12% of £5.

However, equations (2.2) and (2.8) in Chapter 2 show that investors consider the present values of all a security's future returns when they decide how much to pay for it. To take account of the returns from the gilt and the share after the next year, X and Y could consider the values that these securities will have at the end of next year, for these values show what people will pay for them then to secure all the subsequent returns. In fact, X knows that in two years' time, at maturity, the gilt will be worth £100. If it is now worth less than £100, then its value should rise over the next year. As for Y, she may expect the share to earn higher dividends in future and so expect its price to rise as the higher dividends get closer. If X and Y expect to make capital gains as well as earn income, then they may offer to pay more than £93 and £5. Even if they do not intend to sell the securities after one year, the capital gains are relevant as they will mean an increase in wealth.

It follows that the returns to X and Y over the next year have to incorporate the likely price rise over that year as well as the income earned during the year. The relevant concept for the returns that investors like X and Y consider is called the **holding-period return**, R_H. The holding period return on any security in any given period is measured as follows:

$$R_H = [D + (P_1 - P_0)]/P_0 \tag{3.1}$$

where D is the dividend or coupon payment over the period, P_1 is the price at the end of the period, and P_0 is the current price. In (3.1), it is assumed that the dividend or coupon payment is paid at the end of the period. If it is paid during the period, then (3.1) will slightly underestimate the return as the income could be lent between the payment date and the end of the period.

In the example, X and Y were taken to be interested in a holding period of one year, but (3.1) can be used for holding periods of any length. Over long periods, of course, investors will hope for more dividends and more capital gains, and hence for greater holding-period returns. For simplicity, this chapter will assume that people are always interested in a holding period of exactly one year. Moreover, it will be assumed that investors look just one period ahead and consider the return they will get over that period. So they are concerned with their wealth in one year's time.

It is easy to work out the holding-period return on a security at the end of the year, but it is rarely possible to predict it accurately at the start of the year. This is partly because the prices that securities will have in one year are usually uncertain. And it is partly because the income payments during the year may be uncertain in the case of equities and variable-interest securities. So investors have to forecast expected returns, and they have to consider the risk that the actual returns will be different from the expected returns. There are several quite separate sources of risk with securities.

Default risk

One source of risk is **default risk**. This is the risk that any promised income or any due redemption payment may not be made. However, this risk does not apply to equities because they have no promised income and are never redeemed. So, as this chapter focuses on equities, it ignores default risk. But it may be noted that it is the default risk on company securities other than equities that leads to them having higher required returns than similar securities issued by the government.

Inflation risk

Another source of risk with securities is **inflation risk**. This means that a holding-period return might turn out to be less than was expected in real terms because inflation turned out to be higher than was expected. For example, suppose that a one-year bond with a coupon of 7% is currently selling at its face value of £100. If X buys this bond, then he will expect to have £107 at the end of the year when it is redeemed for £100 and the £7 coupon payment is made. So he will expect to gain £7 from his £100 investment. This means that he expects a **nominal return** of 7% over the year. Suppose, also, that X expects inflation to be zero over the year. Then he will expect to be 7% better off in real terms at the end of the year, so his expected **real return** is also 7%. But if inflation turns out to be 5%, then his actual real return will be about 2%.

In fact, the actual real return will be just under 2%. To see why, recall that X buys the bond for £100 and will receive £107 in one year. Suppose that he plans to spend this £107 buying widgets which currently cost £1 each. He could, of course, buy 100 widgets today, but he hopes to buy 107 widgets next year and so secure a 7% return in real terms. Next, suppose that the price of widgets rises by 5% over the year to £1.05. Then X's £107 will buy only (107/1.05) widgets, that is 101.9 widgets. So, as Fisher (1930) pointed out, the real interest rate is $[(1 + r)/(1 + p) - 1]$ where r is the nominal interest rate, here 0.07, and p is the inflation rate, here 0.05. So if inflation is 5%, then the real interest rate in the example is $[(1.07/1.05) - 1]$, which is $(1.019 - 1)$, or 0.019, that is 1.9%.

If people actually expect some inflation, then they will require higher nominal returns on all securities in order to secure their desired real returns. So they will require higher discount rates on zero-interest securities and higher nominal interest yields on fixed-interest securities. But they may not require a higher dividend yield from equities in the next holding period. For they may think that most companies can increase their prices roughly in line with inflation, so that their subsequent dividends will rise in line with inflation. The prospect of higher future dividends should cause equity prices to rise, so investors who hold equities will be compensated for inflation over the next holding-period by making a capital gain. So it often happens in periods of inflation that, although the total holding-period returns on equities are higher than those on fixed-interest securities, the interest yields on fixed-interest securities are higher than the dividend yields on equities. If the average interest yield on gilts exceeds the average dividend yield on equities, then there is said to be a **reverse yield gap**. There has been a reverse yield gap in the United Kingdom since about 1960.

Because most companies can raise their prices and dividends in line with inflation, inflation risk is least pronounced on equities. So, as this chapter focuses on equities, it ignores inflation risk.

Interest rate risk

A further source of risk with securities is **interest rate risk**. This risk refers to the fact that, if interest rates rise, then security prices will fall. Suppose, for example, that interest rates rise so that bank deposits offer higher returns. Then securities will be relatively less attractive and their prices will fall. Their prices will fall until the prospective future yields on them in relation to their prices have risen enough to make their future returns attractive compared with other returns. But over the period when their prices fall, the holding-period return is low. This risk applies to all securities except variable-rate bonds and FRNs whose prices are virtually unaffected by interest rate changes.

Uncertain income risk

A final source of risk is **uncertain income risk**. This does not apply to fixed-interest securities, but it is very important with equities. The point is that individual companies may prosper or decline, so their dividends in the next year, and their share prices at the end of the year, may differ markedly from the expected levels. Uncertain income risk on equities is so important that it causes the holding-period returns required from them to exceed the required returns on other securities.

Assessing returns and risk

When investors choose between a number of different securities, they like to estimate the expected return on each of them. They realise that the actual returns may differ from the expected returns, so they also want to know how much uncertainty should be attached to the expected returns. The word risk on its own refers to this uncertainty. One way in which investors may try to assess the expected return and the uncertainty or risk on any given security, and especially on any given equity, is to see what holding-period returns it has secured in the past and to see how varied or volatile those holding-period returns have been. Of course, they know that the past is not always a sure guide to the future, so they may expect the returns to increase for some equities and to decline for others, and they may expect the returns to get more volatile for some equities and to get less volatile for others. But past performance is a useful starting point for their considerations.

Suppose, for simplicity, that for a given company investors expect no change in the general level of its returns, or in the volatility of its returns. Then they will base their forecast for its expected return in the next period solely on its past performance, and they will base their views on the uncertainty attached to this forecast solely on the basis of the volatility of its past returns. Typically, then, they will take a sample of past periods, and look at the holding-period return in each. To see how expected values and volatility can be deduced from samples, it is necessary to look briefly at the use of samples. This is done in Section 3.3, which can be omitted if the concepts are familiar.

3.3 SAMPLES, EXPECTED VALUES, VARIANCE AND STANDARD DEVIATION

To understand some key issues in sampling, it is helpful to consider an analogy. Suppose a coal merchant has a bag-filling machine that is designed to put the same weight of coal into each bag. In practice, some bags will receive a greater weight than others. The merchant may want to estimate the weight of the next bag, and he may want to know how much uncertainty attaches to that estimate. In seeing how the merchant could answer these two questions, it will be supposed that the distribution of the weights of the bags filled by the machine is symmetrical. In other words, it is supposed that as many bags have weights above the mean, or average, weight as have weights below the mean. And it is supposed that as many bags have weights that are, say, 1 kg above the mean as have weights that are 1 kg below, while as many bags have weights that are 2 kg above the mean as have weights that are 2 kg below, and so on.

Estimating a future value

With a symmetrical distribution, the best estimate for the weight of the next bag would be the mean weight of all the bags that the machine has ever filled and could ever fill. For the weight of the next bag is no more likely to be above this mean than it is to be below it. If any other weight were forecast, say one 3 kg above this mean, then the weight of the next bag would most likely be lower than forecast, so this forecast would be a poorer one than the mean.

Unfortunately, there is no way of discovering the mean weight of all the bags that the machine has ever filled or could ever fill, a concept called the **population** of bags. The best the merchant could do is to take a sample of n bags, weigh them each carefully, and work out the mean for the sample. For the mean of the sample gives an **unbiased estimate** of the mean of the population. In other words, the mean of the sample is no more likely to be above the population mean than it is likely to be below it. The sample mean is unlikely to equal the population mean exactly, and it could be very different if the sample happened to be unrepresentative. But, on the basis of the information available from the sample, the sample mean is the best estimate that can be made of the population mean. In turn, the sample mean is the best available forecast of the expected weight of the next bag.

Measuring spread

The sample mean is the best available forecast of the weight of the next bag, but the weight of that bag is unlikely to equal its expected value. So the merchant wants an idea about how far away its weight could be. This depends on the spread of the weights of the coal bags. There is no way in which the merchant could discover the spread of the weights of the population of bags, but he can get some idea of it from the spread of the weights of the bags in the sample. Spreads can be measured in various ways. Two common measures are the **variance** and the **standard deviation**. These can be calculated for the bags in the sample by using five steps:

1. The mean weight of the n bags is found. Say this is 50 kg.
2. Each bag is taken in turn and the difference between its weight and the mean weight of 50 kg is found. This difference is called the bag's **x-value**. The more spread out the weights are, the larger these differences will be. However, it is not possible to add up the x-values to get an idea of spread, because bags with weights over 50 kg will have positive x-values, while bags with weights under 50 kg will have negative x-values. The total value of all the x-values will actually be 0 kg, no matter how spread out the weights are.
3. The x-value for each bag is squared to get the bag's x^2-value. The more spread out the weights are, the larger these x^2-values will be, and each x^2-value will be positive.
4. The x^2-values are summed to get Σx^2. Σ is a Greek letter, a capital sigma, which is often used to indicate sum totals. The more spread out the weights, the larger is Σx^2.
5. The variance of the sample is defined as $\Sigma x^2/n$. The standard deviation of the sample is defined as the square root of its variance, that is $\sqrt{(\Sigma x^2/n)}$; the standard deviation is always in the same units as the x-values and the original observations, so in the example it is in kilograms.

The merchant might wonder if the variance of the sample of n bags gives an unbiased estimate of the variance of the population of bags. In fact, the sample variance gives a slightly biased underestimate of the population variance. Fortunately, an unbiased estimate of the population variance can be found by using instead the formula $\Sigma x^2/(n-1)$; in turn, $\sqrt{[\Sigma x^2/(n-1)]}$ is taken as an estimate of the population standard deviation. The Greek letter σ, a small sigma, is used for the population standard deviation and σ^2 for the population variance. These letters or symbols are often also used for estimates of the population standard deviation and variance.

3.4 EXPECTED RETURNS AND THEIR RISKS

The merchant in Section 3.3 used a sample of bags to estimate the weight of the next bag that will be filled by a machine and to see how spread out the weights of the bags are. Investors are in a similar position. For a given security, they can look at its holding-period returns in a sample of past periods and, assuming the distribution of returns is symmetrical, use the sample mean as the **expected return** in the next period. They can also use the sample to estimate the standard deviation, σ, and variance, σ^2, of the holding-period returns, for these measures of spread show the uncertainty or risk of the returns from the security. The chief difference between investors and the merchant is that the machine should perform in future as it has in the past, whereas a security may not. So, in estimating future returns and risks, investors may modify the figures derived from the sample to allow for their hunches about future changes.

To see how expected returns and risks for securities can be estimated, an example will be used of an imaginary country which has just four different risky assets, namely the shares issued by Aco, Bco, Cco and Dco. Suppose that investors want to estimate the expected returns and risk for each company over the next year. In each case, they use a sample of returns in recent years. Suppose that their samples contain the returns in each of the last four years, so that the sample size, n, is four, and suppose that the holding-period returns for each company in each of year are as shown in columns (1) to (4) of Table 3.1. Bearing in mind that these returns cover both dividends and changes in the share prices, they are all relatively stable, but they are useful for illustrating many of the concepts covered in this chapter.

In practice, investors would regard samples with four observations as far too small to be reliable. However, the aim of the example is simply to show the general principles of what investors might do. To get larger samples, investors could go back over more than four years, but they rarely do that because returns do in fact vary over time, which means that old data are of limited use. Instead, they might get larger samples by dividing the returns over the last four years into 48 monthly returns. They could then work out the means and variances of the monthly returns, and multiply the results by 12 to estimate the annual means and variances.

Estimating expected returns for individual shares and the market

The bottom line of Table 3.1 shows the mean returns over the last four years. For example, in Aco's case the mean of 4% is found by adding up Aco's four returns, to give a total of 16%, and then dividing by n, or four. This mean is an unbiased estimate of the population mean, that is the mean of all the returns that Aco shares could have produced over the years covered by the sample. Investors will use these means as their expected returns for each company in the next year, unless they modify them because they think the means will change in future.

Table 3.1 Returns for four companies and the market as a whole over four years

Year	Aco (%) (1)	Bco (%) (2)	Cco (%) (3)	Dco (%) (4)	Market (%) (5)
1	1	11	13	27	13
2	3	9	18	30	15
3	7	13	21	11	13
4	5	7	12	20	11
Total	16	40	64	88	52
Mean or expected return	4	10	16	22	13

Column (5) of Table 3.1 gives the return in each year from shares as a whole, that is from the equity market as a whole. Some care is needed in calculating these market returns. For example, if the total value of all issued Aco shares was £397m, while the total values of the shares issued by each of Bco, Cco and Dco was £1m, then virtually all the money that investors between them held in shares would be invested in Aco shares, and the annual returns from their portfolios would closely match the performance of Aco. Suppose, however, that each company has actually issued 100 million shares and that each share has had a price of about £1 over the last four years. In that case, investors between them will have invested about equal amounts in each company, and the performance of shares as a whole will depend in about equal measure on the performance of each company. So the performance of the market will be taken to be as shown in column (5) where each year's figure is the average of the returns in that year for the four companies. The mean value of the four annual returns given in column (5) is 13%, and this shows the return that investors will expect next year from shares as a whole unless, of course, they think that the mean will change in the future.

The returns shown in column (5) would be secured by any portfolio of shares that contained shares in every company in proportion to the numbers issued. Here, each company has issued 100 million shares, so such a portfolio would contain equal numbers of each. Also, the proportion of such a portfolio's value accounted for by any company would equal the proportion of the total value of all shares accounted for by that company's shares. As each company has issued 100 million shares priced at about £1, each accounts for about a quarter of the value of all shares. So each would account for about a quarter of the portfolio's value. Such a portfolio is often called a market portfolio, as it represents the equity market, though a **market portfolio** should strictly represent *all* risky assets, including assets such as currencies and commodities held for resale.

Column (5) shows that year 2 was the best year for shares as a whole; perhaps there was a mini-boom that year. Year 4 was the worst year; perhaps there was a mini-recession that year. No individual equity conformed very closely to the market as a whole, but at least Bco and Cco were at their worst in year 4, while Dco was at its best in year 2, so there was some relationship between these three equities' performances and the market. This was not true of Aco, though, for it was at its best in year 3 and its worst in year 1. Perhaps Aco is a firm of receivers which does well in the years after a boom and badly in the years up to a boom.

Estimating risk for individual shares

Although the mean returns shown in Table 3.1 may be used as estimates of the next year's returns, investors will want an idea of the uncertainty attached to these estimates. So they will want to know the variance and standard deviation of each share's returns. Table 3.2 shows how these measures can be calculated. Columns (1), (4), (7) and (10) of Table 3.2 repeat the returns for each share from Table 3.1.

Table 3.2 Variance and standard deviation for four companies' equities

	Aco			Bco			Cco			Dco		
	(1)	(2) x	(3) x^2	(4)	(5) x	(6) x^2	(7)	(8) x	(9) x^2	(10)	(11) x	(12) x^2
	R_H	R_H-M	$(R_H-M)^2$	R_H	R_H-M	$(R_H-M)^2$	R_H	R_H-M	$(R_H-M)^2$	R_H	R_H-M	$(R_H-M)^2$
Year 1	1	−3	9	11	1	1	13	−3	9	27	5	25
Year 2	3	−1	1	9	−1	1	18	2	4	30	8	64
Year 3	7	3	9	13	3	9	21	5	25	11	−11	121
Year 4	5	1	1	7	−3	9	12	−4	16	20	−2	4
Total	16	0	20	40	0	20	64	0	54	88	0	214
Mean	4			10			16			22		
σ^2			6.67			6.67			18.00			71.33
σ			2.58			2.58			4.24			8.45

The first step in working out the variances is to find the mean return for each share, and these means are repeated from Table 3.1 in columns (1), (4), (7) and (10) of Table 3.2. The second step is to work out for each year the difference between that year's return and the mean, that is the x-value. The x-values are shown in columns (2), (5), (8) and (11). For example, the first figure in column (2), –3%, shows that Aco's return of 1% in year 1 was 3% below its mean return of 4%. The third step is to work out the x^2-values, as is done in columns (3), (6), (9) and (12). For example, Aco's x-value of –3% in year one becomes an x^2-value of 9. The fourth step is to sum the x^2-values, as is done also in columns (3), (6), (9) and (12). For example, Aco's total x^2-value is 20.

If investors wanted to know the variance of Aco's returns in the sample of four years, they would divide this total of 20 by the number of years, or n, that is four, and get the answer as 5.00. But instead they want to estimate the variance of all the returns that could possibly have occurred in the period covered by the sample, that is the population of returns. They can get an un-biased estimate of this variance, σ^2, by dividing the total of 20 by $(n-1)$, or three, to get 6.67. They can then take the square root of 6.67 to estimate the population standard deviation, σ, as 2.58. Similar procedures are used for Bco, Cco and Dco. In practice, of course, investors may adjust past figures for variances and standard deviations to account for expected changes in volatility.

Expected returns and volatilities for portfolios

Assume, for simplicity, that investors in the country covered by the example expect no significant changes in the means or standard deviations of any equity's returns. Then the past figures in Tables 3.1 and 3.2 can be taken to indicate the investors' expectations for the future.

Suppose Y is an investor in this country. She may look at Table 3.2 and see that she could use her funds to buy Aco shares, with a mean or expected return of 4%, or Bco shares with an expected return of 10%, or Cco shares with an expected return of 16%, or Dco shares with an expected return of 22%. But the shares with the highest expected returns tend also to have the most risky returns. For example, although Dco has the highest mean return, at 22%, its returns also have the highest standard deviation. One drawback of this volatility arose in Year 3 when its 11% return was below the 13% and 21% returns secured by Bco and Cco, even though they have lower mean returns. The combination of expected return and volatility for each share is marked by points A, B, C and D on Fig. 3.1. Here, the vertical axis measures the mean or expected return, while the horizontal axis measures the estimated volatility or standard deviation of the possible returns.

Y need not invest in just one company. She might use her funds to buy a **portfolio** comprising two or more different assets. Consider three possible port-folios of two shares: Aco plus Bco, Bco plus Cco, and Cco plus Dco. Assume that each time Y considers placing half her funds with each company. On the basis of the last four years, she wonders what her expected returns would be and what the estimated standard deviation of the possible returns would be. The results are given in columns (1) to (9) of Table 3.3.

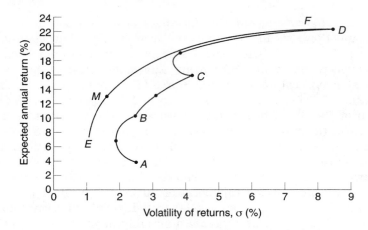

Figure 3.1 Mean–volatility relationships for selected portfolios.

For example, columns (4) to (6) consider a portfolio that is divided equally in value terms between Bco shares and Cco shares. In year 1, when Bco had a return of 11% and Cco had a return of 13%, this mixture would have secured a return half-way between at 12%, as shown in column (4). The figures for the three other years are found likewise, and the mean return of the portfolio is found as 13%, half-way between Bco's mean of 10% and Cco's mean of 16%. However, the standard deviation is *not* half-way between the figures of 2.58% and 4.24% which applied to Bco and Cco, for the figure half-way between these is 3.41%, while the standard deviation for the combined portfolio is found in the normal manner and is 3.14%. The calculations are shown in columns (5) and (6) and begin by working out the x-values for each year, that is each year's return minus the mean of 13%. Then each year's x^2-value is worked out, and then the four x^2-values are added to give a total of 29.50. This must be divided by $(n-1)$ to give 29.50/3 or 9.83, and then its square root must be found, that is $\sqrt{9.83}$, to get the standard deviation, which is 3.14%.

The reason this figure is below the half-way value of 3.41% for Bco and Cco shares alone is that the returns from the two shares do not move up and down in exactly matching steps. So, when they are combined in a portfolio, the movements in their returns offset each other to some extent. The standard deviation for a portfolio comprising two assets in equal proportions is exactly half-way between the separate standard deviations *only* if the two sets of returns do move in exactly matching steps *or* if one set is constant so that it has no movements to offset movements in the other.

As it happens, the returns on Bco and Cco shares did move fairly closely together, so the standard deviation of a portfolio that is divided equally in value terms between each company is not far below the half-way value. A different situation arises for the Cco plus Dco portfolio where column (9) shows that the standard deviation is 3.83%. This is well below the standard deviation of 8.45% which applies to Dco, and it is even below the 4.24% which applies to Cco, so it is way below the half-way value of these two figures, which is 6.35%. The

Table 3.3 Returns and volatilities for four portfolios

	Aco plus Bco			Bco plus Cco			Cco plus Dco			All four companies		
	(1)	(2)	(3)	(4)	(5)	(6)	(7)	(8)	(9)	(10)	(11)	(12)
		x			x			x			x	
Year	R_H	$R_H{-}M$	x^2 $(R_H{-}M)^2$	R_H	$R_H{-}M$	x^2 $(R_H{-}M)^2$	R_H	$R_H{-}M$	x^2 $(R_H{-}M)^2$	R_H	$R_H{-}M$	x^2 $(R_H{-}M)^2$
1	6	−1	1	12.0	−1.0	1.00	20	1	1	13	0	0
2	6	−1	1	13.5	0.5	0.25	24	5	25	15	2	4
3	10	3	9	17.0	4.0	16.00	16	−3	9	13	0	0
4	6	−1	1	9.5	−3.5	12.25	16	−3	9	11	−2	4
Total	28	0	12	52.0	0	29.50	76	0	44	52	0	8
Mean	7			13.0			19			13		
σ^2			4.00			9.83			14.67			2.67
σ			2.00			3.14			3.83			1.63

big difference between the standard deviation for the combined portfolio and the half-way value for Cco and Dco shares alone means that the movements in those shares' returns offset each other considerably in a combined portfolio.

There is a similar result for the Aco plus Bco portfolio. Aco's shares are unusual in that they did worse in the boom year 2 than in the recession year 4, while Bco's shares are typical in that they did not. A portfolio combining these two shares has fairly stable returns. Indeed, the standard deviation of each share on its own was 2.58%, so a half-way value must also be seen as 2.58%, but the standard deviation of the Aco plus Bco portfolio is shown in column (3) to be just 2.00%.

The fact that the standard deviation for a portfolio comprising equal values of two shares is almost always less than half-way between the two separate standard deviations is reflected in Fig. 3.1 by the dots on the curves between A and B, B and C, and C and D. These dots show the combinations of volatility and expected returns for portfolios that combine the two shares concerned, that is Aco and Bco, Bco and Cco, and Cco and Dco in equal values. The dots show that the expected returns from such two-share portfolios are exactly half-way between the returns of the separate shares, whereas the standard deviation is less than half-way. For example, the dot on the curve between B and C shows that the mean return is 13%, half-way between Bco's mean return of 10% and Cco's of 16%, but the standard deviation at this point is 3.14%, which is less than half-way between Bco's standard deviation of 2.58% and Cco's 4.24%. In other words, the dot is half-way between B and C in terms of its vertical position, but it is less than half-way in terms of its horizontal position. Points on the curve to the left of this dot show the results for portfolios comprising Bco and Cco shares in which the value of Bco shares counts for progressively more than half the total value, while points on the curve to the right of this dot show the results for portfolios comprising Bco and Cco shares in which the value of Bco shares counts for progressively less than half the total value.

The efficient frontier

Investors could have other portfolios comprising mixes of two shares, such as Aco plus Cco, Aco plus Dco and Bco plus Dco. They could also have portfolios with mixes of three or four shares, but it is not possible to show with a single line on the figure the relationship between the volatility and the returns of a portfolio that mixes more than two shares, say Aco plus Bco plus Cco, because there are so many ways in which the proportions of the these shares could be varied. Typically, though, the returns become less volatile when more than two shares are combined. In turn, this means that it is usually possible to find portfolios with more than two shares that have a higher expected return for any degree of volatility than could be obtained from any two-share portfolios.

Investors like Y like to know the highest expected return they can secure for any degree of volatility. For example, take a degree of volatility indicated by a standard deviation of 3.00. This could be secured by a portfolio that comprised one particular mix of Bco and Cco shares. It could also be secured by one particular mix of Aco and Cco shares, and by one particular mix of Bco and Dco shares, and by one particular mix of Aco and Dco shares. Moreover, it could be secured by several different mixes of Aco shares, Bco shares and Cco shares, where these three shares were combined in various proportions, and from several different mixes that included other combinations of three shares. And it could be secured by several different mixes of all four shares. All of these portfolios with standard deviations of 3.00% are likely to have different expected returns. But one of them is likely to have a higher expected return than the others, say about 17.5%. Likewise for any other degree of volatility there is likely to be just one portfolio with the highest expected return.

In Fig. 3.1, the curve *EF* shows the highest expected or mean return that is attainable for any given standard deviation. This curve is called the **efficient frontier** because it is efficient for investors to choose portfolios that end them up on it. That is because, for any degree of risk or standard deviation that they take, the frontier shows the highest expected return they can get. Although this curve shows points that are efficient in terms of their combinations of expected or mean returns and standard deviations, it is always said to show points that are **mean–variance efficient**. As variance is simply the square of the standard deviation, portfolios which are on *EF* also offer the highest expected or mean return for any given level of variance.

For reasons that will become clear later, a market portfolio of all risky assets should end up on the efficient frontier. So, in the example, a portfolio which combined Aco, Bco, Cco and Dco shares in proportion to the numbers issued should end up on *EF*. Columns (10) to (12) of Table 3.2 show the mean return and standard deviation of such a portfolio. It has a mean of 13% and a standard deviation of 1.63%, and it is shown on Fig. 3.1 by point *M*. In this example, the market portfolio has the same mean return of 13% as a portfolio that comprises Bco plus Cco shares alone in equal values, but its standard deviation of 1.63% is much lower than the 3.14% which applies to a portfolio containing Bco and Cco shares in equal values. This is because the market portfolio also contains Aco and Dco shares which partly offset the volatilities of Bco and Cco shares. In fact, in this example, the market portfolio's standard deviation is less than that of any individual share.

3.5 ATTITUDES TO RISK

Section 3.4 considered an imaginary country where the only securities available are equities. It showed how investors like Y could work out an efficient frontier of portfolios from which to choose. But Y needs to decide which efficient portfolio to choose. Her choice will depend on her attitudes to risk and returns, so this section considers how people view returns and risk. It does so by using a simple but quite separate example which continues with the assumption that people look just one period ahead, the period being just one year. For simplicity, no currency will be specified.

Consider an investor Z who has a wealth of 1,000 which he intends to invest in a portfolio. Suppose that Z considers two different possibilities. One is to buy some one-year government bonds which will mature next year for 1,050 and which will also give him an interest payment of 50. If he buys these bonds, then he is sure to end up with a wealth of 1,100, so he will gain 100 and his holding-period return will be 10%. Moreover, the risk attached to this return is zero.

Alternatively, Z might buy equities, say shares in a hypothetical company LML which, on past form, generate a mean holding-period return of 10%. Strictly, then, the expected return from these shares is also 10%. However, these returns are volatile. Suppose, for simplicity, that LML shares only ever produce returns of 4% and 16%. If they produce a return of 16% next year, then X's wealth will end up at 1,160. But if they generate a return of 4%, then his wealth will be 1,040.

Compared with the bonds, the equities could bring in 60 more, which would be pleasant, or 60 less, which would be unpleasant. Z's choice between them will depend on how he views the possible pleasantness and unpleasantness. The three parts of Fig. 3.2 illustrate three possible views that he could take. Each part begins with points B and E which show the expected risk–return combinations that Z would face with the bonds and the equities respectively. The two securities have the same mean or expected 10% return, but the equities have a high standard deviation, while the bond has none.

Risk-taking

First, Z might reckon that if he got the 60 more, then he could afford to go and see his new baby grandchild who lives overseas. Thus the extra 60 would add greatly to his satisfaction or utility. On the other hand, if he got the 60 less, then he would merely keep his car a little longer before replacing it, and this would take little away from his utility. So, as he attaches much more weight to the possibility of 60 more than to the possibility of 60 less, he would choose the equities. And he would be called a **risk-taker** because he would take the riskier investment, even though its mean or expected return was the same. Although Z would choose the equities in the situation considered here, he would have been more tempted by the bonds if their return was higher. Maybe a 13% return on them would have made him indifferent between them and the equities. With a 13% return, the bonds would be represented in Fig. 3.2(a) by the point C.

So Z might be indifferent between points C and E, and also between other points in between them like those lying on curve I_2. This curve is called an **indifference curve** as it shows points between which Z is indifferent. Figure 3.2(a) includes two more indifference curves. I_1 shows another set of risk–return combinations between which Z might be indifferent, though these are all less appealing than those shown by I_2 because, for any level of risk, they offer lower expected returns. I_3 shows yet another set of risk–return combinations between which Z might be indifferent, and these are all more appealing than those shown by I_2 because, for any level of risk, they offer higher expected returns.

Risk-aversion

Alternatively, Z might reckon that if he got the extra 60, then he would merely use it to buy a rather more expensive model of a car. But if he got the 60 less,

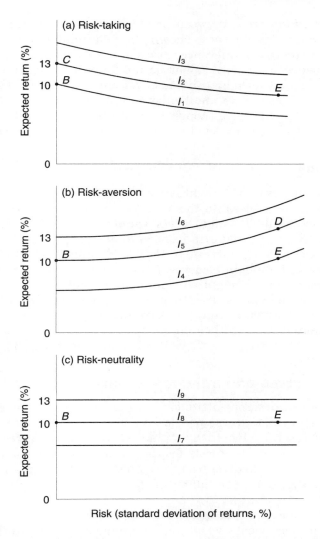

Figure 3.2 Indifference curve maps for different attitudes towards risk.

then he could not even afford to go and see his older grandchildren who live in a distant town. In this case, Z would attach much more weight to the possibility of the 60 less than to the possibility of the 60 more, so he would take the bond. And he would be said to be **risk-averse** because he would take the less risky investment even though its expected return is the same. Although Z would choose the bonds in the situation considered here, he would have been more tempted by the equities if their expected return had been higher. Maybe a 13% return on them would made have him indifferent between the bonds and the equities. With a 13% return, the equities would be represented in Fig. 3.2(b) by the point *D*.

So Z might be indifferent between points B and D, and also between other points in between them like those shown lying on indifference curve I_5. Figure 3.2(b) includes two more indifference curves. I_4 shows another set of risk–return combinations between which Z might be indifferent, though they are all less appealing than those shown by I_5 because, for any level of risk, they offer lower expected returns. I_6 shows yet another set of risk–return combinations between which Z might be indifferent, though they are all more appealing than those shown by I_5 because, for any level of risk, they offer higher expected returns.

Risk-neutrality

The third possibility is that Z might be quite indifferent between the possibility of the 60 more or the 60 less. In this case he would be indifferent between the two securities and would be said to be **risk-neutral**. Here, Z would be indifferent between points B and E, and also between other points in between them like those lying on indifference curve I_8 in Fig. 3.2(c). Figure 3.2(c) is completed by including two more indifference curves. I_7 shows another set of risk–return combinations between which Z might be indifferent, though they are all less appealing than those shown by I_8 because, for any level of risk, they offer lower expected returns. I_9 shows yet another set of risk–return combinations between which Z might be indifferent, though they are all more appealing than those shown by I_8 because, for any level of risk, they offer higher expected returns.

Indifference curves and attitudes to risk

Two implications of different attitudes towards risk can be deduced from Fig. 3.2. First, the more risk-averse people are, the more their indifference curves will slope upwards from left to right. Indeed, their indifference curves might be very steep at high levels of risk, for they would typically want progressively higher and higher expected returns to compensate them for every increase in risk. Secondly, the more risk-taking people are, the more their indifference curves will slope downwards.

It is generally believed that most investors are risk-averse. This stems from a belief that, for most people, wealth has a diminishing **marginal utility**. That means, for example, that if someone was given successively more and more pounds, then each extra pound would generate less extra **utility** or satisfaction than the last one. In turn, most people would find that a rise in wealth by 60 at the end of the holding period being considered would add less utility than a fall in wealth by 60 would remove.

3.6 PORTFOLIO CHOICE

Choice with equity-only portfolios

It is now possible to see how investors might select their portfolios. This will be done by using as an example the country considered in Section 3.4 where the only risky assets are equities. However, the analysis of portfolio choice given here requires a number of assumptions. The first three are as follows:

1. Investors are risk-averse. This means that their indifference curves slope upwards.
2. Investors seek to maximise the utility they will get from their wealth at the end of the period under consideration, which is taken here to be one year, so they will select the portfolios that take them to the highest indifference curves they can reach.
3. Investors compare different portfolios on the basis of their expected returns and standard deviations. In other words, they refer to the efficient frontier when they make their choice.

In addition, it will be supposed that all investors agree on the position of the efficient frontier and on the composition of all the portfolios that lie upon it. This requires five further assumptions:

4. Investors must all have free access to all information about each security. Otherwise, they would undoubtedly form different views about the expected return and standard deviation for each security and so, in turn, for each possible portfolio.
5. When they use this complete information, all investors must end up agreeing on the expected future return and standard deviation for each security and so, in turn, for each possible portfolio. This means that they must all make similar hunches about how far, if at all, past mean returns and volatilities need to be adjusted when forecasting future ones.
6. All investors must have identical time horizons. Otherwise, if they allowed for future changes in the performances of different equities, then the forecasts of expected returns and standard deviations that they used would differ, depending on how far ahead they looked.
7. There must be no taxes which distort the choice of securities. Ultimately, investors are concerned about the return they secure net of taxes such as income tax and capital gains tax. If income and capital gains are taxed differently, then, depending on their individual situations, some investors will prefer securities whose returns arise chiefly in the form of income, while others will prefer securities whose returns arise chiefly in the form of capital gains. So different investors will have different views about the net returns from identical portfolios.
8. There must be no **transactions costs** such as stockbrokers' **commissions** or fees. For investors are concerned about their returns net of these costs, so if different investors face different costs, then they will not necessarily regard identical portfolios as securing identical net returns.

Suppose that X and Y both live in the country considered in Section 3.4, and suppose that they agree that the efficient frontier is as shown in Fig. 3.1. This is reproduced in Fig. 3.3, though here the horizontal axis is drawn to a different scale. Figure 3.3 includes two of Y's indifference curves which are labelled Y_1 and Y_2. Y chooses the portfolio that takes her to position y_1, for this portfolio puts her on to her highest attainable indifference curve. Figure 3.3 also

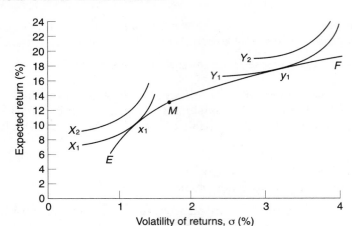

Figure 3.3   Choices of equity-only portfolios.

includes two indifference curves for X who is more risk-averse. His curves are labelled X_1 and X_2, and he chooses position x_1. His portfolio has much less volatility or risk than Y's, but it also has a much lower expected return.

This analysis of portfolio choice was put forward by Markowitz (1952). It argues that different investors want different portfolios of risky assets depending on how risk-averse they are. In turn, it offers no neat way of working out the returns that investors will require from different assets. However, these two results are radically altered if just one extra element of choice is allowed for.

Allowing for risk-free lending and borrowing

Suppose now that X and Y are allowed to widen their portfolios a little from having equities alone. This means making a further assumption:

9. In addition to investing in equities, investors may all lend **risk-free** by buying a risk-free asset. Moreover, they may all borrow at the same risk-free rate that is available on the risk-free asset.

The risk-free asset is usually taken to be a Treasury bill because its short-term life makes its price very insensitive to interest rate changes, while its government backing eliminates any default risk. The assumption that investors can also borrow at the same risk-free rate as the government is clearly unrealistic, but it will be assumed for the moment.

When investors can lend and borrow at the risk-free rate, they will choose their portfolios as shown in Fig. 3.4. This resembles Fig. 3.3 except that it includes a line labelled *LMN*. This line is included because the highest expected return for each level of risk is now shown by *LMN* rather than by *EF*. So investors will choose portfolios that take them to points on *LMN*. This line starts on the vertical axis at the risk-free rate, r_F, which is assumed here to be 7%, and it touches the original efficient frontier, *EF*, at *M*. The reason that

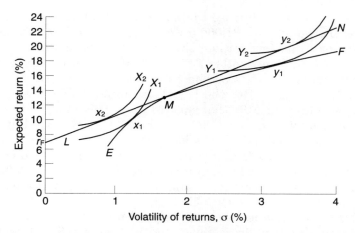

Figure 3.4 Choices of portfolios with equities and with risk-free borrowing and lending.

it touches *EF* at the point that applies to the market portfolio is explained shortly; meanwhile, the fact that *M* represents the market portfolio can be ignored.

To get to *M*, investors would buy equities alone and have a mean or expected return of 13% and a standard deviation of 1.63%. To get to *L*, they would buy the risk-free asset alone and have a return of 7% with a standard deviation of zero, for the return on the risk-free asset is certain.

Investors could also end up at a position on *LMN* between *L* and *M*, such as x_2, which is half-way in between *L* and *M*. Suppose X wants to end up at x_2, and suppose his initial wealth is £2,000. To get to x_2, he would use half his wealth to buy the risk-free asset and half to buy the share mix that on its own results in position *M*. Thus he would have £1,000 invested in the risk-free asset at 7%, guaranteeing a return of 7%, or £70, and he would have £1,000 in a share mix with an expected return of 13%, or £130. So X's total expected return is £200, that is 10% of his wealth of £2,000, as shown at x_2. As half of his wealth is invested in the risk-free asset, which has a zero standard deviation, and half in the share portfolio represented by position *M*, which has a standard deviation of about 1.63%, it might be expected that the standard deviation of the combination would be less than half-way, as occurred with portfolios of two shares shown in Fig. 3.1. But this time the standard deviation *is* half-way between the two separate ones at about 0.82% because the stable returns on the risk-free asset do nothing to offset the volatile returns of the equity portfolio represented by *M*. The standard deviation of the portfolio represented by x_2 is below that of the portfolio represented by *M* only because the former partly comprises a risk-free asset, whereas the latter does not.

Investors could even end up at a position on *LMN* to the right of *M*, such as y_2, which is as far to the right of *M* as *M* is to the right of *L*. Suppose Y wants to end up at y_2, and suppose her initial wealth is £1,000. To get to y_2, she would use all this on buying the share mix that on its own results in position M. So she would have £1,000 invested in this portfolio with an expected return of 13%, or £130. In addition, she would borrow another £1,000 at the risk-free rate of 7% and buy another £1,000 worth of shares in another identical mix to the first and so secure a second expected return of £130. In total, then, Y expects a return of £260. But she has to pay interest of £70 on her loan, so she expects to end up with £190 that she can keep. This represents an expected 19% return on her wealth of £1,000, as shown by point y_2. But while her expected return is higher than it would be if she had just invested £1,000 in the portfolio represented by M, the volatility of her returns is double, at 3.26%, for she has twice as many volatile shares in relation to her £1,000.

Given their indifference curves, X and Y will, in fact, settle at x_2 and y_2. Moreover, all investors, will reach their highest possible indifference curves by settling on LMN. This line is called the **capital market line**. It must be seen as a new efficient frontier, for it shows the highest possible expected return for each possible degree of risk, once lending or borrowing at the risk-free rate is permitted.

The separation theorem

It was seen in Fig. 3.4 that X wants a portfolio of equities which, on its own, would take him to M, though he will also lend some money on the risk-free asset and so end up at x_2. Y also wants a portfolio of equities which, on its own, would take her to M, though she will also borrow some money at the risk-free rate and so end up at y_2. In fact, all investors want an *identical* portfolio of risky assets which, on its own, would take them to M. This conclusion is quite different from the one reached when there was no risk-free asset, for then X and Y and other investors wanted different portfolios of risky assets depending on how risk-averse they were. But once a risk-free asset is available, investors' choices over risky-asset portfolios become quite separate from their attitudes towards risk. Following Tobin (1958), this result is called Tobin's **separation theorem**.

The fact that everyone wants an identical portfolio of risky assets such as equities means they must each want shares in every company. It also means they must each want the proportion of their portfolio's value that is accounted for by any given company's shares to equal the proportion of the value of all issued shares that is accounted for by that company's shares. The reason for these conclusions is that, if everyone wants the same portfolio, then there cannot be any shares which no-one wants, nor can there be any shares which are specially disfavoured or favoured. If there were any such shares, their prices would soon change to make them more attractive or less attractive. These conclusions actually mean that the portfolio shown by position M must be a market portfolio.

Although Fig. 3.4 implies that all investors want to end up with a market portfolio, it would actually be absurd for every investor to seek a portfolio with shares from every company. This is because such portfolios would include a huge range of equities in negligible quantities, and in practice the transaction costs of buying them would be huge. So most investors actually try to have equity portfolios of perhaps 20 or 30 different shares, and they may try to get a portfolio that has a very similar mean–volatility position, or mean–variance position, to a market portfolio of equities.

Systematic risk and diversifiable risk

Figure 3.4 shows that both X and Y end up with some volatility or risk because their portfolios contain some equities. The risk on any given equity arises from two groups of factors. One group comprises firm-specific factors like new products and management changes. The risk generated by these factors is called **non-systematic risk** because it is not shared by a range of shares in a systematic way. It is also called **diversifiable risk** because investors can almost entirely diversify it away by **diversification**, that is by buying shares in a range of companies, perhaps as few as 20 or 30; for then, bad results by some companies should be offset by good results from others. Because this risk can be diversified away, investors cannot expect to earn high returns for bearing it.

Each factor in the other group of factors that generate risk tends to affect all equities, albeit to varying extents. These factors include the level of industrial production, the level of consumer spending, interest rates and exchange rates. The market portfolio itself is affected by these factors, even though it is as diversified as possible, and this is why the standard deviation of its returns is not zero. The risk generated by these factors is called **systematic risk**, because it affects all equities. It is also called **non-diversifiable risk** because it cannot be diversified away by buying many equities. And it is called **market risk** because it affects the equity market as a whole.

It is because the market portfolio has some systematic risk that investors would require a higher expected return from it than they require from the risk-free asset. In other words, to compensate for its systematic risk, people will offer sufficiently low prices for shares in general that a market portfolio will end up with a higher expected return than the return on the risk-free asset. The size of the market portfolio's extra return, or **risk premium,** depends on how much systematic risk it involves and on the average degree of risk-aversion in the economy. In Fig. 3.4, the mean return on the market portfolio is 13%, while the risk-free asset has a return of 7%, so the market portfolio has a risk premium of 6%. In practice, its risk premium varies a little over time and is often around 8%.

3.7 THE CAPITAL ASSET PRICING MODEL (CAPM)

The model of portfolio choice shown in Fig. 3.4 suggests that all investors will combine a market portfolio, which contains all risky assets, with some lending or borrowing at the risk-free rate. In a country with many different risky assets, investors may select only 20 to 30 equities, but this will be ignored here for simplicity. By combining a market portfolio with risk-free lending or borrowing, investors end up on the line *LMN* which is the tangent to *EF* from the point on the vertical axis that shows the risk-free rate of interest. *EF* derives from the expected returns of all risky assets, and the volatilities of those returns. The example involved only four risky assets. Their expected returns were 4% for Aco shares, 10% for Bco shares, 16% for Cco shares and 22% for Dco shares.

If investors expect that next year they could get a 4% return from Aco shares and a 22% return from Dco shares, then it might seem that the demand for Dco shares should rise, so causing their price to rise and their expected return to fall. And it might seem that the demand for Aco shares should fall, so causing their price to fall and their expected return to rise. The reason that this does not happen must be that investors *require* a higher return from Dco than Aco. Likewise, they must also require different returns from Bco and Cco. The **capital asset pricing model** (CAPM) is a hypothesis about what determines the different returns that investors require on different assets. It derives chiefly from the work of Sharpe (1963, 1964), Lintner (1965) and Mossin (1966).

Individual share returns

The discussion of Fig. 3.2(b) suggests one possible reason why required returns might vary. There, X compared a bond with a certain return of 10% and an equity whose return might be 4% or 16%. The average or expected return from the equity was the same as the return on the bond. But X was risk-averse, so he preferred the bond because its return was certain. However, he might have chosen the equity if its expected return had exceeded that of the bond. On this basis, it might seem that all that matters in determining the required return from any given equity is the volatility of its returns, so that the higher the standard deviation, or total risk, the higher the required return will be.

However, the CAPM argues that required returns do *not* depend on total risk. That is because the non-systematic part of the risk on any given share can be almost wholly diversified away. What matters is the remaining systematic part of the risk. Investors dislike shares with a high systematic risk, because including them in their market portfolios aggravates the volatility of their market portfolios. So, these unpopular shares are the ones where investors require the highest returns.

The argument can be illustrated with an example. Suppose that the risk-free rate is 7% and that the expected return on the market portfolio is 13%. The returns on the market portfolio will vary over time, tending, for example, to rise in booms and fall in recessions. Imagine two companies whose shares have returns that are equally volatile, so that they rise and fall to similar extents over time. But suppose that one company is a hotel whose returns tend to rise and fall at the same time as, and to the same extent as, those of the market portfolio, while the other is a firm of receivers whose returns tend to rise and fall at the opposite times to those of the market portfolio.

Although the two shares have identical volatilities, investors will not require equal returns from them. Investors will like the receivers' shares because including them in their market portfolios reduces the uncertainty about the overall return they will get in the next period. In contrast, the hotel shares have no such effect. As the receivers' shares will be more popular in terms of the timing of the rises and falls in their returns, no-one will buy the hotel shares unless they have a higher expected return. In other words, investors will *require* a higher return from the hotel shares. In turn, the prices that investors will pay for the two shares will settle at levels which ensure that the expected return from each is equal to its required return. In fact, because the returns from the hotel shares mimic those of the market portfolio, their required return will equal the expected 13% return of the market portfolio. But the receivers' shares might have a required return of, say, only 5%.

Next, consider a company whose shares have returns that tend to rise and fall at the same time as the market portfolio, but which rise and fall to a smaller extent. The CAPM argues that, unlike the hotel shares, these shares will tend to reduce the overall volatility of the returns from a market portfolio, though they will do so less effectively than the receivers' shares. So they will have a required return between 5% and 13%. In contrast, a company whose shares have returns that tend to rise and fall at the same time as the market portfolio, but which rise and fall to a greater extent, will be very unpopular in terms of aggravating the volatility of the returns from the market portfolio, so the required return on them will exceed the 13% that is required for the hotel and for the market portfolio. So, to predict the required or expected return for any given shares, it is necessary to measure the extent to which their returns tend to move at the same time as those of the market portfolio, and also to see how significant these movements are compared with the volatility of the market portfolio. There is a measure which does this. It is called a beta coefficient.

Beta coefficients

The **beta coefficient** or **beta** (β) for a company's shares depends on two factors. One is the **covariance** between the returns on its shares and the returns on the market portfolio. This measures how closely the two returns tend to move together. The other is the variance of the returns of the market portfolio. This is needed to see how significant the covariance is in relation to the volatility of the market portfolio. To estimate the beta for a share, it is necessary to estimate the covariance of all the combinations of returns that could arise between the share's returns and the market portfolio's returns. It is also necessary to estimate the variance of all the returns that could arise on the market portfolio. The following paragraphs show how the beta coefficients can be worked out for all the four companies in the country considered in Section 3.4.

Table 3.3 (on p. 75) showed how the variance of all the possible returns from the market portfolio there could be estimated from a sample of its returns in n periods. The variance of the returns in the sample is $\Sigma x^2/n$, where the x-value for each period equals that period's return minus the mean return. This variance is a biased estimate of the variance of all the returns that there could be, but fortunately $\Sigma x^2/(n-1)$ gives an unbiased estimate. In the example this is 2.67.

Likewise, the covariance between the returns on a given company's shares, such as Aco's, and the returns of the market portfolio can be estimated by looking at the returns of the share and the returns of the market portfolio in a sample of n periods. For each period, it is necessary to work out the x-value for the share and also the x-value for the market portfolio, called here x_M. The covariance between the two sets of returns in the sample is defined as $\Sigma(xx_M)/n$. This slightly underestimates the covariance between all the returns that could arise. Fortunately, $\Sigma(xx_M)/(n-1)$ gives an unbiased estimate.

Table 3.4 shows how the beta can be worked out for each of the four companies. The four x-values for the market portfolio are used to calculate each beta, so they are taken from column (11) of Table 3.3 and repeated four times in Table 3.4, in columns (2), (5), (8) and (11), where they are called x_M. In the mini-boom year 2, x_M was positive at 2%, showing that the return of the market portfolio was then 2% above its mean value, but in the mini-recession year 4, x_M was negative at −2%, showing that the return of the market portfolio was then 2% below its mean value. Columns (1), (4), (7) and (10) of Table 3.4 repeat the four x-values for each share from columns (2), (5), (8) and (11) of Table 3.2. In each case, these are positive when the company had above average returns and negative when it had below average returns. Columns (3), (6), (9) and (12) of Table 3.4 give all the values for xx_M and $\Sigma(xx_M)$ for each share.

Aco's shares have returns that tend to move up and down at different times from those of the market portfolio. Most notably, Aco had below average returns in year 2, when the market portfolio had above average returns, and it had above average returns in year 4 when the market portfolio had below average returns. So in year 2, Aco had a negative x-value while x_M was positive, so that xx_M was negative, and in year 4, Aco had a positive x-value while x_M was negative, so that xx_M was again negative. These negative xx_M figures led to a negative $\Sigma(xx_M)$ of −4, and hence to a negative covariance, $\Sigma(xx_M)/(n-1)$, of −4/3, that is −1.33.

In contrast, the shares in the other companies have returns that broadly tend to move up and down at the same times as those of the market portfolio. For example, in years 2 and 3, Cco had returns that were above average, as shown by its positive x-values in those years, while the market portfolio had returns that were either average or above average, so no negative xx_M figures arose in either year. Also, in years 1 and 4, Cco had returns that were below average, as shown by its negative x-values in those years, while the market portfolio had returns that were either average or below average, so again no negative xx_M figures arose. The absence of any negative figures for xx_M led to a positive $\Sigma(xx_M)$ of 12, and hence to a positive covariance, $\Sigma(xx_M)/(n-1)$, which was 12/3 or 4.00.

It follows that a positive covariance arises for shares whose returns tend to move up and down at the same times as those of the market portfolio, as with Bco, Cco and Dco, while a negative covariance arises for shares whose returns tend to move up and down at opposite times to those in the market portfolio, as with Aco. However, investors need to know how significant these covariances are in relation to the volatility of the market portfolio. So they need to know the beta coefficients which are defined as the covariances divided by the variance of the market portfolio's returns. It was shown in column (12) of Table 3.3 that the variance, or σ^2, for the market portfolio is 2.67.

Table 3.4 Beta coefficients for four shares

	Aco			Bco			Cco			Dco		
	(1)	(2)	(3)	(4)	(5)	(6)	(7)	(8)	(9)	(10)	(11)	(12)
	x	x_M	xx_M	x	x_M	xx_M	x	x_M	xx_M	x	x_M	xx_M
Year 1	−3	0	0	1	0	0	−3	0	0	5	0	0
Year 2	−1	2	−2	−1	2	−2	2	2	4	8	2	16
Year 3	3	0	0	3	0	0	5	0	0	−11	0	0
Year 4	1	−2	−2	−3	−2	6	−4	−2	8	−2	−2	4
Total	0	0	−4	0	0	4	0	0	12	0	0	20
Covariance			−1.33			1.33			4.00			6.67
Market σ^2			2.67			2.67			2.67			2.67
β coefficient			−0.50			0.50			1.50			2.50
Risk premium			−3%			3%			9%			15%
Required return			4%			10%			16%			22%

The market portfolio's σ^2 of 2.67 is repeated in columns (3), (6), (9) and (12) of Table 3.4 which give the calculations needed to get each of the betas. For example, Aco's covariance is −1.33, so its beta coefficient is −1.33/2.67, or −0.50. The other betas are calculated in a similar way as 0.5, 1.5 and 2.5. Each beta reflects the extent to which the returns on the company's shares tend to rise and fall at the same time as the returns on the market portfolio, and it also reflects the size of those rises and falls in relation to the volatility of the market portfolio. So a company's beta indicates the systematic risk on its shares. Of course, investors are really interested in the future systematic risk of its shares, so when they estimate future betas they may adjust past betas in the light of any hunches they have about possible changes.

It is possible to work out covariances and beta coefficients for portfolios as well as for individual shares. In the case of the market portfolio, beta must be one, because its returns necessarily move perfectly in line with those of the market portfolio. In the case of a portfolio comprising the risk-free asset alone, beta must be zero, for the returns on the risk-free asset never move at all, so they do not vary at all in line with the returns of the market portfolio. In the case of a portfolio like the one X chose in Fig. 3.4, half of which was the risk-free asset and half of which was a market portfolio of shares, it can readily be shown that the beta is 0.5; one of the questions at the end of this chapter asks for the relevant calculations.

Figure 3.5 is a graph whose horizontal axis measures beta coefficients and whose vertical axis measures expected rates of return. However, as noted earlier, security prices settle so that expected rates of return equal required rates of return, so this axis also measures required rates. Point F shows the position of a portfolio comprising the risk-free asset alone, with β = 0.0 and a rate of return of 7%. Point B shows the position of X's portfolio with β = 0.5 and an expected rate of return of 10%. And point M shows the position of the market portfolio with β = 1.0 and an expected rate of return of 13%. These three points fall on a straight line, called the **security market line**, and it

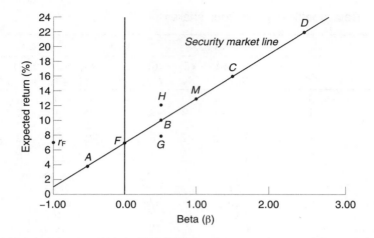

Figure 3.5   The security market line.

can be readily shown that the combinations of beta and expected rate of return for all the portfolios on the efficient line *LMN* in Fig. 3.4, that is all combinations of the market portfolio and the risk-free asset, will also fall on this line.

The CAPM hypothesis

The CAPM hypothesis is that the relationship between the beta and the required return for each individual security also falls on the security market line so that there is a linear relationship between different assets' betas and their required returns. As asset prices adjust to ensure that expected returns equal required returns, the CAPM also argues that there is a similar linear relationship between different assets' betas and their expected returns.

The insight behind this hypothesis is the CAPM's view that shares with betas greater than one are unpopular in terms of the relationship between their volatility and that of the market portfolio, because they aggravate the volatility of the market portfolio. So the CAPM argues that, on these shares, investors require high returns which exceed the return of the market portfolio. Conversely, the CAPM argues that companies whose betas are less than one are popular in terms of the relationship between their volatility and that of the market portfolio, because they reduce the volatility of the market portfolio. So the CAPM argues that on these shares investors require low returns which are below the return of the market portfolio.

More specifically, the CAPM argues that each asset has its own risk premium which is directly proportional to its beta. Consider the country in the example where the risk-free rate is 7% and the expected return of the market portfolio is 13%, so that the market portfolio has a risk premium of 6%. This portfolio has a beta of 1.0, so a beta of 1.0 leads to a risk premium of 6%. The CAPM argues that Bco shares, whose beta is 0.5, will have a risk premium of 3%, and hence a required return that is 3% above that of the risk-free asset at 10%, as shown by point B in Fig. 3.5. But Aco shares, whose beta is -0.5, will have a risk premium of -3%, and hence a required return that is 3% *below* the risk-free rate at 4%, as shown by point A.

More formally, the CAPM says that the risk premium for any asset, $(r - r_F)$, is given by:

$$(r - r_F) = \beta(r_M - r_F) \tag{3.2}$$

where r is the asset's required rate of return, r_F is the risk-free rate, β is the asset's beta, and r_M is the return on the market portfolio. (3.2) can be rearranged to give this formula for r:

$$r = r_F + \beta(r_M - r_F) \tag{3.3}$$

For example, (3.2) shows that the risk premiums for Cco and Dco shares, whose betas are 1.5 and 2.5, are $1.5(13\% - 7\%)$ and $2.5(13\% - 7\%)$ respectively, that is 9% and 15%. (3.3) shows that their required returns are $7\% + 9\%$ and $7\% + 15\%$ respectively, that is 16% and 22%. These results are shown by points C and D in Fig. 3.5. It will be found from Table 3.1 that the mean returns for Cco and Dco, and also Aco and Bco, correspond precisely to the values that the CAPM believes investors require from them, but this does not mean the CAPM hypothesis is correct. It merely means that the example was constructed to be consistent with the CAPM.

The formal proof that, under the CAPM assumptions, the relationship between assets' betas and their required returns follows the straight security market line is not given here because it requires calculus. Instead, an intuitive argument will be given. Suppose, for example, that a new company, Gco, is launched in the country in the example, so that some Gco shares are now included in the market portfolio. Imagine for simplicity, however, that Gco has so few shares that the expected return and volatility of the market portfolio remain unaltered at point M in Fig. 3.5. Suppose, also, that Gco's beta is estimated at 0.5. According to (3.3), the price of these shares should settle so that, like Bco, they have an expected return of 10%.

But suppose the price of Gco shares settles so high that their expected return is 8%, as shown by point G in Fig. 3.5. This point is below the security market line. This means that, for a systematic risk represented by a beta of 0.5, Gco's shares offer a lower expected return than could be secured by a portfolio, like X's original portfolio, where half the funds were invested in the risk-free asset and half in a combination of all other shares. So investors who own Gco shares would sell them and use the money raised to buy portfolios like that. So the price of Gco shares would fall and their expected return would rise. Conversely, if the price of Gco shares settles so low that they have an expected return of 12%, as shown by point H, then for a systematic risk measured by a beta of 0.5, they would offer an attractive expected return. Admittedly investors would not want to replace all their other assets with Gco shares as they would then be highly exposed to the non-systematic risk on Gco shares. Even so, Gco shares would be in great demand, so their price would rise and their expected return would fall.

Is the CAPM correct?

The CAPM rests on the model of portfolio choice that was developed in Section 3.6. So it is a model which explains how securities should be priced if those assumptions hold. In practice, some of these assumptions are more plausible than others, as noted below.

1. *Investors are risk-averse.* The widespread incidence of gambling shows that people are not always risk-averse. But it is widely believed that most people are risk-averse most of the time.
2. *Investors seek to maximise the utility they will get from their wealth at the end of the period.* This is not contentious.
3. *Investors compare different possible portfolios on the basis of their expected returns and standard deviations.* The main issue here is whether investors always measure risk solely in terms of the standard deviation of the expected future returns. For example, they could use other measures, such as the standard deviation of the natural logarithms of the expected returns. If investors use another measure, then they will end up with different efficient frontiers that are plotted on graphs with this alternative measure on the horizontal axis. In turn, all the expected CAPM results will need modifying. Past standard deviations are widely quoted, so presumably investors do use standard deviations, but whether they are the *only* factors that investors use to measure risk is, to say the least, far from certain.
4. *Investors all have free access to all information about different securities.* Most of the value of equities is accounted for by large companies, and information on them is widely disseminated. But information on some risky assets, such as shares in small companies, is not widely available.
5. *All investors agree on the expected future mean return and standard deviation for each security.* This is implausible as investors are likely to have different hunches about how mean returns and volatilities will alter in the future.
6. *Investors have identical time horizons.* This is implausible.
7. *There are no taxes which distort the choice of securities.* This is implausible.
8. *There are no transactions costs.* This is implausible.
9. *All investors can borrow or lend at the same risk-free rate.* They cannot all borrow at this rate.

As several of these assumptions are implausible, no-one would expect to find that the prices of different equities adjust to give them expected returns whose differences from the return available on a risk-free asset can be explained wholly with reference to their betas. Indeed, the world of assets is so complex that no model could hope to explain their expected returns fully. What matters is whether the CAPM explains expected returns reasonably well, or whether it turns out to be a seriously flawed model that should be replaced by another.

Unfortunately, it is hard, and perhaps impossible, to test the CAPM. There are two main difficulties. First, the CAPM argues that the prices of assets adjust so that their expected returns equal their required returns, and these in turn depend on their betas, or, more precisely, on their expected betas. Thus it argues that expected returns are related to expected betas. But for data reasons, tests of CAPM have to see whether realised returns relate to realised betas. If these tests show little relationship, then it could be because realised betas or returns were quite different from the expected ones. That would not necessarily invalidate the CAPM.

Secondly, different assets' betas should in principle be measured by relating their varying returns to the varying returns of the true market portfolio. But, as Roll (1977) pointed out, the true market portfolio contains *all* risky assets, including commodities, currencies and works of art which can be bought in the hope of selling them at a profit, yet in practice no-one could work out the returns from such a diverse portfolio. So, in practice, tests of the CAPM measure betas by relating the returns on different assets to the returns of a much narrower and hence incomplete market portfolio, such as the equities represented in a FTSE index. Because these tests use an incomplete market portfolio, their results are inevitably controversial.

Despite these problems, many tests have been made, but because of these problems, it is not clear how seriously to take them. An important early test in the United States was made by Black, Jensen and Scholes (1972) who found that high betas were associated with higher returns, but they also found that low-beta securities seemed to get higher returns than the CAPM would predict, while high-beta ones got lower returns than the CAPM would predict. The CAPM received further modest support from study by Fama and MacBeth (1973), but Fama and French (1992) have argued that the relationship between betas and returns is very weak. Instead, they agree with some other studies that, for some reason, required returns tend to be highest for small companies, and also for companies whose assets, as valued on their balance sheets, are high compared with the values of their shares. But the conclusion reached by most studies is, perhaps, that the CAPM seems to do a tolerable but far from perfect job.

3.8 ARBITRAGE PRICING THEORY (APT)

The CAPM seems to do a far from perfect job at predicting required rates of return, or, equivalently, asset prices, so there has been much search for a different model of asset prices. As the CAPM rests on the portfolio choice model presented in Section 3.6, so any different model has to rest on a modified model of portfolio choice. Ross's (1976) **arbitrage pricing theory** (APT) is the leading alternative to the CAPM. A key feature of the APT is that it makes no reference to a market portfolio. This means that the APT cannot and does not see all investors wanting an identical market portfolio of risky assets, as implied by Fig. 3.4 in the model of portfolio choice given in Section 3.6. It also means that the returns on different portfolios cannot be explained simply with reference to betas that relate their returns to the returns of the market portfolio, as implied by Fig. 3.5 in the CAPM. Instead, the APT assumes that portfolio returns depend on several different factors.

It is helpful to approach the APT by seeing that it takes a different view of investor behaviour from the CAPM. In the CAPM, investors are very concerned about the betas of different assets and portfolios, that is about their systematic risk. But they do not consider *why* systematic risk arises. In contrast, the APT sees investors as having a list of systematic factors which cause returns to be volatile, so they care about each asset's sensitivity to each of those factors. Unfortunately, the APT leaves it to others to try and identify the relevant factors. The most promising ones include the level of industrial production, the level of retail sales, the real interest rate, the inflation rate, and the exchange rates for sterling and other currencies.

To see how these factors may be relevant, suppose that investors require a return of 12% from the shares on some company, say LML. Then the price of LML's shares will adjust so that their expected return in the next period is 12%. This expected return depends in part on the levels that investors expect industrial production, consumption, and the other factors to take. However, investors know that LML's return may not turn out as expected, and this is why LML shares are a risky asset. A major source of risk is systematic factors that are common to LML shares and other assets, such as the levels of industrial production and consumption. Ultimately, the reason that there is a systematic risk attached to LML's shares is that the levels of industrial production, consumption and so on may be different from their expected values. So the ultimate sources of systematic risk are changes, or more specifically *unexpected changes*, in industrial production, consumption, and so on. So investors want to know how sensitive the returns of assets like LML shares are to such unexpected changes.

Another source of risk is non-systematic factors that are unique to LML. The APT expects investors to make non-systematic risk a negligible problem by having **well-diversified portfolios**. A well-diversified portfolio is one that is diversified over a large enough number of assets, usually securities, each of which comprises a small enough proportion of the whole, that the portfolio's returns are not significantly affected by the effects of the non-systematic factors on any one security. Moreover, because non-systematic factors are likely to affect different securities in different directions, so the combined impact of all the non-systematic factors of all the securities in a well-diversified portfolio are likely to cancel each other out. So the APT expects the required or expected returns on any given well-diversified portfolio to depend only on its sensitivities to the various systematic factors. Incidentally, the APT accepts that a well-diversified portfolio may include holdings of the risk-free asset or, indeed, holdings of equities financed by borrowing at the risk-free rate.

The APT hypothesis for the returns on well-diversified portfolios

The APT makes a specific claim about the relationship between the expected return on any given well-diversified portfolio, r, and the expected sensitivity of that portfolio to the factors that cause systematic risk. This claim is that there is a linear or proportional relationship between the expected return and each factor, as shown in the following equation:

$$r = r_F + \beta_1(r_{F1} - r_F) + \beta_2(r_{F2} - r_F) + \beta_3(r_{F3} - r_F) + \ldots \tag{3.4}$$

where r_F is the risk-free rate. Unlike the CAPM equation *(3.3)*, this equation does not use the required return on the market portfolio, r_M, as a benchmark. Instead, it uses as **benchmarks** the required returns on several different port-folios called **factor portfolios**. These returns are termed r_{F1}, r_{F2} and so on. A factor portfolio is one whose returns are sensitive to only one systematic factor. For example, a portfolio whose returns were sensitive to changes in real interest rates but not to changes in any of the other factors would be a factor portfolio.

To use *(3.4)* for a given well-diversified portfolio, it is first necessary to work out a series of betas for it. For example, its β_1 is the expected covariance of its returns with the returns of the factor portfolio that is sensitive only to factor 1, divided by the expected variance of that factor portfolio's returns. There might be several alternative portfolios whose returns were sensitive only to factor 1, but, as explained shortly, it would not matter which was used as a benchmark. Likewise, the portfolio's β_2 is the expected covariance of its returns with the returns of the factor portfolio that is sensitive only to factor 2, divided by the expected variance of that factor portfolio's returns.

Suppose, for example, that there are three systematic factors, and suppose that the required returns on the three benchmark portfolios are 9% for the factor 1 portfolio, 12% for the factor 2 portfolio, and 13% for the factor 3 port-folio, so that $r_{F1} = 0.09$, $r_{F2} = 0.12$, and $r_{F3} = 0.13$. Suppose, also, that a given portfolio has $\beta_1 = 1.5$, $\beta_2 = 0.8$, and $\beta_3 = 0.5$. Finally, suppose that the risk-free rate is 7%. Then the required return for that given portfolio will be 7% plus 1.5(9% – 7%) plus 0.8(12% – 7%) plus 0.5(13% – 7%), which is 17%.

It might seem that *(3.4)* could fail to deliver a unique required return for any given portfolio if there was, say, more than one factor 1 portfolio. For example, suppose there was a second factor 1 portfolio that was more sensitive to factor 1. If this was used as the benchmark portfolio, then the β_1 for the portfolio considered in the last paragraph might be exactly 1.0 as it might be no more sensitive to factor 1 than the new factor 1 benchmark portfolio. However, the required return on the new factor 1 benchmark portfolio would be higher than 9%, for it would be riskier. This is because it would have more volatile returns as it is more sensitive to factor 1. So this time r_{F1} might be 10%. So *(3.4)* would now give the required return for the portfolio under consid-eration as 7% plus 1.0(10% – 7%) plus 0.8(12% – 7%) plus 0.5(13% – 7%), which is 17% once again.

One problem with the APT is that it does not explain what determines the required returns on the factor portfolios. All that can be said is that these returns clearly depend on the average degree of risk-aversion to the risk gener-ated by each of those factors.

The role of arbitrage

The reason why the APT claims that well-diversified portfolios must have expected returns that accord with *(3.4)* stems from the fact that, if they do not, then people can make riskless profits, or make more profits without taking any

Table 3.5   Required returns on three well-diversified portfolios

Portfolio	r_F (%)	$\beta_1(r_{F1}-r_F)$ (%)	$\beta_2(r_{F2}-r_F)$ (%)	Required r (%)
P	7	0.25(4) = 1	0.50(2) = 1	9
Q	7	1.00(4) = 4	1.00(2) = 2	13
R	7	1.75(4) = 7	1.50(2) = 3	17

more risks, by means of arbitrage. Arbitrage will continue until the expected returns do accord with (3.4). It is this arbitrage activity that gives the theory its name. To see how it operates, consider three different well-diversified portfolios, P, Q and R. And suppose this time that there are just two relevant factors.

Table 3.5 shows how the required return for each portfolio is worked out. These required returns have three components. The first component is the risk-free rate, r_F, which is taken to be 7%. Secondly, there is the portfolio's β_1; this is multiplied by $(r_{F1}-r_F)$, that is the risk premium on the factor 1 portfolio, which is taken to be 4%. Thirdly, there is the portfolio's β_2; this is multiplied by $(r_{F2}-r_F)$, that is the risk premium on the factor 2 portfolio, which is taken to be 2%. The total required returns are 9% for P, 13% for Q and 17% for R.

Assume for the moment that all securities are priced so that each portfolio's expected return equals its required return. Then it can be shown that investors would regard £200 invested in Q as equivalent to £100 invested in each of P and R. The Q portfolio and the P + R portfolio would certainly have identical expected returns. For £200 invested in Q would be expected to secure 13% of £200, or £26, while £100 invested in each of P and R would be expected to secure 9% of £100 plus 17% of £100, which is £9 plus £17 and so also £26. The Q portfolio and the P + R portfolio would also have identical risks. The β terms measure the sensitivity of each portfolio to the two factors. Take, for example, the β_1 terms of 0.25, 1.00 and 1.75. These imply that a change in factor 1 which caused the return on, say, £100 invested in P to change by £1 would cause the return on £100 invested in Q to change by £4 and the return on £100 invested in R to change by £7. So the effect on £200 invested in Q would be £8 which equals the effect on £100 invested in P plus the effect of £100 invested in R. As the β_2 terms for P and R add up to double the β_2 term for Q, a similar result holds there too.

Suppose, next, that some of the securities in the Q portfolio are priced in a way which means that its expected return differs from its required return. Maybe the expected return is 12%, whereas the required return is 13%. Then people who own the Q portfolio should sell their securities and divide the proceeds equally between buying the securities included in the P and R portfolios. Each time they sell £200 worth of Q portfolio securities they lose expected earnings of £24, but they can buy £100 worth of P portfolio securities and £100 worth of R portfolio securities with combined expected earnings of £26. Their overall risk position will be unaltered as their new purchases have exactly the same overall sensitivity to factors 1 and 2 that the sold securities had. So large sales of securities in the Q portfolio are likely to occur, forcing their prices down until the expected return on the Q portfolio equals the required 13%.

The APT hypothesis for the pricing and returns of individual assets

The APT argues that the prices of *almost all* individual assets will adjust so that their expected returns are as given by *(3.4)*. Otherwise, arbitrageurs will seek riskless profits by selling overpriced assets and buying underpriced ones. However, a few securities could remain mispriced. This is because all investors are assumed to have well-diversified portfolios in which no individual assets form a substantial proportion. So if X finds that his portfolio contains one or two overpriced assets, then he may not bother to replace them because the impact on his portfolio might be trivial. And if Y identifies one or two under-priced assets that she does not own, then she may not bother to buy them. But this argument can allow only a few assets to be mispriced. If a significant number were mispriced, then significant profits could be made through selling them or buying them, and these opportunities would be taken.

Tests of APT

Tests have been made to compare the APT with the CAPM, but the results are mixed. A major problem with testing the APT is that it does not specify the factors that should be included. Another problem is that, like the CAPM tests, the APT tests tend to relate realised returns to realised betas, whereas the APT itself actually relates expected returns to expected betas. Some research, but by no means all, implies that the APT explains asset prices better than the CAPM. But fund managers probably use the CAPM more than the APT because it is simpler and because the APT has not been shown to be greatly superior. However, it is possible that future developments will be made to the APT which improve its performance.

3.9 MARKET EFFICIENCY

The CAPM rests on the portfolio theory of Section 3.6 where investors choose a point on the line *LMN* in Fig. 3.4 that gives them their preferred combination of expected return and risk. They all have portfolios which in principle include a market portfolio of all risky assets together with a holding of the risk-free asset or some borrowing at the risk-free rate. In practice they would probably confine their risky assets to the shares in relatively few companies, but they might well select them so that the combination of volatility and expected return from their share portfolio closely matched the combination for the equity market as a whole.

The APT simply regards investors as selecting well-diversified portfolios which will also include shares in a number of companies and which may also include the risk-free asset or shares bought by borrowing at the risk-free rate.

It also envisages investors as selecting portfolios whose overall combinations of return and risk matches their preferences, though it does not think that a single beta captures all there is to say about systematic risk.

In each case, it seems that once investors have made a selection of shares, they should buy and sell shares only if the performance of some shares changes so that the combination of expected return and risk for their overall portfolio moves away from their desired combination. However, investors may wonder if they could instead buy and sell shares more frequently in an effort to secure higher returns than would be expected for their chosen level of systematic risk.

Trying to achieve a better portfolio performance

To see how this might be done, suppose that X and Y have identical portfolios which have total values of £100,000. Maybe each portfolio includes 1,000 shares in LML which are currently worth £5 each and so worth £5,000 in all. Suppose, next, that news arrives which leads people to expect LML's share price to double. Maybe the news suggests that LML's future profits will double. Or maybe it suggests that LML's beta will fall dramatically; this will reduce the risk premium on LML shares and so cause their price to rise until there is an appropriate fall in the expected return. In either case, the value of the LML shares held by X and Y should rise by £5,000, so the values of their portfolios should rise to £105,000.

Imagine, though, that most investors react slowly to news. Then the price of LML shares might take a long time to adjust fully. This means that ordinary slow reactors like, say, X, could be outperformed by quick reactors like, say, Y, for Y could increase the value of her portfolio by more than £5,000. When the news arrives which leads Y to expect the LML share price to rise, she might sell £45,000 worth of her shares in other companies and use the money to buy 9,000 more LML shares before their price rises. At this moment, she has £50,000 invested in LML and £50,000 invested in other companies. Next, she waits for the LML share price to double. So she now has £100,000 invested in LML and £50,000 in other companies. Her portfolio has risen much more than X's. She may worry that she is over-exposed to non-systematic risk on LML shares, so she may finally sell most of her LML shares and spread the money round on other shares. However, her gain has been made and she still has a portfolio worth £150,000.

Types of market efficiency

Whether investors can actually act like Y and outperform other investors like X, whose portfolios have the same level of systematic risk, depends on what is termed **market efficiency**. Consider, first, an asset market where prices fully and correctly reflect all the currently available information and where these prices react instantly to relevant news; such a market is called **strong form efficient**. Here, if news arrives that makes LML shares more attractive, then LML share prices will instantly rise. So Y could not buy extra LML shares before the price rose, so neither she nor anyone else could have a superior investment performance. In practice, most portfolios contain relatively few companies. As good and bad news arrives randomly, so some well-diversified portfolios will outperform others with the same degree of risk. But this should happen only by luck and, usually, only temporarily.

Consider, next, an asset market where prices fully reflect all the information that is available to most people, and where these prices react instantly to new publicly available information. But suppose, also, that share prices do not reflect any **insider information** that is available to only a few people. Such a market is called **semi-strong form efficient**. Here, it is impossible for outsiders to outperform other people whose portfolios have comparable levels of systematic risk, but it *is* possible for insiders. Suppose, for example, that LML's researchers have just invented something which will make LML's profits soar. If this is not widely known, then it will not be reflected in LML's share price, so they could buy extra LML shares now and outperform other investors. However, acting on inside information, or **insider trading**, is illegal, so their gains might be offset by fines or denied to them while they served prison sentences!

Finally, consider an asset market where prices fully reflect any information that can be derived by looking at the past, such as past asset prices and trading volumes, but where prices do not fully reflect any other publicly known information. Such a market is said to be **weak form efficient**. Here, if news arrives that leads people to expect the price of LML's shares to rise, then the price will not immediately react to reflect this news, so quick reactors like Y could outperform slow reactors like X whose portfolios have similar levels of systematic risk.

These three forms of efficiency were formalised by Fama (1970). They can be contrasted with an asset market that is not even weak-form efficient so that prices do not even fully reflect all information that can be derived by looking at the past. Here, it would be possible to achieve a superior investment performance without even having to react to news. For example, suppose a trend developed for the price of LML shares to fall in June and rise in September. Smart investors could sell LML shares in June and buy them back in September for less money, using their savings to expand their portfolios. This would not be possible in a weak-form efficient market where, once the trend emerged, the demand for LML shares would rise in June, raising the June price, and fall in September, reducing the September price, so eliminating the opportunity for smart investors to outperform others.

The efficient markets hypothesis

The **efficient markets hypothesis** (EMH) is a belief that financial asset markets are fully strong-form efficient and thus correctly reflect all information. It evolved in the wake of work by Kendall (1953). He studied security prices and commodity prices in the hope of finding patterns. Instead, he found that these prices seemed to follow **random walks**, so that future price changes could not be predicted on the basis of past prices. At the time this was thought surprising, but it was soon seen as evidence that the markets studied by Kendall were at least weak-form efficient. For if he had found patterns, then investors would have been missing opportunities to use past information to secure a superior performance. The fact that the price changes seemed random implied that they were responses to news, for news, by definition, comes in at random. The importance of news for asset prices led to the idea of the EMH.

For a market to be efficient, three assumptions are needed, as shown below. The first two, at least, are not fully met in any asset market, but any short-comings in the extent to which they are met are unlikely to create much difference between actual asset prices and correct prices.

1. All information relevant to financial asset prices must be costlessly, widely and quickly available. If information is costly to secure, or is known only to some investors, or spreads slowly, then asset prices might not reflect all information. In practice, information can be hard to obtain, and large institutions such as life insurance companies often spend huge sums acquiring it. But this does not necessarily mean that asset prices are far from their correct levels. To see why, suppose Z runs a fund with assets of £1,000m. If Z could raise next year's return by just 0.1%, then the return would rise by £1m. So Z would be willing to spend up to £1m to secure information which would secure such a tiny rise. Paradoxically, the activities of fund managers like Z, who look for and buy underpriced securities, make it very unlikely that many securities end up significantly underpriced.

2. There must be no transactions costs in purchasing or selling financial assets. Otherwise, if news arrives that leads people to believe that some assets are more attractive, then their price may not rise to reflect this because the transactions costs involved in buying them could outweigh the gains that might be made. In practice, there are transactions costs, but these are small relative to asset prices, so they are unlikely to cause much inefficiency.

3. Investors must act rationally on the information they have, for otherwise asset prices will not correctly reflect available information. To test the EMH, researchers compare observed asset prices with what they believe to be the correct asset prices, so they use an asset-pricing model to give them the correct prices. They usually use the CAPM. But suppose they find that observed asset prices differ from those given by the CAPM. This could mean that the EMH is wrong and that investors do not properly reflect all available information in the prices they pay. But it could instead mean that the CAPM is wrong and does not predict the prices that rational investors will pay. It is a pity that the EMH can only be tested jointly with an asset-pricing model such as the CAPM or the APT.

Evidence on the EMH

Although formal tests of the EMH have to be joint tests on some asset pricing theory such as the CAPM, it is possible to do informal tests by seeing whether any investors consistently beat other investors whose portfolios have similar levels of systematic risk. It should be possible for some investors to do so if share prices do not properly reflect all known information, no matter how 'properly' is defined. The investors who might be thought most likely to achieve consistent superior performances are professional fund managers, but there is scant evidence that any of them have done *consistently* better than would be predicted, given the systematic risk they are accepting. Of course, even if the EMH is correct, half the fund managers who take any given degree of risk will have above average returns this year. Also, half of these, one quarter in all, will secure superior returns next year as well. And one eighth in all will secure superior returns in the following year too. But there is little or no evidence that the number of fund managers with successful track records over several years is more than would be expected by chance.

The formal tests on the EMH suggest that the typical financial market is at least weak form efficient. Indeed, the typical financial market seems to be substantially, if not wholly, semi-strong form efficient. Some markets may even be strong form efficient. However, investors who lack insider information should focus on the conclusion on semi-strong form efficiency, for it implies that they will find it very hard to achieve a superior investment performance.

However, there are a few observations which seem inconsistent with the EMH. Perhaps the most significant and intractable of these is the spectacular world-wide stock market crash that occurred on 19 October 1987. Massive selling caused share prices to fall by 20% or more on many stock markets, yet there was no specially significant news that day to cause this selling.

A more modest exception is evidence that the prices of small companies' shares often rise at the start of each tax year, that is in January in the United States and April in the United Kingdom. Apparently this is because many investors sell loss-making shares in the previous month in order to realise some capital losses before the end of the tax year, and then they reinvest a little later, so pushing share prices up. The reason that the effect is most noticeable with small companies' shares is that these companies have the most volatile performances and share prices, so people who sell loss-making shares typically sell shares in small companies. To maintain well-diversified portfolios, they then replace them with shares in different small companies, so causing a rise in those companies' share prices. From an EMH perspective, it seems odd that other investors do not exploit the chance to buy towards the end of the tax year those shares whose prices are likely to rise shortly, with a view to selling them a few weeks later. Such activity would raise the end-of-year price and reduce the start-of-year price. Related to this **month-of-the-year effect**, some researchers have found **day-of-the-week effects**, such as share prices tending to fall on Mondays, and also **time-of-the-day effects**, such as prices rising over lunch and falling afterwards, but these effects are very small.

There are other oddities. For example, small companies' shares often seem underpriced in relation to their betas. And Reinganum (1991) and Fama and French (1992) found that, in the United States, companies whose shares have low market values in relation to the balance sheet values of the companies' assets also seem underpriced in relation to their betas. However, these results probably reflect a weakness in the CAPM, which may not properly assess the risks of the shares in the companies concerned, rather than a weakness in the EMH.

Implications of the EMH

One implication of the EMH is that companies contemplating takeover bids for other companies, say LML, should rarely defend their bids on the grounds that the market has undervalued LML's shares, for the market probably reflects all information except that which is known only to insiders. Usually, their main defence should be that their superior management skills will improve LML's performance, or that the two companies would benefit from joining forces.

However, the most debated implications of the EMH are those for portfolio management. The EMH suggests that investors who lack insider information will rarely be able to achieve superior investment performances, given the systematic risk they are adopting. This implies that investors should adopt **passive portfolio management** and not try to achieve a superior performance. However, this does *not* mean that they should do nothing. At the very least, investors should discover the expected returns and systematic risks of their portfolios, and then consider whether they wish to take more risk in the search for higher expected returns, or vice versa. Also, they must monitor their portfolios and adjust them if their combinations of expected return and risk ever move away from their preferred combinations. Furthermore, they may adjust their portfolios in an effort to switch from returns in the form of income to returns in the form of capital gains, or vice versa, according to changes in their tax position.

There may be little more that private individuals can do, but there are many fund managers, and also many financial advisers, who advocate **active portfolio management**. This means that they try to find underpriced shares, and then buy them in an effort to have a superior investment performance. There are perhaps two main justifications for this approach.

First, they may believe they can exploit market inefficiencies. Certainly not all markets are strong form efficient, and some fund managers have clients with access to insider information. There are laws against using such information, but it may still be used. Moreover, most markets are probably not wholly semi-strong form efficient, so there may be rewards for those who respond most quickly to information. This is not just, or even chiefly, a matter of quick reactions. Rather, there are hundreds of equities available, so fund managers who undertake **fundamental analysis**, that is a careful analysis of different companies' prospects, may occasionally find some shares that seem underpriced in relation to currently available information. Some managers go beyond fundamental analysis because they believe that the markets are not always even weak-form efficient, so they undertake **technical analysis** of past prices in an effort to find recurring patterns which they can exploit. These managers are often called **chartists** because they study graphs of past share prices in an effort to find patterns.

Secondly, there is a dimension to fund management that has not been mentioned so far. Share indices rise and fall, and one way of trying to achieve a superior investment performance is to forecast the falls and the rises. If large numbers of shares could be sold before the falls and bought again afterwards before the rises, then portfolios could grow rapidly. Of course, this growth would be at the expense of people who buy and sell at the wrong times. The possibility of prospering in this way means that managers will try to make good market forecasts and buy and sell at appropriate times. Even so, there is no firm evidence that professionally managed funds tend to beat the market, either by smart timing or by exploiting market inefficiencies.

3.10 TERM STRUCTURES

This chapter has said little about the returns on fixed-interest securities. The returns or yields required on them tend to depend more on the perceived default risk than on the past volatility of the returns. Indeed, the holding-period returns on these securities should be very stable, though some fluctuations will arise when interest rate changes lead to price changes.

However, when a variety of fixed-interest securities is issued by one borrower, the yields seem to vary between different securities. This even applies with the gilts issued by the government where there is no risk of default. The varying returns depend chiefly on the varying terms, or times to maturity, of the varying securities. The relationship between the returns and the time to maturity for gilts is called the **term structure**. Figure 3.6 shows some different relationships which could arise. The most usual case is where the redemption yields increase with the time to maturity. This produces an upward-sloping term-structure curve like the one in Fig. 3.6(a). In this case, the highest returns come on undated consols, although, as noted in Section 2.3, their returns are expressed only in terms of interest yield. Occasionally, there is little or no difference in the returns from gilts with different terms, and this leads to a 'flat' curve like the one in Fig. 3.6(b). But quite often, the returns decrease with the time to maturity, and this leads to a downward-sloping curve like the one in Fig. 3.6(c).

When the term-structure curve slopes upwards, it implies that people require higher returns on longer period loans, so, in general, undated securities and longs have the highest returns. When the curve slopes downwards, it implies that people require lower returns on long-period loans, so, in general, undated securities and longs have the lowest returns. There are at least three reasons why people might require different returns on different-length loans and they will be discussed here. Two of them were noted in Section 1.9, though the discussion there concerned bank deposits and CDs, not securities.

Expectations

One reason why different maturity fixed-interest securities may have different yields concerns expected future interest rates. If interest rates are expected to rise, then lenders will be unwilling to buy longs and commit their funds to long-term loans, for they will think that they could soon lend at a higher rate. Thus lenders will wish to lend short. Consequently, people wishing to borrow long will have to offer lenders a margin over short-term rates. So, for example, new gilts with long lives will have to offer relatively high coupons, and people

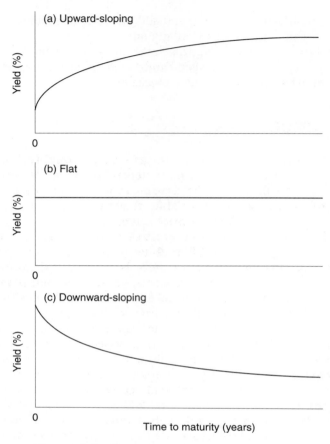

Figure 3.6   Three possible term structures.

selling existing longs and consols will have to accept low prices so that the buyers are able to secure high redemption yields.

Conversely, if lenders expect interest rates to fall, then they will be very willing to commit their funds to long-term loans at today's high interest rates. The difficulty here is persuading anyone to lend short, so short-term loans must offer relatively high returns. Therefore, people selling existing shorts will have to accept low prices so that the buyers are able to secure high redemption yields on them.

Liquidity premiums

If expectations were the only factor at work, then the term-structure curve should slope upwards and downwards with roughly equal frequencies. So longs should have higher returns than shorts no more often than they have lower returns. But in practice, longs have higher returns far more often than they have lower returns. This suggests that there is another factor at work which creates a permanent pressure for longs to have higher returns. For then they will have lower returns only if the effect of an expected fall in interest rates was strong enough to offset the other factor.

The most promising suggestion for this other factor is that lenders may typically wish to lend for shorter periods than borrowers wish to borrow. Suppose that the companies and governments which issue fixed-interest bonds wish, on average, to borrow for 20 years. Then they will usually wish to issue 20-year bonds. If they issue shorter-term ones, then they will have to repay these by borrowing again at mid-term, and they run the risk that interest rates might then be much higher. Of course interest rates might be lower, but such borrowers will usually prefer to avoid any risk of having to borrow again at higher rates which they can do by issuing 20-year bonds.

Suppose, also, that typical lenders, such as households saving for retirement, wish to lend for 10 years. Then they will usually prefer to buy 10-year bonds. If they buy 20-year ones, then they will have to sell their bonds when they want their money back, as redemption will be another 10 years away. They run the risk that interest rates could be much higher when they sell their bonds in 10 years' time, so that the security prices will be much lower, and in that case they would make a capital loss. Of course, interest rates may turn out to be lower, so they could make a capital gain. But such lenders will usually prefer to avoid any risk of a capital loss by buying 10-year bonds. For these will mature at a guaranteed face value when they want their money back.

In these circumstances, maybe only 20-year bonds will be issued, yet households will prefer second-hand ones with 10 years to run. So the prices of the second-hand 10-year ones will be bid up and their redemption yields will fall. This fall in their yields will make them less attractive, and eventually some households will be tempted to buy 20-year bonds and thereby lend longer than they would ideally prefer. The higher return they will get is called a **liquidity premium** as they have made their funds less liquid. Their funds are less liquid because the value of their bonds is more volatile. This, in turn, is because their bonds are further from maturity, so they have high durations, and hence, as explained in Section 2.8, their prices will be more sensitive to interest rate changes.

Market segmentation

Another possible explanation for different returns on longs and shorts is **market segmentation**. The argument here is that there are some people who only lend long and some people who only borrow long, and it is their activities which determine long-term yields. Likewise, there are some people who only lend short and some people who only borrow short, and it is their activities that determine short-term yields. If this is the case, then it would be quite possible for different yields to emerge in these different markets.

SUMMARY

3.1   Aside from cash, virtually all financial claims secure returns for their holders. These returns vary greatly between different claims.

3.2   When analysing different returns, the focus is on expected holding-period returns. These include any expected capital gain or loss as well as any expected income. Actual returns may differ from expected returns because of various types of risk.

3.3   A security's returns vary over time. Often, a sample of its past returns is analysed to give an idea of its future returns. If the distribution of its varying returns is symmetrical, then the mean of the sample gives an unbiased estimation of the population mean, that is the mean of all the returns there could have been. If the population mean is thought unlikely to change in future, then the sample mean is also the best available estimate of the return in the next period. The risk or uncertainty attached to this estimate depends on the spread of the population of returns, as indicated by their variance or standard deviation. These values can be estimated from the sample.

3.4   Portfolios of shares offer more attractive combinations of risk and return than individual shares because the fluctuations in the shares in a portfolio offset each other to some extent. The efficient frontier shows the portfolios of shares with the highest expected return for each possible degree of risk. A market portfolio is, strictly, a portfolio in which all risky assets are represented. In practice, it is often thought of as a portfolio of equities that reflects only the equity market, but this means that it must include shares from all companies.

3.5   Most investors are risk-averse. Given the choice of two portfolios with equal expected returns, they would prefer the one whose actual return was likely to be closest to the expected return.

3.6   If investors invested in risky assets alone, then they would each seek different portfolios of risky assets according to their degrees of risk-aversion. But if they can borrow and lend at the same risk-free rate, then, under certain assumptions, they will all want market portfolios of risky assets combined with either borrowing or lending at the risk-free rate. Each risky asset has some specific diversifiable risk which can be diversified away by having a portfolio with a range of assets. It also has some systematic non-diversifiable risk stemming from factors that affect a wide range of assets and so also affect the market portfolio.

3.7   The CAPM argues that the required return on a given asset depends on its systematic risk, that is the extent to which its returns tend to move in line with the returns of the market portfolio. This risk is indicated by the asset's beta, β. The CAPM argues that the asset's price will adjust so that its required return, r, equals $r_F + \beta(r_M - r_F)$ where r_M is the expected return on the market portfolio and r_F is the rate on the risk-free asset.

3.8   The APT argues that investors should have well-diversified portfolios. It also argues that the required return for any given well-diversified portfolio, and the required return for almost any given risky asset, depends on a series of betas, β_1, β_2 etc., which relate the movements in the returns on the portfolio or security to the returns of a series of factor portfolios. Each factor portfolio is sensitive to only one of the factors that causes systematic risk, so $r = r_F + \beta_1(r_{F1} - r_F) + \beta_2(r_{F2} - r_F) + \beta_3(r_{F3} - r_F) + \ldots$, where r_{F1}, r_{F2} etc. are the required returns on the factor portfolios.

3.9   The EMH argues that most financial asset markets are efficient so that prices reflect all the currently available information and react instantly to relevant news. The evidence suggests that most capital markets are close to being at least semi-strong form efficient, where only insider information is not reflected in prices. In a market which is semi-strong form efficient, only insiders are in a position to ensure a superior investment performance than other investors who accept a similar degree of risk.

3.10 The term structure shows the relationship between the returns on the fixed-interest securities of any given borrower, such as the government, and their time to maturity. The returns on different length securities are usually different. These differences may be caused by expectations of interest rate changes, by a liquidity premium on longer term loans, and by market segmentation.

QUESTIONS

1.   What are the chief sources of risk on equities?

2.   What is meant by: (a) a holding-period return; (b) a market portfolio; (c) mean–variance efficient; (d) risk-averse; and (e) semi-strong form efficiency?

3.   What is meant by the efficient frontier? What is the shape of an efficient frontier faced by investors who can invest only in equities? What effectively happens to the efficient frontier if they can also lend and borrow at the risk-free rate? What is meant by the separation theorem?

4.   Distinguish between the following pairs: (a) the capital market line and the security market line; (b) systematic risk and diversifiable risk; (c) a well-balanced portfolio and a factor portfolio.

5.   Why is the term-structure curve normally upward-sloping? What could be inferred about a situation where it was downward-sloping?

6.   Assume that half of X's wealth is invested in a risk-free asset earning a constant 7% and half in a market portfolio like the one shown in Table 3.1 (on p. 70). So in the four years covered by that table, half his portfolio earns 7%, while the other half earns 13%, 15%, 13% and 11%. Work out the expected return for X's portfolio in the next period and also its expected variance and standard deviation. Then work out the beta for X's portfolio. How does this relate to the separate betas for each half of his portfolio?

7.   What are the assumptions of the EMH? Does it matter if these assumptions do not hold? What sort of market inefficiencies do insiders, fundamental analysts and chartists hope to exploit?

REFERENCES

Black, F., Jensen, M.C. and Scholes, M.S. (1972) 'The capital asset pricing model', in M.C. Jensen (ed.) *Studies in the Theory of Capital Markets* (New York: Praeger).

Fama, E.F. (1970) 'Efficient capital markets: a review of theory and empirical work', *Journal of Finance*, **25** (May), 383–417.

Fama, E.F. (1991) 'Efficient capital markets II', *Journal of Finance* **46** (December), 1575–617.

Fama, E.F. and French, K.R. (1992) 'The cross-section of expected stock returns', *Journal of Finance*, **47** (June) 427–65.

Fama, E.F. and MacBeth, J.D. (1973) 'Risk, return and equilibrium: empirical tests', *Journal of Political Economy*, **81** (May/June), 607–36.

Fisher, I. (1930) *The Theory of Interest* (New York: Macmillan).

Kendall, M. (1953) 'The analysis of economic time series, part I: prices', *Journal of the Royal Statistical Society*, **116** (Part I) 11–25.

Lintner, J. (1965) 'The valuation of risky assets and the selection of risky investments in stock portfolios and capital budgets', *Review of Economics and Statistics*, **47** (February), 13–37.

Markowitz, H.M. (1952) 'Portfolio selection', *Journal of Finance*, **7** (March), 13–37.

Mossin, J. (1966) 'Equilibrium in a capital assets market', *Econometrica*, **34** (October), 768–83.

Reinganum, M.R. (1991) 'The anatomy of a stock market winner', *Financial Analysts Journal*, (March–April), 272–84.

Roll, R. (1977) 'A critique of the asset pricing theory's tests, part 1: on past and potential testability of the theory', *Journal of Financial Economics*, **4** (March), 129–76.

Ross, S.A. (1976) 'The arbitrage theory of capital asset pricing', *Journal of Economic Theory*, **13** (December), 341–60.

Sharpe, W.F. (1963) 'A simplified model for portfolio analysis', *Management Science*, **9** (January), 277–93.

Sharpe, W.F. (1964) 'Capital asset prices: a theory of market equilibrium under conditions of risk', *Journal of Finance*, **19** (September), 425–42.

Tobin, J. (1958) 'Liquidity preference as behavior toward risk', *Review of Economic Studies*, **25** (February), 65–86.

4 FORWARDS

The remaining chapters in this book study **derivatives**. Most derivatives are **financial derivatives**, which are financial instruments that concern, or derive from, financial claims. But some derivatives are **commodity derivatives**, which concern commodities. Financial derivatives and commodity derivatives come in many forms, but these fall into four broad groups: forwards, futures, options and swaps. This chapter looks at forwards, while the following chapters look at the other groups.

4.1 WHAT ARE FORWARDS?

Forwards are contracts in which two parties agree to trade an item on a future date at a price that is agreed in the contract. A number of technical terms are used in association with forwards. The item concerned is called an **underlying asset**. The party who agrees to buy it, and who will thus receive a delivery, is said to have a **long** position in forwards, while the party who agrees to sell it, and who will thus make a delivery, is said to have a **short** position in forwards. The future date when the trade will take place may be called the **maturity date** or the **expiry date**, and on that date the contract may be said to reach its **maturity**, **expiry** or **expiration**. Finally, the price at which the trade will take place is called the **forward price**.

Forwards compared with futures

Parties who wish to trade an item on a future date at a price agreed today do not have to make forward contracts. Instead, they often make futures contracts, which are discussed in Chapter 5. The boundary between forwards and futures is not entirely sharp. However, this book adopts the normal convention of regarding forwards as contracts where the buyer and seller may agree their own terms. So they may agree to trade any quantity they wish on any maturity date they wish; moreover, in the case of commodity forwards, they may agree to trade any quality they wish at any **delivery point** they wish. In contrast, the futures contracts considered in Chapter 5 are all agreed on exchanges which limit the terms which the parties may agree. For example, the exchanges specify the quantity that must be agreed in each contract and they greatly restrict the choice of maturity dates, perhaps to only four a year; also, in the case of commodities, they specify the quality and restrict the delivery points.

Topics covered in this chapter

Section 4.2 discusses the parties who buy and sell forward and their reasons for doing so; it also explains why, generally, one party ends up making a gain while the other ends up making a loss. Then there are three sections which look at forward prices: Section 4.3 explains that forward buyers and forward sellers often face slightly different forward prices; Section 4.4 explains how these prices are related to current spot prices; and Section 4.5 explains how they are related to expected future prices. Section 4.6 outlines what the parties who have agreed to buy or sell forward might try to do if they change their minds before the maturity day arrives.

Most forwards are for trades in commodities or currencies, so most forwards are either **commodity forwards** or **currency forwards**, and Section 4.7 gives some examples of each. However, there is a variant of forwards called forward rate agreements which concern interest rates, and these are discussed in Section 4.8. Finally, Section 4.9 takes a brief look at repurchase agreements (repos) which are, arguably, a variant type of forward which concerns securities.

4.2 THE PARTIES WHO MAKE FORWARD CONTRACTS

Any two parties can make a forward contract. Sometimes both parties are households. For example, X might agree to buy a puppy from a neighbour for £25 in one month's time. Sometimes one party is a household and one is a business. For example, Y might agree to sell her car to a garage for £5,000 next 1 August when she also agrees to buy a new car for £15,000. However, most forwards involve agreements between two businesses. These businesses fall into four groups.

Businesses who need the underlying asset in future

One group of businesses which make forward contracts are businesses which need the underlying asset on a future date. For example, a distillery might agree a forward contract to buy some barley next September, a galvanised-iron manufacturer might agree a forward contract to buy some zinc next December, and a car importer might agree a forward contract to buy some yen next March.

These parties could simply buy barley, zinc or yen in future when they need them. But if they fear that the actual price of the underlying asset, that is the **spot price**, may be high on the day when they need it, then they might well prefer to make forward contracts now. In that case, they would be **hedging** against a high future spot price by buying forward at a forward price agreed now. As they would become long in forwards, their hedges would be **long hedges**. Sometimes long hedges are instead called **anticipatory hedges**.

As an alternative to forwards, these fearful **hedgers** could hedge their positions by using the **cash markets** or the **spot markets**, that is by buying the underlying asset today and keeping it until required. But hedging with **forward markets**, that is using forwards, has several advantages. First, it means that buyers who do not have enough money to make a purchase today need not borrow, while buyers who do have enough money today need not spend it now and lose interest. Secondly, it means that buyers who want commodities on a future date do not have to buy them now and then pay to store them. Thirdly, it gives buyers a chance to change their minds about making a purchase, for if they change their minds before the maturity date, then they may be able to find a way out of their obligations to buy the underlying asset.

Businesses who want to supply the underlying asset in future

Another group of businesses which make forward contracts are businesses which want to supply the underlying asset on a future date. For example, a farmer might agree a forward contract to sell some barley next September, a zinc producer might agree a forward contract to sell some zinc next December, and a clothes exporter might agree a forward contract to sell some yen next March.

These parties could simply sell barley, zinc or yen when they wish to sell them. But if they fear that the spot price of the underlying asset may be low on the day when they want to sell it, then they might well prefer to make forward contracts today to sell these items in future. In that case, they would be hedging against a low future spot price by selling forward at a forward price agreed now. As they would become short in forwards, their hedges would be **short hedges**.

As an alternative to forwards, these fearful hedgers could sometimes hedge their positions by using the cash or spot markets, that is by selling the commodity or currency today. But short hedgers usually wish to hedge against low prices for items that they do not yet have. Thus a farmer may wish to hedge against a low price for barley that will be harvested next September, a zinc producer may wish to hedge against a low price for zinc that will be produced next December, and a clothes exporter may wish to hedge against a low price for yen that will be received next March.

Speculators

Forward contracts are also made by speculators. A speculator who expects the spot price at maturity to exceed the forward price may agree to buy the underlying asset at maturity at the forward price, intending to sell it just after maturity at the spot price applying then. He will make a profit if the spot price at maturity is indeed over the forward price. Another speculator, who expects the spot price at maturity to be below the forward price, may agree to sell the underlying asset at the forward price at maturity, intending to buy it just before maturity at the spot price applying then. She will make a profit if the spot price at maturity is indeed below the forward price.

Intermediaries

Sometimes, each party to a forward contract belongs to one of the groups just described. Thus a distillery might agree to buy forward barley from a farmer, while a speculator might agree to sell forward yen to a car importer. But very often one party to a forward contract is an intermediary, such as a merchant, or a dealer, or a financial intermediary. These intermediaries make forward contracts to buy from many people, and they make forward contracts to sell to many other people. For example, commodity forwards may be agreed for gold and silver with around 20 dealers on the London bullion market, while currency forwards may be agreed with many financial intermediaries. Indeed, most people who want to buy or sell currencies on a future date agree currency forward contracts with a bank or another money market dealer. The intermediaries who offer to make forward contracts can be seen as providing a market for forward contracts. This market is called an over-the-counter market. This means that the intermediaries do not offer standardised contracts like the standardised futures exchange contracts discussed in Chapter 5.

Why forward parties make gains or losses

When any forward contract matures, one party usually makes a gain while the other party usually makes a loss. To see why, suppose it is 30 March and suppose X agrees to buy five tonnes of barley from Y on 30 September at £100 a tonne. On 30 September, X will pay £500 and Y will deliver five tonnes of barley. If the spot price on 30 September is over £100 a tonne, say £120, then the five tonnes of barley will actually be worth £600. So X will gain £100 because he is paying £500 for a delivery of barley that is worth £600, while Y will lose £100 because she is receiving £500 in return for making a delivery of barley that is worth £600. If the 30 September spot price is under £100 a tonne, say £90, then the barley will actually be worth £450. So X will lose £50 and Y will gain £50. The only way in which neither party would make a gain or a loss is if the maturity day spot price *exactly equalled* the forward price agreed in the contract, but this is very rare.

4.3 FORWARD BID AND ASK PRICES

Intermediaries who make forward contracts try to minimise the chances of making losses on maturity days. The most effective way for them to do this is to agree many contracts for each maturity day, with the total value of the purchases they have agreed to make exactly matching the total value of the sales they have agreed to make. For example, suppose it is 21 May and a firm of dealers is willing to make forward agreements to buy and sell lead on 21 August. It will try to set its forward price for 21 August so that the total quantity of lead which forward buyers agree to buy forward from it exactly matches the total quantity which forward sellers agree to sell forward to it. Maybe it finds that a forward price of £500 a tonne achieves this result, and maybe it finds that, at this price, it ends up agreeing to buy a total of 1,000 tonnes on 21 August and also agreeing to sell a total of 1,000 tonnes on 21 August. Then, on 21 August, it will spend £500,000 and receive £500,000, and so break even, no matter what the spot price then is. For example, if the spot price that day is, say, £525 a tonne, then it will lose £25 on every tonne it sells, or £25,000 in all, but it will also gain £25 on every tonne it buys, or £25,000 in all. So overall it neither gains nor loses.

This analysis suggests that the intermediaries make no profits out of handling forwards. In practice, of course, the only reason they deal in forwards is to make profits, and they do so by having a bid–ask spread or bid–offer spread. This means that they actually have two forward prices, for they agree to buy at a **forward bid price** that is slightly below the **forward ask price** or **forward offer price** at which they agree to sell. They tend to keep a fairly constant small gap between their bid and ask prices. For a firm dealing in forward contracts for lead, the bid–ask spread might be around £1 a tonne. Thus on 21 May it might agree to buy 1,000 tonnes on 21 August at £499.50 and sell 1,000 tonnes at £500.50. So its total profit for the day on 21 August will be £1 per tonne, or £1,000 in all.

The need for many bid and ask prices

In principle, on any given day such as 21 May, forward dealers can make forward agreements for any subsequent maturity date. In practice, they may be more restrictive. The widest choice of maturity dates usually arises with currencies. With many currencies, the banks will allow any maturity date within the next year, provided it is a business day, and with a few major currencies, such as United States dollars, German marks, Japanese yen and Swiss francs, they may allow maturity dates up to five years ahead. For each currency, the banks like to balance the total values of their purchases and their sales on each available maturity date. This means that they generally have to set a different forward bid price and a different forward ask price for each available date.

Currency dealers often agree forward contracts that are more flexible than conventional forwards. Conventional forwards are called **fixed-date forward contracts** because they mature on a particular day, but currency dealers often also offer **option-date forward contracts** where they give a client a single bid or ask price and allow the client to trade with them, at that price, an agreed quantity of an agreed currency on any day chosen by the client within an agreed period. Thus X might have agreed to sell $1m to a bank on any business day next April at a bid price of £0.63 per dollar, while Y might have agreed to buy $2m on any business day in the first week of July at an ask price of £0.64 per dollar. Inevitably, option date contracts tend to have wider bid–ask spreads than fixed-date contracts. Option date contracts are just a variant type of forward contract and should not be confused with currency options, which are discussed in Chapters 6 to 8.

With commodities, it is much harder for an intermediary to match the purchases and sales that must be made on each of a wide variety of days. For example, an intermediary might find that it deals with many different commodities, each of which can be traded in many different qualities and at many different delivery points. The intermediary will not only want to balance its financial position on each future date for which it will make contracts. It will also try to balance the amount it buys and sells of each quality of each item at each delivery point. Accordingly, intermediaries may not guarantee to make any specific contract that any given forward buyer or seller wishes to make. So there is no guarantee exactly how many dates will be offered for any particular commodity. However, there is sometimes a wide choice. For example, forward contracts for silver and gold can be made on the London bullion market for any business day for at least two years ahead. And once any intermediary has decided which dates to offer for any given commodity, it will have to quote separate bid and ask prices for each of these dates to try and balance its purchases and sales on every one.

Frequent changes in bid and ask prices

It has been seen that dealers or other intermediaries have to quote both a bid price and an ask price for any maturity day which they will allow in their forward contracts. A further complexity for them is that they usually have to alter their bid and ask prices frequently. To see why, consider a firm of dealers which on 21 May offers forward contracts for lead maturing on a variety of dates including 21 June and 21 August.

At the start of 21 May, the firm will quote forward prices for both 21 June and 21 August, and it will wait to see how much lead other parties want to sell forward to it and buy forward from it on each date. If the quantity of lead that various people want to sell forward to it on 21 June exceeds the quantity that other people want to buy forward from it on 21 June, then it will reduce its bid price for 21 June to deter some people from selling forward lead to it on 21 June, and it will reduce its ask price for 21 June to tempt more people to buy forward lead from it on 21 June. In contrast, if the quantity of lead that various people want to sell to it forward on 21 August is less than the quantity that other people want to buy forward from it on 21 August, then it will raise its forward prices for 21 August to tempt more people to sell forward lead to it and to deter some people from buying forward lead from it.

To keep the total value of the lead that it must buy on 21 June exactly equal to the total value that it must sell, it may have to alter its forward prices for 21 June frequently during 21 May. Likewise, it may have to adjust its forward prices for 21 August frequently during 21 May.

4.4 FORWARD PRICES AND SPOT PRICES

When forward contracts are agreed with intermediaries, it is the intermediaries who set the forward prices. Although they actually set slightly different forward bid and ask prices for each maturity date, the rest of this chapter will ignore this small difference and will instead refer to a single forward price for each date. The intermediaries will be assumed to set the forward price for any given future maturity day, P_F, so that the total value of the forward sales that they will make that day exactly matches the total value of the forward purchases that they will make that day.

Very often this forward price, P_F, exceeds the current spot price, P_S. In this case, the forward market displays **contango**. But sometimes P_F is below P_S, and in this case the market displays **backwardation**. Either way, the relationship between P_F and P_S is usually related to the **cost of carrying**, C. This is the cost that is incurred by anyone who holds the underlying asset from now until maturity. With a commodity, the cost of carrying is chiefly the interest lost on the money that is used to buy the commodity *plus* the cost of storing it. With a foreign currency, the cost of carrying is the interest lost on the domestic currency that is used to buy it *minus* the interest that the foreign currency itself earns; the interest that it earns is effectively a negative storage cost. The relationship between P_F, P_S and C, will now be discussed, taking currencies and commodities in turn.

The relationship between P_F and P_S for currencies

With currencies, the relationship between P_F and P_S is:

$$P_F = P_S + C \qquad\qquad (4.1)$$

To see what this means, suppose that it is 4 June and that the P_S of \$1 is 64p, while the P_F for \$1 in one year's time is 66p. Then (4.1) implies that the cost of carrying \$1 for 12 months, C, must be 2p. In other words, if someone bought \$1 today for 64p, and held it until 4 June next year, then the interest they would lose on the 64p would be worth 2p more than the interest they would earn on the \$1. This implies that United Kingdom interest rates exceed United States interest rates. For instance, United Kingdom interest rates on 12-month deposits might be 7.80% per year and United States ones 4.53%. At 7.80%, 64p would earn 4.99p interest over one year, while at 4.53%, \$1 would earn 4.53 cents; and these 4.53 cents could be exchanged in one year for just 2.99p at the forward rate of 66p for a dollar.

Suppose the relationship in (4.1) did not hold. Maybe P_S is 64p and P_F is 67p, so that the difference between them exceeds C which is 2p. Then many people with sterling which they did not intend to spend for a while would buy dollars spot at 64p and agree to sell them forward next 4 June at 67p, for the 3p per dollar gain from selling the dollars for more than they cost would more than offset the 2p per dollar carrying cost. This means that the supply of forward dollars would rise and also that the demand for dollars today would rise. In turn, P_F would fall and P_S would rise, causing the gap between P_F and P_S to diminish to 2p.

Conversely, suppose that the gap between P_S and P_F was narrower than 2p, with P_S at 64p and P_F at, say, 65p. In this case, many people with dollars which they did not intend to spend for a while would sell them spot at 64p, and they would agree to buy dollars forward next 4 June at 65p, for the 1p per dollar loss from having to buy dollars back at a higher price than the price at which they sold them would be more than offset by the 2p per dollar saving in carrying costs, that is by the higher interest they would get on the sterling. This means that the demand for forward dollars would rise and also that the supply of dollars today would rise. In turn, P_F would rise and P_S would fall, causing the gap between P_F and P_S to widen to 2p.

It follows that, for currencies, P_F will always settle at P_S plus C, as given in (4.1). Recall that C with currencies is created by differences in interest rates. The **interest rate parity theorem** states that all differences between spot and forward exchange rates are offset by differences in interest rates. More precisely, P_F is related to P_S by the domestic interest rate, r_D, the foreign interest rate, r_F, and the time to maturity in years, T, as follows:

$$P_F = P_S[(1 + r_D)/(1 + r_F)]^T \tag{4.2}$$

In the present example, $P_S = 0.64$, $r_D = 7.80\%$ or 0.0780, $r_F = 4.53\%$ or 0.0453, and $T = 1.0$. So P_F is given by $0.64(1.0780/1.0453)$, which is 66p.

The relationship between P_F and P_S for storable commodities that are in constant production

With commodities, the relationship between forward and spot prices depends on the nature of the commodity itself. Consider, first, storable commodities which are in constant production. There are many examples such as silver, tin, oil and hides. Further examples include coffee and sugar, for these are each harvested throughout the year, albeit in different places at different times. For commodities like these, (4.1) does not hold. Instead the relationship between P_F and P_S is given by:

$$P_F \leq P_S + C \tag{4.3}$$

To see why, consider silver. Suppose it is 12 December and that the spot price of silver, P_S, is £3.00 an ounce, and suppose it costs £0.04 to carry one ounce of silver for three months. Then (4.3) states that the P_F for next 12 March could not exceed £3.04. Suppose P_F was higher, say £3.05. Then many people who wanted silver next March and who had thought of buying it forward would instead buy silver today. For by paying £3.00 an ounce, and also accepting that they will have to pay £0.04 an ounce in carrying costs, they would still save £0.01 compared with buying silver forward at £3.05. Also, many speculators would buy silver today for £3.00 and sell it forward for £3.05, the £0.05 per ounce gain more than covering their £0.04 carrying costs. So the demand for forward silver would fall and the demand for silver today would rise. In turn, P_F would fall and P_S would rise, and so the gap between P_F and P_S would diminish to £0.04.

Suppose, next, that P_F for 12 March was lower than £3.04, say £3.03. Then, if anyone happened to be holding stocks of silver which they did not intend to use before 12 March, they would certainly be willing to sell it today at £3.00 an ounce and agree to buy silver forward on 12 March at £3.03. For the £0.03 per ounce loss from buying silver at a higher price than the price at which they sold it would be more than offset by the £0.04 per ounce saving in carrying costs, to give a net £0.01 per ounce gain. Such actions would increase the demand for forward silver and increase the supply of silver today. So P_F would rise and P_S would fall, and thus the gap between P_F and P_S would widen.

However, not many people will be holding silver which they do not intend to use before 12 March. Some stocks of silver are held by firms who intend to use it soon, perhaps to make silver cutlery or silver ornaments, and some stocks are held by households who already own items such as silver cutlery and silver ornaments. It is most unlikely that a gain of £0.01 per ounce would tempt any firms to sell off their silver and close their factories until March, or that it would tempt any households to sell any cutlery or ornaments. So (*4.3*) states that P_F *can* settle below P_S plus C because, if that did happen, very few people would react by selling silver today. Strictly, any gains that would be made by selling silver today and buying it forward would be lower than the return or **convenience yield** from using it meanwhile in production or as a consumer good. A similar result applies to many commodities where too few people would react if P_F was below P_S plus C to cause a significant change in P_F or P_S.

The relationship between P_F and P_S for storable commodities that are in periodic production

Some storable commodities are not in constant production. The classic examples are crops like wheat and barley. Here, the relationship between P_F and P_S depends on how far ahead the forward date is. For a forward date *before the next harvest*, the relationship is:

$$P_F = P_S + C \qquad\qquad (4.4)$$

while for a forward date *after the next harvest*, the relationship is:

$$P_F \leq P_S + C \qquad\qquad (4.5)$$

To see why these different relationships occur, consider barley which is harvested each August. At harvest time, many merchants buy stocks of barley which they sell on the spot market, over the 12 months before the next harvest, to users of barley. These merchants incur carrying costs which they aim to pass on to the buyers. So they aim to charge progressively higher prices as each month passes, to reflect the extra costs of carrying for a longer period. So the spot price of barley tends to rise gradually as time passes between harvests, and then it drops back sharply at harvest time. The merchants aim to sell all their stocks before the next harvest, for they could not pass on a full 12 months' carrying costs to buyers, because buyers could purchase newly harvested barley instead.

Suppose it is 30 March and the spot price of barley, P_S, is £100 a tonne. And suppose it costs £1 to carry a tonne of barley for one month. Then (*4.4*) implies that the P_F for 30 June, which is before the August harvest, cannot settle above

P_S plus three months' carrying costs, and so cannot exceed £103. Also, (4.5) implies that the P_F for 30 September, which is after the summer harvest, cannot settle above P_S plus six months' carrying costs, and so cannot exceed £106. In either case, if the forward price did exceed the spot price plus carrying costs, then merchants would buy barley at the spot price and immediately agree to sell it later at the forward price. Their profit from selling at the higher forward price would more than cover their carrying costs. Their actions would drive the spot price up and the forward price down, and so reduce the gap between them.

(4.4) also implies that the P_F for 30 June, which is before the summer harvest, *cannot* settle below P_S plus three months' carrying costs, and so cannot be below £103. Suppose it was lower at £102. Then any merchants who were today planning to sell some of their current stocks of barley in June would instead sell their barley now at the spot price of £100 and immediately agree to buy some barley forward in June at £102, ready for their planned June sales. They would lose £2 a tonne by selling at £100 a tonne and having to buy at £102, but this loss would be more than offset by saving £3 in carrying costs. Their actions would drive the spot price down and the forward price up, and so widen the gap between them.

In contrast, (4.5) implies that the P_F for 30 September, which is after the summer harvest, *can* settle below P_S plus six months' carrying costs, and so can be below £106. Suppose it was lower at £105. Then it might seem that any merchants who were today planning to sell some of their barley in September would instead sell their barley now, at the spot price of £100, and buy forward in September at the forward price of £105, ready for their planned September sales. For the loss of £5 a tonne by buying at a higher price than the selling price would be more than offset by saving six months' carrying costs. So it might seem that the forward price would rise and the spot price would fall, causing the gap between them to widen. But, in fact, no merchants will have planned to hold on to any barley for sale at a date after the next harvest. Instead, as noted above, they always plan to sell all their stocks before the next harvest. So no merchants will sell their barley today just because there is a low P_F in September. So P_F *can* settle below P_S plus C, for dates after the next harvest.

The relationships between spot and forward prices can become complex with crops like cocoa and soyabeans which are harvested somewhere in the world in many months but not in all months. For these crops, forward prices will never exceed P_S plus C, but they may be below P_S plus C if there are some harvests due between the day the contract is agreed and its maturity date.

The relationship between P_F and P_S for unstorable commodities

Some commodities cannot easily be stored. Examples include fresh milk and many fresh fruits and vegetables. It is not clear how their carrying costs should be defined. If they are defined as the cost of storing the commodities without keeping them edible, then P_F could well be above P_S plus C. For if it was, then no-one who wanted the commodity in future would react by buying it now and storing it meanwhile, so there would be no pressure for the prices to change.

Also, P_F could well be below P_S plus C, for if it was, then no-one would be holding stocks that they did not intend to use for a while, so no-one would react by selling the commodity now and agreeing forward contracts to buy the commodity later. So, again, there would be no pressure for the prices to change.

However, it is arguable that carrying costs should be defined as the cost of storing the commodities in an edible condition. In that case C would be effectively infinite, so that the relationship between P_F and P_S would be given by $P_F < P_S + C$. But with $C = \infty$, this is not a useful statement.

The relationship between different forward prices for one underlying asset

It has been seen that for currencies, the forward price equals the spot price plus the cost of carrying. Thus on 4 June, the P_F for the dollar on 4 July equals the P_S on 4 June plus the cost of carrying dollars from June to July, and the P_F for the dollar on 4 September equals the P_S on 4 June plus the cost of carrying dollars from June to September. This means that the two forward prices differ by an amount equal to the cost of carrying one dollar from July to September. More generally, then, the gap between the forward prices for a currency on two different future dates equals the cost of carrying the currency between those two dates.

With storable commodities, the gap between any two forward prices cannot exceed the cost of carrying the commodity between those dates. But the gap can usually be below the cost of carrying between those two dates because forward prices can usually be below the spot price plus carrying costs to maturity.

4.5 FORWARD PRICES AND EXPECTED FUTURE PRICES

In addition to being related to the current spot price, a forward price, P_F, is also related to the spot price that people, on average, expect to apply on the maturity day. This **expected price** will be expressed as P_E. Unfortunately, the average expected price is not readily measurable, so it is easier to express views about the relationship between P_F and P_E than it is to prove them.

Expected prices and forward prices with commodities

For commodities, it is generally thought that P_F will be close to P_E, but it is also thought that P_F will usually be slightly below P_E by an amount that reflects the risk premium which faces investors who agree forward contracts on those commodities. This belief has long been associated with two British economists, John Maynard Keynes and Sir John Hicks; their views are here termed the traditional view. The belief is also supported by the modern portfolio theories, like those given in Section 3.4. The following paragraphs look in turn at the traditional view and the modern view.

The traditional view for commodities

The reasoning on the traditional view was as follows. Suppose that, on 18 June, the P_F for zinc for contracts maturing on 18 June next year is some way below P_E. In this case, few zinc producers will wish to supply forward zinc, but many speculators will demand forward zinc, expecting to sell zinc immediately after maturity for more than the P_F they will pay. Of course, these speculators will make losses if the spot price at maturity is in fact below P_F. The combination of a low supply of forward zinc and a high demand for forward zinc means that P_F will rise and so get closer to P_E.

Next, suppose P_F is some way above P_E. In this case, few zinc users will wish to buy forward zinc, but many speculators will supply forward zinc, expecting to buy zinc immediately before maturity for less than the P_F at which they will then sell it. Of course, these speculators will make losses if the spot price at maturity is in fact above P_F. The combination of a high supply of forward zinc and a low demand for forward zinc means that P_F will fall and so get closer to P_E.

On this approach, speculators play a crucial role in holding P_F close to P_E. However, speculating is risky. So individual speculators will buy or sell forward only if P_F is below or above the spot price which they personally expect at maturity by a sufficient amount to tempt them to risk making a loss.

The traditional view added that most commodities, such as zinc, are a major output for many sellers, like zinc producers, and are a minor input for many buyers, like galvanised-iron makers. So sellers may fear low future prices much more than buyers fear high future prices. This means that, if there were no speculators, then there would be far more enthusiasm for forward sales than for forward purchases, so that forward prices would probably be some way below expected future prices. Thus the traditional view felt that speculators would usually be entering forward markets as buyers, and their purchases would raise P_F until it was only slightly below P_E. A forward market where P_F is below P_E displays **normal backwardation**. Very occasionally, speculators might enter a market where forward buyers outnumbered forward sellers so that forward prices were some way above expected future prices. Here, speculators would be forward sellers, so P_F would fall until it was only slightly above P_E. A market where P_F is above P_E displays **normal contango**.

The modern view for commodities

The modern view is based on the portfolio theory of Section 3.4. It suggests that forward prices will always be below expected future prices for all those commodities whose prices tend to rise when the economy expands and whose prices tend to fall when the economy contracts. This may apply to most commodities. For any commodities where the converse holds, the modern view suggests that forward prices would always be above the expected future prices.

To see this view, suppose that investors can lend risk-free at a rate, r, that is currently 7% per year. Section 3.4 implies that a typical investor, say X, will either lend or borrow at the risk-free rate and will also have a market portfolio of shares whose average return exceeds the risk-free rate by that portfolio's risk premium of, say, 6%. But Section 3.4 also noted that investors need not limit their investments in risky assets to shares. They could also make speculative forward purchases or sales of commodities or currencies. Assume that they do this and that the market portfolio is now defined to include these risky investments as well as shares. Assume, too, that this wider market portfolio also has a risk premium, p, of 6%, so that its expected return is also 13%.

Now consider an individual asset whose beta, or β, is, say, 0.5. X would require a risk premium on this asset of $0.5p$, or 3%, so he would require an expected return that was 3% above the 7% return on the risk-free asset, that is 10%. And on any asset with a β of, say, −0.5, X would require a risk premium of −$0.5p$, or −3%, so he would require an expected return that was 3% below the 7% return on the risk-free asset, that is 4%. He would require a very low expected return on an asset with a negative β because its return would be high if the returns on most other assets were low, and vice versa, and this would reduce the riskiness of his portfolio as a whole.

Next, suppose the returns from regularly buying forward zinc and aiming to sell it for a profit have a β of 0.5. The positive β means that forward buying secures the greatest returns, as a result of spot zinc prices rising above forward prices, when the economy expands. It follows that the β from regularly selling forward zinc and aiming to buy it for less on the spot market is −0.5. The negative β means that forward selling secures the greatest returns, as a result of spot zinc prices falling below forward prices, when the economy contracts. In these circumstances, investors who agree to buy forward zinc will require a return of 10%, while investors who agree to sell forward zinc will require a return of 4%. Both, these returns will be secured provided that P_F is related to P_E as follows:

$$P_F = P_E(1 + r)/(1 + r + \beta p) \qquad (4.6)$$

where β is taken as the 0.5 for buying forward. In the example, $P_F = P_E$ $(1 + 0.07)/(1 + 0.07 + 0.03)$, which is $P_E(1.07)/(1.10)$, or $0.97P_E$. In fact, (4.6) ensures that P_F will be less than P_E, if the β for buying forward is positive.

To see why (4.6) holds, suppose that on 18 June X has £1,000 which he considers using as part of a speculative strategy with zinc. And suppose P_E for 18 June next year is £1,100 a tonne. Then (4.6) implies that P_F for next 18 June must be £1,100(1.07)/(1.10) which is £1,070 a tonne. Suppose P_F is indeed £1,070. Then, for example, X could lend his £1,000 risk-free and secure £1,070 next June, and he could also commit himself to spending that £1,070 next 18 June to buy a tonne of zinc, because he can agree a forward contract with that price. If he expects to sell this tonne for £1,100 immediately after his forward contract matures, then he expects a return of £100 on the £1,000 that he commits to the strategy today. This is a return of 10%. So X and others will regard buying forward zinc as yielding just the expected 10% return they want. So, with P_F at £1,070 they will be willing to buy forward zinc. If P_F was below £1,070, so that the gap between P_F and P_E was any wider and the expected return exceeded the 10% they want, then they would buy forward zinc in large amounts, so raising P_F and causing the gap to shrink.

Equally, though, X would be happy to sell tin forward at £1,070, being content with the following two-part strategy. First, he would lend his £1,000 risk-free and secure £1,070 next 18 June, so making a gain of £70 that day; secondly, he would hope to buy a tonne of zinc next 18 June for £1,100, and he would agree today to sell it forward at £1,070, so making an offsetting loss of £30 that day. Taken together, these two activities would give a combined return of £40, which is 4% on the £1,000 that he commits to them today. X is happy to take an expected 4% return on an investment with a negative β of −0.5; for with this investment, he will gain if the economy contracts so that the zinc he will buy costs less than £1,100, for then his return from buying and selling zinc will be higher than £40 and will offset the poor returns that the contraction causes for his other investments. So, if P_F is £1,070, then X and others will regard selling forward zinc as yielding just the expected 4% return they want, and they will be willing to sell it. If P_F was above £1,070, so that the expected loss next 18 June was less than £30, then the expected combined return would exceed the 4% they want. Thus they would sell forward zinc in large amounts, so reducing P_F and causing the gap to widen. And if P_F exceeded P_E, so that there was an expected gain next 18 June, then they would sell huge quantities of forward zinc and P_F would plummet.

On this approach, forward prices are slight underestimates of expected future prices. So they are estimates with a downward bias. However, a study by Dusak (1973) argued that, for many commodities, β was close to zero. In this case, (4.6) shows that P_F would be very close to P_E, so P_F would give a virtually unbiased estimate of P_E. Some other studies imply that a few commodities have negative betas for forward buyers, in which case P_F would overestimate P_E.

Forward prices and expected prices with currencies

With currencies, as with commodities, there could be risk premiums that drive a wedge between forward prices and expected future spot prices. Suppose, for example, that it is 18 January and that P_E for the dollar on 18 November is 64.9p. If there was no risk premium on the dollar, then P_F for the dollar on 18 November would also be 64.9p. If there was a risk premium on the dollar, then P_F for the dollar on 18 November would be lower, perhaps 64.1p.

In this case, it would follow that there was a *negative* risk premium on the pound. To see why, consider the above figures from the perspective of someone holding dollars who contemplates buying forward sterling. The expected price for the dollar on 18 November of $1 = 64.9p is equivalent to an expected price for sterling on 18 November of £1 = $1.54. And the forward price for the dollar of $1 = 64.1p is equivalent to a forward price for sterling of £1 = $1.56. This forward price is *above* the expected value of sterling which implies that sterling has a negative risk premium.

It is likely that some currencies do have positive risk premiums and others have negative ones, but it is hard to show whether these risk premiums are sizeable or trivial. Copeland (1994) has pointed out that the empirical tests are ambiguous, not least because this is a very difficult research area. The most direct method would be to do a survey of many people at a particular moment on a particular day, say 1130 on 18 January, and see if their average expectation for the future price of a currency, such as the dollar on 18 November, was close to the forward price for 18 November that applied at 1130 on 18 January. However, it is hard and costly to undertake such research, though more efforts are now being made to undertake it.

In practice, there is a widespread feeling, albeit not a unanimous one, that currencies have negligible risk premiums, in which case forward exchange rates are very good estimates of average expected future exchange rates. Moreover, there is substantial evidence to show that currency markets are at least semi-strong form efficient, so that forward prices should reflect all publicly available information that could affect people's expectations. In these circumstances, it may seem odd that some companies pay large sums to private analysts for exchange rate forecasts. There is, of course, no mystery about why companies want forecasts, for the profits they will make from future trading may depend greatly on future exchange rates. But why do they buy private forecasts when forward prices, which give average expectations or forecasts, are available from banks and the press?

Some companies may buy forecasts because they believe that risk premiums are large and drive a significant wedge between forward rates and average expected future rates. Other companies may buy forecasts as a way of assuring their shareholders that they have done everything possible to get 'good' forecasts. But probably a major reason why most companies pay for private forecasts is that, even if risk premiums are negligible, forward prices only tell them the average prices that are expected on the maturity day. A private analyst could go beyond this to consider, for example, a range of values within which the future rate might lie, and also whether the currency is very stable or volatile, and hence how likely its price is to end up close to the expected value.

Implications of the relationship between expected prices and forward prices

The fact that forward prices for commodities and currencies are probably closely related to the prices expected at maturity has three implications:

1. It means that forward prices change whenever expected future prices change, which is very frequently. The reason for this is that all forward markets are probably at least semi-strong form efficient, so that forward prices reflect all the publicly known information which affects expected future prices. New information comes in all the time, so expected future prices alter all the time, and so, in turn, do forward prices. Thus on 12 December, the forward price for silver in contracts maturing on 12 March might be £3.03 an ounce in contracts agreed at 1000, £3.05 in contracts agreed at 1430, and £2.98 in contracts agreed at 1615.

2. It means that forward prices are useful for **price discovery**. In other words, by looking at the current forward price, people can get a good idea of the average spot price that people currently expect to apply at maturity. However, as just noted, expectations and forward prices tend to change frequently. So the forward price may change frequently before maturity,

and the actual price at maturity may be very different from the current forward price.

3. It means that forward prices and spot prices converge as maturity gets closer. To see why, consider forward contracts for oil maturing at 1100 on 8 August. Suppose, first, that today is 8 February. If the price of oil is widely expected to rise or fall sharply over the next six months, then the forward price will be well over or well under the current spot price. Next, suppose that today is 7 August. It is unlikely that the spot price expected for 8 August will be very different from the spot price today, so it is unlikely that the forward price for 8 August will be very different from the spot price for today. Finally, suppose today is 8 August and it is 1058. It is most unlikely that people will expect any change in oil prices over the next two minutes, so the forward price for today should be effectively identical to the current spot price.

4.6 CLOSING OUT WITH FORWARDS

Why forward parties might want to close out their positions

Parties to forward contracts do not always want to take or make a delivery at maturity. Consider a manufacturer who uses potatoes in her products. She might predict on 30 March that she will run out of potatoes in about three months. To hedge against a high price, she agrees to buy some forward potatoes on 30 June. But she might run out of potatoes in early June and so not want to wait until maturity for a delivery. Alternatively, she might not run out until mid-July and might regret having to take and pay for a delivery before she needs one. In such circumstances, she would like to escape from the delivery obligation agreed in her forward contract; that is, she would like to **close out** her position. Consider, also, a merchant who supplies potatoes. He might agree on 30 March to sell some forward potatoes on 30 June. But he might later wish to close out his position and escape from the delivery obligation agreed in his forward contract. For example, he might sell far more potatoes than he expected in May, and so be unable to deliver any on 30 June.

As for speculators, they are almost always keen to close out. For example, one speculator might agree on 30 March to buy some forward potatoes on 30 June. He could sell them just after maturity and make a gain if, as he hopes, the spot price then exceeds the forward price, or make a loss if it does not. But he would prefer to make any due gain or loss in a way that avoided the need to receive and store any potatoes, even briefly. So he would like to escape from the delivery obligation of his contract. Likewise, another speculator might agree on 30 March to sell some forward potatoes on 30 June. She could buy some potatoes just before maturity and make a gain if, as she hopes, the spot price then is below the forward price, or make a loss if it is not. But she would prefer to make any due gain or loss in a way that avoided the need to buy and store potatoes, even briefly. So she would like to escape from the delivery obligation of her contract.

How forward parties can try to close out

A forward contract is a binding agreement, so parties who wish to close out cannot have their contracts annulled. However, there are two ways in which they can try to close out. One way is to try and make a second offsetting contract. This is called making a **reversing trade**. The other way is to try and trade the original contract, either by selling it to someone else or by paying someone else to take it over. These two ways will be illustrated in the case of a food manufacturer who on 8 August wants to buy some forward barley next May. She goes to a dealer and negotiates a forward contract with him. He may not be able to sell forward barley on every future business day for the exact quantity and quality she desires, and at a delivery point convenient to her. But suppose the two parties eventually agree on a forward contract in which she will buy 200 tonnes of barley next 10 May at £100 a tonne. Later, on 1 March, she decides that she wishes to close out.

Closing out with a reversing trade

First, she might try to make a reversing trade in which she would sell 200 tonnes of barley forward on 10 May. In this way, on 10 May, she would receive 200 tonnes of barley under her first contract and immediately dispose of these 200 tonnes under her second contract, so she would effectively not have to receive or deliver any barley on 10 May. The obvious person with whom she could try to agree the reversing trade is the dealer who agreed the first contract. But it is possible that, on 1 March, this dealer will be reluctant to make an exactly offsetting agreement. For example, there might be too many people trying to deliver barley to him at the point where she would deliver, or too many people trying to sell to him the quality that she now wishes to sell.

However, if the dealer was willing to make a reversing trade, then she would not only escape from any deliveries on 10 May. She would also determine whether she would gain or lose on 10 May. Under her first contract, she must pay £20,000 on 10 May to buy 200 tonnes of barley at £100 each. Under her second contract, she must agree a price for the 200 tonnes that she will sell on 10 May. For example, if the forward price for 10 May when she closes out on 1 March is £105, then under her second contract she will receive £21,000 for her 200 tonnes. So, no matter what the spot price of barley is on 10 May, she will pay £20,000 that day and receive £21,000, and so make a gain of £1,000. In contrast, if the forward price for 10 May on 1 March is £95, then she will receive £19,000 on 10 May from her second contract. So, no matter what the spot price of barley is on 10 May, she will pay £20,000 that day and receive £19,000, and so lose £1,000.

Closing out by trading a contract

If the dealer would not agree a reversing trade, then the manufacturer might try to close out by using the second method which means finding someone else to take over her first contract. This might prove tricky, for there might be few people who want to buy exactly the same quality and quantity of barley from the same delivery point on the same date. Moreover, even if someone was in principle prepared to take over her contract, it could take some time to negotiate the terms. However, if she did make an agreement with another party, then she would not only escape her delivery obligation. She would also determine on 1 March how much she would gain or lose. For example, suppose she agreed with the party taking over her contract that a suitable forward price for 10 May was now £105 per tonne. Then that party would give her £5 a tonne, or £1,000 in all, for the right to buy barley at the forward price in the contract of £100 per tonne. Conversely, if she agreed with the party taking over her contract that a suitable forward price for 10 May was now £95 per tonne, then that party would demand £5 a tonne from her, or £1,000 in all, for taking over the right to buy barley at the forward price in the contract of £100 per tonne.

Closing out in practice

It is clear that the manufacturer may find it tricky to close out, and closing out commodity forwards can sometimes prove hard. So with many commodities, parties who want the option of closing out prefer futures contracts, which are discussed in the next chapter, to forwards. In contrast, closing out currency forwards is usually easy, for currency dealers will offer reversing trades for almost any existing forward contracts. So currency forwards are widely used by both hedgers and speculators.

4.7 EXAMPLES OF FORWARDS

Commodity forwards

Most commodity forwards are agreed on an individual over-the-counter basis, so few forward prices are published. However, the major London bullion dealers agree some **fixing prices** each day which apply for one trading session of the day, and these fixing prices are published. Table 4.1 shows some fixing prices for silver which applied on 21 May 1998. These prices are mid-prices which are mid-way between the bid and ask prices. The spot price was 328.00p per troy ounce. The forward prices rise 3.55p an ounce, or less, for every quarter of a year. For example, the three month price is 3.55p above the spot price. As (4.3) applies to silver, so that $P_F \leq P_S + C$, it is clear that the carrying cost for an ounce cannot be less than about 3.55p per quarter.

Table 4.1   Examples of silver forwards (21 May 1998)

Silver fix	Spot	Three months	Six months	One year
p per troy oz.	328.00	331.55	334.15	336.30

Currency forwards

Figures for currency forwards are readily available from currency dealers and are widely published. Table 4.2 gives examples of forward prices for sterling in terms of Greek drachmas (Dr) and Japanese yen (Y). The figures are based on those supplied by a number of London banks at about 1700 on 21 May 1998. The table begins with information about the spot prices for sterling that day. The 'close' figures show the closing bid, offer and mid-point spot prices. Thus at the close of business, banks would buy £1 for Dr494.317 or Y220.973, and they would sell £1 for Dr494.832 or Y221.272, so the mid-prices were Dr494.574 and Y221.122. The 'change' figures show the change in the mid-point price since the previous day: the pound was worth 4.684 fewer drachmas and 0.999 fewer yen. The 'high–low' prices are the highest and lowest prices at which deals took place during the day. Finally, the one-month and three-month figures reflect the closing mid-point prices at which dealers agreed to buy and sell sterling forward on 21 June or 21 August.

The one-month price for sterling in terms of the drachma was 496.539. The spot price was 494.574, so the banks were offering 1.965 more drachmas for one pound in forward sales of sterling than in spot sales, that is about 0.40% more drachmas. Equivalently, they wanted about 0.40% more drachmas for one pound in forward purchases of sterling than in spot purchases. Assuming that the forward price indicates the expected price in one month, the price of sterling in terms of drachmas was expected to rise by about 0.40%. Equivalently, the value of the drachma against the pound was expected to fall by about 0.40% in one month. The table expresses this by saying that, over the next month, the drachma was expected to fall in value at a rate equivalent to –4.8% per year. It seems that the banks expected that rate of fall to persist. For example, the three months price of sterling, of 500.628 drachmas, was about 1.22% above the spot price. So the drachma was expected to fall in value by about 1.22% against sterling over three months, and this is shown as an annual rate of –4.9%.

The one-month price for sterling in terms of the yen was 219.817. The spot price was 221.122, so the banks were offering 1.305 fewer yen for one pound in forward sales of sterling than in spot sales, that is about 0.59% fewer yen. Equivalently, they wanted about 0.59% fewer yen for one pound in forward purchases of sterling than in spot purchases. Assuming that the forward price indicates the expected price in one month, the price of sterling in terms of yen was expected to fall by about 0.59%. Equivalently, the value of the yen against the pound was expected to rise by about 0.59% in one month. The table expresses this by saying that, over the next month, the yen was expected to rise in value at a rate equivalent to +7.1% per year. It seems that the banks also expected that rate of increase to persist. For example, the three months price of sterling, of 217.267 yen, was about 1.74% below the spot price. So the yen was expected to rise in value by about 1.74% against sterling over the next three months, and this is shown as an annual rate of +7.0%.

Like most published tables of forward exchange rates, Table 4.1 covers only a few future dates, even though, as noted in Section 4.3, banks will make forward contracts for a wide range of future dates. All banks have close at

Table 4.2 Examples of currency forwards (end of 21 May 1998)

Currency	Close bid–offer	Close mid	Change	High–Low	One-month	Three months
Greece	494.317–494.832	494.574	–4.684	499.432–493.177	496.539 (–4.8%)	500.628 (–4.9%)
Japan	220.973–221.272	221.122	–0.999	221.930–219.790	219.817 (+7.1%)	217.267 (+7.0%)

hand their spot rates and their forward prices for some future dates, such as one, three, six and 12 months ahead. Their computers can use these forward rates to work out the expected percentage changes in the prices of various currencies over the next one month, three months, six months and 12 months. When the banks are asked to quote forward prices for other dates, their computers use those expected rates of change to produce suitable figures.

4.8 FORWARD RATE AGREEMENTS

Forward rate agreements (FRAs) can be seen as a type of forward contract because two parties agree to do a deal on a future date on terms that are agreed today. But FRAs differ from conventional forwards in that they do not concern deals to trade anything. So FRAs are not made by parties who wish in future to buy or sell something and who respectively fear a high price or a low price. Instead, FRAs are agreed by two other main groups of parties.

The two main groups of parties who make FRAs

The first group is people who wish in future to lend money by making a short-term deposit, say a three-month bank deposit with a fixed rate, and who fear that short-term interest rates will be low when the time comes. Parties like these can hedge by making an FRA with a bank. Although they are just making an agreement, they are referred to as FRA buyers. In principle, they agree with the bank today an interest rate which will be paid on their deposit, irrespective of what the spot interest rate may be when the day comes. They will gain, and the bank will lose, if the spot interest rate at maturity turns out to be below the one agreed in the FRA, and vice versa. In practice, they may deposit their money in the bank where they agreed the FRA, or indeed at any other bank, and either way they will actually earn interest at the current spot rate, but the bank where they made the FRA will pay them compensation if its spot rate is below the agreed rate, while they will pay compensation to the bank if it is above the agreed rate.

The second group is people who wish in future to borrow short-term from banks, say a three-month bank loan with a fixed rate, and who fear that interest rates will be high when the time comes. Parties like these can also hedge by making an FRA with a bank. Although they are just making an agreement, they are referred to as FRA sellers. In principle, they agree today with the bank an interest rate which they will be charged on their loan, irrespective of what the spot interest rate may be when the day comes. They will gain, and the bank will lose, if the spot interest rate at maturity turns out to be above the one agreed in the FRA, and vice versa. In practice, they may borrow from the bank where they agreed the FRA, or they may borrow from any other bank, and they will actually pay interest at the current spot rate, but the bank where they made the FRA will pay them compensation if its spot rate is above the agreed rate, while they will pay compensation to the bank if it is below the agreed rate.

On any given day, a bank will usually agree FRAs starting on any business day in the next year, but most agreements start three, six, nine or 12 months hence, and a few start over a year hence. FRAs are almost always made for periods of exactly three, six, nine or 12 months. So, each day, a bank must set a whole raft of FRA rates, one for each available length FRA on each possible starting date. More precisely, it must set two rates for each available length FRA on each available starting date, one rate being the **bid rate** which it will agree for deposits and the other being the **offer rate** which it will agree for loans. Its lending rate will usually be about ⅛% higher than its deposit rate, so there is bid–offer spread, just as banks always offer less on other deposits than they charge on other loans. However, in the interests of simplicity, the rest of this section ignores the fact that banks have a spread between their FRA borrowing and lending rates.

The meaning of forward/forward rates

The interest rates agreed in FRAs apply to deposits or loans that start in the future. However, no interest is actually due on those deposits or the loans until they end, which is some months after they start. Consequently, the rates agreed in FRAs are called **forward/forward rates**. And this name is used even though, in practice, the compensation payments that arise with FRAs are actually made at the beginning of the period of the deposit or loan, not at the end. Of course, the compensation payments are small compared to the interest payments that are made when the deposits or loans end, for the compensation payments only cover the difference between the interest that is due at the actual spot rates and the interest that would be due at the agreed FRA rates.

Just as the forward prices for commodities and currencies are linked by carrying costs to current spot prices, so the forward/forward rates agreed on FRAs are linked to current spot interest rates. The link in the case of FRAs is a little complex and will be explained with an example. This example also illustrates the fact that people who want to hedge against high or low interest rates do not have to use FRAs. They could instead hedge by using the cash or spot market for loans.

FRAs and future lenders

Suppose it is 15 March and that the spot interest rate which banks will pay on 91-day deposits and charge on 91-day loans is 7.60%. Suppose, also, that the spot rate on 182-day deposits and loans is 8.00%. Finally, suppose that X expects to have £100 to lend on deposit from 14 June to 13 September and that he fears that 91-day rates will be low on 14 June. To hedge against this, X could adopt the following strategy. He could borrow £98.14 now for 91 days at 7.60% and lend it at 8.00% in a 182-day deposit. He would actually need £100 on 14 June to repay the borrowed £98.14 with interest, and for this purpose he could use the £100 which he expects to have then. On 13 September, his lent £98.14 plus interest would be worth £102.05. Thus, on this strategy, he would get £102.05 on 13 September, irrespective of what the 91-day spot rate of interest turned out to be on 14 June, because he would be making no new agreements on 14 June.

As another hedging strategy, X could agree an FRA with his bank with an agreed forward/forward rate for a 91-day deposit starting on 14 June. Using the FRA would be a little more straightforward, so X would doubtless choose this alternative provided that the forward/forward rate agreed in it ensured that he would end up with at least £102.05 on 13 September. This actually means that the forward/forward rate agreed in the FRA must be at least 8.24%, for £100 lent for 91 days at 8.24% will secure £102.05 after 91 days.

FRAs and future borrowers

Suppose that, on 15 March, Y anticipates needing to borrow £100 from 14 June to 13 September. She fears that 91-day rates will be high on 14 June. To hedge against this, Y could adopt the following strategy. She could borrow £98.14 now for 182 days at 8.00% and lend it at 7.60% in a 91-day deposit. When the lent £98.14 was repaid with interest on 14 June, she would get the £100 she antic-ipates needing then. On 13 September, Y would need £102.05 to repay the borrowed £98.14 with interest. She would need £102.05 irrespective of what the spot 91-day interest rate turned out to be on 14 June, because she would be making no new agreements that day.

Y could instead hedge by making an FRA with her bank with an agreed forward/forward rate for 91-day loans starting on 14 June. Using the FRA would be a little more straightforward, so Y would doubtless choose this alternative provided she would end up owing at most £102.05 on 13 September. This actually means that the forward/forward rate agreed in the FRA must be at most 8.24%, for the repay-ment and interest due on a £100 loan after 91 days at 8.24% is £102.05.

A formula for the forward/forward rate

Banks always wish to attract both depositors and borrowers. If the banks approached by X and Y in the above examples are to do this, then they *must* set their 91-day forward/forward rate for 14 June at 8.24%, given the current spot 91-day interest rate of 7.60% and the current spot 182-day interest rate of 8.00%. Any rate below 8.24% would drive away people like X who might make deposits using FRAs, while any rate above 8.24% would drive away people like Y who might borrow using FRAs.

The forward/forward rate for any period from A days hence to B days hence, r_{B-A}, is linked by a formula to the current spot rate for the period from now to A days hence, that is r_A, and the current spot rate for the period from now to B days hence, that is r_B. The formula is as follows:

$$r_{B-A} = \{[1 + r_B(B/365)]/[1 + r_A(A/365)] - 1\}[365/(B-A)] \qquad (4.7)$$

In the example, $A = 91$ days, $B = 182$ days, $r_A = 7.60\%$ or 0.076, and $r_B = 8.00\%$ or 0.080. So:

$$r_{B-A} = \{[1 + 0.080(182/365)]/[1 + 0.076(91/365)] - 1\}[365/(182-91)]$$

Thus r_{B-A} equals $\{[1.0399/1.0189] - 1\}[365/91]$ which is $\{0.0206\}[4.0110]$, or 0.0824, or 8.24%.

This forward/forward rate of 8.24% can be related to the spot rates of 7.60% and 8.00% with a simple example. Suppose that on 15 March a depositor places £98.14 in a 182-day deposit at 8.00%. Then the depositor will secure £102.05 on 13 September. The depositor might instead place the £98.14 in a 91-day deposit at 7.60% to get £100 by 14 June. If this £100 could be lent for 91 days from 14 June at 8.24%, then the depositor would once again get £102.05 by 13 September. The forward/forward rate makes the return on two consecutive 91-day deposits equivalent to the return on one 182-day deposit.

Forward/forward rates and expected rates

Just as the forward prices for commodities and currencies are probably close to the average prices that are expected on the maturity date, so forward/forward rates are probably close to the average expected future spot interest rates. However, forward/forward rates will slightly exceed expected rates if longer-term bank deposits have higher interest rates than short-term deposits. It was explained in Section 1.9 that this is the normal situation because longer-term deposits are rewarded with a liquidity premium.

To see why the existence of liquidity premiums pushes forward/forward rates above expected rates, suppose first that there is no liquidity premium. Suppose, also, that people expect interest rates to be constant. In that case, as explained in Section 1.8, the current quoted rates on three-month deposits will be slightly lower than the quoted rates on rates on six-month deposits. In the example given in Section 1.8, the three-month or 91-day rate was 7.60%, while the six-month or 182-day rate was 7.67%. In this case, the FRA rate for 91 days starting in 91 days' time is given by (4.7) with $A = 91$ days, $B = 182$ days, $r_A = 7.60\%$ or 0.0760, and $r_B = 7.67\%$, or 0.0767. So:

$$r_{B-A} = \{[1 + 0.0767(182/365)]/[1 + 0.0760(91/365)] - 1\} \ [365/(182 - 91)]$$

Thus r_{B-A} equals $\{[1.0382/1.0189] - 1\} \ [365/91]$ which is $\{0.0189\} \ [4.011]$, or 0.0760, or 7.60%. This means that the 91-day FRA rate is identical to the expected 91-day rate, for that rate is expected to remain unchanged from the present 91-day rate, and hence is expected to be 7.60%.

Next, suppose there is a liquidity premium, and suppose once again that people expect interest rates to be constant. In this case, the liquidity premium means that the gap between the current 182-day rate and the current 91-day rate will be higher than the gap supposed in the last paragraph. Say the 91-day rate is 7.60% as before, but that the 182-day rate is 8.00%. As people expect interest rates to be constant, they expect the 91-day rate in 91 days to be 7.60%. Yet (4.7) has been used to show that the FRA rate in these circumstances will be 8.24%. So the existence of a liquidity premium means that FRA rates will overestimate expected future interest rates.

Settling FRA contracts

It was mentioned earlier that FRAs are actually settled with compensation payments. Recall X who agreed an FRA with his bank. This FRA quoted a forward/forward rate of 8.24% for a 91-day deposit starting on 14 June. It might seem that X would, indeed, deposit £100 from 14 June for 91 days at 8.24% and so secure £102.05 91 days later. But, in practice, he would deposit his money at the bank, or elsewhere, and get the spot interest rate on fixed-term 91-day deposits. If this was, say, 8.00%, then he would end up with only £102.00 after 91 days. The bank could pay him 6p compensation at the end of the term of the deposit, but it would normally compensate him at the start. As he would get the compensation before he needed it, the bank would give him a shade less than 6p. It would give him a sum which he could lend at 8.00% to secure 6p after 91 days, that is 5.88p. This is a trivial sum, chiefly because the £100 involved is small. FRAs are typically made for large sums, £1m or more being very common.

4.9 REPURCHASE AGREEMENTS

A **repurchase agreement**, or **repo** for short, is a sale and repurchase agreement that concerns a security. As it concerns a financial claim, it is a form of financial derivative. Repos are not normally classed as forwards, but essentially they share the characteristics of forwards in that two parties agree to trade something on a future date at a price that is agreed today.

With a repurchase agreement, an investor, say X, may sell a security to a bank today and agree to buy it back tomorrow for a slightly higher amount. In effect, X is getting an overnight loan, but instead of paying interest he will repurchase the security for a slightly higher price than the price at which he sold it. Repos usually involve gilts. Most repos are **overnight repos** which involve repurchases the next day, but some are **term repos** where the repurchase might be a week or two away. They are used as a means of securing funds for a short time.

For example, suppose X suddenly decides to buy £100,000 worth of tin because he thinks tin prices may soon rise. To raise the money quickly, he sells £100,000 worth of gilts to a bank, agreeing to buy them back next day by which time he hopes to have fixed up another source of funds for his tin purchase. The bank agrees to sell the gilts back next day for £100,016. The cost of X's loan is £16 for one day which is equivalent to a rate of interest of 6% per year. To see this, suppose the bank lent £100,000 for one day and secured £100,016 the next day, that is £100,000(1.00016). It could lend the £100,016 the next day for one day at the same rate and have £100,016(1.00016) or, equivalently, £100,000(1.00016)(1.00016), that is £100,000$(1.00016)^2$, on the following day. If it did this for 365 days, then it would end up with £100,000$(1.00016)^{365}$, which is about £106,000. So it would get a 6% return over the year.

Banks are very happy to lend large sums to people under repo agreements because they can hold on to the securities whenever a loan is not repaid. So the securities provide some guarantee or **collateral** that the loan will be repaid, and such repos are called **general collateral repos**. Incidentally, the bank in this example does not have to deliver the exact gilts that it bought from X. It is merely obliged to sell equivalent gilts, that is the same number of gilts of the same type.

The fact that the identical gilts need not be involved facilitates a different sort of repo called a **special repo**. These are agreed with banks by people who need gilts in a hurry. For example, Y may have agreed to sell £100,000 worth of gilts today to Z but may not actually have any gilts to sell. To enable the sale to proceed, she might buy some gilts from a bank under a repo agreement and agree to sell back equivalent gilts the next day. Here she would actually sell to Z the gilts which she receives from the bank, so she can only sell back to it equivalent gilts which she will try to obtain by the next day. In this example, Y is effectively lending to the bank. She will be rewarded by being paid a slightly higher price for the gilts that she sells back to the bank than the price which she paid for the ones that she bought from them. But the repurchase price set by the bank will most likely ensure that her return is equivalent to a much lower annual rate than the 6% which was charged to X.

SUMMARY

4.1   Forwards are contracts in which two parties agree to trade an underlying asset on a future maturity date or expiry date at a price that is agreed in the contract. The forward buyer has a long position and the forward seller a short position. Most forwards concern commodities or currencies.

4.2   The parties who agree forwards include speculators and intermediaries as well as people who really want to buy or sell the underlying asset. Almost invariably, one party gains at maturity, while the other loses.

4.3   Intermediaries who make forward contracts quote a separate bid and ask price for each available maturity date. They constantly adjust these prices to try and ensure that the total value of their sales and purchases on any maturity date are precisely equal. Their bid–ask spreads ensure that they make profits.

4.4   The cost of carrying a commodity is chiefly the interest lost on the money that would be used to buy the commodity plus the cost of storing it. The forward price for a storable commodity will not exceed the spot price plus the cost of carrying, but it may be below, except in the case of storable crops between harvests. The cost of carrying a foreign currency is the interest lost on the domestic money used to buy it minus the interest that the foreign currency itself earns. The interest rate parity theorem argues that all differences between spot and forward exchange rates are accounted for by different interest rates in the countries concerned.

4.5   Forward prices are likely to be close to expected future prices, but they may be slightly lower to allow for any risk premiums that speculators require.

Speculators may require risk premiums with both commodities and currencies, but it is hard to estimate the size of these risk premiums.

4.6   Parties with forwards can try to close out their positions either by making offsetting reversing trades or by trading their contracts. It can prove tricky to close out commodity forwards, but it is easy to close out currency forwards with reversing trades.

4.7   Few figures are published for commodity forward prices, but currency forward prices are widely published.

4.8   A forward rate agreement is an agreement about an interest rate, the forward/forward rate, which will apply to a fixed-term deposit or to a fixed-term loan that is due to start on a future date. The agreed rate will slightly overestimate the expected future interest rate if, as is usually the case, long-term bank deposits have higher interest rates than short-term deposits.

4.9   A repurchase agreement, or repo, is an agreement whereby a party will either sell a security to a bank and buy an equivalent one back later for slightly more, or buy a security from a bank and sell an equivalent one back later for slightly more.

QUESTIONS

1.   Explain whether it is feasible for long hedgers and short hedgers to hedge against adverse future commodity prices by using spot markets alone.

2.   It is 18 January. Explain with reasons which of the following underlying assets, if any, could have a forward price for 18 June that is below the current spot price plus five months' carrying costs: (a) copper; (b) coffee; (c) oil; (d) Spanish pesetas; and (e) wheat. Could any of these underlying assets have a forward price that exceeds the current spot price plus five months' carrying costs?

3.   Explain why forward prices are volatile and why they converge with spot prices at maturity.

4.   Explain what is meant by the following terms: (a) an anticipatory hedge; (b) a risk premium; (c) closing out; (d) a reversing trade; and (e) a general collateral repo.

5.   Suppose that interest rates on six-month deposits are 6.5% in the United Kingdom, 5.5% in the United States and 0.5% in Japan. The current values of sterling are £1 = $1.70 and £1 = Y200. Estimate the forward six-month rates using the interest rate parity theorem formula.

6.   Explain how people who agree FRAs could make equivalent hedges without using them. Suppose the current rate on 91-day deposits is 6.25% while the current rate on 182-day deposits is 6.50%. What will the forward/forward rate be for 91-day deposits starting 91 days hence?

REFERENCES

Copeland, L. S. (1994) *Exchange Rates and International Finance*, 2nd edition (Wokingham: Addison-Wesley).

Dusak, K. (1973) 'Futures trading and investor returns: an investigation of commodity market risk premiums', *Journal of Political Economy*, **87** (November/December), 1387–1406.

5 FUTURES

5.1 WHAT ARE FUTURES?

Futures, or futures contracts, are contracts that resemble forwards in many ways. Like forwards, they oblige the parties to do a deal on a future **maturity date** or **expiry date**, which is usually within the next year. Also, they specify a **futures price**, or some other value, to determine the terms under which the deal will be made. Further, they are used by both hedgers and speculators who stand to make gains or losses depending on the gap between the spot price or value at maturity and the agreed futures price or value. However, there are two key distinguishing features of futures contracts.

First, futures contracts may be agreed only on recognised **futures exchanges**, whereas forward contracts may be agreed anywhere. Secondly, the exchanges insist on standardised contracts. Thus they stipulate the quantity that must be agreed in each contract, they restrict the choice of maturity dates, sometimes to only four a year, and they even constrain the futures price or value that may agreed; for example, they might stipulate a **tick** of £5 per tonne, in which case the agreed futures price per tonne would have to be a multiple of £5. Furthermore, in the case of commodity futures, they specify the quality that must be agreed, and they restrict the permitted delivery points. In contrast, the parties to a forward contract may agree any quantity, maturity date and forward price they choose, and with a commodity forward they may agree any quality and delivery point they choose.

Topics covered in this chapter

Section 5.2 looks at some general features of futures contracts, explaining how they are made and how they can be closed out easily. Section 5.3 explains many of the varied futures contracts that are available, and it shows that although all futures are agreements to do a deal on a future date, the deal is not always one to buy and sell, so that not all futures involve a futures price. Section 5.4 looks at the timing of payments between the parties to futures contracts. The payments are timed differently from those on forwards; for whereas forwards involve just one payment, futures involve a whole series of payments. Section 5.5 looks at some of the issues that arise when futures positions are closed out. Section 5.6 notes some of the exchanges where futures can be made, and looks closely at some examples of their futures contracts. Section 5.7 explains some of the difficulties that arise when people hedge with standardised futures contracts, and it explains some of the hedging techniques that may be used to try and overcome these difficulties. Finally, Section 5.8 looks at some uses of futures that are not covered earlier in the chapter.

5.2 GENERAL FEATURES OF FUTURES CONTRACTS

Exchanges and clearing houses

Say X wants to agree a futures contract to buy 300 tonnes of coffee. Unless he happens to work for a firm that operates on an exchange where these futures may be agreed, he must contact a firm that does operate on one and ask them to agree a contract on his behalf. In fact, they may have to agree many contracts. For example, if the exchange only allows contracts to be made for 5 tonnes of coffee, then X requires 60 contracts. The firm X contacts has to find a futures seller. On advanced exchanges, they would find a seller by using a computer network, but this section focuses on the traditional method.

Traditionally, the firm will send a **broker** to the exchange **floor**. This floor is divided into **pits**, one for each type of contract, and the broker will go to the pit used for coffee futures. All the people she meets there will work for firms that operate on the exchange, but they can be divided into two groups. Some of them will be there like her, acting as brokers for clients who wish to make contracts. Others will be acting as **traders**, which means that they will make contracts on behalf of their firms, not on behalf of clients. Traders make many contracts to buy and sell on each available maturity date, and they try to agree slightly higher prices in the contracts where they will sell than in those where they will buy. X's broker will look around the two groups until she finds someone who will agree to sell 60 contracts worth of coffee on the maturity date that X requires. If several people are willing to do this, then she must find the one who will agree the lowest futures price. Prices and quantities are shouted out on the pits in a system called **open outcry**.

Suppose she agrees to do a deal with another broker who is acting on behalf of Y who wants to sell coffee. Then it is often convenient to assume that the brokers will agree a single contract in which X will be a futures buyer and Y will be a futures seller, and much of the discussion of futures makes this assumption. But it is a simplifying assumption, for what happens is more complex. The brokers will actually contact a **clearing house** which is a firm that has a branch at the exchange. X's broker will agree on X's behalf

60 five-tonne futures contracts to buy coffee *from the clearing house* at the price and on the maturity date agreed with Y's broker, and Y's broker will agree on Y's behalf 60 five-tonne futures contracts to sell coffee *to the clearing house* at the same price and on the same date. So X and Y both have 60 contracts with the clearing house, not with each other.

The advantage of this arrangement is that X need not worry about whether Y will default, nor need Y worry about X, for their contracts are with the clearing house. It is up to the clearing house to get money from X and coffee from Y, and in fact it will demand money and coffee from their brokers and leave it to them to get money and coffee from X and Y. The clearing house and the brokers make profits by charging commissions. Clearing houses only ever agree contracts with brokers or traders when they arrive as a pair who have agreed to make matched trades, like those made on behalf of X and Y. Consequently, a clearing house only ever agrees futures contracts to buy when it simultaneously agrees other futures contracts to sell the same amount at the same time and at the same futures price. So it is not at all concerned about how many contracts the two brokers or traders want to make, nor is it concerned about the futures price that they have agreed.

In this example, two brokers struck a deal, so the futures price which X will pay is the same price that Y will receive. But X's broker might have struck a deal with a trader, and that trader might moments later have struck a deal with Y's broker. In this case, the trader would try to make a profit by agreeing a higher price in the deal with X's broker than in the deal with Y's broker, for in the former case the trader would end up selling coffee to the clearing house and in the latter case he would end up buying coffee from it. Traders use the open outcry system to indicate their different bid and ask prices. The bid–ask spread applied by traders may make them seem less satisfactory than other brokers for X's broker and Y's broker to deal with for, by dealing directly with each other, the brokers cut out the trader's spread. But traders are valuable because they ensure that brokers can always make a quick deal on the exchange. In the example, X's broker readily found another broker willing to make an offsetting deal, but often she would have to wait some time before finding such a broker. When none is to hand, it is convenient to agree a deal with a trader.

Contract dates

Much of the discussion of futures assumes that each contract concerns a deal that must be made on a specific maturity date, but in practice the situation is a little more complex. Each exchange restricts the dates for which deals may be agreed by first stipulating a number of **delivery months** for each type of contract. Maybe for coffee futures the delivery months are January, March, May, July, September and November. The exchange then stipulates a **last trading day**, and indeed a precise time on that day, which is the last moment in each delivery month that contracts maturing in that month can be agreed. Thus the last trading day might be 1232 on the last business day of the delivery month. In theory, all the contracts made for a given delivery month actually mature at this moment. However, it is clearly impracticable for many trades to take place at precisely 1232. So the exchanges also stipulate the times when the trade may actually take place.

For futures contracts concerning commodities, a few exchanges set a **prompt date** and require the trade to take place that day. Prompt dates are usually two days after the last trading day to give the parties time to prepare their final payments and arrange for deliveries. However, most exchanges give futures sellers of commodities a **tender period** during which they make their deliveries and receive payment. This tender period might be any business day in the month up to the last trading day. Suppose the last trading day in Y's contract is Friday 31 May, yet she decides on 21 May that she wants to deliver as soon as possible. She notifies the clearing house via her broker, and 21 May is called the **position day**. On the next business day, 22 May, which is the **notice of intention day**, the clearing house notifies someone who has agreed to buy 300 tonnes of coffee from it on 31 May that they must instead take delivery of Y's coffee on the following business day, 23 May, which is the **delivery day**. There may be many people with appropriate contracts whom the clearing house could notify. In this case, it may select the holder of the oldest contracts, or else choose someone at random. Either way, it is unlikely to be X who ends up receiving Y's coffee.

This sort of flexibility rarely applies to futures contracts that do not concern commodities. With these, the exchanges usually specify that the deal has to take place on a specified delivery date which is generally only one or two days after the last trading day.

Why futures are easier to close out than forwards

It was explained in Section 4.6 that closing out with forwards can be hard. For example, suppose that on 8 August a manufacturer expects to need some barley next spring. She fears that barley prices will then be high. She could hedge against a price rise by going to a dealer and, after some negotiation, agree a forward contract to buy, say, 200 tonnes of barley of a certain quality from a certain delivery point on 10 May. But if she later wished to close out, then she might find it tricky. Say she wished to close out on 1 March. She might try to make a second offsetting contract, or reversing trade, with the same dealer. But that dealer might be reluctant to agree to a precisely offsetting contract in which she would sell 200 tonnes of the same quality of barley at the same delivery point on 10 May. So she might instead try to find someone else to take over her contract, but with forward contracts there are so many different maturity dates, quantities, qualities and delivery points, that it could be hard to find someone willing to take over her specific contract.

In contrast, if on 8 August the manufacturer contacts a futures exchange, then she might find that she can make barley futures contracts for perhaps only six maturity days a year, say the third Wednesdays in January, March, May, July, September and November. Also, she will be given no choice over the quality or quantity, and little choice over the delivery points. So she will probably not be able to agree exactly the contract she would ideally like. Some appropriate responses to this situation are outlined in Section 5.7, and it will be seen that it is far less of a problem than it might appear. The offsetting advantage of the standardised futures contracts is that the people who agree to them must accept the specifications laid down by the exchange, and, in practice there are always plenty of people, including traders, who are willing to agree to them. Consequently, it is always easy to agree futures contracts, and thus it is also always easy to agree precisely offsetting contracts.

Suppose each contract has to be for 100 tonnes of barley. Then on 8 August the manufacturer will find it easy to agree two futures contracts to buy a total of 200 tonnes of barley on the third Wednesday in May. If she decides to close out on 1 March, then she can contact the exchange that day and she will find that she can just as easily agree two offsetting contracts for the same maturity day. So she can easily close out by making a reversing trade, and this is how futures are closed out. Because futures are so much easier to close out than forwards, they are said to be more liquid assets.

Suppose the manufacturer makes her first two contracts on 8 August and agrees to buy 200 tonnes of barley on the third Wednesday in May. Suppose, too, that the futures price agreed in these contracts is £100 a tonne. If later, say on 1 March, she closes out by making two offsetting contracts to sell a total of 200 tonnes on the third Wednesday in May, then she will effectively have no delivery obligations on the maturity day, so the clearing house will regard her position as closed. Moreover, she will settle her financial position on 1 March. On 8 August she agreed to buy two tonnes of barley at £100 each. If, on 1 March, the futures price for barley for the third Wednesday in May is, say, £105 a tonne, then she will agree to sell 200 tonnes for £105 each, so she will gain £5 a tonne whatever the spot price of barley is at maturity. Alternatively, if on 1 March the futures price for barley for the third Wednesday in May is, say, £95 a tonne, then she will agree to sell 200 tonnes for £95 each, so she will lose £5 a tonne whatever the spot price of barley is at maturity. In practice, she will not even have to wait until the maturity date to secure her gain or pay her loss, for, as explained in Section 5.4 below, payments with futures are timed in a way which means that all gains and losses are realised by the time that closing out occurs.

The term closing out may be applied to parties who are long in futures and who make an offsetting contract to sell, and to parties who are short in futures and who make an offsetting contract to buy. But in the latter case, the term **covering** is sometimes used instead of closing out.

The reasons why people close out

Almost all futures positions are closed out. There are several reasons for this. The manufacturer in the example might have closed out on 1 March because she actually needed some barley before the maturity date. So she closed out and bought some barley on the spot market. She might have known all along that she would probably need barley some time before the third Wednesday in May, and hence that she would close out and buy on the spot market. But the futures contract enabled her to hedge against a rise in barley prices. For if the spot price rose before she closed out, then the futures price would also rise, and the profit she made on closing would be used to offset the rise in the spot price.

Alternatively, she might have closed out because she decided on 1 March that she no longer wanted any barley until after the maturity date. Maybe she decided that she did not need any until early next July. In this case, she might decide on 1 March that she should hedge against high prices in July. So she would probably close out her May position with two offsetting contracts to sell barley, and then make two new futures contracts to buy barley as soon as possible after early July, that is on the third Wednesday in July. By extending the period of time over which she has hedged, she would be **rolling over** her futures position.

Even if the manufacturer really did want to receive a delivery on the maturity date, she would still probably close out and instead buy barley on the spot market. One reason for this is that she may end up having to take a delivery earlier, for it has been seen that futures sellers of commodities have the right to sell on a wide range of dates. Another reason is that the seller has the right to choose the delivery point from a selection approved by the exchange. These delivery points are often widely scattered around the world, so she might have to take a delivery from an inconvenient place. Of course, these two reasons for closing out apply only to commodities futures.

Finally, many futures contracts involve parties who are traders on exchanges or speculators. Neither of those groups really wants to buy or sell anything, so they almost always close out.

5.3 TYPES OF FUTURES CONTRACT AND THEIR AGREED VALUES

There are six main types of futures contract:

1. Commodity futures.
2. Currency futures.
3. Long-term interest rate futures.
4. Short-term interest rate futures.
5. Stock index – or FTSE index – futures.
6. Freight index futures.

Types 1, 2 and 3 are contracts to buy and sell commodities, currencies and gilts, so any contracts which run to maturity involve a delivery and payment. In contrast, types 4, 5 and 6 are not contracts to buy and sell, so any contracts which mature do not involve a delivery. Strictly speaking, the parties to types 4, 5 and 6 do not agree a futures price. Instead, they agree some other futures value, such as an interest rate, a FTSE index or a freight cost index. For convenience, however, the term futures price will often be used in this chapter to cover also agreed futures interest rates or indices.

The following paragraphs describe each type of contract and explain why they are used by hedgers. However, futures are also used by speculators who hope that the spot price at maturity will be different from the futures price agreed in the contract. In each case, the agreed futures price will always be close to the price that people on average expect at maturity. So, like a forward price, a futures price converges with the spot price as maturity draws near. For, as maturity approaches, there is less time for the spot price to change, so the price expected at maturity, and hence the price agreed in the futures contract, will get closer to the current spot price.

Some of the terms used in forward markets are also used in futures markets. Thus a futures market displays backwardation if the spot price is expected to fall, so that P_F, which in this chapter means the futures price, is below the current spot price, P_S; and it displays contango if the spot price is expected to rise, so that P_F is above P_S. Also, it displays normal backwardation if P_F is below the spot price that people on average expect at maturity, P_E, and normal contango if P_F is above P_E.

Commodity futures

Commodity futures, like commodity forwards, can be used by long hedgers and short hedgers. Suppose X wants to buy nickel in future and fears high nickel prices when the time comes. He may make a long hedge by agreeing a futures contract to buy nickel at an agreed futures price. If he does not close out, he will gain at the other party's expense if the spot price of nickel at maturity is above the futures price, and lose if it is below. If he does close out, he will gain if the futures price when he closes out is above the one he agreed in his first contract, and lose if it is below.

Suppose Y wishes to sell nickel in future and fears low nickel prices when the time comes. She may make a short hedge by agreeing a futures contract to sell nickel at an agreed futures price. If she does not close out, she will gain at the other party's expense if the spot price of nickel at maturity is below the futures price, and lose if it is above. If she does close out, she will gain if the futures price when she closes out is below the one in her first contract, and lose if it is above.

As commodity futures are similar to commodity forwards, so the futures prices for commodities are very similar to their forward prices. Thus the future price for a commodity, P_F, is related to the spot price, P_S and the carrying cost, C, in the same way as a forward price, as explained in Section 4.4. So, for storable commodities, P_F never exceeds P_S plus C, which chiefly comprises the interest lost on the money needed to buy the commodity plus the cost of storing it until the futures contract matures. Moreover, for storable crops between harvests, P_F should always equal P_S plus C.

However, P_F for an unstorable commodity can exceed P_S plus C. An example occurs in the United States where there is a futures market for cattle under a certain weight. If the P_F for these light young cattle exceeds P_S plus C, then it might seem that profits could be made by buying light cattle spot and at once agreeing futures contracts to sell them later, storing them meanwhile. In turn, it seems that P_S would rise and P_F would fall, so that the gap between them would shrink. However, it is not possible to store light young cattle as such until maturity, for they grow rapidly and may well exceed the permitted weight at maturity. So here P_F can stay above P_S plus C.

Commodity futures prices are also related to the spot price that people, on average, expect to apply on the maturity day, that is P_E. The relationship is the same as that for commodity forward prices, as explained in Section 4.5. So, for commodities whose prices tend to rise and fall when the returns from a market portfolio rise and fall, P_F will be slightly below P_E. The gap will reflect the risk premiums that are required by people who make futures purchases and sales of the commodity.

Although the same principles govern both forward prices and futures prices, very slight differences can arise between the forward price and the futures price of a commodity for contracts that mature on the same day. This is because people are not wholly indifferent between forwards and futures. For example, futures are easier to close out than forwards and their payments are timed differently. Also, there is negligible risk of the other party to a futures defaulting as it is a clearing house, but there may be a risk of the other party to a forward defaulting, especially if it is not an intermediary.

Currency futures

Currency futures can be used by hedgers in the same way as currency forwards. Suppose X wants to buy dollars in future and fears a high dollar price when the time comes. He may make a long hedge with a futures contract in which he will buy dollars at an agreed futures price. If he does not close out, he will gain at the other party's expense if the spot price of dollars at maturity is above the futures price, and lose if it is below. If he does close out, he will gain if the futures price when he closes out is above the one he agreed in his first contract, and lose if it is below.

Suppose Y wants to sell dollars in future and fears a low dollar price when the time comes. She may make a short hedge with a currency futures contract in which she will sell dollars at an agreed futures price. If she does not close out, she will gain at the other party's expense if the spot price of dollars at maturity is below the futures price, and lose if it is above. If she does close out, she will gain if the futures price when she closes out is below the one in her first contract, and lose if it is above.

As currency futures are similar to currency forwards, the futures prices of currencies are very similar to their forward prices. So, just like a forward currency price, the futures price of a currency, P_F, equals the current spot price, P_S, plus the cost of carrying the currency until maturity, C. C for a foreign currency is the interest lost on the money used to buy it minus the interest that it earns. So any gaps between P_F and P_S are caused by differences in the interest rates on the two currencies concerned, as noted in the interest rate parity theorem explained in Section 4.4.

Also, the P_F for a currency is very close to the average expected maturity-day spot price, P_E, unless there is a significant risk premium. Section 4.5 explained that the risk premium on a currency might be positive or negative. This means that the P_F for a currency could be below or above P_E.

In practice, very slight differences can arise between the forward price and the futures price of a currency for contracts with the same maturity. This is because people are not wholly indifferent between currency forwards and futures, chiefly because their payments are timed differently.

Long-term interest rate futures

Some long hedgers are people who wish in future to lend long-term and who fear that long-term interest rates in future may be low. Suppose X is such a person. To gain some compensation if long-term interest rates do turn out to be low, he may agree a **long-term interest rate futures** contract in which he will buy some gilts at an agreed futures price, P_F. If X does not close out, he will gain at the other party's expense if spot long-term interest rates at maturity are low, for then spot gilt prices will be high. This means that the P_F at which he will buy gilts will be below the spot price. However, he will lose if spot long-term interest rates at maturity are high, for then the spot price of gilts will be below the P_F at which he will buy them. If X does close out, he will gain if the futures price in his offsetting contract is above the P_F agreed in his initial contract, and vice versa.

Some short hedgers are people who wish in future to borrow long-term and fear that long-term interest rates in future may be high. Suppose Y is such a person. To gain some compensation if long-term interest rates do turn out to be high, she may agree a futures contract in which she will sell some gilts at an agreed P_F. If Y does not close out, she will gain at the other party's expense if spot long-term interest rates at maturity are high, for then spot gilt prices will be low. This means that the P_F at which she will sell gilts will exceed the spot price. However, she will lose if spot long-term interest rates at maturity are low, for then the spot price of gilts will be below the P_F at which she will sell them. If Y does close out, she will gain if the futures price in her offsetting contract is below the P_F agreed in her initial contract, and vice versa.

In these futures, the P_F agreed for gilts will equal the current spot price of gilts, P_S, plus the cost of carrying gilts until the futures contract matures. This cost, C, is the interest lost on the money used to buy gilts minus the income from the gilts. If P_F exceeded P_S by more than C, then people would make profits by buying gilts now and selling them in futures contracts, carrying them meanwhile. So P_S would rise and P_F would fall, and the gap between them would shrink. If P_F was below P_S plus C, then people who now hold gilts would make profits by selling them and agreeing to buy them back later in futures contracts, for their saving in carrying costs would more than offset any difference between the P_F at which they would buy them back and the P_S at which they sold them. So P_S would fall and P_F would rise, and the gap between them would widen.

The P_F of gilts should be very close to the spot price that people on average expect to apply on the maturity day, P_E. The only reason that it may differ is that gilt prices are a little volatile as they change when interest rates change, as shown in Section 2.3. This volatility means that investors who buy and sell gilts in futures contracts require a risk premium. If the returns from agreeing to buy gilts in futures contracts tend to rise and fall at the same time as the returns on a market portfolio, then the P_F of gilts will be a little below P_E, and vice versa. The reasons are the same as those explained in Section 4.5 for commodities.

One problem which arises for an exchange which offers long-term interest rate futures is deciding which gilt to use. If just one gilt was allowed, then there might be too few available for easy delivery by all the futures sellers who held their contracts until maturity. One solution would be to have several different futures contracts, each with a different underlying gilt. Usually, though, the exchanges devise a **notional gilt** or **hypothetical gilt**, and then they allow a selection of actual gilts to be delivered at maturity as substitutes.

Like the sellers in commodity futures contracts, the gilt sellers in long-term interest rate futures contracts usually have some choice over when to make their delivery, subject to giving two days' notice. The period over which a seller may give notice is called the **notice period**. This might last for some weeks before the maturity date. Whenever a notice is received, the clearing house will select a buyer who must then make the purchase. Delivery will take place two days later.

Short-term interest rate futures

Some long hedgers are people who wish to lend short-term in future and fear that short-term interest rates will be low when the time comes. Suppose X is such a person. He can agree a **short-term interest rate futures** contract. This will specify an agreed interest rate – the **futures rate** – for the maturity date. The deal here is that if the spot short-term rate at maturity is lower than the agreed futures rate, then the other party will pay X some compensation the amount depending on the gap between the futures rate and the spot rate. But if the spot rate exceeds the agreed futures rate, then X will pay some money to the other party. X could later close out by making an offsetting contract in which he would pay the other party compensation if the spot rate at maturity was below the futures rate agreed in his second contract, and vice versa. He would gain if the futures rate agreed on the day when he closes out is below the futures rate in his first contract.

Likewise, Y may be a short hedger who wishes to borrow short-term in future and fears high short-term interest rates when the time comes. She can agree a short-term interest rate futures contract which will specify an agreed futures interest rate for the maturity date. The deal here is that if the spot short-term rate at maturity exceeds the agreed futures rate, then the other party will pay Y some compensation the amount depending on the gap, but if the spot rate is below the agreed futures rate, then Y will pay some money to the other party. Y could close out by making an offsetting contract in which she would pay the other party compensation if the spot rate at maturity exceeds the futures rate agreed in her second contract, and vice versa. She would gain if the futures rate agreed on the day when she closes out is above the futures rate in her first contract.

These futures do not concern an underlying asset that is traded at maturity. All that happens at maturity is that one party pays compensation to the other.

However, even though there is no underlying asset that can be bought or carried, short-term futures interest rates will be linked to current spot rates in the same way that applies to the forward/forward rates agreed in FRAs, as given in (4.7), for short-term interest rate futures are similar to FRAs.

The similarity between short-term interest rate futures and FRAs also means that the relationship between short-term interest rate futures rates and expected future interest rates is the same as the relationship between FRA interest rates expected future interest rates. As discussed in Chapter 4.8, this relationship depends on whether long-term bank deposits tend to attract higher interest than short-term deposits in the form of a liquidity premium. If there is no liquidity premium, then futures rates, like FRA rates, will equal the expected future rates. If, as is likely, there is a liquidity premium, then futures rates, like FRA rates, will slightly exceed expected future rates.

Short-term interest rate futures rates should be very close to FRA rates for contracts with the same maturity dates. More precisely, as LIFFE (1995) points out, the futures rate should be about half-way between the FRA bid and offer rates. The futures rate may at times move away from this central value, but if it does, then it is likely to be brought back by arbitrageurs. They may simply agree to borrow in future at whichever rate is lower and agree to lend at whichever is higher.

Stock index futures

Some long hedgers are people who wish to buy equities in future and fear that equity prices will be high when the time comes. If X is such a person, then he can agree **a stock index futures** contract. This will specify an agreed FTSE index for the maturity date. This is called the **futures index,** I_F. The deal here is that if the spot FTSE index at maturity, I_M, exceeds I_F, then the other party will pay X compensation, say £25 for each point that I_M is above I_F; but if I_M is below I_F, then X must pay £25 to the other party for each point that I_M is below I_F. If X does not close out, then his gain or loss at maturity will be £25$(I_M - I_F)$, so he will gain if I_M is above I_F and lose if it is below. Suppose, instead, that X closes out on a day when the futures index agreed for contracts maturing on the same day as his first contract is I_C. X closes out by making an offsetting contract where he will pay £25 to the other party for each point that I_M is above I_C and receive £25 from that party for each point that I_M is below I_C, so his gain or loss will be £25$(I_C - I_M)$. His overall gain or loss will be £25$(I_M - I_F)$ + £25$(I_C - I_M)$ which is £25$(I_C - I_F)$. So he will gain if I_C is above I_F, and vice versa.

Some short hedgers wish to sell equities in future and fear that equity prices will be low when the time comes. If Y is such a person, then she can agree a stock index futures contract which will specify an agreed FTSE index, I_F, for the maturity date. The deal here is that if the spot index at maturity, I_M, is below I_F, then the other party will pay X £25 compensation for each point that it is below I_F; but if the spot index is above I_F, then X must pay £25 to the other party for each point that it is above I_F. If Y does not close out, then her gain or loss at maturity will be £25$(I_F - I_M)$, so she will gain if I_M is below

I_F and lose if it is above. Suppose, instead, that Y closes out on a day when the futures index agreed for contracts maturing on the same day as her first contract is I_C. Y will close out by making an offsetting contract where she will pay £25 to the other party for each point that I_M is below I_C and receive £25 from that party for each point that I_M is above I_C, so her gain or loss will be £25$(I_M - I_C)$. Her overall gain or loss will be £25$(I_F - I_M)$ + £25$(I_M - I_C)$ which is £25$(I_F - I_C)$. So she will gain if I_F is above I_C, and vice versa.

The agreed futures index will be below the average **expected index** by an amount that covers the risk premiums from buying and selling the equities in the index in futures contracts. Also, although there are no purchases and deliveries with stock index futures, they effectively concern a bundle of equities like the one whose prices are used to calculate the relevant FTSE index. So an agreed I_F will be related to the current spot index, I_S, by the carrying costs of equities, C, that is the interest lost by buying them less the dividends they produce. To see this relationship, consider an example.

Suppose that anyone who spends £150,000 buying a bundle of equities that matches the bundle used in the index will incur C of £500 over the next six months. In other words, the interest they will lose on the £150,000 used to buy the equities is £500 more than the dividends they will earn from them. So C over six months is 1/300th of the value of the equities. Next, suppose I_S is 6,000. Then I_F for futures maturing in six months must be *about* 6,000 plus 1/300th of 6,000, that is 6,020. To see why, consider in turn what would happen if I_F was above 6,020 and then below 6,020.

Suppose first that I_F is above 6,020, say 6,030. In this case, suppose Y buys a bundle of securities for £150,000 and also agrees a six-month futures contract in which, if I_M is under 6,030, she will be paid £25 by the other party for each point by which it is under 6,030, whereas if I_M is over 6,030, she will pay the other party £25 for each point that it is above. Suppose Y sells her securities on the maturity date and that I_M is then 6,000. Y will receive £150,000 for her securities, for their value will be the same as it is now, but she will lose C of £500 as the equities will have produced £500 less in dividends than she would have earned in interest on the £150,000 if she had kept it. However, she will also receive £750 from the other party to the futures contract as I_M is 30 points below the I_F of 6,030. So she will make a net gain of £250. For every point that I_M might be below 6,000, Y's securities would be worth 1/6,000th less, that is £25, so she would get £25 less from selling them, but she would gain £25 more from her futures contract, so she would still make a net gain of £250. And for every point that I_F might be above 6,000, Y would get £25 less from the futures contract, actually losing from it if I_M is over 6,030, but this would be offset by the £25 more that she would get from selling her securities. So again, her net gain would still be £250.

There would be massive demand to adopt Y's strategy of buying securities and selling them later, and also agreeing stock index futures contracts like hers. So I_S would rise and I_F would fall and the gap between them would narrow. Suppose for simplicity that I_F fell, while I_S stayed at 6,000. Then it might seem that I_F would continue to fall until it reached 6,020 and so made the gap equal to 1/300th of I_S, for this gap would reflect the fact that C over six months is 1/300th of the cost of buying shares. However, the high trans-actions costs of buying and selling a wide array of shares mean the gap could settle a shade wider than that. So I_F could settle a little above 6,020.

Next, suppose that I_F was below 6,020, say 6,010. In this case, suppose X sells a bundle of securities worth £150,000 that matches the bundle used in the index, and suppose he also agrees a stock index futures contract in which, if I_M is over 6,010, he will be paid £25 by the other party for each point by which it is over 6,010, whereas if I_M is under 6,010, he will pay the other party £25 for each point that it is below 6,010. Suppose I_M is 6,000. Then X could use the £150,000 he received for his securities to buy the bundle back again, and he would pay £250 compensation to the other party to his futures contract as the index would be 10 points below the I_F of 6,010. But he would have gained £500 because the interest he earned on the £150,000 raised from selling his securities would be £500 more than the dividends he would have lost, so he would make a net gain of £250. For every point that I_M might be below 6,000, X would have to spend 1/6,000th less to buy his securities back, that is £25, but he would also have to pay £25 more to the other party to the futures contract, so his net gain would still be £250. And for every point that I_M might be above 6,000, X would save £25 from the futures contract, actually gaining from it if I_M is over 6,010, but this would be offset by the £25 more that he would need to pay to buy his securities back. So again, his net gain would still be £250.

There would be massive demand to adopt X's strategy of selling securities and buying them back later, and also agreeing stock index futures contracts like his. So I_S would fall and I_F would rise and the gap between them would widen. Suppose for simplicity that I_F rose while I_S stayed at 6,000. Then it might seem that I_F would continue to rise until it reached 6,020 and so make the gap equal to 1/300th of I_S, for this gap would reflect the fact that C over six months is 1/300th of the cost of buying shares. However, the high trans-actions costs of selling and buying a wide array of shares mean the gap could settle a shade narrower than that. So I_F could also settle a little below 6,020.

Freight index futures

Some long hedgers will be people who wish to shift cargo by freight ships in future and fear high freight charges when the time comes. If X is such a person, he can agree a **freight index futures** contract which will specify an agreed index of freight costs for the maturity date. The deal here is that if the spot freight index at maturity date exceeds the futures index, then the other party will pay X some compensation, but if the spot index is below the agreed futures index, then X must pay some money to the other party. If X does not close out, he will gain if the spot index at maturity is above the futures index in his contract, and vice versa. If he does close out, he will gain if the futures index on the day when he closes exceeds the index in his initial contract, and vice versa.

Likewise, some short hedgers will be people who wish to offer freight services in future and fear low freight charges when the time comes. If Y is such a person, she can agree a freight index futures which will specify an agreed index of freight costs for the maturity date. The deal here is that if the spot freight index at maturity date is below the futures index, then the other party will pay Y some compensation, but if the spot index exceeds the agreed futures rate, then Y must pay some money to the other party. If Y does not close out, she will gain if the spot index at maturity is below the futures index in her contract, and vice versa. If she does close out, she will gain if the futures index on the day when she closes is below the index in her initial contract, and vice versa.

There are no purchases and deliveries with these futures, so there is no underlying asset that can be bought now and stored. In turn, there is no clear link between the futures indices and current indices of freight costs. However, there should be a link between the agreed future index and the expected index on maturity day. For a futures index should be less than the expected future index by an amount that reflects the risk premiums on making these sorts of contract.

5.4 PAYMENT TIMES AND MARKING-TO-MARKET

Payment timing with forwards

The timings of payments on futures are different from those on forwards. The difference will be explained with the help of an example which concerns two commodity futures, but identical arrangements apply also to currency futures and long-term interest rate futures. The slight differences that apply with other sorts of futures are noted at the end of the section. For simplicity, the example will consider contracts with very short lives.

Suppose it is Wednesday 10 April. X wants to buy one tonne of tin next week on 17 April and Y wants to sell one tonne. X wants to hedge against a high price and Y against a low price. They could agree a forward contract with each other with a forward price of, say, £4,000. If they did, then the only payment would be one of £4,000 made on 17 April. A snag here is that X would have an incentive to default if the 17 April spot price was below £4,000, for he would then prefer to buy on the spot market. Likewise Y would have an incentive to default if the 17 April spot price was above £4,000, for she would then prefer to sell on the spot market.

To make default less likely, X and Y might instead each make separate forward contracts with an intermediary. The intermediary might then ask each of them to place a deposit of, say, 10% of the contract value, that is £400. This would be refunded to each party on 17 April. In this case, any temptation that X or Y might have to default and trade on the spot market should be more than offset by knowing that they would then lose their £400 deposit. With these forward contracts, X and Y would both pay £400 on 10 April. On 17 April, X would receive his £400 back but pay £4,000 for the tin, while Y would receive her £400 back and also receive £4,000 for the tin.

Suppose the spot price on 17 April is £4,200. X will gain £200 by buying one tonne of tin for £200 less than the spot price, while Y will lose £200 by selling one tonne for less than the spot price. The intermediary could, in principle, make X's gain very explicit by telling X that on 17 April he must actually pay them the current spot price of £4,200, and then refund him £200 as the spot price was £200 over the agreed price of £4,000. If the intermediary did this, then X would face three payments on 17 April: he would get his £400 back, he would pay the spot price of £4,200, and he would receive the £200 refund. The intermediary could also make Y's loss very explicit by telling Y that on 17 April she would receive the current spot price of £4,200 from them, and then making her refund them £200 as the spot price was £200 over the agreed price of £4,000. If the intermediary did this, then Y would also face three payments on 17 April. She would receive her £400 deposit back, she would receive the spot price of £4,200, and she would pay a refund of £200. In essence, futures contracts work just like this except that the refunds are spread out over the whole life of the contract and are not made in one payment at the end. It is because these payments are spread out that the timings of payments with futures differ from those with forwards.

Payment times with futures

To see how payments arise with futures contracts, suppose that X and Y make futures contracts for tin. They find an exchange where futures contracts mature on the third Wednesday of each month, so that some will mature a week today on 17 April. Their brokers agree the current futures price of £4,000. Then both X and Y have separate futures contracts with the clearing house. Their financial relationships with it are shown in Table 5.1. The first payments arise when the contracts are agreed. The clearing house opens one account for X and one for Y, and it requires them each to place in their accounts a deposit called an **initial margin** of, say, 10% of the value of the contract. So, as soon as the contracts are agreed on 10 April, they each make a payment of £400 and each has a balance of £400. They must maintain a balance of at least £400 in their accounts until their contracts mature, or until they close out. Interest is paid on these accounts.

At the end of each business day until maturity, the clearing house works out the average spot futures price agreed on the last few contracts of the day for new futures contracts maturing on 17 April. This is called the **settlement price**. The clearing house then looks separately at all the people with futures contracts to see who would lose at maturity, and who would gain, if the spot price then equalled the settlement price. Those who would lose must increase their margins by the amount of their potential loss. But these extra **variation margins** are not kept in their accounts. Instead, they are paid into the accounts of those who would gain, so these receipts effectively form negative variation margins to the gainers. The gainers may keep their receipts in their accounts or withdraw them. For simplicity, the example supposes that the gainers always withdraw them.

Table 5.1 shows the settlement price for each business day. On days when this is below the futures price of £4,000, X is required to have a variation margin equal to the gap; for he would lose at maturity if the spot price then equalled the settlement price, as he would pay £4,000 instead of a lower spot price. On days when the settlement price is above the futures price, Y is required to have a variation margin equal to the gap; for she would lose at maturity if the spot price then equalled the settlement price, as she would receive £4,000 instead of a higher spot price.

At the end of 10 April, the settlement price is £3,950. If that was the spot price at maturity, then X would lose by £50. So X has a variation margin of £50, while Y has one of –£50, and X must pay the clearing house £50. The payments from losers like X are used to finance payments to gainers like Y who receives and withdraws £50. So X and Y each end up with £400 still in their accounts. At the end of 11 April, the settlement price is £3,850. If that was the spot price at maturity, then X would lose by £150. So X has a variation margin of £150, while Y has one of –£150. X's variation margin has risen by £100 from the previous day, so he must pay the clearing house £100, while Y receives and withdraws £100. So again X and Y end up with £400 in their accounts. At the end of 12 April, the settlement price is £4,050. If that was the spot price at maturity, then Y would lose by £50. So now Y has a variation margin of £50, while X has one of –£50. Y's variation margin has risen by £200 from the previous day's value of –£150, so she has to pay the clearing house £200 while X receives and withdraws £200, so yet again X and Y end up with £400 in their accounts.

This process takes place each business day until maturity. Whenever the settlement price moves against X, as it did, for example, between 10 and 11 April, X pays money to the clearing house which is effectively transferred to Y. And whenever the settlement price moves against Y, as it did, for example, between 11 and 12 April, Y pays money to the clearing house which is effectively transferred to X. The only time when no payment would be made is if the settlement price remained unchanged between one day and the next, an event which does not occur in the example.

The contracts mature on 17 April. They mature at a specified time, say 1230. At that moment, the clearing house effectively works out three separate payments for X and Y. These are shown separately on the table, though in practice one net payment to or from either party would take place. First, the clearing house determines a final settlement price called the **exchange delivery settlement price** (EDSP). As spot prices and futures prices converge at maturity, this price also equals the spot price at maturity. The table shows the futures price at maturity on 17 April, that is the EDSP, as £4,200. This is £50 above the settlement price on 16 April, so Y has to pay £50 more variation margin, while X receives and withdraws £50, to leave them both with balances of £400. The final spot price equals the EDSP and is £200 above the futures price, and this means that X gains £200 in all through the variation margins, while Y loses £200 in all. Secondly, X pays the maturity spot price of £4,200 and receives one tonne of tin, while Y delivers one tonne of tin and is paid £4,200 for it. Thirdly, X and Y have their initial margins of £400 returned.

This system of daily payments between potential gainers and losers is called **marking-to-market**. Its chief aim is to minimise any risk of default. Consider X at the end of 11 April when he is required to make an additional payment

Table 5.1 An example of variation margins and marking-to-market

April	Event	Current futures price	X's variation margin	X's payments and receipts (−)	X's balance	Y's variation margin	Y's payments and receipts (−)	Y's balance
10	Contract	4,000	0	400	400	0	400	400
10	Settlement	3,950	50	50	400	−50	−50	400
11	Settlement	3,850	150	100	400	−150	−100	400
12	Settlement	4,050	−50	−200	400	50	200	400
15	Settlement	3,900	100	150	400	−100	−150	400
16	Settlement	4,150	−150	−250	400	150	250	400
17	Settlement	4,200	−200	−50	400	200	50	400
17	Buy/sell tin	4,200	0	4,200	400	0	−4,200	400
17	Margin refund	4,200	0	−400	0	0	−400	0
	Total			4,000	−		−4,000	−

of £100. If he defaults, then the clearing house will at once terminate his contract and he will lose his £400 deposit.

Payments with contracts which do not run to the maturity day

Spme modifications to the process outlined in Table 5.1 are needed with futures contracts that do not run until the maturity day. For example, with commodity futures and long-term interest rate futures, sellers may often choose to make a delivery before maturity, in which case the clearing house makes someone else receive it and pay for it. In these cases, both parties still effectively have three payments at their final settlements. First, they pay or receive any changes in the variation margin since the day before. Secondly, the buyer makes a purchase payment that is based on the latest settlement price, and this sum is transferred to the seller. Thirdly, their initial margins are returned.

Another possibility is that a party may close out. Imagine that X actually closed out on 12 April at a moment when the current futures price was £3,900. He would have made an offsetting contract to sell a tonne of tin to the clearing house for £3,900, and this would have been matched by another party who would have agreed to buy a tonne from the clearing house for £3,900. The clearing house would have had no further interest in X as he would have agreed to buy one tonne for £4,000 and sell one tonne for £3,900. All it would have wanted from him is a net sum of £100. So it would have repaid him his margin payments to date, £400 initial margin plus £150 variation margin, minus this £100. So X would have lost £100 overall. Imagine, next, that Y had actually closed out on 12 April at a moment when the current futures price was £3,950. She would have made an offsetting contract to buy a tonne of tin from the clearing house for £3,950. This would have been matched by another party who would have agreed to sell a tonne to the clearing house for £3,950. The clearing house would have had no further interest in Y as she would have agreed to sell one tonne for £4,000 and buy one for £3,950. It would simply have settled up by giving her a net payment of £50. As she would have already removed £150 in variation margin, it would have ensured a net payment of just £50 by repaying her only £300 from her initial margin of £400.

Settlement with other types of futures contracts

The settlement terms for short-term interest rate futures, stock index futures and freight index futures differ slightly from the arrangements shown in Table 5.1 because no final purchase or delivery is made with these. Otherwise, the arrangements are exactly as shown in Table 5.1.

The absence of a final purchase and delivery does not affect the parties' gains or losses. To see why, recall from the example in Table 5.1 that on 17 April X paid £4,200 for a tonne of tin. This price equalled that day's spot price. So X paid £4,200 for one tonne of tin which was worth £4,200. Likewise, Y sold for £4,200 one tonne of tin that was worth £4,200. So X and Y could have eschewed the receipt and the delivery of tin, and the associated £4,200 payments, without affecting their financial gain and loss. X would still have gained £200 through his variation margin receipts while Y would have lost £200 through her variation margin payments. These variation margins arose because the maturity day spot price was £200 above the futures price of £4,000. With short-term interest rate futures, stock index futures and freight futures, variation margins still occur, so the parties still gain or lose if the maturity day spot value differs from the agreed futures value.

An implication of marking-to-market

Marking-to-market means that a futures contract can, in effect, be seen as a series of one-day forward contracts, each one having the previous business day's futures settlement price as its maturity value. For, each day, a party loses money through its variation margin if the settlement price has moved against it since the day before, and it gains if it has moved in its favour.

5.5 OPPORTUNITIES AND RISKS WITH CLOSING OUT

Section 5.2 showed how futures are closed out with reversing trades. It also showed that people who close out will gain or lose depending on the relative futures prices in their original contracts and their reversing trades, and Section 5.4 showed that their gains or losses will be realised by the time they close. This section looks at some implications of closing out for speculators and hedgers.

Closing out and speculators

The fact that the gains or losses which people make when they close out depend only on the relative futures prices in their original contracts and their reversing contracts is very important for speculators who enter futures markets. For it means that they do not have to consider whether they expect the spot price at maturity to be higher or lower than the current futures price. They need only consider whether the futures price might rise or fall some time before maturity. If they think the futures price will rise at some stage, then they may make futures contracts to buy and hope to close out later when there is a higher futures price. If they think the futures price will fall at some stage, then they may make futures contracts to sell and hope to close out later when there is a lower futures price. Much speculation is done by traders, and traders who speculate are often divided into three groups according to the time gap they leave between their initial and closing contracts.

Scalpers are traders who hope to gain through favourable moves in the futures price over the next few minutes. They try to make many tiny gains each day. **Day traders** hope to gain through favourable moves in the futures price over the rest of the day. Even if no favourable move occurs, they will close out at the end of the day to avoid the risk of adverse overnight changes. **Position traders** hope to gain through favourable moves over any period from overnight to some weeks. Of course, any trader may act at different times as a scalper, a day trader, and a position trader.

The effect of closing out on hedgers' profits and losses

Hedgers are said to use futures to hedge against **price risk** because they use them to hedge against adverse prices in the underlying asset. It can be shown that if hedgers do not close out, then futures contracts give them perfect hedges. This means that the futures allow the hedgers to predict their future payments or receipts precisely at the outset. However, if they do close out, then the hedge is not perfect because their future payments or receipts are not certain at the outset. This point is important because most people do close out. Nevertheless, the uncertainty which arises from using futures and then closing out is much smaller than the price risk which is avoided by using futures.

All of this will be illustrated with an example of a barley futures contract for one tonne of barley. This futures is agreed on 23 March for maturity on 23 June, but the example will show what happens if it is closed out. It will consider the effects of closing out either just before maturity or on 23 April. Table 5.2 gives the necessary information. The spot price is £100 per tonne on 23 March, £94 on 23 April, and £107 at maturity on 23 June. As the contract matures before the next harvest, the futures price each day for a futures contract maturing on 23 June equals the current spot price plus the cost of carrying until 23 June. Say the carrying cost is £1 a month. Then on 23 March it will cost £3 to carry one tonne until maturity, so the futures price that day is £100 + £3 or £103. On 23 April it will cost £2 to carry one tonne until maturity, so the futures price that day is £94 + £2 or £96. On 23 June it will cost £0 to carry one tonne until maturity, so the futures price that day is £107 + £0 or £107. Finally, Table 5.2 gives figures each day for what is called the **basis**, which is the spot price minus the futures price; so it is –£3 on 23 March, –£2 on 23 April and £0 on 23 June. In this example, each day's basis is simply the negative of the carrying cost to maturity.

Suppose it is 23 March and X wants to acquire one tonne of barley at some time in the future. If he makes no futures contract, then he is exposed to price risk. He does not know what the future spot price will be, but Table 5.2 illustrates the price risk he faces, for it shows that he will have to pay £94 if he buys spot on 23 April and £107 if he buys spot on 23 June. X can fix his future payment on 23 March if he make a futures contract to buy one tonne on 23 June at the current futures price of £103 and holds his contract until maturity. For then, at maturity, he will acquire one tonne for which he will have paid £103. He will pay £3 more than the current spot price, and so make a loss of £3 compared with buying barley now, but this loss can be seen merely as a payment to the person from whom he buys the barley for effectively carrying it for three months on X's behalf.

Table 5.2   An example of a barley futures contract

Date	Spot price (£)	Carrying cost to maturity (£)	Futures price (£)	Basis (£)
23 March	100	3	103	–3
23 April	94	2	96	–2
23 June	107	0	107	0

But suppose X closes out at some time, T. He does so by making an offsetting futures contract to sell barley on 23 June, and then buying the one tonne of barley that he wants to acquire on the spot market. The profit, Π, which he will make compared with buying barley on 23 March is given by:

$$\Pi_{\text{LONG HEDGE}} = (P_S - P_{SC}) + (P_{FC} - P_F) \tag{5.1}$$

Here, P_S and P_F are the spot and future prices when the contract is made and P_{SC} and P_{FC} are the spot and future prices when it is closed out. For example, suppose X closes out just before maturity. The first bracketed expression shows that X will make a gain of –£7, that is a loss of £7, by buying barley at the closing-day spot price of £107 instead of the 23 March spot price of £100. The second expression shows that his futures position does much to offset this loss, for he makes a new futures contract to sell at £107 to close out his existing contract to buy at £103, and this gains him £4. So $\Pi_{\text{LONG HEDGE}}$ is $(-£7) + (£4)$, or –£3. This is a loss, but it is of no significance as it equals the three months' carrying costs that are effectively borne on X's behalf by the person from whom he actually buys. If he closes out on 23 April, then $\Pi_{\text{LONG HEDGE}}$ is $(£100 - £94) + (£96 - £103)$ which is $(£6) + (-£7)$ or –£1, and this is also of no significance as it equals the one month's carrying costs that are borne on his behalf.

(5.1) can be re-expressed as:

$$\Pi_{\text{LONG HEDGE}} = (P_S - P_F) - (P_{SC} - P_{FC}) \tag{5.2}$$

which shows that $\Pi_{\text{LONG HEDGE}}$ equals the original basis minus the basis at closure. If X closes out just before maturity when the basis is zero, then $\Pi_{\text{LONG HEDGE}}$ equals the original basis and so is a loss of –£3. If he closes out on 23 April when the basis is –£2, then $\Pi_{\text{LONG HEDGE}}$ is $(-£3) - (-£2)$ which is a loss of –£1.

Next consider Y who wants to sell one tonne of barley at some time in the future. If she makes no futures contract, then she is exposed to price risk. She does not know what the future spot price will be, but Table 5.2 illustrates the price risk she faces, for it shows that she will receive £94 if she decides to sell spot on 23 April and £107 if she sells spot on 23 June. Y can fix her future receipt on 23 March if she makes a futures contract to sell one tonne on 23 June at the current futures price of £103 and holds her contract until maturity. For then, at maturity, she will sell one tonne for £103. This means she will receive £3 more than the current spot price, and so make a gain of £3 compared with selling now, but this gain can be seen as merely offsetting the carrying costs that she bears while carrying the barley over the next three months for the eventual buyer.

But suppose Y closes out at some time, T. She does so by making an offsetting futures contract to buy barley on 23 June, and then selling the one tonne of barley that she wants to sell on the spot market. The profit, Π, which she will make compared with selling barley now is given by:

$$\Pi_{\text{SHORT HEDGE}} = (P_{SC} - P_S) + (P_F - P_{FC}) \tag{5.3}$$

Here P_S and P_F are the spot and future prices when the contract is made and P_{SC} and P_{FC} are the spot and future prices when it is closed out. For example, suppose Y closes out just before maturity. The first bracketed expression shows that Y will gain £7 by selling barley at the closing day spot price of £107, instead of selling it at the 23 March spot price of £100. The second expression shows that her futures position does much to offset this gain, for she makes a new futures contract to buy at £107 to close out her original contract to sell at £103, and this produces a gain of –£4, that is a loss of £4. So $\Pi_{\text{SHORT HEDGE}}$ is (£7) + (–£4) or £3. This profit simply offsets the three months' carrying costs which Y bears. If she closes out on 23 April, then $\Pi_{\text{SHORT HEDGE}}$ is (£94 – £100) + (£103 – £96), which is (–£6) + (£7), or £1, which offsets the one month's carrying cost she bears.

(5.3) can be re-expressed as:

$$\Pi_{\text{SHORT HEDGE}} = (P_{\text{SC}} - P_{\text{FC}}) - (P_{\text{S}} - P_{\text{F}}) \qquad (5.4)$$

which shows that Y's gain equals the basis at closure minus the original basis. If Y closes out just before maturity, when the basis is zero, then $\Pi_{\text{SHORT HEDGE}}$ is zero minus the original basis which is (£0) – (–£3) or £3. If she closes out on 23 April when the basis is –£2, then $\Pi_{\text{SHORT HEDGE}}$ is (–£2) – (–£3) or £1.

Hedgers and basis risk

In the example, it seems that it does not matter when X and Y close out. If X closes out just before maturity, then he makes a loss of –£3 which matches the carrying costs that are borne by the eventual seller on his behalf over three months, while if Y closes out just before maturity, then she makes a profit of £3 which offsets the carrying costs that she bears on behalf of the eventual buyer. Likewise, if they close out after one month, they will respectively make a loss of –£1 and a profit of £1. It also seems that their futures contracts give them perfect hedges, for it seems that on 23 March they could predict their future payments or receipts precisely for any closing date they might choose. However, the example has ignored **basis risk**, that is the risk that the basis may change.

Suppose that sometime after 23 March, carrying costs fall to £0.50 a month. Then the gap between the spot and forward prices on, say, 23 April will equal two months' carrying costs at £0.50 a month, which is £1. So the basis will be –£1. (5.2) shows that X's loss, if he closes out that day, will now be (–£3) – (–£1), or –£2, instead of the –£1 that it would have been if carrying costs had not altered. And (5.4) shows that Y's profit would be (–£1) – (–£3), or £2, instead of £1. This situation, where the gap between the futures price and spot price has narrowed, is called a **strengthening basis**. It means that a long hedge makes a bigger loss or a smaller gain, while a short hedge makes a smaller loss or bigger gain.

Suppose, instead, that after 23 March, carrying costs rise to £1.25 a month. Then the gap between the spot and forward prices on, say, 23 April will equal two months' carrying costs at £1.25 a month, which is £2.50. So the basis will be –£2.50. (5.2) shows that X's loss, if he closes out that day, will be (–£3) – (–£2.50) or –£0.50, instead of the –£1 that it would have been if carrying costs had not altered. And (5.4) shows that Y's profit will be (–£2.50) – (–£3) or £0.50

instead of £1. This situation, where the gap between the futures price and spot price has widened, is called a **weakening basis**. It means that a long hedge makes a smaller loss or a bigger gain, while a short hedge makes a bigger loss or a smaller gain.

This example shows that hedgers who close out before maturity are not wholly protected by their futures contracts as they cannot actually be sure at the outset what their financial position will be. By using futures, they replace price risk with basis risk. However, basis risk is typically much smaller than price risk. For example, the carrying cost of barley is much more stable than the spot price of barley. Moreover, basis risk becomes negligible as maturity approaches, for then the carrying cost to maturity becomes negligible, and hence so also does the basis.

The basis risk with the barley futures was small because the basis on any day, that is $(P_S - P_F)$ that day, was always tied precisely to C which is fairly stable. With some futures contracts, however, $(P_S - P_F)$ is not tied precisely to carrying costs. Consequently the basis can fluctuate quite widely, so that basis risk may be important. This situation actually applies to all commodities futures – except those for crops that are stored between harvests – for here the gap between P_F and P_S can be less than C. It also applies to short-term interest rate futures and freight index futures where there is no underlying asset that can be carried, so that here P_S and P_F are not linked by any carrying costs.

Basis risk can also be significant if the asset that is being hedged is different from the asset that underlies the futures contract that is being used. For in this case, the basis is the difference between the spot price of the asset being hedged and the futures price of the asset underlying the futures contract, and this basis may be quite erratic. This situation always occurs with long-term interest rate futures contracts, for here the underlying asset is a hypothetical or notional bond, whereas hedgers can only buy or sell real bonds. It also occurs with stock index futures, for here the underlying asset is effectively a bundle of securities like those used in a FTSE index, yet these futures are almost invariably used by people who are hedging rather different portfolios.

5.6 EXAMPLES OF FUTURES EXCHANGES AND FUTURES CONTRACTS

There are exchanges for commodity futures and financial futures in many countries. Table 5.3 lists the exchanges whose futures prices are most often quoted in the United Kingdom press together with some of the futures contracts that they offer. Many of these exchanges are in the United States. Further details of some of the futures contracts noted on Table 5.3 are given below. In each of these cases the details include some information about the futures that applied about 21 May 1998, as published the next day in the *Financial Times*.

This information includes figures for open interest and volume. The **open interest** figures show the number of contracts that were held for a given type of futures contract, at the start of the day, by people who had not closed out. If the open interest was, say, 750, then there were 750 outstanding contracts

Table 5.3 Some major futures exchanges and their main futures contracts

Futures exchanges		Main futures offered
Commodity futures exchanges		
The Chicago Board of Trade	CBT	maize, soyabeans, wheat
The Chicago Mercantile Exchange	CME	lean hogs, live cattle, pork bellies
The Commodity Exchange, New York	COMEX	copper, gold, silver
The Coffee, Sugar and Cocoa Exchange, New York	CSCE	cocoa, coffee, sugar
The International Petroleum Exchange, London	IPE	crude oil, gas oil, natural gas
The London International Financial Futures and Options Exchange	LIFFE[1]	barley, cocoa, coffee, potatoes, sugar, wheat; also BIFFEX freight index futures
The London Metal Exchange	LME	aluminium, copper, lead, nickel, tin, zinc
The New York Commodity Exchange	NYCE	cotton, orange juice
The New York Mercantile Exchange	NYMEX	crude oil, gasoline, heating oil, natural gas, palladium, platinum
Financial futures exchanges		
The Chicago Board of Trade	CBT	interest rate futures
The International Monetary Market (a part of CME)	IMM	currency futures
The London International Financial Futures and Options Exchange	LIFFE[1]	long- and short-term interest rate futures, stock index futures
Le Marché à Terme des Instruments Financiers, Paris	MATIF	interest rate futures
El Mercado Español de Futuros Financieros, Madrid	MEFF	interest rate futures

[1]LIFFE is pronounced 'life'. It absorbed the London Commodity Exchange (LCE) in 1996 and acquired most of its commodity futures from the LCE, but its BIFFEX futures were initially offered on the Baltic International Freight Futures Exchange in London, now the Baltic Exchange.

to buy from the clearing house and 750 outstanding contracts to sell to it. The **volume** figures show how many contracts were agreed during the day. If the volume was, say, 50, then 50 contracts were made that day to buy from the clearing house and 50 contracts were made to sell to it. However, this does not mean that the open interest necessarily rose by 50 over the day, for some contracts were probably made by people who were closing out. Indeed, if every contract was made by someone who was closing out, then the open interest would *fall* by 50. The main use of volume figures is to draw attention to days when there is a low volume or **thin trading**. On such days, the agreed futures prices reflect the views of very few people and so might not be as close as usual to the average expected prices.

LIFFE commodity futures

Table 5.4 gives four examples of LIFFE wheat futures, each one having a different maturity date. The figures applied at the close of business on 21 May 1998. LIFFE allows six maturity dates each year with these futures: these are the 23rd day of alternate months, or the previous business day if the 23rd is not a business day. The contracts mature at 1230 on the maturity day. Each contract is for 100 tonnes and has a tick of 5p per tonne.

The open interest figures show how many contracts were held at the start of 21 May by people who had not closed out, while the volume figures show how many contracts were made during 21 May. The other figures show the highest, lowest and settlement futures prices that applied on 21 May, and the change in the settlement price from the close of business on 20 May. These prices are in £ per tonne. There was a gap of about £2 between the September and November settlement prices, and also between the November and January settlement prices, which suggests that the carrying cost of wheat was about £1 a tonne a month. Surprisingly, the settlement price for September was above the July price, despite the harvest in between. As discussed further below, people must have expected a relatively poor harvest.

To see some implications of these figures, consider the settlement price of £78.50 for futures maturing on 23 November. This was the price agreed in the last few contracts made for that day on 21 May and will be near the spot price that people expected to apply on 23 November. If the 23 November spot price for wheat was, say, £85.00, then futures buyers who had agreed a futures price of £78.50 and who had not closed out would gain by trading at £78.50 while futures sellers would lose. More precisely, the buyers and sellers would trade at £85.00, but they would have respectively received their gains and paid their losses through the marking-to-market process. If a futures seller elected to deliver some days before the maturity date, as is allowed with these futures, then the final payments for gains and losses would depend on the settlement price at that time.

The futures price for January 1999 was £80.65, so people expected a spot price of about £80.65 in late January. Allowing for carrying costs of about £1 per month, people must also have expected a spot price for July 1999 of about £86.65. This is well above the expected price for July 1998 as indicated by the settlement price for July 1998 of £75.25. Presumably people expected the 1998 harvest to be poorer than the 1997 one, so that prices in 1998–99 would be higher than in 1997–98.

Table 5.4 Examples of LIFFE wheat futures (end of 21 May 1998)

Commodity	Maturity	Open interest	Volume	High	Low	Sett.	Change
Wheat	Jul 98	1,250	62	75.50	75.20	75.25	+0.60
	Sep 98	165	20	76.25	76.25	76.50	+0.85
	Nov 98	3,154	90	78.65	78.15	78.50	+0.85
	Jan 99	710	16	80.65	80.65	80.65	+1.00

LME commodity futures

Table 5.5 gives an example of an LME copper futures and an example of an LME zinc futures. The figures applied at the close of business on 20 May 1998. These contracts are sometimes called forwards because the LME operates differently from other futures exchanges. For example, it allows far more maturity dates than most exchanges, as it allows any business day within the next three months, any Wednesday from three to six months ahead, and the third Wednesday of any month up to 27 months ahead. Also, separate bid and ask prices are always quoted and published. However, the LME conforms with other exchanges in most salient respects. For it places some limits on the available maturity dates, it specifies the quantity and quality of metal that is to be traded in any contract, it restricts the number of delivery points around the world, and it operates a marking-to-market system. Despite being in London, the LME quotes prices in US dollars. For copper and zinc futures, each contract is for 25 tonnes, and the tick is $0.50 per tonne. The copper must meet a British Standards specification and the zinc must be at least 99.995% pure.

The open interest figures show the total number of futures contracts, for all maturity dates, held at the start of 20 May by people who had not closed out. The total daily turnover figures show the number of contracts made on 20 May. The cash figures show the spot bid and ask prices (in $ per tonne) at the close of business on 20 May. Thus people could then sell copper at a spot price of $1,677.5 and buy it at $1,678.5. The **AM official prices** show the prices on the last contracts made in the main trading period of the day, called the **ring**, which ends at 1255. It may seem odd to call these 1255 prices AM (i.e. morning) prices, but the LME does not regard the morning as finished until 1330 when the next period of trading, the **kerb**, is completed. The AM official prices are of no significance to the futures contracts, but they do have two uses. First, they are used around the world by many traders who often agree to trade at LME prices. Secondly, the average of these prices is worked out each month, and the average is used to settle the LME's Asian options which are noted in Section 6.7. As these official prices are used to settle options, they are sometimes called settlement prices, but they are *not* used for settlement purposes with LME futures contracts.

For the futures contracts, the three-month close figures show the bid and ask prices for a maturity date on 20 August. These three-month futures prices would have been near the prices that people, on average, expected for 20 August. The futures prices for copper and zinc were above the current spot prices, so

Table 5.5 Examples of LME copper and zinc futures (end of 20 May 1998)

Commodity	Open interest	Total daily turnover	Cash	AM official	Three-month		
					close	previous	high/low
Copper	176,425	78,709	1,677.5–78.5	1,695–96	1,695–96	1,678–79	1,718/1,675
Zinc	81,328	19,095	1,039.5–40.5	1,051.5–52	1,066–67	1,073–73.5	1,079/1,066

people expected copper and zinc prices to rise. The futures prices for copper and zinc were $17.50 and $26.50 above the current cash prices, so the carrying costs of copper and zinc for three months cannot have been below $17.50 and $26.50 respectively. The three-month previous figures show the closing three-month futures prices on 19 May. In the case of copper, these were lower than the closing prices on 20 May, so people's expectations about copper prices in August must have risen between the end of 19 and 20 May. The converse applied to zinc. Finally, the three-month high/low prices show the highest and lowest forward prices for 20 August that applied on 20 May. These are the highest and lowest mid-point prices, which are midway between the bid and ask prices.

The press rarely gives the settlement prices used in the LME's marking-to-market calculations. Each evening, the clearing house there works out over 90 settlement prices for each metal. This is because, for each metal, the available futures contracts will have over 90 different maturity dates.

IMM currency futures

Table 5.6 gives two examples of IMM currency futures. Both examples are for sterling, with prices given in dollars, but they have different maturity dates. The figures applied at the close of business on United Kingdom markets on 21 May 1998. Each IMM sterling contract is made for £62,500, so that people who want to trade large amounts need 16 contracts per £1m. The tick is just $0.0001 per pound; but a price change of $0.0001 per pound alters the price of a contract by $6.25.

Figures for the IMM go to press in the United Kingdom before the IMM closes. So the volume figures in the table show the number of contracts agreed on the previous day, 20 May. Also, the open interest figures show how many contracts were held at the start of 20 May by people who had not closed out. The other figures show the opening prices for 21 May, together with the highest, lowest and latest futures prices that applied when United Kingdom markets closed. The contracts made at that latest price for maturity in June agreed a futures price of $1.6278 for £1. This price was $0.0028 lower than the price that applied at the same time on the previous day.

Table 5.6 Examples of IMM sterling futures (late on 21 May 1998)

Currency	Delivery	Open interest	Volume	Open	High	Low	Latest	Change
Sterling	Jun 98	51,409	13,205	1.6306	1.6328	1.6242	1.6278	−0.0028
	Sep 98	972	80	1.6184	1.6220	1.6180	1.6204	−0.0036

LIFFE long-term interest rate futures

Table 5.7 gives two examples of LIFFE long-term interest rate futures, each one having a different maturity date. The figures applied at the close of business on 21 May 1998. LIFFE allows only four delivery months a year with these futures. The contracts mature at 1100 two business days before the last business day of the delivery month, that is 26 June and 28 September 1998 for the examples shown. The prices are in pounds and pence, and the tick is 1p or £0.01.

The open interest figures show the total numbers of contracts held at the start of 21 May by people who had not closed out. The volume figures show the number of contracts made during the day. The other figures show the opening, highest, lowest and settlement futures prices for the day, together with the change in the settlement price since the end of the previous day. The settlement figure of 108.60 for the 28 September futures means that typical contracts made for 28 September at the end of 21 May agreed a gilt price of £108.60. If the spot long-term interest rate at 1100 on 28 September was low enough to send the gilt price over £108.60, then futures buyers who had agreed that price and who had not closed out would by then have received payments through the marking-to-market process, while sellers would by then have made payments, and vice versa. If a seller chose to deliver gilts some days before the maturity date, as is allowed, then the payments would be based on the settlement price on the day selected. The futures price for September was above that for June, which implies that people expected interest rates to fall in between, causing gilt prices to rise.

Each LIFFE long-term interest rate futures contract is for 500 hypothetical gilts or notional gilts. This term arises because LIFFE does not specify a particular gilt. Instead, its only requirement is that, in principle, the gilt delivered should have a 7% coupon and a redemption date between 10 and 15 years after the maturity date of the futures contract. So the obligation in these contracts is merely for futures sellers to deliver 500 7% gilts with between 10 and 15 years to redemption. If, when the futures contract is agreed, the futures price is, say, £108.60, then the futures buyer agrees to pay £54,300, that is £108.60 for each of 500 gilts, and will expect to receive 500 7% coupon gilts in return. There may be several 7% gilts in circulation, and their prices will all tend to be slightly different. So futures sellers will choose to deliver the one with the lowest price.

In practice, sellers need not even deliver gilts with a 7% coupon, for LIFFE also allows them to deliver many others with redemption dates between 10 and

Table 5.7 Examples of LIFFE notional UK gilt futures (end of 21 May 1998)

Future	Maturity	Open interest	Volume	Open	High	Low	Sett.	Change
Long gilt	Jun 98	230,119	110,573	108.08	108.49	108.08	108.38	+0.29
	Sep 98	2,164	822	108.43	108.67	108.43	108.60	+0.31

15 years. These non-7% coupon gilts may have very different prices from any 7% coupon gilts, because gilts with the highest coupons tend to have the highest prices. So, as the buyer must pay £54,300, the seller need not deliver exactly 500 of any non-7% gilt, and LIFFE works out how many must be delivered. It does so by working out what price each **deliverable gilt** would have if it had the redemption yield that would give every 7% gilt a price of £100. If a 7% gilt has a price of £100, then it earns a return of 7% on a six-month basis. Using the formula given in Chapter 1.9, it can be shown that this is equivalent to an annual rate of about 7.12%. So 7% gilts will have prices of £100 if their redemption yields are about 7.12%. If the redemption yields on all other gilts were also about 7.12%, then, for example, a 6% gilt with 10 years to run would have a price of £92.89. As £92.89 is 0.9289 times the £100 price of a 7% coupon gilt, the 6% gilt has a **conversion factor** of 0.9289 and the number to be delivered would be 500/0.9289 or 538. In contrast, a 12% gilt with 15 years to run would have a price of £145.98 and a conversion factor of 1.4598, so the number of gilts to be delivered would be 500/1.4598 which is 343.

The conversion factors, and thus the numbers of gilts to be delivered, reflect the prices which deliverable gilts would have *if* each had a 7.12% redemption yield. But on any given day, few if any gilts have prices that give them yields of just 7.12%, so their prices vary by slightly different amounts from those which would give them yields of 7.12%. So, for example, the actual costs of bundles of 538 6% 10-year gilts, 343 12% 15-year gilts, and various 500 7% coupon gilts will all differ slightly from each other. As futures sellers can choose between all of these bundles, they will prefer to deliver the bundle whose current cost is the lowest. The gilt concerned in this bundle is called the **cheapest to deliver** (CTD) gilt. The CTD gilt may change several times over the lifetime of a futures contract, but at any moment in time people can readily work out which gilt it is.

Identifying the CTD gilt helps investors to work out how much the price of the notional futures gilt will change if interest rates change. To see this, suppose that the CTD gilt is the 12% 15-year gilt. The price of the notional 7% gilt is equal to 1/1.4598 that of the CTD gilt. So the price of the notional gilt should change by 1/1.4598 times any change in the price of the CTD gilt. If interest rates change, then the required yield on the CTD will change, and its price will change to ensure that its actual yield equals its required yield. The change in its price in relation to a one basis point change in its yield is given by its basis point value, as explained in Chapter 2.8. If its basis point value is BPV_C, then the basis point value of the notional futures gilt, BPV_F, will be BPV_C/CF_C, where CF_C is the conversion factor of the CTD gilt.

In addition to notional UK gilt futures on 7% gilts with 10–15 years to run, LIFFE offers so-called '5-year gilt futures' on 7% gilts with 4–7 years to run. It also offers several other similar long-term interest rate futures that are based on notional foreign central government bonds. Thus it offers Bund futures on notional German bonds with 8½–10½ years to run, Bobl futures on notional German bonds with 3½–5¼ years to run, and also futures on notional Italian bonds and notional Japanese bonds.

LIFFE short-term interest rate futures

Table 5.8 gives two examples of LIFFE short-term sterling interest rate futures, each one having a different maturity date. The figures applied at the close of business on 21 May 1998. LIFFE offers only four delivery months a year with these futures. The contracts mature at 1100 on the third Wednesday of the delivery month, that is 16 December and 17 March for the ones shown.

The open interest figures show the total numbers of contracts held at the start of 21 May by people who had not closed out. The volume figures show the numbers of contracts made during the day. The other figures show the opening, highest, lowest and settlement futures prices for the day and the change in the settlement price since the end of the previous day. The settlement figure of 92.97 for the March 1999 futures means that typical contracts made at the end of 21 May for 17 March agreed an interest rate of 7.03%, that is $(100 - 92.97)\%$. The settlement figure was 0.10 higher than the day before, so the figure then was 92.87, which means the agreed interest rate then was 7.13%. Thus a rise in the settlement figure corresponds to a fall in the agreed interest rate.

By 17 March, any long and short hedgers who agreed a futures figure of 92.97, and who had not closed out, would have respectively paid or received compensation through the marking-to-market process if the spot short-term interest rate, specifically the three-month LIBOR, exceeded 7.03% at 1100 that day. LIFFE sets the compensation at the difference in interest that is due on a £500,000 deposit over three months. Suppose the maturity day spot rate was 1.6% over the agreed futures rate at 8.63%. A three-month £500,000 deposit would earn £10,787.50 at 8.63% and £8,787.50 at the futures rate of 7.03%, so the compensation would be (£10,787.50 − £8,787.50), that is £2,000. This figure could be more readily calculated as ¼(1.6%), or 0.4%, of £500,000, that is £2,000. The tick on these futures is 0.01. A change of 0.01% in the agreed figure, say from 92.97 to 92.98, would change the compensation payments due by ¼(0.01%) of £500,000, that is by £12.50.

LIFFE offers several other short-term interest rate futures contracts. These include futures that offer compensation payments which are based on the London banks' interbank three-month deposit rates for Euromarks, Eurolira, Euroswiss francs, Euryen and euros. It also has futures that offer compensation payments which are based on one month London deposit rates for Euromarks.

Table 5.8 Examples of LIFFE three-month sterling futures (end of 21 May 1998)

Future	Maturity	Open interest	Volume	Open	High	Low	Sett.	Change
Three-month	Dec 98	124,176	37,540	92.70	92.79	92.70	92.78	+0.09
sterling	Mar 99	104,760	27,471	92.90	92.98	92.90	92.97	+0.10

LIFFE stock index futures

Table 5.9 gives an example of a LIFFE FTSE 100 Index futures contract. The figures applied at the close of business on 21 May 1998. LIFFE allows only four delivery months a year with these futures. The contracts mature at 1030 on the third Friday of the delivery month, which is 19 June 1998 for the example shown. The tick is 0.5 index points. LIFFE also offers two similar futures contracts that are based on the FTSE 250 index and the FTSE Eurotop 100 index.

The open interest figure shows how many contracts were held at the start of 21 May by people who had not closed out. The volume figure shows how many contracts were made during the day. The other figures show the opening, highest, lowest and settlement futures indices for that day, and the change in the settlement figure since the end of the previous day. The 5,979.0 means that typical contracts made at the end of 21 May for 19 June agreed a FTSE index of 5,979.0. Each contract requires compensation of £12.50 for each half-point that the average FTSE 100 index between 10.10 and 10.30 on the maturity day differs from the agreed level. So if the average on 19 June was, say, 50 points below 5,979.0, then any long and short hedgers who had agreed a futures index of 5,979.0, and who had not closed out, would by then have respectively paid or received compensation of £1,250 through the marking-to-market process, that is £25 for each point.

Table 5.9 Example of LIFFE FTSE 100 Index futures (end of 21 May 1998)

Period	Open interest	Volume	Open	High	Low	Sett.	Change
Jun 98	157,962	20,366	5970.0	6024.0	5951.0	5979.0	+54.0

LIFFE freight index futures

Table 5.10 gives an example of a LIFFE BIFFEX freight index future. The figures applied at the close of business on 21 May 1998. These futures mature at 1200 on the last business day of the month, which is 31 July 1998 in the example shown. The tick is one whole index point.

The open interest figure shows how many contracts were held at the start of 21 May by people who had not closed out. The volume figure shows how many contracts were made during the day. The other figures show the highest, lowest, and settlement futures indices for that day, and the change in the settlement price since the end of the previous day. The 880 means that typical contracts

Table 5.10 Example of LIFFE BIFFEX index futures (end of 21 May 1998)

Period	Open interest	Volume	High	Low	Sett.	Change
Jul 98	384	129	891	880	880	−15

made at the end of 21 May for 31 July agreed a Baltic Freight Index of 880; the **Baltic Freight Index** is calculated daily by the Baltic Mercantile and Shipping Exchange – or, more simply, the Baltic Exchange – in London, and it is an index of the cost of carrying dry freight by cargo ship. Each LIFFE contract requires compensation of $10 for each point that the average index on the maturity date and the previous four days differs from the agreed level. If the 31 July index was, say, 35 points below 880, then any long and short hedgers who had agreed a futures index of 880 and who had not closed out would by then have paid or received through the marking-to-market process the sum of $350, that is $10 for each of those 35 points.

5.7 HEDGING WITH STANDARDISED CONTRACTS

The standardisation of futures contracts means that hedgers can rarely make precisely the hedges they want. This section considers some of the problems this poses and some appropriate responses.

Timing problems

One problem with futures is that they rarely mature on the day which hedgers would most like. Suppose it is 10 April and a company wishes to borrow £1m short-term on 10 October. It wishes to hedge against high interest rates by using a LIFFE short-term interest rate futures, but no futures contracts mature on 10 October. The closest available maturity dates are the third Wednesdays of September and December, say 17 September and 17 December. It may seem that the best strategy is to use the 17 September futures. However, there is a risk that interest rates might be very stable until 17 September, so that the marking-to-market payments made by or to the company by 17 September might be very small, yet interest rates might rise sharply between 17 September and 10 October. It is always wise to use futures that mature after the required date and close out on that date. So here the company should use the December futures and close out on 10 October.

Strip hedges and stack hedges

Sometimes with futures it is appropriate to make a series, or strip, of futures contracts and so create a **strip hedge**. This occurs when people want to hedge over more than one point in time. Suppose, for simplicity, that it is the third Wednesday in December so that LIFFE short-term interest rate futures contracts will be maturing in exactly three, six, nine and 12 months. A company has £10m. It does not expect to have to spend this for at least a year, but it wants to place it in a succession of three-month deposits so that it could withdraw the money fairly quickly if necessary. The rate on each of these deposits will be linked to LIBOR at the start of the relevant three months. The company is worried that LIBOR could soon fall, so that it might get low rates on all the three-month deposits except the first one.

The company can hedge against low short-term interest rates by buying a series of three short-term interest rate futures contracts which will mature in three, six and nine months respectively. For then, if the three-month LIBOR on any of those days turns out to be below the futures rate agreed in the relevant contract, the company will have received compensation through the marking-to-market process. This compensation will offset the lower rates earned on the following three-month deposit. As each LIFFE contract gives compensation on a deposit of £500,000, the company will need 20 contracts for each date. Of course, if interest rates rise and the company gets more interest on its deposits, then it will also have to pay compensation on its futures contracts through the marking-to-market process, so it will not gain any benefit for itself through the higher rates.

If the company did not expect to need the money for a much longer period, say three years, then it might seek a longer strip hedge. However, there is a problem here in that futures contracts are rarely agreed for maturity dates much over a year or two ahead. The best response is simply to make new contracts as soon as they become available, while also carrying each existing contract until maturity, or closing out just before maturity. This is called a **stack hedge** or a **rolling hedge**.

Cross and weighted hedges

Suppose that X wants to buy 100 tonnes of oats in one year's time and that he wants to hedge against a rise in the spot price from today's price. Oats are a grain crop, like barley and wheat, but futures contracts are not available for oats, even though they are available for barley and wheat. X's best strategy using futures might seem to be to make a futures contract to buy 100 tonnes of wheat in one year and to close out just before maturity. For if grain prices rise over the year, then futures prices should also rise, so X should make a gain when the wheat futures contract is closed out with a reversing trade to sell wheat at the new higher futures price. This gain will offset the loss he incurs by buying oats at a price higher than today's price. Using a futures contract on one underlying asset to hedge against changes in the price of another is called making a **cross hedge**.

However, suppose that oats prices are more volatile than wheat prices. Suppose, also, that grain prices rise. Then wheat futures prices will rise but oats spot prices will rise even more. So the gain that X makes by closing his wheat futures at a higher wheat futures price will be too small to compensate him for having to buy oats at a higher oats spot price. In this situation, the appropriate response is for X to make a **weighted hedge** by agreeing a futures contract to buy more than 100 tonnes of wheat, perhaps 105 tonnes. In other words, X needs a futures **hedge ratio** of 1.05.

It is possible that a hedge ratio of 1.05 will give a perfect hedge in that the compensation secured is exactly what is needed. But it would only be possible to work out in advance the ratio that would secure a perfect hedge if the spot prices of the two assets involved always moved by identical percentage amounts, and they rarely do. However, hedgers can look at the past movements of the two asset prices and see what the outcomes would have been for different possible hedge ratios. Some ratios might have secured results which would have ranged from large gains to large losses while others might have given a smaller range or spread of outcomes. Many hedgers try to discover and use the ratio which would previously have given the smallest spread of outcomes.

The profits or losses from weighted cross hedges can be measured by adaptations of (5.1) and (5.3). Those formulae assumed that hedgers would in future buy or sell on the spot market a particular quantity of a particular asset, say one tonne of barley, and that they would hedge against price changes by today making a futures contract to buy or sell the same quantity of the same asset. But consider hedgers who wish in future to trade one tonne of oats on the spot market and who hedge by making a futures contract today to buy or sell H tonnes of wheat, so that H is the hedge ratio. Suppose, finally, that they will close out at the time when they make their trades on the spot market. Then the adapted formulae for their profits and losses for a tonne of oats are:

$$\Pi_{\text{LONG HEDGE}} = (P_S - P_{SC}) + H(P_{FC} - P_F) \tag{5.5}$$

$$\Pi_{\text{SHORT HEDGE}} = (P_{SC} - P_S) + H(P_F - P_{FC}) \tag{5.6}$$

(5.5) and (5.6) can be rearranged and re-expressed as:

$$\Pi_{\text{LONG HEDGE}} = -\Delta P_S + H\Delta P_F \tag{5.7}$$

$$\Pi_{\text{SHORT HEDGE}} = \Delta P_S - H\Delta P_F \tag{5.8}$$

Δ is the Greek letter delta which is used for changes. ΔP_S is $(P_{SC} - P_S)$, that is the change in the spot price of the asset to be hedged between the day when the futures contract is closed out and the day when it is agreed. ΔP_F is $(P_{FC} - P_F)$, that is the change in the futures price of the asset underlying the futures contract between the day when the contract is closed out and the day when it is agreed.

Suppose the hedgers want to set whatever H would have secured the lowest possible spread of figures for Π. Section 3.3 noted that spreads can be measured by variances, so the hedgers may set the **minimum variance hedge ratio**. It can be shown mathematically that this means setting H so that:

$$H_{\text{LONG HEDGE}} = \text{covariance}(\Delta S, \Delta F)/\text{variance}(\Delta F) \tag{5.9}$$

$$H_{\text{SHORT HEDGE}} = -\text{covariance}(\Delta S, \Delta F)/\text{variance}(\Delta F) \tag{5.10}$$

The minus sign in (5.10) means that a short position should be adopted in the futures contract.

It will be recalled from Sections 3.3 and 3.5 that variances and covariances are estimated from samples. A series of n periods, such as days or weeks, is needed, and in each period the value for ΔS and ΔF must be observed. Then the mean values for ΔS and ΔF must be calculated. Then, in each period, the difference between the observed ΔS and the mean ΔS must be worked out, and also the difference between the observed ΔF and the mean ΔF. These differences may be defined respectively as x_S and x_F. Then it can readily be shown that (5.9) and (5.10) can be re-written as:

$$H_{\text{LONG HEDGE}} = \Sigma(x_S x_F)/\Sigma(x_F)^2 \tag{5.11}$$

$$H_{\text{SHORT HEDGE}} = -\Sigma(x_S x_F)/\Sigma(x_F)^2 \tag{5.12}$$

Weighted cross hedges with long-term interest rate futures

Hedging with long-term interest rate futures always involves a cross hedge because they concern notional gilts, whereas hedgers can only buy or sell actual gilts. Suppose Y owns 50,000 gilts and wishes to sell them in six months. She hedges against a fall in their price by agreeing some long-term interest rate futures for the first available maturity date after six months. In these contracts, she will sell notional gilts at an agreed futures price. She will close out her futures position in six months when she sells her own gilts. She trusts, reasonably enough, that if interest rates rise and push down the spot price of the gilts that she owns, then they will also push down the spot price of the notional gilts in the futures contracts. This means that the futures price of those gilts should also fall, so that she will make a gain by the time she closes out with a reversing trade to buy gilts at the new lower futures price. This gain will compensate her for the fall in the price of her gilts.

Y finds that LIFFE offers long-term interest rate futures contracts which will mature soon after the time when she wishes to sell her gilts. Each LIFFE contract is for 500 gilts. Y owns 100 times as many gilts, so it may seem that she should make 100 futures contracts. However, it might be better for her to make a weighted hedge with a different number of contracts. The reason is that the impact on the price of her gilts of, say, a 0.01% rise in interest rates or yields, that is a one basis point rise, may be different from its impact on the price of the notional gilts in the futures contract.

To investigate this, Y compares the basis point value of the gilts which she wishes to hedge, BPV_H, with the basis point value of the gilts in the futures contract, BPV_F. Section 5.6 showed that BPV_F equals BPV_C/CF_C, where BPV_C and CF_C are the basis point value and the conversion factor of the cheapest to deliver gilt. Suppose that BPV_C is 9p, so that the price of the CTD gilt changes by 9p for each one basis point change in interest rates, and suppose its conversion factor is 1.2. Then BPV_F equals 9/1.2 or 7.5p, so that the price of the gilts in the futures contract changes by 7.5p for each one basis point change in interest rates. Finally, suppose the basis point value of Y's gilts, BPV_H, is 6p, so that the price of her gilts changes by 6p for each one basis point change in interest rates.

In this case, Y needs 80 futures contracts for 500 notional gilts each, or 40,000 in all. For if interest rates rise by, say, one basis point, then the value of her gilts will fall by 50,000 times 6p, which is £3,000. Yet at the same time, the value of the notional gilts will fall by 40,000 times 7.5p, which is also £3,000. In turn, the futures price of those gilts should fall by about 7.5p. This means that Y could secure a gain of about £3,000 by closing out with reversing trades to buy 40,000 notional gilts at the new lower futures price. In general, the futures hedge ratio required, that is the required ratio of futures gilts to actual gilts, is given by BPV_H/BPV_F, which here is 6/7.5 or 0.8. So Y needs futures contracts for 40,000 notional gilts to hedge the 50,000 gilts she owns.

Weighted cross hedges with stock index futures

Weighted cross hedges may also be used for hedging portfolios of shares with stock index futures. Suppose a fund manager has a well-diversified portfolio worth £96,000,000. He fears that the FTSE 100, which is currently standing at 6,000, may soon fall sharply. He might reckon that each one point fall will reduce the value of his portfolio by 1/6,000th or £16,000. He might also recall that with a LIFFE FTSE stock index futures contract, he could secure £25 worth of compensation for each point that the index was below the futures level on a given maturity day. So 640 contracts would secure him £16,000 compensation for every one point fall.

However, this approach overlooks the fact that his portfolio might be more or less volatile than the FTSE 100. Suppose it is more volatile, so that a one point fall in the FTSE 100 index would reduce the value of his portfolio by 1/4,800th instead of 1/6,000th. Then each one point fall would reduce the value of his portfolio by £20,000. With compensation at £25 a point, he would need 800 futures contracts to ensure that he was compensated by £20,000 for each one point fall. In this example, his portfolio is assumed to move in the same direction and at the same time as the FTSE 100, but to be more sensitive. Thus it is reckoned to have a β of 1.25 with respect to the FTSE 100, for a change of 1/4,800 is 1.25 times a change of 1/6,000.

5.8 FURTHER USES OF FUTURES CONTRACTS

This section illustrates five further uses of futures contracts.

Using commodity futures to speculate on changes in carrying costs

Suppose it is 23 January and the spot price of wheat is £100 per tonne. The carrying cost is currently £1 per tonne per month. Recall from Section 5.3 that for storable crops between harvests, the futures price for any given maturity date should always equal the spot price plus the cost of carrying until that date. So the futures prices for 23 March and 23 May will be £102 and £104. X believes that the carrying cost will rise. Maybe X believes that interest rates will rise or that storage costs will rise. If X is confident, then he can speculate as follows. He can agree one futures contract to sell some wheat on 23 March at £102, and he can agree another futures contract to buy some wheat on 23 May at £104. Suppose he makes one contract for each day, each contract involving 100 tonnes. An investor who adopts two futures positions for the same underlying asset, with a different maturity date for each position, is said to be making a **calendar spread**.

Suppose, too, that X is proved right, and that by February carrying costs have risen to £1.50 per tonne per month. No matter what the spot price might be, X can then close out both his futures positions and make a gain. Suppose, for example, that he closes out on 23 February when the spot price is £S per tonne.

The futures price for 23 March will now be £S + £1.50, while the futures price for 23 May will now be £S + £4.50. Under his first March contract, X agreed to receive 100(£102); by closing it out with an offsetting contract to buy wheat in March, he agrees to pay 100(£S+£1.50). Under his first May contract, X agreed to pay 100(£104); by closing it out with an offsetting contract to sell wheat in May, he agrees to receive 100(£S + £4.50). His net income, that is his gain, will be 100(£102 – £S – £1.50 – £104 + £S + £4.50), which is 100(£1), or £100.

Using currency futures to speculate on changes in interest rates

Calendar spreads may also be used with currency futures. Suppose it is 15 March. Suppose, too, that the spot price of sterling in terms of United States dollars is $1.65, while the futures price for £1 on 15 June is $1.66 and the futures price for £1 on 15 September is $1.67. The fact that the futures prices of sterling exceed the spot price means that there is a positive carrying cost for sterling, which in turn means that United States interest rates exceed United Kingdom interest rates. For the discussion in Chapter 4 of formula (4.1) implies that a carrying cost for sterling will arise if the interest lost on the dollars used to buy sterling exceeds the interest which sterling itself earns.

Next, suppose that an investor Y believes that, from May, United States and United Kingdom interest rates will be the same. Then she will expect that, in May, the futures prices of sterling for both June and September will equal the current May spot price. Thus she believes that the carrying cost of sterling will fall; indeed, in this example, she believes that it will fall to zero. If Y is confident, then she can speculate as follows. She can agree today, on 15 March, to buy some sterling on 15 June at a futures price of $1.66, and she can agree to sell some sterling on 15 September at a futures price of $1.67. Say she agrees to buy £1m on 15 June and to sell £1m on 15 September.

By May, Y expects the two futures prices to equal the current spot price. Suppose that by 21 May she is proved right and the two futures prices are equal to the current spot price. Then Y can close out both her futures positions and gain, no matter what the 21 May spot price is. To see this, suppose that the spot price and the futures prices of sterling on 21 May are all £1 = $$D$. Then, on 21 May, she can close out her June futures position by agreeing to sell £1m on 15 June at $$D$. Thus she is agreeing to pay $1.66m under her first June contract and to receive $$D$m under her second. Also, on 21 May, she can close out her September futures position by agreeing to buy £1m on 15 September at $$D$. Thus she is agreeing to receive $1.67m under her first September contract and to pay $$D$m under her second. Taking the four payments together, she will make a net gain of $(–1.66 + D + 1.67 – D)m. This is $0.01m, or $10,000, and is independent of D.

Using short-term interest rate futures to speculate on changes in the time structure of interest rates

Suppose today is 18 June and that, at present, interest rates on all deposits are at rates equivalent to 7.82% a year. Then, as noted in Section 1.9, three-month deposits will have quoted rates of 7.60%, while six-month deposits will have quoted rates that are 0.07% higher at 7.67%. Moreover, as noted in Section 4.8, the FRA rate for three-month deposits starting in three months will be 7.60%, and the same rate should apply to three-month interest rate futures contracts maturing in three-months' time on 18 September. Thus the September short-term interest rate futures price will be quoted as 92.40. Suppose, too, that most investors expect spot interest rates to remain constant. Then they will expect the three- and six-month rates on 18 September to equal their present rates, so that the current futures price for short-term interest rate futures contracts maturing on 18 December should also be 92.40.

Suppose, next, that X has different expectations from most investors, for he believes that, before 18 September, the true annual rates on six-month deposits will exceed those on three-month deposits, so that the gap in the quoted rates will widen from the current 0.07%. There are various ways in which this gap could widen. For example, the six-month rate could rise, or the three-month rate could fall, or they could both rise with the six-month rate rising more than the three-month rate, and so on. X is unsure which of these possibilities will occur, but suppose, for the moment, that he thinks the most likely possibility is that the three-month rate will remain at 7.60%, while the six-month rate will rise to 8.00%. If the three-month and six-month rates on 18 September are indeed 7.60% and 8.00%, then the FRA rate on 18 September for three-month deposits starting on 18 December will be 8.24%, as shown in Section 4.8. Thus the futures price for 18 December should be quoted as 91.76.

If X is confident of his expectation, then he can speculate by making a calendar spread using LIFFE short-term interest rate futures. He could today agree a futures contract in which he will receive compensation in September if the interest rate is then below 7.60%, and vice versa, as given by the current September futures price of 92.40. He can also agree another futures contract in which he will receive compensation in December if the interest rate then is above 7.60%, and vice versa, as given by the current December futures price of 92.40. Both sets of compensation will refer to three-month deposits of £500,000.

When September comes, X can close out both positions, and he will make a profit if his expectations prove correct. Say he closes them out just before his September contract matures. He will close out this contract with an offsetting one in which he will receive compensation on 18 September if the interest rate is then above 7.60%, and vice versa, as given by the current September futures price of 92.40, and so he will make neither a gain nor a loss on his two September contracts taken together. He will also close out his December contract with an offsetting contract in which he will receive compensation in December if the interest rate on 18 December is below 8.24%, and vice versa, as given by the current December futures price of 91.76. This means he will make a gain on his two December contracts taken together. This can be seen most simply by supposing he allows both contracts to run to maturity. For then, if the spot rate in December is between 7.60% and 8.24%, he will receive compensation under both contracts. Conversely, if the spot rate is above 8.24%, then he will receive more compensation under his first contract than he pays under the second, and if the spot rate is below 7.60%, then he will receive more compensation under his second contract than he will pay under the first. But, in fact X, will receive his net gain through the marking-to-market system by the time he closes out in September.

In this example, X neither gained nor lost by making and closing out his September contract. However, it would be worth making this contract because then X would be protected against any general fall in interest rates. For example, if the three-month rate on 18 September was 5.00% while the six-month rate was 5.40%, then it can be shown using formula (4.7) that the three-month FRA rate for 18 December, and hence the futures rate for that day, would be 5.73%. In this case, X would lose when he closed out his December contract to pay compensation if interest rates were below 7.60% with an offsetting one to receive compensation if interest rates were below 5.73%, but this loss would be more than offset by the gain that he would make when he closed out his September contract to receive compensation if interest rates were below 7.60% with an offsetting one to pay compensation only if interest rates were below 5.00%.

Using long-term interest rate futures to change the duration and BPV of a portfolio

Suppose Y manages a fund that contains £50m invested in five year 9% gilts. Y expects interest rates to fall. This fall will raise the value of her gilts, but it would have more impact on the value of her portfolio if that comprised gilts with a higher duration, for Section 2.8 showed how the prices of long duration securities react more than the prices of short duration securities to changes in interest rates and yields. To get more benefit from the expected rise in interest rates, Y could sell the five-year gilts and use the proceeds to buy, say, 15-year gilts. This strategy would lengthen the duration of her portfolio, and so raise the benefit she would get from a rise in interest rates, but it has the disadvantage that it would incur significant costs such as stockbrokers' commissions.

Y could instead get more benefit from a fall in interest rates if she made some LIFFE long-term interest rate futures contracts to buy gilts. For then, a rise in interest rates would raise gilt prices and so raise the futures price of the gilts in the futures contract, and thus Y could close out her futures position at a profit. So making these futures contracts has the same effect as increasing the duration of her portfolio. Indeed, the more futures contracts Y agrees, the longer will be the effective duration of her portfolio. Another way of seeing the effect of buying the futures is to realise that it means that the value of her portfolio will rise more if there is a fall in interest rates. Thus it changes the basis point value, BPV, of her portfolio.

The BPV of Y's final portfolio can be found from the following formula:

$$BPV_{\text{final portfolio}} = BPV_{\text{initial portfolio}} - N(BPV_{\text{notional futures gilt}}) \qquad (5.13)$$

where N is the number of futures gilts bought. For example, suppose that Y's five-year gilts have a price of £112,80. Then, as noted in section 2.8, they will have a required yield of 6% and a Duration, D, of about 8.39 six month periods, which is about 4.19 years. It was also shown that their modified duration, D^*, was 8.15 six month periods or 4.075 years. The $BPV_{\text{initial portfolio}}$ is given by (2.17) as $-0.0001P_0D^*$, where P_0 here can be taken as the initial price or value of the portfolio. So $BPV_{\text{initial portfolio}}$ is $-0.0001.£50m(4.075)$ which is $-£20,337$.

Suppose Y wants to achieve a $BPV_{\text{final portfolio}}$ of $-£30,000$. And suppose $BPV_{\text{notional futures gilt}}$ is 9.1p or £0.091. Then Y must buy a number of futures gilts, N, such that $-30,000 = -20,375 - 0.091N$. This can be solved to show that N must equal 105,769. So, with 500 gilts per futures contract, Y must agree 105,769/500 futures contracts, that is about 212 contracts. In short, buying 212 futures contracts means that each 0.01% fall in interest rates will raise the value of her portfolio by £30,000, even though it will only raise the value of her gilts by £20,375.

Using stock index futures to speculate on changes in share prices

Suppose that most investors expect little change in share prices before the next FTSE 100 Index futures mature. Then the futures index currently being agreed will be close to the current spot index. Suppose, also, that X has different expectations from most investors, for he believes that share prices will rise. In turn, X also expects the futures index to rise. A simple way of speculating here is to buy some shares now, hoping to sell at a profit when share prices rise. However, this entails spending money and meeting two lots of commissions. An even simpler way to speculate is to agree to some LIFFE FTSE 100 Index futures contracts in which X agrees to pay compensation if the spot index at maturity is below the agreed futures index, an outcome which X deems unlikely, and in which X agrees to receive compensation if the spot index at maturity is above the agreed futures index, an outcome which Y deems likely.

However, X might try to be more subtle. For example, if share prices generally rise, then the rise must be caused by some systematic factor, so the shares with the highest betas will react the most. These shares tend to be those in the smaller companies. So the FTSE 250 Index may rise more than the FTSE 100 Index, for, as noted in Section 2.7, the FTSE 100 Index is based on the 100 largest United Kingdom companies, while the FTSE 250 Index is based on the 250 next largest companies. So X may prefer to make LIFFE futures contracts concerning the FTSE 250 Index futures rather than futures contracts concerning the FTSE 100 Index futures. The only problem is that X would run the risk of losing large sums if share prices fell.

A more conservative speculative strategy would be to agree to FTSE 100 Index futures contracts whereby X would *pay* compensation if the index rose, and also to agree to FTSE 250 Index futures contracts whereby X would *receive* compensation if the index rose. Simultaneously making two related contracts for two different items is often called making a **commodity spread**, even if the underlying assets are not actually commodities. With this particular spread, X will gain if the FTSE 250 Index rises more than the FTSE 100 Index, as should happen if share prices generally rise. For in this case, X could close out both his futures contracts, and the gain he would make by closing out the FTSE

250 Index contract would more than offset the loss that he would make by closing out the FTSE 100 Index contract. X will make only a modest gain with this conservative strategy, but simultaneously he will restrain his loss should share prices fall. For then, the loss that he would make by closing out his FTSE 250 Index contract should be substantially offset by the gain that he would make by closing out his FTSE 100 Index contract. It will not be wholly offset because the FTSE 250 Index will tend to fall more than the FTSE 100 index.

SUMMARY

5.1   Futures are contracts to do deals on future dates at terms agreed when they are made. The contracts are made on exchanges which specify the contracts that must be adopted.

5.2   One party to each futures contract is a clearing house at the exchange. Futures positions are easy to close out by using reversing trades. Most parties do close out before the maturity date.

5.3   There are six main types of futures contract. Commodity futures, currency futures and long-term interest rate futures are agreements to buy and sell and are settled by a delivery. Short-term interest rate futures, stock index futures and freight index futures are agreements that involve a compensation payment. In each case, the agreed futures value, be it a price or interest rate or index, is likely to be close to the value expected at maturity.

5.4   Futures contracts involve a daily system of marking-to-market whereby potential losers and gainers secure their losses and gains as they arise. People who close out realise all their gains and losses by the time they close out.

5.5   Many parties use futures to speculate, often over very short time spans. Hedging with futures gives good protection against adverse changes in the price of the underlying asset, though this protection may be imperfect if the asset being hedged is different from the underlying asset of the futures contract. Also, people who close out may find that the performance of the hedge is affected by changes in the basis, that is in the gap between the spot price and the futures price.

5.6   Major United Kingdom futures exchanges include the London International Financial Futures and Options Exchange (LIFFE) and the London Metal Exchange (LME). Both offer some commodity futures, though the LME contracts have some characteristics of forwards. LIFFE also offers a wide range of financial futures and freight futures. Its long-term interest rate futures relate to notional government bonds but may be settled with actual bonds. Its short-term interest rate futures relate to the three-month interest rate loans made between banks in London. Its stock index futures relate to stock indices. Its freight index futures relate to Baltic Freight indices

5.7   The limited range of futures contracts available means that hedgers can rarely do the precise hedges they would like. Various ways of responding to this problem include strip hedges, stack or rolling hedges, cross hedges and weighted hedges.

5.8   There are several less straightforward uses of futures. Many of these appeal to speculators and involve the use of time spreads or calendar spreads.

QUESTIONS

1.   What is meant by: (a) a scalper; (b) basis; (c) open interest; and (d) a notional gilt?

2.   Two brokers, acting respectively on behalf of X and Y, agree one potato futures contract. What will happen to the open interest figures for this futures if: (a) X and Y have no previous potato futures contracts; (b) X is using the new contract to offset an earlier one; and (c) both X and Y are using the contract to offset earlier contracts?

3.   A trader at the exchange referred to in Table 5.1 (on p. 153) often makes contracts at the close of day at the settlement price. Suppose he makes some tin futures contracts with a maturity date of 17 April at the settlement prices shown in the table. On 10 April he makes a contract to buy 100 tonnes. On 12 April he makes another contract to buy 100 tonnes. On 16 April he closes out both contracts. Assume that the clearing house sets its initial margins as 10% of the contract value, and assume that the trader withdraws any variation margin owing to him at the end of each day. Work out his total variation margin, payments, receipts, and balance for each day.

4.   Suppose it is 21 May. A company treasurer expects to receive £10m on 19 December which is the third Wednesday in December. He plans to place the money in a three-month deposit at LIBID but fears LIBID may fall beforehand. So he agrees some LIFFE three-month sterling futures contracts which happen to mature on 19 December and under which he will be compensated if interest rates are below the futures rate for LIBOR that is agreed in his contract. This rate is implied by the futures price of 93.25. (a) Explain why he might decide to buy 20 LIFFE contracts. (b) What LIBOR rate does 93.25 correspond to? (c) Suppose the EDSP price is 94.50. How much compensation will he receive per contract? (d) Suppose LIBID is always ⅛% below LIBOR. What lending rate does the treasurer effectively guarantee by taking a futures position?

5.   Suppose that the treasurer in Question 4 does indeed buy 20 LIFFE short-term interest futures. Also, interest rates drop, as he predicted. By 1 November, he believes that interest rates have bottomed out, and he decides to close out. The current futures price for the December sterling futures when he closes out is 95.00. (a) Why might he decide to close out? (b) What precisely would

he do to close out? (c) What total payment should he have received through the marking-to-market arrangements when he closes out?

6. Suppose it is 4 June. A fund manager wishes to sell 500,000 identical gilts at the end of September but fears gilt prices may fall. She decides to hedge against a fall in the value of her gilts by making futures contracts to sell many notional LIFFE gilts. The contracts will mature on 28 September and she proposes to close out just before maturity. (a) Assume that BPV_C is 12p and that CF_C is 1.2, and work out BPV_F. (b) Assume also that BPV_H is 5p and work out an appropriate hedge ratio. (c) How many LIFFE contracts should she sell?

7. Consider the following situations and determine whether a long or a short hedge is appropriate. (a) A company plans to issue some debentures in three months' time and fears interest rates may rise. (b) A life insurance company with a large portfolio fears there could be a sharp fall in share prices. (c) An importer suspects that freight costs may soon fall.

8. It is 18 January and the price of barley is £100 a tonne, while the price of wheat is £101 per tonne. Y is unsure whether grain prices will rise or fall before the next harvest, but she is convinced that the gap between wheat and barley prices will soon widen to £2 per tonne. She wants to speculate on this expectation by making a commodity spread. Outline a suitable spread strategy for her.

REFERENCE

LIFFE (1995) *Short-term interest rates: futures and options*. (London: LIFFE).

6 OPTIONS

6.1 WHAT ARE OPTIONS?

Options are contracts which resemble forwards and futures in that two parties agree to do a deal on a future date at terms that are agreed in the contract. These terms often specify a price at which a purchase and delivery will take place, just like the terms in forwards and many futures. But occasionally the terms specify some other value, such as an interest rate or FTSE index, on which a compensation payment will be based. The agreed price or value is called the **exercise price** or **strike price**, and the future date written in the contract is called the **exercise date**, the **expiry date** or the **last trading day**.

However, there is a crucial difference between options and forwards or futures. This difference is that with options one party is allowed to call off the deal. With a **call option**, the party intending to buy has this option or right. With a **put option**, the party intending to sell has this right. In return for having this right, the party who has it pays a non-refundable **premium** or **price** to the other party. So the party who holds the option is seen as *buying* that option. Thus the holder of a call option buys an option to buy something at a later date, while the holder of a put option buys an option to sell something at a later date. The premiums are usually paid at the time when the contracts are agreed. The factors that affect the sizes of option premiums, that is the prices which are paid for options, are discussed at length in the next two chapters.

Topics covered in this chapter

Section 6.2 looks more closely at call options and put options, and it explains who might agree them. Section 6.3 explains that some call and put options are American style options, while others are European style options. Section 6.4 explains that some options are agreed over-the-counter on a tailor-made basis with banks and other dealers, while other options are agreed on **options exchanges** which lay down detailed specifications for the contracts; the latter are called traded options because they can effectively be closed by trading them. Section 6.5 notes some major exchanges for traded options and describes some of the options that they offer. Section 6.6 looks at some so-called 'exotic' options which have special features. Section 6.7 explains why many people simultaneously have two or more different types of option on the same underlying asset. Finally, Section 6.8 looks at warrants which are financial instruments that closely resemble call options.

6.2 CALL OPTIONS AND PUT OPTIONS

How do call options work?

Suppose it is 30 March. X wants to buy one tonne of tin on 30 June and he wants to hedge against a high price. He could agree a futures contract maturing on 30 June in which he would agree to buy one tonne at a futures price of, say £4,000. The gain or loss to X from this futures contract on 30 June will depend on the spot price that day. In Fig. 6.1, the dashed diagonal line marked *Futures* shows the gain or loss that X would secure for a range of possible spot prices running from £0 to £7,000 a tonne. The horizontal axis shows these possible 30 June spot prices, while the vertical axis measures the gain or loss. The futures contract will protect X from spot prices over the futures price, so if the spot price on 30 June exceeds £4,000, then X will gain from the futures contract by buying at £4,000. But the futures contract has the drawback that if the spot price on 30 June is below £4,000, then X must still pay £4,000, so he will lose by paying more than the spot price.

Ideally, X would like a contract that secured the results shown by the kinked line marked *Ideal* in Fig. 6.1. With this contract, if the 30 June spot price was above an agreed figure, say £4,000, then the other party would sell tin to X at £4,000, so X would gain by buying for less than the spot price; but if the 30 June spot price was below £4,000, then X could cancel the agreement and buy at the

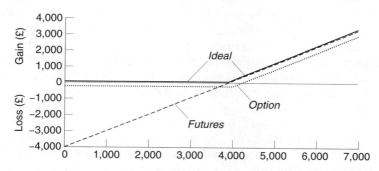

Figure 6.1   Gains and losses from a futures contract, an ideal contract and a call option.

spot price. With this contract X would never lose, but no-one else would agree to it because the other party would never gain. For if the 30 June spot price was above £4,000, then the other party would lose by selling tin to X at £4,000, yet if the spot price was below £4,000, X would buy tin elsewhere so that the other party would sell nothing and gain nothing.

Although X could not hope to agree this ideal contract, he could agree a fairly similar contract by buying a call option. He might pay a non-refundable premium, say £250, to an option seller or **writer**. With a call option, if the 30 June spot price exceeds an agreed exercise price, say £4,000, then X will exercise his option and buy tin from the writer at that agreed price of £4,000; yet if the spot price is below £4,000, X will call off the deal and buy at the spot price. So, like a futures contract, the call option will protect X against his main fear, which is a high spot price on 30 June; but, unlike a futures contract, the option has the extra advantage that X could buy tin at the future spot price if it is low. Admittedly X has to pay the premium to secure this extra advantage.

The gains and losses from the option contract are shown in Fig. 6.1 by the dotted line marked *Option*. If the spot price on 30 June is below £4,000, then X will buy at the spot price, but he will make a £250 loss because of the premium. If the spot price is above £4,000, then X will exercise his option and buy at £4,000, but his gain will be £250 less than the difference between the spot price and £4,000 because of the premium. X may gain a lot if the spot price is high, yet the most he can lose if the spot price is low is his premium. So he has great **upside potential** and little **downside risk**. The converse applies to the writer. She may lose a lot if the expiry day spot price is high and she has to sell tin to X at £4,000 a tonne, while if the spot price is low, she will gain only the premium. To minimise her risks, she will want a high premium or a high exercise price.

Writers of call options often offer call option buyers a variety of exercise prices, charging higher premiums for lower exercise prices. Buyers often respond by selecting low premiums and high exercise prices that are unlikely to be reached. Thus their hedges are often against prices that may exceed the prices used in forward or futures contracts, and so may, in turn, exceed the expected future prices. As a result, call options are often not exercised, in which case all that happens is that their holders just lose the premiums and their writers just gain the premiums. Writers also offer a variety of expiry dates. They charge higher premiums for distant dates because the spot price is likely to move more over a long period, so it could end up very high.

If the writer of a call option already owns the underlying asset, which is tin in the present example, then the option is a **covered call option**; if not, then it is a **naked call option**. A covered call occurs when the writer has a long position in the underlying asset, and thus owns some, and simultaneously has a short position in the option, and is thus liable to have to make a delivery. With a covered call option, if the spot price rises and the option is exercised, thereby causing a loss for the writer, then at least the writer will have made a gain on the asset that was already owned.

How do put options work?

Suppose it is 30 March. Y wants to sell one tonne of tin on 30 June and she wants to hedge against a low price. She could agree a futures contract maturing on 30 June in which she would agree to sell one tonne at a futures price of, say £4,000. The gain or loss to Y from this futures contract on 30 June will depend on the spot price that day. In Fig. 6.2, the dashed diagonal line marked *Futures* shows the gain or loss that Y will secure for a range of possible spot prices running from £0 to £7,000 a tonne. The horizontal axis shows these possible spot prices, while the vertical axis measures the gain or loss. The futures contract will protect Y from spot prices below the futures price, so if the spot price on 30 June is under £4,000, then Y will gain from the futures contract by selling at £4,000. But the futures contract has the drawback that if the spot price on 30 June is above £4,000, then Y must still sell at £4,000, so she will lose by selling for less than the spot price.

Ideally, Y would like a contract that secured the results shown by the kinked line marked *Ideal* in Fig. 6.2. With this contract, if the 30 June spot price was below an agreed figure, say £4,000, then the other party would buy Y's tin at £4,000, so Y would gain by selling for more than the spot price; but if the 30 June spot price was above £4,000, then Y could cancel the agreement and sell at the spot price. With this contract Y would never lose, but no-one else would agree to it because the other party would never gain. For if the 30 June spot price was below £4,000, then the other party would lose by buying Y's tin at £4,000, yet if the spot price was above £4,000, Y would sell her tin elsewhere so that the other party would buy nothing and gain nothing.

Although Y could not hope to agree this ideal contract, she could agree a fairly similar contract by buying a put option. She might pay a non-refundable premium, say £250 a tonne, to an option seller or writer. With a put option, if the 30 June spot price is below an agreed exercise price, say £4,000, then Y will exercise her option and sell tin to the writer at that agreed price of £4,000 a tonne; yet if the spot price is above £4,000, Y will call off the deal and sell her tin at the spot price. So, like a futures contract, the put option will

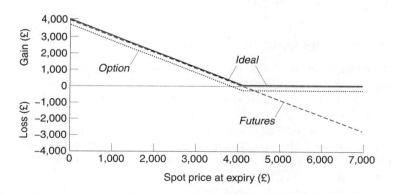

Figure 6.2 Gains and losses from a futures contract, an ideal contract and a put option.

protect Y against her main fear, which is a low spot price on 30 June; but, unlike a futures contract, the option allows Y to sell her tin at the future spot price if it is high. Admittedly X has to pay the premium to secure this extra advantage.

The gains and losses from the option contract are shown in Fig. 6.2 by the dotted line marked *Option*. If the spot price on 30 June is above £4,000 a tonne, then Y will sell at the spot price, but she will make a £250 loss on her option because of the premium. If the spot price is below £4,000, then Y will exercise her option and sell her tin at £4,000, but her gain will be £250 less than the difference between £4,000 and the spot price because of the premium. Y may gain a lot if the spot price is low, yet the most she can lose if the spot price is high is her premium. So she has great upside potential and little downside risk. The converse applies to the writer. He may lose a lot if the expiry day spot price is low and he has to buy Y's tin at £4,000 a tonne, while if the spot price is high, he will gain only the premium. To minimise his risks, he will want a high premium or a low exercise price.

Writers of put options often offer put option buyers a variety of exercise prices, charging higher premiums for higher exercise prices. Buyers often respond by selecting low premiums and low exercise prices that are unlikely to be reached. So their hedges are often against prices that may be below the prices used in forward or futures contracts, and so, in turn, may be below the expected future prices. As a result, put options are often not exercised, in which case all that happens is that their holders just lose the premiums and their writers just gain the premiums. Writers also offer a variety of expiry dates. They charge higher premiums for distant dates because the spot price is likely to move more over a long period, so it could end up very low.

In the example considered here, Y owned some tin which she wanted to sell. Because she had an option to sell some tin which she already owned, her put option is called a **protective put option**. Not all puts are protective ones. For example, a speculator who believes that tin prices will fall below £4,000 may buy a put option with that exercise price. If he is right, he could buy some tin at the spot price just before expiry, and then exercise his option to sell it for £4,000 and so make a profit.

Who buys and sells options?

Hedgers often buy options to secure protection against adverse price movements. Long hedgers, who want to buy the underlying asset, like to buy call options which protect them against high prices, while short hedgers, who want to sell the underlying asset, like to buy put options which protect them against low prices. But options are also very attractive to speculators.

For example, suppose the spot price of the shares in a hypothetical company, LML, is now 200p and suppose X believes it will rise over the next three months to 230p. And suppose X has £2,000 to invest. X could speculate by buying 1,000 shares. If he is right and the spot price in three months is 230p, then his shares will be worth £2,300. But suppose X can buy call options on LML shares with an exercise price of 210p and an expiry date in three months, and suppose the option premium is 12½p per share. Then X can use his £2,000 to buy options on 16,000 shares. If he is right, and the price of LML shares rises to 230p, then these options will be worth 20p each at expiry because they will allow people to buy for 210p shares that are worth 230p. So they will be worth a total of £3,200. So speculators who expect the price of the underlying asset to rise, and who buy call options instead of the asset itself, will gain far more if they are right. However, they will also lose far more if they are wrong. If the spot price ended up below the exercise price at, say, 205p, then the 1,000 shares would be worth £2,050, whereas the options would be worth nothing, because no-one would want an option to buy at 210p shares that were worth less.

Speculators who expect price falls may buy put options. Suppose Y also has £2,000 to invest and she expects the price of LML shares to fall over the next three months to 190p. She may be able to buy put options with an exercise price of 200p for a premium of only 5p each, so she could buy 40,000 options. If the price does fall to 190p, then her options will be worth 10p each at expiry as they allow people to sell for 200p shares that are worth 190p. So her 40,000 options will be worth £4,000. However, they would be worthless if the spot price at expiry was over the exercise price, because no-one would want an option to sell at 200p shares that were worth more.

Writers have a riskier position than option holders. Consequently, most options are written by speculators. Their main hope is that the spot price at expiry will be at a level which ensures that the holders will not exercise their options, in which case the writers will simply keep the premiums. However, options are sometimes written by hedgers, but only if they are making two or more option contracts at the same time. The reasons why they might do this are outlined in Section 6.7.

6.3 AMERICAN STYLE OPTIONS AND EUROPEAN STYLE OPTIONS

The discussion so far has implied that option holders are allowed to exercise their options only on the expiry date. This is true with some options, and options like this are called **European style** options. However, many options permit **early exercise** whereby their holders may exercise the option either at expiry or at any time up to expiry, and options like this are called **American style** options. With both styles, the actual settlement in terms of delivery and payment takes place on a **settlement day** which is usually a day or so after the option is exercised. This slight delay gives the parties time to organise the delivery and the payment once the option has been exercised.

The names European style and American style are misleading because they have absolutely *nothing* to do with the types of option that are most common in America or Europe. On both continents, the vast majority of traded options and many over-the-counter options are American style.

6.4 OVER-THE-COUNTER OPTIONS AND TRADED OPTIONS

People who wish to make option contracts have two alternatives. One is to negotiate a tailor-made over-the-counter option with a specialised intermediary, often a bank. The other is to agree a standardised contract on an exchange; such options can be traded, so they are called traded options.

Over-the-counter options

With **over-the-counter options**, people who want to buy or write options can negotiate with the intermediary and can often agree any expiry date, quantity and strike price that meets their requirements; and in the case of commodities, they can also negotiate the quality and the delivery point. However, this flexibility has the disadvantage that it may make it hard for a party to close out by trading the contract, should the party wish to do so, for it may prove hard to find anyone who is willing to have a contract with the exact specification concerned. However, intermediaries sometimes facilitate closing out by agreeing to make second reversing contracts.

There are many types of over-the-counter option, and these often have slightly different arrangements for settlement. They fall into five main groups, as follows:

1. **Commodity options.** These concern commodities and are settled by a purchase and a delivery.
2. **Currency options.** These concern currencies and are settled by a purchase and a delivery.
3. **Equity options.** These concern individual equities and are usually settled by a compensation payment.
4. **Interest rate options.** These concern gilts and are usually settled by a compensation payment.
5. **Swaptions.** These concern swaps and are discussed in Chapter 9.

Traded options

Traded options are agreed on exchanges which are usually the same exchanges that handle futures. These exchanges insist on standardised contracts. Thus they stipulate the quantity that must be agreed in each contract, they restrict the choice of expiry dates, perhaps to only four each year, and they greatly limit the available strike prices, perhaps to only three. They even constrain the premium that may be agreed; for example, they might stipulate a tick of £1 per tonne, in which case the agreed premium per tonne would have to be a multiple of £1. Furthermore, in the case of commodity futures, they specify the quality and restrict the permitted delivery points. This standardisation makes it easy for parties to close out their positions, as explained shortly.

Most traded options fall into seven groups, as follows:

1. **Commodity options.** These concern commodities; most of them are **commodity futures options** which are settled by the delivery of a commodity futures contract.

2. **Currency options.** These concern currencies. They are sometimes settled by a purchase and a delivery, and are sometimes **currency futures options** settled by the delivery of a currency futures contract.
3. **Equity options.** These concern individual equities and are settled by a purchase and a delivery.
4. **Short-term interest rate futures options.** These concern short-term interest rates and are settled by the delivery of a short-term interest rate futures contract.
5. **Long-term interest rate futures options.** These concern bonds and are settled by the delivery of a long-term interest rate futures contract.
6. **Stock index options.** These concern a FTSE index and are settled by a compensation payment.
7. **Freight index futures options.** These concern the Baltic Freight Index and are settled by the delivery of a BIFFEX futures contract.

Opening a traded option position

To see how traded options are agreed, suppose X wants to buy an American call option for 1,000 LML shares with a strike price of 210p and expiration on 30 June. Suppose each option contract is for 1,000 shares. X contacts a broker who goes to the relevant pit on the exchange floor. She meets brokers acting for clients who wish to write options, and she meets traders who will always buy and write options and who quote separate bid and ask premiums for them. She finds out who will write an option like the one X wants for the lowest premium. Say this is a broker acting for Y who offers a premium of 20p per share. Then the two brokers report to the clearing house which itself agrees *two* call option contracts at this premium. One contract is a call held by X's broker on X's behalf, where the clearning house is the writer, and the other is an identical call where it is the holder and Y's broker is the writer on Y's behalf. So the clearing house receives a premium from X, and then at once pays the same premium to Y. Clearing houses only ever agree options in matching pairs with the same exercise prices, expiry dates and premiums.

The clearing house has no risks. If X ever exercises his option, then it can shift its obligation to sell him 1,000 LML shares at 210p on to someone else by at once exercising an identical option that it holds, like the one with Y. On any given day, the clearing house may be the holder and writer of many identical options. So if X exercises his option, then it may hold many identical options which it could exercise. If so, then it may choose the oldest one or a random one, so it will be most unlikely to select Y's. The clearing house and the brokers make profits by charging commissions. So X has to pay two commissions plus the premium, whereas Y pays two commissions and receives the premium. At 20p per share, the total premiums for their option contracts are £200.

Closing out a traded option position

Suppose X later decides to close out. He asks his broker to make an **offsetting trade**. Strictly, X has to write a call option on 1,000 LML shares with a

210p strike price and expiration on 30 June. The broker goes to the pit to find out who will now pay the highest premium for such an option. Say a trader will pay 22p per share. Then the broker and the trader report to the clearing house. The clearing house could agree a new pair of offsetting call options, buying one from X where he would be the writer, and selling the other to the trader where it would be the writer. But, instead, the trader takes over X's original contract. The trader pays X the premium of 22p per share for this option, so X sells it for £220 in all. So, in this case, X gains £20 from his option, minus all his commissions. It is because option holders like X can sell them, or trade them, that they are called traded options.

If Y later closes out, she must strictly buy an offsetting call option. Her broker must find out who will now write such an option for the lowest premium. Say this is a trader who will today accept 24p per share. Then her broker and the trader report to the clearing house. It could agree a new pair of options, with Y buying one from it, and it buying the other from the trader. Instead, it just transfers Y's writing obligations in her first contract to the trader. Y pays the trader the agreed premium, which is £240 for the 1,000 shares. In this way, Y is said to 'buy her contract back'. She buys it back for £20 more than she originally received, so she loses £20 plus all her commissions.

Margins

People who buy options limit their possible losses to the value of their premiums which are usually paid when the options are agreed. As they can make no further losses, clearing houses require no other payments from them. However, option writers can lose large sums. To cover themselves against writers who might default, clearing houses typically make each writer place *two margins* in an account when the option is written. This account earns interest. One margin is an initial margin which is set at an amount appropriate to the option involved. The other margin is a variation margin which equals the current value of the option, as shown by its current premium or price. So, on the day when the contract is agreed, the writer must pay into the account a sum equal to the initial margin plus the premium received. Thereafter, the writer's position is marked-to-market at the end of each business day. This means that the variation margin must be increased on any day when the option price rises, but may be reduced on any day when the option price falls.

If an option is exercised, either before or at expiry, then its writer must make the required delivery or compensation. After that, any money left in the margin account may be withdrawn. If an option passes expiry without being exercised, then its writer may withdraw all the money in the margin account. Of course, options which are not exercised at expiry are either calls to buy something for more than its current spot price or puts to sell something for less than its current spot price. In either case, these options are worth nothing at expiry. So, here, the variation margin requirements will have fallen to zero. Hence the only money left in the accounts will be the initial fixed margins.

Futures options

Several types of traded option are settled with the delivery of a futures contract rather than with a conventional purchase and delivery. Options like these are called **futures options**. To see how they work, suppose X gets his broker to agree on his behalf a futures call option for one tonne of tin with a strike price of £4,000. As with other traded options, this option will actually be agreed between X and the clearing house. So if X later exercises his option, then the clearing house must itself make an appropriate delivery to X, and in this case it must deliver a futures contract that entitles its holder to buy one tonne of tin at £4,000 when that futures contract matures. To obtain this contract, the clearing house will exercise an equivalent futures call option that it holds against another writer. X will exercise the option only on a day when the futures price of tin is currently over £4,000. Say he exercises it on a day when the futures price is £4,100. Then the writer selected by the clearing house will first have to agree with the clearing house a matched *pair* of futures contracts whose futures price equals the exercise price of the option. One of these contracts will be to buy one tonne of tin at £4,000, and this will be given to X. The other will be to sell one tonne of tin at £4,000, and this will be kept by the writer.

The clearing house will at once ask both the writer and X for initial margins on their new futures contracts. It will also ask the writer for an immediate variation margin of £100, because the writer would lose £100 if the spot price of tin was equal to the current futures price of £4,100 when the writer's futures contract to sell tin matured. But it will give X £100, effectively giving him a negative variation margin payment, because he would gain £100 if the spot price of tin was equal to the current futures price of £4,100 when his futures contract to buy tin matured. In practice, X might at once close out his futures position by making an offsetting futures contract to sell one tonne of tin at the current futures price of £4,100. In this case, there would be no need for him to place an initial margin as his futures position would be closed out, but he would still keep his £100.

Futures options are very suitable for commodity options. If the underlying asset for a commodity option was a commodity, then the writer would have to be prepared to deliver that commodity whenever the option was exercised, which could be on any day over a period of some months. It is much more convenient for the writer to deliver a futures contract. Indeed, futures options are always very convenient for writers, and this has helped to make them popular. Currently, they are the norm for traded interest rate options as well as for traded commodity options.

6.5 EXAMPLES OF OPTION EXCHANGES AND OPTION CONTRACTS

There are exchanges for commodity options and financial options in many countries. Table 6.1 lists the exchanges whose option prices are most often

Table 6.1 Some major options exchanges and their main option contracts

Options exchanges		Main options offered
Commodity options exchanges		
The International Petroleum Exchange, London	IPE	crude oil
The London Metal Exchange	LME	aluminium, copper, lead, nickel, tin, zinc
The London International Financial Futures and Options Exchange	LIFFE[1]	barley, cocoa, coffee, potatoes, sugar, wheat; also BIFFEX freight index futures
Financial options exchanges		
The London International Financial Futures and Options Exchange	LIFFE[1]	equity options, long- and short-term interest rate futures options, stock index options
Le Marché à Terme des Instruments Financiers, Paris	MATIF	interest rate options
The Philadelphia Stock Exchange	PHLX	currency options

[1]LIFFE is pronounced 'life'. It absorbed the London Commodity Exchange (LCE) in 1996 and acquired its commodity futures options from the LCE, but its BIFFEX futures options were initially offered on the Baltic International Freight Futures Exchange in London, now the Baltic Exchange.

quoted in the United Kingdom press, together with some of the option contracts that they offer.

The rest of this section describes some of some of the options noted in Table 6.1. In each case, a table is given showing the premiums that applied on these options at the close of business in the United Kingdom on or about 21 May 1998. The descriptions begin with some ordinary options and then consider some futures options. All of these options could be bought or written by hedgers or speculators, but the descriptions focus chiefly on hedgers.

Philadelphia Stock Exchange currency options

Table 6.2 gives some premiums for American style currency options on the PHLX. The premiums shown are for options for sterling, and they applied at the close of business in United Kingdom markets on 21 May 1998. At that time, the spot exchange rate was about £1 = $1.63. The PHLX allows a wide range of expiry dates and strike prices, but the table covers only three expiry days and two strike prices. Each option expires on the Friday before the third Wednesday in the expiry month. The premiums are in cents per pound, and the tick is $0.01. However, each PHLX sterling option contract is made for £31,250, so anyone buying one contract would pay 31,250 times the premiums shown in the table and, if they exercised it, would buy or sell £31,250. The figure of £31,250 is used so that people need just 32 options contracts per £1m.

Table 6.2 Premiums for some Philadelphia stock exchange sterling options (late on 21 May 1998)

Strike price	Calls			Puts		
	Jun	Jul	Aug	Jun	Jul	Aug
1.62	1.68	2.19	2.66	0.72	1.40	2.17
1.64	0.69	1.22	1.78	1.66	2.46	3.21

Suppose that on 21 May, X anticipated buying sterling in August, using dollars. He hedged against a high price by buying from the clearing house one $1.64 call option contract. This entitled him to buy 31,250 pounds at $1.64 each at any time up to its expiry on 14 August. He paid a premium of 31,250($0.0178), that is $556.25. X would exercise his option only if the price rose above $1.64, and the clearing house would then meet its obligations by exercising another $1.64 call option where it was the holder and making its writer sell it 31,250 pounds at $1.64. In fact, at the moment X bought his option, the clearing house agreed another $1.64 call option where it was the holder, but it would be unlikely to exercise that particular call option if X exercised his. The writers of the $1.64 call options hoped the price would not go above $1.64, or at least not go far above. For if it went above $1.64, then the options would be exercised, and the losses they would make by selling pounds at $1.64 could far exceed the value of the premiums they received.

In contrast, Y anticipated selling pounds in July for dollars. She hedged against a low price by buying from the clearing house one $1.62 put option contract which entitled her to sell 31,250 pounds at $1.62 each at any time up to its expiry on 10 July. She paid a premium of 31,250($0.0140), that is $437.50. Y would exercise her option only if the price fell below $1.62, and the clearing house would then meet its obligations by exercising a $1.62 put option where it was the holder and making its writer buy 31,250 pounds from it at $1.62. In fact, at the moment when Y bought her option, the clearing house agreed another $1.62 put option where it was the holder, but it would be unlikely to exercise that particular put if Y exercised hers. The writers of the $1.62 put options hoped the price would not go below $1.62, or at least not go far below. For if it went below $1.62, then the options would be exercised, and the losses they would make by buying pounds at $1.62 could far exceed the value of the premiums they received.

LIFFE equity options

LIFFE offers American style equity options on the equities of about 75 different United Kingdom companies. Table 6.3 gives the premiums for options on British Petroleum (BP) shares which applied at the close of business on 21 May 1998. At that time, the spot price of BP shares was 930½p. The exchange allows three expiry dates and three exercise prices on each equity option. The table covers all the dates and two of the prices. Each option expires on the third

Table 6.3 Premiums for some LIFFE BP equity options (end of 21 May 1998)

		Calls			Puts		
	Series	Jul	Oct	Jan	Jul	Oct	Jan
BP	900	67½	99	119	28	53½	62½
(930½)	950	41½	76	94	49	77½	86

Wednesday in the expiry month. The premiums are in pence per share, and the tick is ½p. However, each LIFFE equity option contract concerns 1,000 shares, so people buying one contract would pay 1,000 times the premiums shown in the table.

Suppose that on 21 May, X anticipated buying BP shares in July. He hedged against a high price by buying from the clearing house one 950p call option contract which entitled him to buy 1,000 BP shares at 950p at any time up to its expiry on 15 July. He paid a premium of 1,000(41½p), that is £415. He would exercise this option only if the spot price rose above 950p, and the clearing house would then meet its obligations by exercising a 950p call option where it was the holder and making its writer sell 1,000 BP shares to it at 950p. In fact, at the moment when X bought his option, it agreed another 950p call option where it was the holder, but it would be unlikely to exercise that particular call option if X exercised his. The writers of the 950p call options hoped the price would not go above 950p, or at least not go far above. For if it went above 950p, then the options would be exercised, and the losses they would make by selling BP shares at 950p could far exceed the value of the premiums they received.

In contrast, Y anticipated selling BP shares in October. She hedged against a low price by buying from the clearing house one 900p put option contract which entitled her to sell 1,000 BP shares at 900p at any time up to its expiry on 21 October. She paid a premium of 1,000(53½p), that is £535. She would exercise it only if the spot price fell below 900p, and the clearing house would then meet its obligations by exercising a 900p put option where it was the holder and making its writer buy 1,000 BP shares from it at 900p. In fact, at the moment when Y bought her option, it agreed another 900p put option where it was the holder, but it would be unlikely to exercise that particular put if Y exercised hers. The writers of the 900p put options hoped the price would not go below 900p, or at least not go far below. For if it went below 900p, then the options would be exercised, and the losses they would make by buying BP shares at 900p could far exceed the value of the premiums they received.

LIFFE American style stock index options

Table 6.4 gives some premiums for American style stock index options on LIFFE. The premiums shown are for options on the FTSE 100 Index, and they applied at the close of business on 21 May 1998 when the index stood at 5,961.

Table 6.4 Premiums for some LIFFE American FTSE 100 options (end of 21 May 1998)

		FTSE 100 Index (5,961)			
		5,800	5,900	6,000	6,100
Calls	Jul	330½	267	208	154½
	Aug	403½	344	284½	232½
	Sep	462	403	343½	287½
Puts	Jul	125½	161½	203½	256
	Aug	188	226	265½	315
	Sep	216	257	298	344

The exchange allows several expiry dates and also several exercise indices, which it calls exercise prices. However, the table covers only three dates and four exercise prices. Each option expires on the third Friday in the expiry month. As explained below, these options entitle their holders to compensation if the spot FTSE 100 Index on exercise differs in the appropriate direction from the exercise price. The premiums are shown in pence and are the premiums needed to secure 1p compensation for every point difference between the spot FTSE 100 Index and the exercise price. However, each LIFFE contract actually secures £10 compensation for every point difference and requires a payment of 1,000 times the premiums shown on the table. The tick for the premiums shown for 1p per point compensation is ½p.

Suppose that on 21 May X speculated that the FTSE 100 Index would rise by August. In the hope of gaining from the rise, X paid 1,000(232½p), that is £2,325, to the clearing house for one 6,100 call option contract. Then, at any time up to its 21 August expiry date when the FTSE 100 Index was above 6,100, he could exercise it and claim £10 compensation for each point that the index was above 6,100. The clearing house would then meet its obligations by exercising a 6,100 call option where it was the holder and demanding compensation from its writer. The writers of the 6,100 call options hoped the FTSE 100 Index would not go above 6,100, or at least not far above. For if it went above 6,100, then the options would be exercised, and the losses they would make paying compensation could far exceed the value of the premiums they received.

In contrast, Y speculated that the FTSE 100 Index would fall by July. In the hope of gaining from the fall, Y paid 1,000(125½p), that is £1,250, to the clearing house for one 5,800 put option contract. Then, at any time up to its 17 July expiry date when the FTSE 100 Index was below 5,800, she could exercise it and claim £10 compensation for each point that the index was below 5,800. The clearing house would then meet its obligations by exercising a 5,800 put option where it was the holder and demanding compensation from its writer. The writers of the 5,800 put options hoped the FTSE 100 Index would not go below 5,800, or at least not far below. For if it went below 5,800, then the options would be exercised, and the losses they would make by paying compensation could far exceed the value of the premiums they received.

LIFFE European style stock index options

LIFFE also offers some similar European style FTSE 100 Index options. These have slightly different exercise prices from the American style FTSE 100 Index options to avoid confusion. In addition, LIFFE offers European style FTSE 100 Index **FLEX® options**. ® indicates that FLEX, which stands for flexible, is a registered trade mark: it belongs to the Chicago Board Options Exchange Inc (CBOE). These resemble the ordinary European style FTSE 100 Index options except that the parties who agree matched pairs of contracts can agree almost any exercise price they like and almost any expiry date they choose within the next two years. The only constraints are that the expiry day must be a business day, and the parties cannot have a combination of a date and a price that coincides with a combination offered on an ordinary European style LIFFE FTSE 100 Index option. As there are so many different FLEX® contracts, no premiums are given in the press. Finally, LIFFE also offers European style options on the FTSE Eurotop 100 index.

LIFFE commodity futures options

Table 6.5 gives some premiums for American style commodity futures options on LIFFE. The premiums shown are for options on coffee futures and they applied at the close of business on 21 May 1998. The exchange allows several expiry dates and three strike prices. The table covers two dates and all the prices. Each option actually expires on the third Wednesday of the month *before* the expiry month shown in the table. The premiums are in dollars per tonne and the tick is $1 per tonne. However, each LIFFE coffee futures option contract is made for five tonnes of coffee, so anyone buying one contract would pay five times the premium shown in the table and, if they exercised it, would secure a coffee futures contract concerning five tonnes. The futures contract would mature on the last business day of the option's expiry month.

Suppose that on 21 May X anticipated buying coffee in September. He hedged against a high price by buying from the clearing house one $1,950 futures call option contract. He paid a premium of 5($120) or $600 for it. It entitled him to demand, at any time up to its expiry on 19 *August*, a futures contract to buy five tonnes of coffee at a futures price of $1,950. The maturity date of the futures contract would be 30 September. X would exercise his option only if the spot futures price being agreed for coffee futures contracts maturing on

Table 6.5   Premiums for some LIFFE coffee futures options (end of 21 May 1998)

Series	Calls		Puts	
	Jul	Sep	Jul	Sep
1,850	80	164	58	164
1,900	55	125	83	218
1,950	38	120	116	263

30 September rose above $1,950. Say the futures price rose to $2,020 and he exercised the option. Then the clearing house would give him the futures contract and a marked-to-market variation margin payment of $70 per tonne. It would secure the contract and the payment by exercising an identical futures call option where it was the holder. In fact, when X bought his option, the clearing house itself bought an identical one, though it would be unlikely to exercise that particular option if X exercised his.

The writers of the $1,950 futures call options hoped the futures price would not go above $1,950, or at least not go far above. For if it went above $1,950, then the options would be exercised, and they would make losses that could far exceed the value of the premiums they received. A writer whose option was exercised would have to agree two offsetting futures contracts with the clearing house, each at a futures price equal to the strike price of $1,950. One contract would be to buy coffee at $1,950, and the writer would give this to the clearing house to give to someone like X. The other would be to sell coffee at $1,950. The writer would keep this one and suffer. For if the current futures price was, say, $2,020, the clearing house would at once demand a variation margin of $70 per tonne.

In contrast, Y anticipated selling coffee in September. She hedged against a low price by buying from the clearing house one $1,900 futures put option contract. She paid a premium of 5($218) or $1,090 for this option. It entitled her to demand, at any time up to its expiry on 19 August, a futures contract to sell five tonnes of coffee at a futures price of $1,900. The maturity date of the futures contract would be 30 September. Y would exercise her option only if the spot futures price being agreed for coffee futures contracts maturing on 30 September fell below $1,900. Say the futures price fell to $1,810 and she exercised the option. Then the clearing house would give her the futures contract and a marked-to-market margin variation payment of $90 per tonne. It would secure both the contract and the payment by exercising an identical futures put option where it was the holder. In fact, when Y bought her option, the clearing house itself bought an identical one, though it would be unlikely to exercise that particular one if Y exercised hers.

The writers of the $1,900 futures put options hoped the futures price would not go below $1,900, or at least not go far below. For if it went below $1,900, then the options would be exercised, and they would make losses that could far exceed the value of the premiums they received. A writer whose option was exercised would have to agree two offsetting futures contracts with the clearing house, each at a futures price equal to the $1,900 strike price. One contract would be to sell coffee at $1,900, and the writer would give this to the clearing house to give to someone like Y. The other would be to buy coffee at $1,900. The writer would keep this one and suffer. For if the current futures price was, say, $1,810, the clearing house would at once demand a variation margin of $90 per tonne.

LIFFE long-term interest rate futures options

LIFFE's long-term interest rate futures options are all American style options to secure a LIFFE long-term interest rate futures contract. Some of these

Table 6.6 Premiums for some LIFFE long gilt futures options (end of 21 May 1998)

Exercise price	Calls			Puts		
	Jul	Aug	Sep	Jul	Aug	Sep
10900	0.41	0.68	0.85	0.81	1.08	1.25
10950	0.26	0.48	0.65	1.16	1.38	1.55

options are options to secure a long gilt futures contract, while others are options to secure similar futures contracts for German government bonds, both Bunds and Bobls, and Italian government bonds. Table 6.6 gives some premiums for options on the long gilt futures contracts. The premiums applied at the close of business on 21 May 1998. The exchange allows few expiry dates and exercise prices, and the table covers three expiry dates and two exercise prices. The premiums are in pounds with a tick of £0.01. The premiums on these options are not paid until the options are exercised or expire.

The futures contracts which underlie these options mature two days before the last business day of the quarter in which the option's expiry month lies; this is because there are no other LIFFE long gilt futures contracts available that will mature any sooner. So the underlying asset for all the options shown was a futures contract that matured on 28 September. The options themselves actually expire six business days *before the first day* of their expiry months. So the expiry dates for the options shown were 23 June, 24 July and 21 August. The premiums shown are the premiums per gilt. However, each option contract concerns one futures contract which itself concerns 500 notional gilts, so anyone buying one option contract would pay 500 times as much as the premiums shown.

Suppose that on 21 May X expected to lend long-term in September. Fearing low interest rates and so, equivalently, high gilt prices, he bought from the clearing house one 10,950 September futures call option contract. He paid a premium of 500(£0.65) or £325 for it. It entitled him to demand, up to its expiry on 21 August, a futures contract to buy 500 notional LIFFE gilts at a futures price of £109.50. The maturity date for the futures contract would be 28 September. X would exercise his option only if the spot futures price being agreed for long gilt futures contracts maturing on 28 September rose above £109.50. Say the futures price rose to £111.50 and he exercised the option. Then the clearing house would give him the futures contract and a marked-to-market variation margin payment of £2 per gilt, that is £1,000. It would secure both items by exercising an identical futures call option where it was the holder and demanding a futures contract and £1,000 from its writer.

The writers of the 10,950 futures call options hoped the futures price would not go above £109.50, or at least not go far above. For if it went above £109.50, then the options would be exercised, and the losses they would make could far exceed the value of the premiums they received. A writer whose option was exercised would have to agree two offsetting futures contracts with the clearing house, each at a futures price equal to the exercise price of £109.50. One contract would be to buy gilts at £109.50, and the writer would give this to the clearing house to give to someone like X. The other would be to sell gilts at £109.50. This would be kept by the writer who would suffer. For if the current futures price was, say, £111.50, the clearing house would at once demand a variation margin of £2 per gilt, that is £1,000.

In contrast, Y anticipated borrowing long-term in August. Fearing high interest rates and so, equivalently, low gilt prices, she bought from the clearing house one 10,900 August futures put option contract. She paid a premium of 500(£1.08), or £540 for it. It entitled her to demand, up to its expiry on 24 July, a futures contract to sell 500 notional LIFFE gilts at a futures price of £109. The maturity date for the futures contract would be 28 September. Y would exercise her option only if the spot futures price being agreed for long gilt futures contracts maturing on 28 September fell below £109. Say the futures price fell to £105 and she exercised the option. Then the clearing house would give her the futures contract and a marked-to-market margin payment of £4 per gilt, that is £2,000. It would secure both items by exercising an identical futures put option where it was the holder and demanding a futures contract and £2,000 from its writer.

The writers of the 10,900 futures put options hoped the futures price would not go below £109, or at least not go far below. For if it went below £109, then the options would be exercised, and the losses they would make could far exceed the value of the premiums they received. A writer whose option was exercised would have to agree two offsetting futures contracts with the clearing house, each at a futures price equal to the exercise price of £109. One contract would be to sell gilts at £109, and the writer would give this to the clearing house to give to someone like Y. The other would be to buy gilts at £109. This would be kept by the writer who would suffer. For if the current futures price was, say, £105, the clearing house would at once demand a variation margin of £4 per gilt, that is £2,000.

LIFFE short-term interest rate futures options

LIFFE's short-term interest rate futures options are all American style options to secure a LIFFE short-term interest rate futures contract. Some of them are options to secure a three-month sterling futures contract, while others are options to secure a similar three-month euro, Euromark, Eurolira or Euroswiss franc futures contract. Table 6.7 gives some premiums for options on the three-month sterling contract. The premiums applied at the close of business on 20 May 1998. LIFFE allows few expiry dates and exercise prices, and the table covers three expiry dates and one exercise price. An exercise 'price' of, say, 92,500 actually means an interest rate of $(100 - 92.500)$ or 7.500%. The options expire on the third Wednesday of the expiry month, and in each case the underlying futures matures on the same day.

At maturity, each LIFFE short-term sterling interest rate futures contract involves one party paying the other some compensation that is based on the interest due on a three-month £500,000 deposit. In turn, the option premiums,

Table 6.7 Premiums for some LIFFE short sterling futures options (end of 20 May 1998)

Exercise price	Calls			Puts		
	Jun	Sep	Dec	Jun	Sep	Dec
92,500	0.025	0.125	0.270	0.055	0.075	0.080

which are expressed in percentages, refer to the interest that would be due on a three-month £500,000 deposit at the percentages shown. So a premium of 0.270% actually means a quarter of 0.270% of 500,000 or £337.50. The tick is 0.005%. The premiums on these options are not paid until the options are exercised or expire.

Suppose that on 20 May X anticipated lending short-term in December. He hedged against low interest rates by buying from the clearing house one 92,500 December futures call option contract. He paid a premium equal to a quarter of 0.270% of £500,000, that is £337.50. This option entitled him to demand, up to its expiry on 16 December, a short-term interest rate futures contract maturing on 16 December. With this futures contract, X would be compensated if the spot three-month LIBOR at maturity was below 7.50%, that is (100 − 92.500), for he would receive the difference between the interest due on a three-month £500,000 deposit at 7.50% and the interest due at the spot LIBOR on 16 December. X would exercise his option only if the spot futures price agreed for short-term interest rate futures contracts maturing in December rose above 92,500. Say it rose above 92,500 by 0.6% to 93,100 and X exercised the option. Then the clearing house would give him the futures contract and a marked-to-market variation margin payment of a quarter of 0.6% of £500,000, that is £750. It would secure both items by exercising an identical futures call option where it was the holder and demanding a futures contract and £750 from its writer.

The writers of the 92,500 futures call options hoped the futures price would not go above 92,500, or at least not go far above. For if it went above 92,500, then the options would be exercised, and the losses they would make could far exceed the value of the premiums they received. A writer whose option was exercised would have to agree two offsetting futures contracts with the clearing house, each at a futures price equal to the exercise price of 92,500. One would be to receive compensation if the spot LIBOR on 16 December was below 7.50%, and vice versa, and this would be given to the clearing house to give to someone like X. The other would be to pay compensation if the spot LIBOR on 16 December was below 7.50%, and vice versa. The writer would keep this one and suffer. For if the current futures price was, say, 93,100, the clearing house would at once demand a variation margin of £750.

In contrast, Y anticipated borrowing short-term in September. She hedged against high interest rates by buying from the clearing house one 92,500 September futures put option contract. She paid a premium equal to a quarter of 0.075% of £500,000, that is £93.75. This option entitled her to demand, up to its expiry on 15 September, a short-term interest rate futures contract maturing on 15 September. With this futures contract, she would be compensated if the spot three-month LIBOR at maturity was above 7.50%, that is (100 − 92.500), for she would receive the difference between the interest due on a three-month £500,000 deposit at 7.50% and the interest due at the spot LIBOR on 15 September. Y would exercise her option only if the spot futures price agreed for short-term interest rate futures contracts maturing on 15 September fell below 92,500. Say it went 0.4% below to 92,100 and she exercised the option. Then the clearing house would give her the futures contract and a marked-to-market variation margin payment of a quarter of 0.4% of £500,000, that is £500. It would secure both items by exercising an identical futures put option where it was the holder and demanding a futures contract and £500 from its writer.

The writers of the 92,500 futures put options hoped the futures price would not go below 92,500, or at least not go far below. For if it went below 92,500, then the options would be exercised, and the losses they would make could far exceed the value of the premiums they received. A writer whose option was exercised would have to agree two offsetting futures contracts with the clearing house, each at a futures price equal to the exercise price of 92,500. One would be to receive compensation if the spot LIBOR on 15 September was above 7.50%, and vice versa, and this would be given to the clearing house to give to someone like Y. The other would be to pay compensation if the spot LIBOR on 15 September was above 7.50%, and vice versa. The writer would keep this one and suffer. For if the current futures price was, say, 92,100, the clearing house would at once demand a variation margin of £500.

By using the futures call option, X effectively ensured that he would not lend for less than 7.50%, for he would receive compensation through the futures contract if interest rates went lower. So X secured an **interest rate floor**, but he paid a premium of 0.270% for it. So his lowest rate of return net of the premium was 7.230%. Likewise, by using the futures put option, Y effectively ensured that she would not borrow for more than 7.50%, for she would receive compensation through the futures contract if interest rates went higher. So Y secured an **interest rate cap**, but she paid a premium of 0.075% for it. So the most she would have to pay, allowing for the premium, is 7.575%.

X and Y could reduce the cost of securing a floor or a cap by also writing short-term interest rate options and so receiving premiums. Thus X might write a 92,250 put option while Y might write a 92,750 call option. The result is that X would also effectively secure a maximum level at which he could lend, here 7.75%, and so have a cap as well as a floor, while Y would effectively secure a minimum level at which she could borrow, here 7.25%, and so have a floor as well as a cap. So X would end up lending within a narrow range and Y would end up borrowing within a narrow range. These ranges are called **interest rate collars**. They are explored further in the questions at the end of the chapter.

6.6 EXOTIC OPTIONS

All the options considered so far have had straightforward rules about what happens if they are exercised. In particular, if they are exercised, then the gains to the holder depend only on the current spot price of the underlying asset and the exercise price. Options with straightforward rules like these are called **vanilla options**. Most over-the-counter options and virtually all traded options are vanilla options. But some options have less straightforward rules, and they are called **exotic options**. This section discusses three of the main types: Asian options, barrier options and conditional premium options. Most exotic options are over-the-counter options, but some exchanges offer Asian options. Asian options have absolutely no special association with Asia, just as European and American options have absolutely no special association with Europe or America.

Asian options

Asian options, or **average price options**, have an unusual payoff condition. To see this, imagine that X holds a call option to buy one tonne of tin. Suppose for the moment that this call is a vanilla European option with a strike price of £4,000 a tonne. In this case, if the spot price at expiry is, say, £4,100, then X will exercise the option and pay the writer £4,000 for a tonne of tin. X will gain £100 by buying the tin for £100 less than its current value, and the writer will lose £100 by selling the tin for £100 less than its current value. But this gain and loss could have been realised just as effectively if the writer had simply paid X the sum of £100. Many Asian options are settled like that, with what might be called a settlement payment instead of a purchase and a delivery.

However, the settlement payment with an Asian option is not based on the difference between an agreed exercise price and the spot price at expiry. Instead, it is based in part on the average spot price over a longer period, perhaps over the whole life of the option or over the last month of its life. Occasionally the payment is the difference between this average price and the spot price at expiry, so that the average price takes the place of an exercise price; but usually the payment is the difference between the exercise price and the average price, so that the average price takes the place of the spot price at expiry. To see this, suppose now that X's call option is an Asian style one where the payment depends on an exercise price of £4,000 and the average spot price over the last month of the option's life. If the average price over that month is £4,070, then the writer will pay X only £70 at expiry, even if the spot price at expiry is £100 above the exercise price at £4,100.

It is possible to have Asian style put options. Y might have an Asian style put option to sell a tonne of tin at an exercise price of £4,100. If the settlement payment is the difference between the exercise price and the average spot price of tin over the last month of the option's life, and if this average is £4,070, then the writer will pay Y £30 at expiry, no matter what the spot price might be.

When Asian style options are offered as traded options on an exchange, they are called **traded average price options** (TAPOs). In 1997, the LME introduced TAPOs for aluminium and copper. On any given day, 27 alternative expiry dates are available, and these are the last business days of the next 27 months. Like vanilla European options, these can only be exercised at expiry. Their settlement terms refer to the **monthly average settlement price** (MASP) for aluminium and copper in the month up to expiry. As noted in Section 5.6, the settlement prices used are the daily AM official prices. Any settlement payments that are due from the clearing house to option holders, or from option writers to the clearing house, are made two days after expiry.

Barrier options

Suppose it is 30 March and the current price of LML shares is 200p. X wants to buy some LML shares in June and fears a sharp rise in the price. Imagine he buys a vanilla American style 200p call option on LML shares with an expiry day on the third Wednesday in June. Then X can exercise his option at any time until that Wednesday and buy LML shares at 200p. However, X may have to pay an appreciable premium for this option, say 10p a share. He could get a lower premium if he agreed a less generous **barrier option**. With a **down-and-out option**, the option would lapse if the spot price fell below a certain barrier before expiry. Thus X might agree to let the option lapse if the spot price fell below 180p at any point. He would then lose the cover that he would have had with the vanilla option if the price subsequently rose above 200p, but he may think that such a rise is unlikely if the price has first dropped to 180p. Alternatively, he may agree an **up-and-in option** which would not come into effect unless the spot price first rose above a certain barrier, say 210p. This option would be exactly like a vanilla 200p call option except that X could not exercise it on a day when the spot price was between 200p and 210p unless it had previously risen above 210p.

Conversely, suppose Y wants to sell some LML shares in June and fears a sharp fall in the price. Imagine she buys a vanilla American style 200p put option on LML shares with an expiry day on the third Wednesday in June. Then Y can exercise her option any time until that Wednesday and sell LML shares at 200p. However, X may have to pay an appreciable premium for this option, say 10p per share. She could get a lower premium if she agreed a less generous option. With an **up-and-out option**, the option would lapse if the spot price rose above a certain barrier before expiry. Thus Y might agree to let the option lapse if the spot price rose above 220p at any point. She would then lose the cover she would have had with the vanilla option if the price subsequently fell below 200p, but she may think that such a rise is unlikely if the price has first risen to 220p.

Alternatively, she may agree a **down-and-in option** which would not come into effect unless the spot price first fell below a certain barrier, say 190p. This option would be exactly like a vanilla 200p put option except that Y could not exercise it on a day when the spot price was between 190p and 200p unless it had previously fallen below 190p.

Conditional premium options

Instead of using barrier options, X and Y might use **conditional premium options**. With one of these, X could agree a call option with a strike price of, say, 200p and pay no premium at all. Moreover, if the June spot price was above 200p, then he could exercise the option to buy shares at 200p, while if the spot price was below 200p, he could cancel the option and buy at the spot price. This resembles the 'ideal' contract illustrated in Fig. 6.1, but there is a catch. If the price falls below an agreed **trigger** level, say 170p, then X would agree to pay a very large premium. Likewise Y might agree a put option with a strike price of 200p and also pay no premium. Moreover, if the June spot price was below 200p, then she could exercise the option to sell her shares at 200p, while if the spot price was above 200p, she could cancel the option and sell at the spot price. This resembles the 'ideal' contract illustrated in Fig. 6.2, but again there is a catch. If the price rises above an agreed trigger level, say 230p, then Y would agree to pay a very large premium.

These options have payoffs which in some respects resemble those of futures more than those of vanilla options. For, as with a futures contract, there is just a gain if the spot price moves adversely, and there is just a loss if it moves favourably. But here the loss is in the form of a premium which may be fixed for all spot prices beyond the trigger level, whereas with a futures contract the loss gets larger the more favourable the spot price is.

6.7 USING A COMBINATION OF OPTIONS

Combinations of options

So far, it has been implied that a hedger or a speculator will either buy a call option or a put option, or else write a call option or a put option. In fact, people often simultaneously agree two or more different options for the same underlying asset, such as buying a call option and writing a put option, or buying two calls and writing two calls. This section explains why they might use more than one type of option. For its examples, it uses options on the equities of the hypothetical company, LML. Most of the discussion will consider the possibility of using two options.

There are six different positions that can be created by having two options for one underlying asset such as LML shares. These are shown – twice each – in Table 6.8. For example, the table shows that simultaneously buying a call and writing a call creates a **call spread**: a call spread is called a **bull call spread** if the bought call has a lower exercise price than the written call, and a **bear call spread** if the bought call has a higher exercise price than the written call. Also, simultaneously buying a put and writing a put creates a **put spread**: a put spread is called a **bull put spread** if the bought put has a lower exercise price than the written put, and a **bear put spread** if the bought put has a higher exercise price than the written put.

Table 6.8 also shows that simultaneously buying a call and buying a put creates a **bought strangle**, though this is sometimes called a **long strangle**;

Table 6.8 Combinations of two options

	Buy a call	Write a call	Buy a put	Write a put
Buy a call	–	Call spread	Bought strangle	Synthetic long
Write a call	Call spread	–	Synthetic short	Written strangle
Buy a put	Bought strangle	Synthetic short	–	Put spread
Write a put	Synthetic long	Written strangle	Put spread	–

and if the two options have the same exercise price, then it is called a **bought straddle** or a **long straddle**. Also, simultaneously writing a call and writing a put creates a **written strangle**, though this is sometimes called a **short strangle**; and if the two options have the same exercise price, then it is called a **written straddle** or a **short straddle**.

Finally, Table 6.8 shows that simultaneously buying a call and writing a put creates a **synthetic long**, while simultaneously buying a put and writing a call creates a **synthetic short**. In each of these two cases, the two options should, strictly, have the same exercise price.

The reason for simultaneously using different options

The reason that people sometimes use more than one option is to secure a different pattern of gains and losses from those which can be secured by using a single option. To illustrate the possible patterns of gains and losses, it is helpful to suppose that no options are exercised until expiry. Then, when the options do expire, the gains and losses to the different parties will depend on only two things: the value of any premiums that they paid or received when they bought or wrote the options, and the gains and losses which result from any options that are exercised at expiry.

As far as the premiums are concerned, suppose that all the options are bought or written on a single day, 26 September. And suppose, for simplicity, that people buy or write options only for a single LML share. Table 6.9 shows the premiums for some equity options on LML shares on 26 September, a day when the spot price of LML shares was 180p. The table gives the premiums for call options and put options that will expire next December, March and June. The premiums have been chosen to give results that are in some cases a shade neater than would be found in practice.

Table 6.9 Option prices on 26 September for the hypothetical company LML

30 Sept	Series	Calls			Puts		
		Dec	Mar	Jun	Dec	Mar	Jun
	150	36	46	50	6	16	25
LML	175	20	31	35	15	26	35
(180)	200	8	20	25	28	40	50

As far as the gains and losses from exercising the various possible options are concerned, these depend on the expiry day spot price for LML shares and also on the exercise prices of the options. Consider, in turn, the gains and losses from the call options and the gains and losses from the put options.

The holders of the 150p call options will exercise them at expiry only if the spot price then is above 150p, for no-one would exercise the right to buy an LML share at 150p if the spot price was lower. The holders will gain if the spot price at expiry is above 150p as they can then exercise the right to buy shares at 150p. For example, they would gain 50p if the spot price was 200p because they have the right to buy shares for 50p less than that spot price. Likewise, the holders of the 175p and 200p call options will exercise them and gain only if the expiry day spot prices are above 175p and 200p respectively. The gains to the holders of the three different call options are shown for a selection of possible expiry day spot prices in rows (1)–(3) of Table 6.10. These gains are mirrored by the losses to the writers of these options at expiry, as shown in rows (7)–(9).

The holders of the 150p put options will exercise them at expiry only if the spot price then is below 150p, for no-one would exercise the right to sell an LML share at 150p if the spot price was higher. The holders will gain if the spot price at expiry is under 150p as they can then exercise the right to sell shares at 150p. For example, they would gain 50p if the spot price was 100p because they have the right to sell shares for 50p more than that spot price. Likewise, the holders of the 175p and 200p put options will exercise them and gain only if the expiry day spot prices are below 175p and 200p respectively. The gains to the holders of the three different put options are shown for various expiry day spot prices in rows (4)–(6) of Table 6.10. These gains are mirrored by losses to the writers of these options at expiry, as shown in rows (10)–(12).

Table 6.10 Gains and losses on LML options with different expiry-day spot prices

Expiry day spot price (p)	0	50	100	150	175	200	250	300	350
1 Gain on bought 150p call	0	0	0	0	+25	+50	+100	+150	+200
2 Gain on bought 175p call	0	0	0	0	0	+25	+75	+125	+175
3 Gain on bought 200p call	0	0	0	0	0	0	+50	+100	+150
4 Gain on bought 150p put	+150	+100	+50	0	0	0	0	0	0
5 Gain on bought 175p put	+175	+125	+75	+25	0	0	0	0	0
6 Gain on bought 200p put	+200	+150	+100	+50	+25	0	0	0	0
7 Loss on written 150p call	0	0	0	0	−25	−50	−100	−150	−200
8 Loss on written 175p call	0	0	0	0	0	−25	−75	−125	−175
9 Loss on written 200p call	0	0	0	0	0	0	−50	−100	−150
10 Loss on written 150p put	−150	−100	−50	0	0	0	0	0	0
11 Loss on written 175p put	−175	−125	−75	−25	0	0	0	0	0
12 Loss on written 200p put	−200	−150	−100	−50	−25	0	0	0	0

Long hedges and bull spreads

Many people who use options want to buy the underlying asset in future and want to make a long hedge against a high price. The simplest way of doing this is to buy a call option. If X is a long hedger, he may spend 50p buying a June 150p call option to hedge against a June price above 150p. X at once loses 50p on the premium. Later, at expiry, he may make a gain, as shown in row (1) of Table 6.10. His net position for each expiry day spot price, allowing for both the premium and any expiry day gain, is shown by the kinked line in Fig. 6.3. With this option, X's gains at expiry will cover him fully against expiry day spot prices over 150p, but he loses 50p paying for this cover.

Instead of just buying a call option, suppose X acquires a bull call spread by buying a 150p June call option and writing a 200p June call option. Bull spreads are used by **bulls**, that is people who expect price rises, as well as by people like X who fear price rises. X pays one premium of 50p and receives one of 25p, and so makes a net payment of 25p. At expiry, X may make both a gain and a loss, as shown in rows (1) and (9) of Table 6.10. Allowing also for the premiums, X's net position for each expiry day spot price is as shown in Fig. 6.4. Compared with just buying the call option, X secures lower gains, and so less cover, at high expiry day spot prices. But for this reduced cover he pays a net premium of only 25p and so loses less at low expiry day spot prices.

As another alternative to just buying a call option, X might acquire a bull put spread, say by buying a 150p June put option and writing a 200p June put option. This involves paying a premium of 25p and receiving one of 50p, to earn a net receipt of 25p. At expiry, X may make both a gain and a loss, as shown in rows (4) and (12) of Table 6.10. Allowing also for the premiums, X's net position for each expiry day spot price is again exactly as shown in Fig. 6.4. In practice, it is rarely possible to get identical returns from the two types of bull spread. However, compared with a call option, all bull spreads secure lower gains at high expiry day spot prices as well as lower losses at low

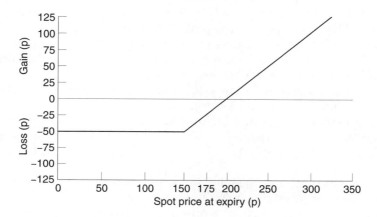

Figure 6.3 The gains and losses from holding a 150p call option.

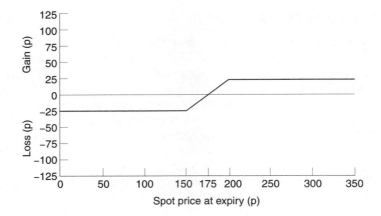

Figure 6.4   The gains and losses from holding a 150p plus 200p bull spread.

expiry day spot prices. In effect, bull spreads mean that X pays less but receives less cover in return.

Short hedges and bear spreads

Many people who use options want to sell the underlying asset in future and want to make a short hedge against a low price. The simplest way of doing this is to buy a put option. If Y is a short hedger, she may spend 50p buying a 200p June put option to hedge against a price below 200p. Y at once loses 50p on the premium. Later, at expiry, she may make a gain, as shown in row (6) of Table 6.10. Her net position for each expiry day spot price, allowing for both the premium and any expiry day gain, is shown by the kinked line in Fig. 6.5. With this option, Y's gains at expiry will cover her fully against expiry day spot prices below 200p, but she loses 50p paying for this cover.

Instead of just buying a put option, suppose Y acquires a bear put spread by buying a 200p June put option and writing a 150p June put option. Bear spreads are used by **bears**, that is people who expect price falls, as well as by people like Y who fear price falls. Y pays one premium of 50p and receives one of 25p, and so makes a net payment of 25p. At expiry, Y may make both a gain and a loss, as shown in rows (6) and (10) of Table 6.10. Allowing also for the premiums, Y's net position for each expiry day spot price is as shown in Fig. 6.6. Compared with just buying the put option, Y secures lower gains, and so less cover, at low expiry day spot prices. But for this reduced cover she pays a net premium of only 25p and so loses less at high expiry day spot prices.

As another alternative to just buying a put option, Y might acquire a bear call spread, say by buying a 200p June call option and writing a 150p June call option. This involves paying a premium of 25p and receiving one of 50p, to earn a net receipt of 25p. At expiry, Y may make both a gain and a loss,

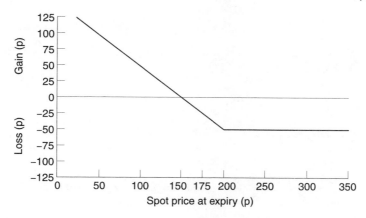

Figure 6.5 The gains and losses from holding a 200p put option.

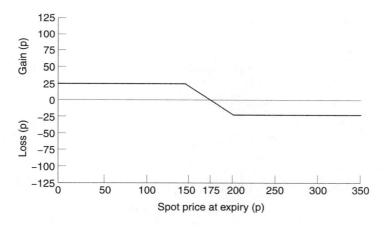

Figure 6.6 The gains and losses from holding a 200p plus 150p bear spread.

as shown in rows (3) and (7) of Table 6.10. Allowing also for the premiums, Y's net position for each expiry day spot price is again exactly as shown in Fig. 6.6. In practice, it is rarely possible to get identical returns from the two types of bear spread. However, compared with a put option, all bear spreads secure lower gains at low expiry day spot prices as well as lower losses at high expiry day spot prices. In effect, bear spreads mean that Y pays less but receives less cover in return.

Strangles and straddles

Suppose now that X is a speculator who thinks that LML shares have a turbulent time ahead. Perhaps LML is buying a subsidiary and X thinks this will affect its share price, but he is unsure which way it will go. He buys a strangle

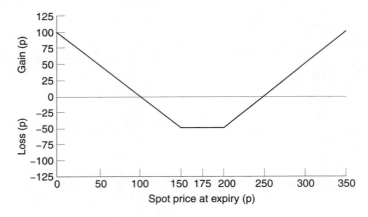

Figure 6.7   The gains and losses from a bought 200p plus 150p strangle.

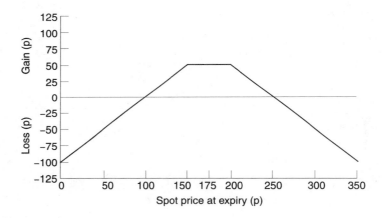

Figure 6.8   The gains and losses from a written 200p plus 150p strangle.

by buying both a 200p June call option and a 150p June put option. X pays a 25p premium for each option and so pays 50p in all. At expiry, X may make some gains, as shown in rows (3) and (4) of Table 6.10. Allowing also for the premiums, X's net position for each expiry day spot price is as shown in Fig. 6.7. X gains at expiry day spot prices below 100p or above 250p. Surprisingly, perhaps, X could here achieve identical gains and losses by buying both a 150p June call option and a 200p June put option. He would pay a 50p premium for each option and so pay 100p in all, and at expiry he may make some gains, as shown in rows (1) and (6) of Table 6.10. In practice, it is seldom possible to secure identical results with two different strangles, but it is possible to get close results. And although X could here secure identical results, he would prefer the first alternative as that alternative requires a lower initial outlay on premiums.

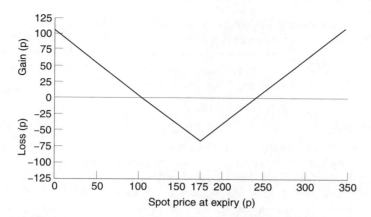

Figure 6.9 The gains and losses from a bought 175p straddle.

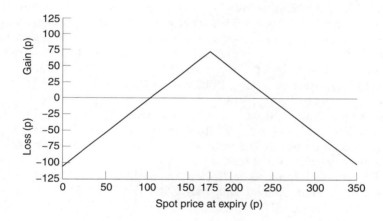

Figure 6.10 The gains and losses from a written 175p straddle.

Suppose Y is a writer who wrote a strangle like the one that X bought by writing a 200p June call option and a 150p June put option. Y's position mirrors X's and her net gains and losses are as shown in Fig. 6.8. Y would write a strangle in LML shares only if she expected the shares to have a stable time ahead, for she gains provided the expiry day spot price is in between 100p and 250p.

Instead of buying a strangle, suppose X buys a straddle, perhaps by buying both a 175p June call option and a 175p June put option. He pays a premium of 35p for each option and so pays 70p in all. At expiry, X may make some gains, as shown in rows (2) and (5) of Table 6.10. Allowing also for the premiums, X's net position for each expiry day spot price is as shown in Fig. 6.9. At high and low expiry day spot prices, X would gain rather more with the straddle than with the strangle, but he would lose more at prices around 175p.

Suppose Y is a writer who wrote a straddle like the one that X bought by writing a 175p June call option and a 175p June put option. Y's position mirrors X's and her gains and losses are as shown in Fig. 6.10. At high and low expiry day spot prices, Y would lose rather more with the straddle than with the strangle, but she would gain more at prices around 175p.

Synthetics

Suppose, next, that X acquires a synthetic long position by buying a 175p December call option and writing a 175p December put option. X pays one premium of 20p and receives one of 15p, and so pays 5p net. At expiry, X may make both a gain and a loss, as shown in rows (2) and (11) of Table 6.10. Allowing for the premiums as well, X's net position is as shown in Fig. 6.11.

Imagine that X had instead bought one LML share on 26 September at that day's spot price of 180p. He would have become long in LML shares. By December he would have made a capital gain if the spot price was above 180p and a capital loss if it was below. His gains and losses would equal those with the synthetic considered here, which is why it is called a synthetic long, though in practice it is rarely possible to acquire a synthetic whose gains and losses exactly replicate the capital gains and losses obtained from buying a share. Acquiring the synthetic has a lower outlay than buying a share, but it secures no dividends and there is a risk that the written option may be exercised at any time.

Suppose, next, that Y secures a synthetic short position by buying a 175p March put option and writing a 175p March call option. Y pays one premium of 26p and receives one of 31p, and so has a net receipt of 5p. At expiry, Y may make both a gain and a loss, as shown in rows (5) and (8) of Table 6.10. Allowing for the premiums as well, her net position is as shown in Fig. 6.12.

Imagine that Y had instead sold one LML share on 26 September at that day's spot price of 180p. She would thereby have become short in LML shares. If the spot price was under 180p by March, then she would have gained, by

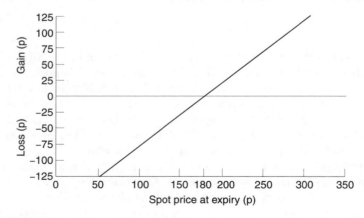

Figure 6.11   The gains and losses from a synthetic long position.

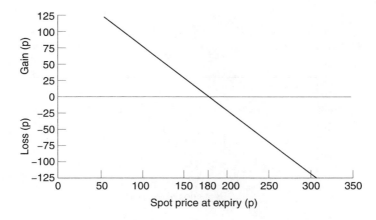

Figure 6.12 The gains and losses from a synthetic short position.

missing a capital loss, but if the spot price was over 180p by March, then she would have lost, by missing a capital gain. Her gains and losses would equal those with the synthetic considered here, which is why it is called a synthetic short, though in practice it is rarely possible to acquire a synthetic whose gains and losses exactly replicate those resulting from selling a share. Y might prefer to use the synthetic so that she could keep the share and still receive dividends; or she might prefer to sell the share and use the money raised to buy something else.

Butterfly spreads

Sometimes people use more than two options for one underlying asset. Often they use either four calls or four puts to acquire what is usually called a **butterfly spread**, though it may instead be called a **sandwich spread**. Each butterfly spread involves either buying two options for a central exercise price and writing one option for each of two outer exercise prices, or writing two options for a central exercise price and buying one option for each of two outer exercise prices. The gains and losses from butterfly spreads tend to be small, so they will be illustrated on figures which have different vertical scales from those used in Figs 6.3 to 6.12.

Suppose that X buys two 175p June call options and also writes one 150p June call and one 200p June call. He pays two premiums of 35p and receives one of 25p and one of 50p, so receiving 5p net. At expiry, X stands to make twice the gains shown in row (2) of Table 6.10 together with the losses shown in both rows (7) and (9). Allowing also for the premiums, his net position will be as shown in Fig. 6.13 . He will make a loss if the expiry day spot price is around 175p, but otherwise he will make a gain of 5p which arises from his net receipts from the premiums. In the present example, X could actually secure an identical net position if he bought two 175p June put options and wrote one 150p June put and one 200p June put. Again he would pay two premiums of

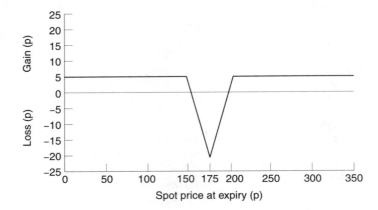

Figure 6.13   The gains and losses from a butterfly spread whose central options are held.

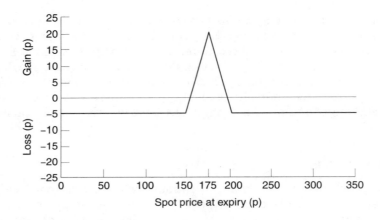

Figure 6.14   The gains and losses from a butterfly spread whose central options are written.

35p and receive one of 25p and one of 50p, so receiving 5p net. He would stand to make twice the gains shown in row (5) of Table 6.10 together with the losses shown in both rows (10) and (12).

These two butterfly spreads secure a modest gain if the spot price ends up either high or low and a very small loss if it ends up in between. Like bought strangles and straddles, they appeal to spectators who believe the spot price will move sharply before expiry but are unsure which way it will move.

Suppose, next, that Y writes two 175p June call options and, also, that she buys one 150p June call option and one 200p June call option. She receives two premiums of 35p and pays one of 25p and one of 50p, so paying 5p net. She stands to make the gains shown in both rows (1) and (3) of Table 6.10 together with twice the losses shown in row (8). Allowing also for the premiums, her net position will be as shown in Fig. 6.14. She will make a gain if the expiry day spot price is around 175p, but otherwise she will make a loss of 5p which arises from her net payment of the premiums. In the present example, Y could actually secure an identical net position if she wrote two 175p June put options and bought one 150p June put and one 200p June put. Again she would receive two premiums of 35p and pay one of 25p and one of 50p, so paying 5p net. She would stand to make the gains shown in both rows (4) and (6) of Table 6.10 together with twice the losses shown in row (11).

These two butterfly spreads secure a modest gain if the spot price ends up close to the central exercise price and a very small loss if it does not. Like written strangles and straddles, they appeal to spectators who believe the price will end up near a central position.

Vertical and horizontal spreads

The bear and bull call spreads and put spreads considered earlier involved simultaneously buying and writing call options with the same maturity date, or simultaneously buying and writing put options with the same maturity date. In each case the two options had different exercise prices. Spreads like these are often called **vertical spreads** because the published prices of the two options appear in vertical columns, as in Table 6.9, but sometimes these spreads are instead called **money spreads**.

Another sort of spread is one which involves two options with the same exercise price but different expiry dates. Spreads like these are usually called **horizontal spreads** because the published prices of the two options appear on the same line in published tables, as in Table 6.9, but sometimes they are instead called **time spreads** or **calendar spreads**. The following paragraphs give an intuitive argument of how people hope to gain from these spreads. The arguments can be proved only by applying the option pricing theory outlined in Chapters 7 and 8.

Suppose that X buys a June 200p LML call option for 25p and writes a March 200p LML call option for 20p, so paying 5p net. His spread position will end in March when the March call expires. X will hope that the spot price of LML shares in March is around the 200p exercise price of his options. Say it is 200p. Then the call that he has written will not be exercised, but the call he holds should be worth more than 5p, so he could sell it and more than recoup the 5p cost of the premiums. But if the spot price is very low, say 150p, then the call he has written will not be exercised, and the call he holds may be worth virtually nothing, so he will simply lose the 5p cost of the premiums. And if the spot price is very high, say 250p, then the call he has written will be exercised and he will lose 50p as a result. Admittedly the call that he holds will be valuable, but it will almost certainly be worth less than the 55p he would need to cover the 50p lost on the March call and the 5p cost of the premiums.

Suppose Y buys a March 150p LML call option for 46p and also writes a June 150p LML call option for 50p, so receiving 4p net. Her spread position will end in March when the March call expires. Y will hope that the spot price of LML shares in March is *not* just about the 150p exercise price of her options.

If it is 150p, then she will gain nothing from the March call that she holds, yet the price of the June call that she has written could well exceed 4p, so she would have to pay more than 4p to get another writer to take it over; so she would make a loss. But if the spot price is well below 150p, say 100p, then although she will still gain nothing from the March call that she holds, the June call that she has written will be virtually worthless; so she should just gain the 4p. And if the spot price is well above 150p, say 200p, then she will gain 50p by exercising her March call to add to the 4p, while the June call that she has written will almost certainly be worth less than 54p, so she would have to pay less than 54p to persuade another writer to take it over; so she would gain overall by spending less than the total of 54p that she has earned from the premium and the March call.

Other types of spread

This section has looked at the most common types of option combination, but there are many other possibilities. For example, it is possible to acquire a **diagonal spread** by buying a call option or a put option with one exercise price and expiry day and simultaneously writing another option of the same type as the first with a different exercise price and a different expiry day. This spread combines the characteristics of vertical and horizontal spreads. Another possibility is to acquire a horizontal type of butterfly spread. Here someone might buy two call options expiring in March and simultaneously write one call option expiring in December and another expiring in June.

Three further types of spread are considered in the questions at the end of the chapter. The first is a **box spread**, which is a combination of a bull call spread and a bear put spread. The second is a **strap**, which resembles a straddle except that it involves two calls and one put. And the third is a **strip,** which also resembles a straddle except that its involves one call and two puts.

6.8 WARRANTS

Warrants are issued by companies. They are agreements between the companies and the warrant holders which entitle the holders to buy ordinary shares, or other securities in the company, on one or more specified future dates at an agreed price. From the holders' point of view, warrants closely resemble equity call options with long lives. However, warrant holders have far less choice over the exercise date than the holders of American options, although they may have rather more choice than the holders of European options.

Most warrants are actually issued by investment trusts. In the case of an ordinary trust, the warrants are usually issued free to the original purchasers of the trust's ordinary shares, and the warrants entitle the holders to buy more ordinary shares later. In the case of split capital trusts, the warrants are usually issued free to the original purchasers of one or more of the trust's various securities, and they entitle the holders to buy more securities of a specified type later. However, warrants are also sometimes issued by other companies.

In this case, the warrants are usually issued free to the purchasers of corporate bonds and entitle the holders to buy ordinary shares.

Warrants have two key advantages for companies. First, a company which is selling some new securities may encourage investors to pay a higher price if it gives them warrants at the same time. Secondly, a company which anticipates needing to raise funds at specific future dates may find it useful to issue warrants that expire around those dates, for then funds may flow into the company without it having to make much effort to secure them.

Warrants can be traded quite separately from the securities alongside which they were issued. They are traded in the capital markets just like equities. The price of any given warrant depends on the same factors that apply to other options, as discussed in the next two chapters. But the main factors are naturally the current spot price of the underlying security which the warrant holder is entitled to buy, along with the exercise price that the warrant holder will have to pay for it.

SUMMARY

6.1   Options are contracts that resemble forwards and futures in that two parties agree to do a deal on a future date at a price or other value agreed in the contract. The agreed value is called the exercise price or strike price. However, with call options the buyer is allowed to call off the deal, while with put options the seller is allowed to call off the deal. The party who holds the option pays a premium to the other party, who is called the writer.

6.2   Options are usually available at a selection of exercise prices. An option holder faces great upside potential and little downside risk, while the opposite applies to the writer. If the writer of a call option already owns the underlying asset, then the option is a covered call. If the holder of a put option already owns the underlying asset, then the option is a protective put.

6.3   American style options can be exercised at any time until expiry. European style options can be exercised only at maturity. American options are just as popular in Europe as America.

6.4   Tailor-made options are agreed over-the-counter with banks and other intermediaries. Standardised options are agreed on exchanges and are called traded options because their holders can readily close out by trading them. Margins are required from writers. Some options have futures contracts as the underlying asset.

6.5   The major option exchanges in London include the London Metal Exchange (LME), which offers some commodity options, and the London International Financial Futures and Options Exchange (LIFFE), which offers equity options, stock index options, some commodity options, freight index options and interest rate options. Traded equity options and stock index options are based directly on equities and stock indices, while commodity options, freight index options and interest rate options generally have futures contracts as the underlying asset. Interest rate options can be used to secure interest rate caps, floors and collars.

6.6   There are many exotic options, most of which are only available over-the-counter. They include Asian options where the payment at expiry includes a reference to the average spot price of the underlying asset over part or all of the option's life.

6.7   There are several ways of combining two or more options to secure specific patterns of gains and losses in respect of possible expiry day spot prices. Some combinations secure less cover from adverse price movements than single options but involve a lower outlay in terms of premiums. Others suit people who believe that the spot price may move sharply before expiry, but are unsure whether it will rise or fall, while yet others suit people who believe that the spot price may move very little before expiry.

6.8   Warrants give security holders the right to purchase securities at agreed prices on specified future dates. They can be seen as a variant of call options.

QUESTIONS

1.   Distinguish between: (a) call options and put options; (b) European style options and American style options; (c) over-the-counter options and traded options; (d) bull spreads and bear spreads; and (e) strangles and straddles.

2.   Refer to the example of X given in the context of short-term interest rate futures options as illustrated for 20 May 1998 in Table 6.7 (on p. 198). X wanted to lend and bought a December 92,500 call option. This ensured that he would not lend for less than 7.50%, but the premium cost 0.27%, so his floor was effectively 7.23%. If spot interest rates at expiry exceeded 7.50%, then X would not exercise the option but would lend at the spot rate. Suppose now that X cuts the cost of his position by also writing a December 92,250 put option for a premium of 0.01%. This raises his floor by 0.01%. But with this option, if interest rates rose above 7.75%, X would end up as the party to a futures contract in which X would compensate the clearing house for any rise in interest rates above 7.75%, so while X could still lend at over 7.75%, he would gain nothing as he would have to pay all the gain to the clearing house. Thus X has also secured an upper limit or cap. What is X's effective floor if interest rates end up at 7.50% or lower? What is his effective cap if they end up at 7.75% or higher? Use these two figures to work out X's effective collar, that is the range within which his net returns will lie.

3.   Refer to the example of Y given in the context of short-term interest rate futures options as illustrated for 20 May 1998 in Table 6.7 (on p. 198). Y wanted to borrow in September and bought a 92,500 put option. This ensured that she would not borrow for more than 7.500%, but the premium cost

0.075% so her cap was effectively 7.575%. If spot interest rates at expiry were below 7.500%, then Y would not exercise the option but would borrow at the spot rate. Suppose now that Y cuts the cost of her position by also writing a 92,750 September call option for a premium of 0.080%. This reduces her cap by 0.080%. But with this option, if interest rates fall below 7.250%, Y would end up as the party to a futures contract in which Y would compensate the clearing house for any fall in interest rates below 7.250%, so while Y could still borrow at under 7.250%, she would gain nothing as she would have to pay all the gain to the clearing house. Thus Y has also secured a lower limit or floor. What is Y's effective cap if interest rates end up at 7.500% or higher? What is her effective floor if they end up at 7.250% or lower? Use these two figures to work out Y's effective collar, that is the range within which her net payments will lie.

4. Refer to the data for LML in Tables 6.9 and 6.10 (on pp. 203–4). Suppose Y constructs a box hedge for December. This is a combination of a bull call spread and a bear put spread. For the bull call spread she buys a 150p call option and writes a 200p call option, while for the bear put spread she buys a 200p put option and writes a 150p put option. What is her total net payment or receipt from the premiums? Calculate, for each expiry day spot price shown in Table 6.10, her total net gain or loss from her box hedge if all the options run until expiry in December. Explain how this spread shows that option premiums must be related to the interest rate on risk-free assets.

5. Refer to the data for LML in Tables 6.9 and 6.10 (on pp. 203–4). Suppose X thinks that the price of LML shares will change sharply, but he is unsure which way it will move. He initially considers holding a straddle by buying both a 175p June call option and a 175p June put option to give the gains and losses shown in Fig. 6.9 (on p. 209). But suppose he thinks that the share price is more likely to rise than it is to fall and he wishes to increase his gains if it does rise. He considers a strap, where he would buy two calls and one put, and a strip where he would buy one call and two puts. Which would be more appropriate? Which should Y use if she was in a broadly similar position to X but thought the price of LML shares was more likely to fall than rise?

6. By combining a position in an asset and an option on it, people can synthesise a different option. To see how, suppose X owns no LML shares. Use Tables 6.9 and 6.10 (on pp. 203–4) to calculate the net position he would secure at each expiry day spot price if he (a) bought a 175p December call, (b) bought a 175p December put, (c) wrote a 175p December call, and (d) wrote a 175p December put. Now suppose he owns one LML share. For each expiry day spot price, calculate the capital gains and losses he would miss by selling the share at its current 180p price, and also calculate the gains and losses he would secure by keeping it. Show that X could replicate his position in (a) with a **synthetic long call** where he keeps his share and buys a 175p December put, and show that he could replicate (b) with a **synthetic long put** where he sells his share and buys a 175p December call. Devise a **synthetic short call** to replicate (c) and a **synthetic short put** to replicate (d).

7 FACTORS AFFECTING OPTION PRICES

7.1 WHY ARE THE FACTORS THAT AFFECT OPTION PRICES IMPORTANT?

When an option is agreed, the parties do more than simply make an agreement, for the option holder also pays a premium, or price, which is transferred to the writer. Some time later, the holder may sell the option for a different price to a new holder. Also, the writer may later pay someone else a different price to take over the writer's obligations. Because options have prices, the people who deal in them need to know what factors affect their prices and how they affect them.

Topics covered by this chapter

This chapter shows that there are six main factors which affect the current price of any given option. These factors are:

1. The exercise price of the option.
2. The current spot price of the underlying asset.
3. The time remaining until the option expires.
4. The rate of interest on risk-free loans.
5. The volatility of the spot price of the underlying asset.
6. The cost of storing the underlying asset from now until maturity. This cost is positive if the underlying asset is a commodity, but it is negative if the underlying asset is a financial asset, such as a currency or a security, which earns interest or dividends.

Sections 7.2 and 7.3 examine the effects of these six factors on the prices of ordinary call options and ordinary put options, while Sections 7.4 and 7.5 examine their effects on the prices of futures call options and futures put options. Section 7.6 summarises all these effects and notes some measures which are related to them. This chapter should be seen as a prelude to Chapter 8 which develops option pricing theory further by discussing methods for estimating exact option prices.

The examples used in this chapter

To illustrate the effects of the six factors, this chapter uses as examples the options on the equities of a hypothetical company, LML. It supposes that an exchange offers ordinary European and American options on single LML shares, and that is also offers European and American futures options on single LML shares. It supposes, too, that the exchange permits four expiry times each year, namely 1300 on the fourth Wednesdays in September, December, March and June, and it supposes that today is the fourth Wednesday in September and that it is coming up to 1300. This means that some options are about to expire, while other options are available that will expire next December, March and June, that is in three months, six months and nine months. In addition, it is assumed that the only exercise prices currently permitted are 150p and 200p. So the available European and American options for each expiry date are 150 and 200 calls, 150 and 200 puts, 150 and 200 futures calls, and 150 and 200 futures puts. Finally, it is assumed that that the current spot price of LML shares is 180p, and that people can lend risk-free for any length of time at a rate equivalent to 6% a year.

The chapter will look in turn at the ordinary calls, the ordinary puts, the futures calls and the futures puts. All prices will be expressed in pence, and the notation used is summarised in Table 7.1.

7.2 CALL OPTIONS

Intrinsic value and time value

Every call option has what is called an **intrinsic value**. This is defined as $\text{Max}\{0,[S-E]\}$ which simply means that it equals whichever is the larger, or maximum, out of zero and the value of $[S-E]$, where S is the current spot price of the underlying asset and E is the exercise price of the option. In the

Table 7.1 Notation

S	Spot price	r	Risk-free rate of interest
E	Exercise price of option	C_A	Price of American call option
S_F	Spot futures price	C_E	Price of European call option
E_F	Exercise price of futures option	FC_A	Price of American futures call option
D	Dividend due before expiry	FC_E	Price of European futures call option
S^*	S minus the present value of D	P_A	Price of American put option
S_C	Critical spot price for early exercise	P_E	Price of European put option
T	Time to expiry (in years)	FP_A	Price of American futures put option
t	Time to dividend (in years)	FP_E	Price of European futures put option

case of a 150 LML call option, the exercise price of 150 is below the current spot price of LML shares, which is 180, so $[S-E]$ is greater than zero; consequently, the intrinsic value equals $[S-E]$ which is 30. In the case of a 200 LML call option, the exercise price of 200 is above the spot price of 180, so $[S-E]$ is less than zero; consequently, the intrinsic value equals zero.

There are two ways of seeing the significance of the intrinsic values of call options:

1. The intrinsic value of an American call shows the gain that its holder could secure by exercising it now. Thus the holder of a 150 American call could gain 30 now by exercising it and buying for 150 a share that is worth 180. But the holder of a 200 American call would gain nothing at all by exercising it now and buying for 200 a share that is worth 180.
2. The intrinsic value of any option that is about to expire shows the gain that holder is about to make. The holder of a 150 call option that expires today is about to gain 30 because, at expiry, the holder will exercise the right to buy for 150 a share that is worth 180. But the holder of a 200 call that expires today is about to gain nothing, for nothing would be gained at expiry by exercising the right to buy at 200 a share that is worth 180.

When a call option has an exercise price that is below the spot price, so that it has a positive intrinsic value, it is called **in-the-money**. So a 150 call is in-the-money. Indeed, it is in-the-money by 30. When a call option has an exercise price that is above the spot price, so that it has a zero intrinsic value, it is **out-of-the-money**. So a 200 call is out-of-the-money. Sometimes an option has an exercise price that is equal to, or close to, the spot price. Such an option is **at-the-money**.

The intrinsic value of any given call depends solely on its exercise price and the current spot price. In Fig. 7.1, the kinked line ABC shows what the intrinsic value of any 150 call would be for all possible current spot prices from zero to 300. In this figure, the horizontal axis gives the possible spot prices while the vertical axis gives the option's value or price. The kinked intrinsic value line ABC shows, for example, that the option's intrinsic value would be zero if the spot price was under 150, so that the option was out-of-the-money, while the option's intrinsic value would be positive if the spot price was above 150, so that the option was in-the-money.

The holder of a call option that is about to expire is about to make a gain equal to its intrinsic value. Consequently, the option has a value or price that is equal to its intrinsic value. So the kinked line ABC in Fig. 7.1 shows what the price of a 150 call would be just before expiry for different possible spot prices at expiry. However, the price of a call option with some time left before expiry rarely equals its intrinsic value and is usually higher. The gap between its price and its intrinsic value is called its **time value**, because this gap diminishes as expiry approaches and disappears entirely at expiry. The reasons why time value arises on call options with some time left are explored shortly.

Today, when the spot price of LML shares is 180, the price of a 150 call option expiring in nine months on the fourth Wednesday of next June might be 75, way

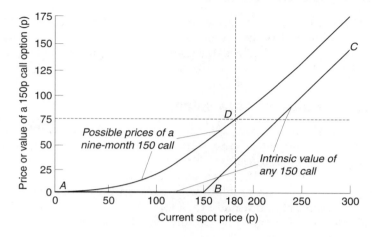

Figure 7.1   The intrinsic value of any 150 call and the possible price of a nine-month 150 call.

above its intrinsic value of 30. Point D in Fig. 7.1 shows this price. The curve through D shows the prices that this nine-month 150 call option might have had today for a wide range of other possible spot prices. As with most call options, it would have a negligible price at low spot prices. Incidentally, if the spot price is very high, then a European call option can have a negative time value. If it does, then the curve showing its price at different spot prices will intersect the sloping part of the intrinsic value line ABC.

Although the price that a 150 call option expiring next June would have today at each possible spot price might be as shown by the curve through D, the price that it would have at each possible spot price when it expires next June is given by the kinked intrinsic value line ABC. In between, as time passes and its time value diminishes, the curve showing its price at each possible spot price will get progressively lower than the one through D until, at expiry, the curve finally 'collapses' on to ABC.

Sources of time value

There are three reasons why a call option with some time left before expiry has some time value, so that its price does not equal its intrinsic value. These sources of time value will be discussed in turn, using the example of a call option that expires in nine months' time next June. It will be seen that the first source is the fact that people can lend money and earn interest at the risk-free rate. This creates positive time value for a call option, so it adds to its value or price. The second source is the fact that the spot price of the underlying asset is volatile and hence unpredictable. This also creates positive time value for a call option, so it also adds to its price. The third source is the fact that storing the underlying asset from now until expiry entails a storage cost. If the storage cost is positive, then it, too, creates positive time value for a call option and so adds to its price. But with an equity option, a storage cost arises only if a dividend is due before expiry, and any such dividend acts as a negative storage cost, which creates negative time for a call option and so reduces its price.

Interest as a source of time value

Suppose for the moment that LML share prices are predictable and that no LML dividends are due before next June. This means that interest is the only source of time value for a June call. To see why it creates time value, consider X who wants to own an LML share in nine months' time. He could decide to buy one then. Normally, the problem with this strategy would be that he would not know how much he would have to spend, because the price of LML shares is unpredictable. So, normally, he might consider other strategies that would enable him to determine his outlay today. In fact, X will not have this problem if, as is presently assumed, LML share prices are predictable. However, it is worth comparing two of the other strategies in these special circumstances, and then seeing the effect of relaxing the assumption that LML share prices are predictable. The two strategies that will be considered are (A) buying an LML share now for 180, and (B) buying a June call option with an exercise price of, say, 150.

(A) requires an outlay today of 180, so (B) would be equally attractive if it also required an outlay today of 180. In fact, (B) would require such an outlay if the option price was 36.41. For in that case, if X laid out 180 today, then he could spend 36.41 buying the option and lend the remaining 143.59 for nine months at the risk-free rate of 6%. When this loan was repaid with interest next June, he would receive exactly 150, which he could use to exercise the 150 option and buy the share. More generally, in the absence of volatility and dividends, the prices of in-the-money American and European calls are given by $[S - E/(1 + r)^T]$, where r is the risk-free rate and T is the time to maturity in years. In the example, r is 6%, or 0.06, and T is nine months or 0.75 years, so the price is $[180 - 150/(1.06)^{0.75}]$, which is $[180 - 143.59]$, or 36.41.

However, if the option had an exercise price that was above 188.04, then $[S - E/(1 + r)^T]$ would deliver a negative price. This is because X would have to lend more than 180 today at 6% in order to have more than 188.04 next June. So he could not reduce his total outlay today to 180 on strategy (B) unless the option had a negative price. In practice, options are never given negative prices. Consequently, options with exercise prices above 188.04 would be quoted as having zero prices, not negative prices, and they would find no buyers. It follows that if $[S - E/(1 + r)^T]$ is negative, then it does not give the correct price. To cover this problem, the following expressions are used for the prices of European and American call options in the absence of volatility and dividends, for these expressions show that the option prices take the maximum value out of zero and the value of $[S - E/(1 + r)^T]$:

$$C_E = \text{Max}\{0, [S - E/(1 + r)^T]\} \qquad (7.1)$$

$$C_A = \text{Max}\{0, [S - E/(1 + r)^T]\} \qquad (7.2)$$

Volatility as a source of time value

The assumption that the price of LML shares has no volatility will now be relaxed. This means that the share price is unpredictable. Recall X who wants to own an LML share in nine months' time and who considers (A) buying a share now for 180, and (B) buying a June call option with an exercise price of, say, 150. In the absence of volatility, X would outlay no more today for (B) than for (A) because (B) would have no advantage over (A). This meant that he would pay only 36.41 for the option. But the presence of volatility gives (B) an advantage over (A). So X will be willing to pay more than 36.41 for the option.

The reason that (B) has an advantage is that the spot price, S, could fall below the exercise price of 150, so that the option would go out-of-the-money. If this happened, then on strategy (B) X need not exercise the option and could instead buy an LML share at the current sub-150 spot price. In contrast, X could not take advantage of any such fall in the spot price if he adopted strategy (A). Even so, X would not be willing to pay much extra for the option. This is because S could well stay above 150. In that case, X would exercise the option and so buy the share for 150, but by paying more than 36.41 for the option, the cost of the share in terms of the outlay required today would exceed 180. Working out precisely how much extra X would pay beyond the amounts given by (7.1) and (7.2) requires exact formulae of the sort discussed in Chapter 8. For this chapter, the extra will be allowed for simply by replacing the '=' in (7.1) and (7.2) by a '≥'. So, in the absence of dividends, the formulae are:

$$C_E \geq \text{Max}\{0, [S - E/(1 + r)^T]\} \tag{7.3}$$

$$C_A \geq \text{Max}\{0, [S - E/(1 + r)^T]\} \tag{7.4}$$

With an in-the-money option, like a 150 call, the time value from volatility arises because there is a chance of the spot price falling enough to take the option out-of-the-money. But this time value naturally depends on how big that chance is. This means that it is higher for options that are just in-the-money than for those which are deeply in-the-money. Indeed, it would be negligible on a 150 call if the spot price was, say, 600, for then the chance of the spot price falling below 150 by expiry would seem negligible.

Volatility also creates time value for out-of-money options. In the absence of volatility, X would not consider buying an out-of-the-money call, or, more strictly, a call with an exercise price above 188.04, because his outlay on strategy (B) would then inevitably exceed the 180 outlay needed for strategy (A). But volatility gives out-of-the-money options some attraction.

To see this, consider X's attitude to an out-of-the-money 200 call. It might seem unlikely that X would pay anything for an option that entitles him to buy for 200 a share that he could buy today for 180. But the attraction of the option is that, if the spot price falls, then X need not exercise the option and could instead buy the share for less than 180. In contrast, he could not take advantage of a fall in the spot price if he bought the share now. Of course, the spot price might instead rise, but if it does, then the option effectively insures X against having to pay more than 200. The time value that volatility creates for an out-of-the-money call is higher if it is just out-of-the-money than if it is deeply out-of-the-money. Indeed, it would be negligible on a 200 call if the spot price was, say, 50, for then the chance of the spot price exceeding 200 at expiry would seem so small that people would pay very little to insure against it.

Dividends as a source of time value

The assumption that there are no dividends due on LML shares before the June options expire will now be relaxed. Suppose a dividend, D, of 7 is due in six months. Recall X who wants to own an LML share in nine months' time and who considers (A) buying an LML share now for 180, and (B) buying a June call option with an exercise price of, say, 150.

Suppose for a moment that there is no volatility. In that case, it was argued previously that X would regard (A) and (B) as equally attractive if they required the same outlay today, and this would occur if the option price was 36.41. However, now that a dividend is due before expiry, X would prefer (A) to (B) if they required the same outlay, because with (A) he will secure a dividend in six months, while with (B) he will not. So he would not consider (B) unless the option price was reduced to offset this drawback. The price does not have to be reduced by the full amount of the forgone dividend, that is 7. Instead, it must be reduced by an amount which X could lend today and have repaid with interest in six months to give him 7 then. With an interest rate of 6%, X actually needs to lend 6.80 today. So the option price must be reduced by 6.80 from 36.41 to 29.61. In general, the price must be reduced by the present value of the dividend, that is $D/(1 + r)^t$, where t is the time in years before the dividend is due. In the example, t is six months or 0.5 years, so $D/(1 + r)^t$ is $7/(1.06)^{0.5}$, or 6.80.

One way of altering (7.1) to reduce C_E by $D/(1 + r)^t$ would be to replace S by $S - D/(1 + r)^t$. However, it is simpler to define $S - D/(1 + r)^t$ as S^* and to replace S by S^*, as in (7.5) below. It is tempting simply to make the same alteration to (7.2) for C_A. But if the dividend was large, then this modified formula might give a price that was below the intrinsic value of $[S - E]$, yet American options are never sold for prices below their intrinsic values, for they can always be exercised to obtain their intrinsic values. So the formula for C_A must be further altered to show that the price cannot be below $[S - E]$. Thus the formulae for call options, if there is no volatility, are:

$$C_E = \text{Max}\{0, [S^* - E/(1 + r)^T]\} \tag{7.5}$$

$$C_A = \text{Max}\{0, [S^* - E/(1 + r)^T], [S - E]\} \tag{7.6}$$

To allow also for the time value created by volatility, (7.5) and (7.6) must be rewritten as:

$$C_E \geq \text{Max}\{0, [S^* - E/(1 + r)^T]\} \tag{7.7}$$

$$C_A \geq \text{Max}\{0, [S^* - E/(1 + r)^T], [S - E]\} \tag{7.8}$$

Graphical representations

The formulae derived above do not give precise values for call options in the presence of volatility, but they do allow some useful graphs of option values to be drawn. Consider two equity calls that are identical except that one is European and the other is American. Figure 7.2(a) illustrates the prices that they would have today at different possible spot prices if no dividend was due before expiry, while Figure 7.2(b) illustrates the prices that they would have today if a sizeable dividend was due before expiry. The horizontal axes show possible spot prices and also mark the exercise price, E.

In part (a), line 1 shows the intrinsic value of the European call and the American call at each possible spot price, S, as given by $\text{Max}\{0,[S-E]\}$. The intrinsic value is positive only when S exceeds E. Line 1, and the later lines, must be regarded as kinked and running along the horizontal axis to the left of the point where they meet it. At expiry, the options will only have the intrinsic value shown by line 1, but before expiry they will also have some time value. If the only source of time value was interest, then they would have some positive time value and would thus have the prices shown by line 2, as given in (7.1) and (7.2).

In part (a), however, both options have some further positive time value created by the volatility of the price of the underlying asset. This raises the option prices above those shown by line 2, especially if the spot price makes the options just in-the-money or just out-of-the-money. The final prices are shown by the curve marked $C_A = C_E$. This curve shows that the American and European calls have the same prices, as given in (7.3) and (7.4). The curve is drawn to reflect the fact that, at low spot prices, the time value created by volatility is negligible. The time value from volatility may also become negligible at very high spot prices when it may be felt that there is a negligible chance of the option ever going out-of-the-money.

In part (b), lines 1 and 2 are the same as in part (a). But here there is also a dividend before expiry which creates negative time value and so reduces the option prices. This reduction occurs because buying call options is now less tempting than buying the share itself, as buying the calls means forgoing a dividend. In the absence of volatility, the price of the European call would be shown by line 3, as given by (7.5). This line is below line 2 to reflect the downward effect a dividend has on the price of a European call, and it is below line 1 because the dividend is a sizeable one. This line cannot apply to the American call because such an option cannot have a price below its intrinsic value, as given by line 1; so in a case where there is a sizeable dividend, but no volatility, the price of the American call would be shown by the intrinsic value line 1, as implied by (7.6). This line is also numbered line 4 to show that it is the price of an American call after allowing for both interest and the dividend.

Allowing in part (b) for the extra positive time value created by volatility takes the final price of the European call from line 3 to C_E and the final price of the American call from line 4 to C_A. The formulae for C_E and C_A are as given by (7.7) and (7.8). These curves are lower than the curve in part (a) because a call option has a lower value when a dividend is due. However, the time

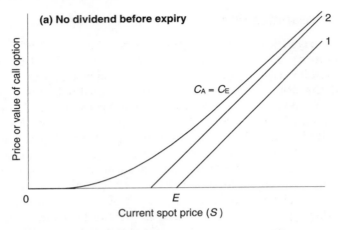

1   Intrinsic value of European and American calls = Max{0, [$S - E$]}
2   Value of European and American calls allowing for interest = Max{0, [$S - E/(1 + r)^T$]}
$C_A = C_E$ Value of European and American calls also allowing for volatility ≥ Max{0, [$S - E/(1 + r)^T$]}

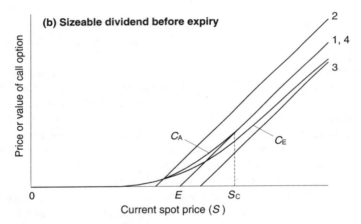

1 Intrinsic value of European and American calls = Max{0, [$S - E$]}
2 Value of European and American calls allowing for interest = Max{0, [$S - E/(1 + r)^T$]}
3 Value of European call also allowing for dividend ≥ Max{0, [$S^* - E/(1 + r)^T$]}
4 Value of American call also allowing for dividend = Max{0, [$S^* - E/(1 + r)^T$], [$S - E$]}
C_E Value of European call also allowing for volatility ≥ Max{0, [$S^* - E/(1 + r)^T$]}
C_A Value of American call also allowing for volatility ≥ Max{0, [$S^* - E/(1 + r)^T$], [$S - E$]}

Figure 7.2 Prices or values of call options

value created by volatility is still greatest for options that are just about at-the-money. This is reflected by the gap between C_E and line 3, and also by the gap between C_A and line 4, for these gaps are widest when the spot price makes the options just about at-the-money.

C_E cuts line 1 and shows that, at high spot prices, the European call can have a price that is below its intrinsic value. That cannot happen with the

American call, so C_A ends up touching line 1 but never goes below it. As the price of the European option can fall below its intrinsic value whereas the value of the American option cannot, the American call is always more desirable and so more valuable. Consequently, C_A lies above C_E at all possible spot prices.

Early exercise of American calls

Suppose, for a moment, that no dividend is due before expiry. Then curve $C_A = C_E$ in Fig. 7.2(a) shows that the prices of both the European call and the American call will always exceed their intrinsic values, which are shown by line 1. So any holder of an American call who wished to dispose of it would receive more by selling it at its current price than by exercising it early to secure its intrinsic value. Thus an American call would never be exercised early. Consequently, it has no advantage over a European call. In turn, it has the same value or price, as shown by $C_A = C_E$. Similar results would apply if there was a modest dividend before expiry, provided that it was too small to take the line equivalent to line 3 in part (b) below the intrinsic value line 1.

When a larger dividend is allowed for, the situation changes. Then, curve C_E in part (b) shows that the price of a European call may be *below* its intrinsic value if S rises high enough for its value to lie on that part of C_E that is below line 1. In contrast, the price of an American call can never fall below its intrinsic value because an American option can always be exercised for its intrinsic value. So, when a dividend is due before expiry, an American option is more desirable and has a higher price or premium. Accordingly, C_A is above C_E.

The gap between C_A and C_E is called an **early exercise premium** because the only reason that the American call is worth more is that it may be worth exercising before expiry if the spot price rises far enough. At high spot prices, the European call is worth less than its intrinsic value and its holder wishes it could be exercised for its intrinsic value. The only advantage of the American option over the European one is that it can be exercised early for its intrinsic value, but to secure this advantage, it must be exercised early when exercise is advantageous. So, broadly speaking, the American call must be exercised at spot prices which would make the holder of a European call wish that it could be exercised. More precisely, the American call should be exercised if the spot price rises to S_C, that is the **critical price** where the option's price ceases to exceed its intrinsic value. But if its holder wished to dispose of it when the spot price was below S_C, then selling it would raise more money than exercising it.

Figure 7.2(b) shows that at spot prices above S_C, C_A coincides with line 1 so that early exercise is advantageous. But, in practice, the only times when C_A and line 1 will coincide before expiry, and thus the only times when early exercise may be advantageous, are the moments just before a dividend is due. In other words, the price of an American call with some time left to expiry will always exceed its intrinsic value except immediately before a dividend is due.

To see why, consider a 150 American call option for an LML share that expires in nine months, and suppose an LML dividend of 7 is due in six months. As the spot price of LML shares today is 180, this call has an intrinsic value of 30. However, its price *must* exceed 30. If its price was only 30, then LML shareholders could make riskless profits. For they could today sell each share for 180. Then they could lend 150 of the 180 raised from each share at the risk-free rate of 6%, and use the remaining 30 to buy a 150 call option. Then, just before the dividend is due in six months, they could demand repayment of the loan with interest, to secure 154.43 in all. They could then exercise the option and buy an LML share for 150. So they would make a profit of 4.43 in the form of interest, and yet lose no dividends. Thus LML shareholders would demand many call options, and this would send the option price above 30.

This example assumed that buying a share just before a dividend is due secures the dividend for the new owner. In fact, securities go ex-dividend a little while before the dividends are paid, as noted in Section 2.3, and LML shares must be owned at that ex-dividend moment to secure the next dividend. Strictly, then, call options should only ever be exercised just before the shares go ex-dividend, which is a little while before the dividends are actually paid.

7.3 PUT OPTIONS

Intrinsic value and time value

Like every call option, every put option has an **intrinsic value**, but for a put option this is defined as $\text{Max}\{0,[E - S]\}$ so that it equals whichever is the larger, or maximum, out of zero and the value of $[E - S]$, where E is the exercise price of the option and S is the current spot price of the underlying asset. In the case of a 200 LML put option, the exercise price of 200 is above the current spot price of LML shares, which is 180, so $[E - S]$ is greater than zero; consequently, the intrinsic value equals $[E - S]$, which is 20. In the case of a 150 LML put option, the exercise price of 150 is below the spot price of 180, so $[E - S]$ is less than zero; consequently, the intrinsic value equals zero.

There are two ways of seeing the significance of the intrinsic values of put options:

1. The intrinsic value of an American put shows the gain that its holder could secure by exercising it now. Thus the holder of a 200 American put could gain 20 now by exercising it and selling for 200 a share that is worth 180. But the holder of a 150 American put would gain nothing at all by exercising it now and selling for 150 a share that is worth 180.
2. The intrinsic value of any option that is about to expire shows the gain that the holder is about to make. The holder of a 200 put option that expires today is about to gain 20 because, at expiry, the holder will exercise the right to sell for 200 a share that is worth 180. But the holder of a 150 put that expires today is about to gain nothing, for nothing would be gained at expiry by exercising the right to sell at 150 a share that is worth 180.

When a put option has an exercise price that is above the spot price, so that it has a positive intrinsic value, it is called **in-the-money**. So a 200 put is in-

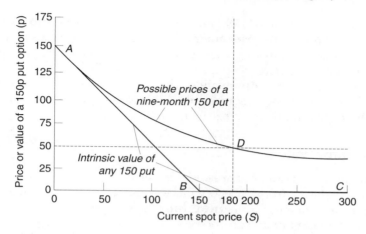

Figure 7.3 The intrinsic value of any 150 put and the possible value of a nine-month 150 put.

the-money. Indeed, it is in-the-money by 20. When a put option has an exercise price that is below the spot price, so that it has a zero intrinsic value, it is **out-of-the-money**. So a 150 put is out-of-the-money. Sometimes an option has an exercise price that is equal to, or close to, the spot price. Such an option is **at-the-money**.

The intrinsic value of any given put depends solely on its exercise price and the current spot price. In Fig. 7.3, the kinked line *ABC* shows what the intrinsic value of any 150 put would be for all possible spot prices from zero to 300. For example, it shows that the intrinsic value would be zero if the spot price was above 150, so that the option was out-of-the-money, while the intrinsic value would be positive if the spot price was below 150, so that the option was in-the-money.

The holder of a put option that is about to expire is about to make a gain equal to its intrinsic value. Consequently, the option has a value or price that is equal to its intrinsic value. So the kinked line *ABC* in Fig. 7.3 shows what the price of a 150 put would be just before expiry for different possible spot prices at expiry. However, the price of a put option with some time left before expiry rarely equals its intrinsic value and is often higher. The gap between its price and its intrinsic value is called its **time value**, because this gap diminishes as expiry approaches and disappears entirely at expiry. The reasons why time value arises on put options with some time left are explored shortly.

Today, when the spot price of LML shares is 180, the price of a 150 put option expiring in nine months on the fourth Wednesday of next June might be 50, way over its zero intrinsic value. Point *D* on Fig. 7.3 shows this price. The curve through *D* shows the prices that this nine-month 150 put option might have had today for a wide range of other possible spot prices. If the spot price is very low, then a European put option can have a negative time value. If it does, then the curve showing its price at different spot prices will intersect the sloping part of the intrinsic value line *ABC*.

Although the price that a 150 put option expiring next June would have today at each possible spot price might be as shown by the curve through D, the price that it would have at each possible spot price when it expires next June is given by the kinked intrinsic value line ABC. In between, as time passes and its time value diminishes, the curve showing its price at each possible spot price will get progressively lower than the one through D until, at expiry, the curve finally 'collapses' on to ABC.

Sources of time value

As with call options, there are three sources of time value on put options with some time left before expiry. These will be considered in turn for put options that expire in nine months' time next June. It will be seen that the fact that people can lend money and earn interest creates negative time value, but the fact that the spot price of the underlying asset is volatile and hence unpredictable creates positive time value. The fact that storing the underlying asset until expiry entails a storage cost creates negative time value if the storage cost is positive, but it creates positive time value if the storage cost is negative. In the case of an option where the underlying asset is an equity on which a dividend is due before expiry, the storage cost is negative.

Interest as a source of time value

Suppose for the moment that LML share prices are predictable and that no LML dividends are due in the nine months before next June. This means that interest is the only source of time value for a June put. To see why it creates time value, consider Y who wants to raise money next June by selling an LML share. She could decide to sell one then. Normally, the problem with this strategy would be that she would not know how much money she would secure, because the price of LML shares is unpredictable. So, normally, she might consider other strategies that would enable her to determine today the amount she will secure. In fact, Y will not have this problem if, as is presently assumed, LML share prices are predictable. However, it is worth comparing two of the other strategies in these special circumstances, and then seeing the effect of relaxing the assumption that LML share prices are predictable. The two strategies that will be considered are (A) selling an LML share now for 180 and lending that 180 risk-free at 6% until June, and (B) buying a European June put option with an exercise price of, say, 200.

(A) secures 180 today, so it will secure 188.04 by June when the loan is repaid with nine months' interest. So (B) would be equally attractive if it also resulted in Y securing 188.04 in June. In fact, (B) would secure 188.04 if the option price was 11.45. In that case, if Y bought the option today for 11.45, then next June she would be worse off by that 11.45 and the interest it would have earned, that is 11.96 in all. However, she could also sell the share for 200. So she could use 11.96 of that to make up her loss and still secure 188.04, as in (A).

More generally, it may seem that in the absence of volatility and dividends, the price of a European put option, P_E, can be found from the expression

$P_E(1 + r)^T = E - S(1 + r)^T$. This can be rearranged to give P_E as $[E/(1 + r)^T - S]$, which in the example is $[200/(1.06)^{0.75} - 180]$, that is $191.45 - 180$ or 11.45. However, if the option had an exercise price under 188.04, then $[E/(1 + r)^T - S]$ would deliver a negative price. This arises because Y would then receive less than 188.04 if she exercised her option in nine months, so she could not secure a sum of 188.04 by using strategy (B) unless the option price was negative. In practice, options are never given negative prices. Consequently, options with exercise prices under 188.04 would be quoted as having zero prices, not negative prices, and they would find no buyers. So if $[E/(1 + r)^T - S]$ is negative, then it does not give the correct price for a European put. This problem can be overcome by using the expression $\text{Max}\{0,[E/(1 + r)^T - S]\}$.

It might be thought that this expression would also apply to American puts, but it does not. That is because $[E/(1 + r)^T - S]$ delivers a value that is less than the option's intrinsic value of $[E - S]$, yet an American option will never be sold for less than its intrinsic value for which it can always be exercised. Admittedly an American 200 put would be worth no more than 11.45 to Y as part of strategy (B). Even so, people would willingly pay up to 20 for it. For with the spot price of LML shares at 180, they could then buy an LML share for 180 today and at once exercise the put to sell it for 200. So they could make instant profits if the option price was below 20. Consequently, the formula for the price of an American put has to show that it cannot be less than its intrinsic value. This means that, in the absence of volatility and dividends, the prices of put options are given by:

$$P_E = \text{Max}\{0,[E/(1 + r)^T] - S\} \tag{7.9}$$

$$P_A = \text{Max}\{0,[E - S]\} \tag{7.10}$$

Volatility as a source of time value

The assumption that the price of LML shares has no volatility will now be relaxed. This means that the share price is unpredictable. Recall Y who wants to raise some money in nine months' time by selling an LML share. She considers (A) selling a share now for 180 and lending that 180 risk-free at 6% to secure 188.04 in nine months, and (B) buying a European June put option with an exercise price of, say, 200. In the absence of volatility, Y would outlay no more today for (B) than the sum that would leave her with 188.04 in nine months because (B) would have no advantage over (A). This meant that she would pay only 11.45 for the option. But the presence of volatility gives (B) an advantage over (A). Consequently, Y will be willing to pay more than 11.45 for the option.

The reason that (B) has an advantage is that the spot price, S, could rise above the exercise price of 200, so that the option would go out-of-the-money. If this happened, then on strategy (B) Y need not exercise the option and could instead sell her LML share at the current above-200 spot price. In contrast, Y could not take advantage of any such rise in the spot price if she adopted strategy (A). Even so, Y will not want to pay much more for the option. This is because S could well stay below 200. In that case, Y would exercise the option and so sell her share for 200, but she would then secure less than 188.04. This is because she will have spent more than 11.45 on the option and so, once the lost interest on its premium is allowed for too, she will have lost more than 11.96 by buying it. Working out precisely how much extra Y would pay over the amounts given by (7.9) and (7.10) requires exact formulae of the sort discussed in Chapter 8. For this chapter, the extra will be allowed for by replacing the '=' in (7.9) and (7.10) by a '≥'. So, in the absence of dividends, the formulae are:

$$P_E \geq \text{Max}\{0,[E/(1 + r)^T - S]\} \tag{7.11}$$

$$P_A \geq \text{Max}\{0,[E - S]\} \tag{7.12}$$

With an in-the-money option, like a 200 put, the time value from volatility arises because there is a chance of the spot price rising enough to take the option out-of-the-money. But this time value naturally depends on how big that chance is. This means that it is higher for options that are just in-the-money than for those which are deeply in-the-money. Indeed, it would be negligible on a 200 put if the spot price was, say, 50, for then the chance of the spot price rising above 200 by expiry would seem negligible.

Volatility also creates time value for out-of-the-money options. In the absence of volatility, Y would not consider buying an out-of-the-money put, or, more strictly, a put with an exercise price below 188.04, because strategy (B) would then secure less than 188.04 next June, and so secure less than strategy (A). But volatility gives out-of-the-money options some attraction.

To see this, consider Y's attitude to an out-of-the-money 150 put. It might seem unlikely that Y would pay anything for an option that entitles her to sell for 150 a share that she could sell today for 180. But the attraction of the option is that, if the spot price rises, then Y need not exercise the option and could instead sell the share for more than 180. In contrast, she could not take advantage of a rise in the spot price if she sold the share now. Of course, the spot price might instead fall, but if it does, then the option effectively insures Y against having to sell her share for less than 150. The time value that volatility creates for an out-of-the-money put is higher if it is just out-of-the-money than if it is deeply out-of-the-money. Indeed, it would be negligible on a 150 put if the spot price was, say, 600, for then the chance of the spot price being under 150 at expiry would seem so small that people would pay very little to insure against it.

Dividends as a source of time value

The assumption that there are no dividends due on LML shares before the June options expire will now be relaxed. Suppose a dividend, D, of 7 is due in six months. Recall Y who wants to raise some money in nine months' time next June by selling an LML share. She considers (A) selling a share now for 180 and lending that 180 risk-free to secure 188.04 in nine months, and (B) buying a European June put option with an exercise price of, say, 200.

Suppose for a moment that there is no volatility. In that case, it was argued previously that Y would regard (A) and (B) as equally attractive if they both secured 188.04 next June from selling her share, and this would occur if the option price was 11.45. However, now that a dividend is due before expiry, Y would prefer (B) to (A) if the price was 11.45. This is because (B) would secure a dividend of 7 after six months, and Y could then lend this 7 at the risk-free rate of 6% for three months and so have an extra 7.10 after nine months. So Y might now select (B), even if the option price was above 11.45. In fact, she would be willing to pay 6.80 extra for the option. For if its price rose by 6.80, then in nine months she would be worse off by that sum plus the interest that it would have earned, which is 7.10, but this would be exactly offset by the 7.10 that she would secure in nine months by receiving the dividend. So if the price was 6.80 higher than 11.45, that is 18.25, then she would once again find (B) equally attractive to (A). The extra price, 6.80, is the present value of the dividend, that is $D/(1 + r)^t$. So, more generally, the price will be $D/(1 + r)^t$ higher than before.

(7.9) could be altered to raise C_E by the amount $D/(1 + r)^t$ if S was replaced by $S - D/(1 + r)^t$, but it is simpler to define $S - D/(1 + r)^t$ as S^* and to replace S by S^*, as in (7.13) below. (7.13) would also apply to an American put except that if the dividend is small, so that S^* is large, (7.13) could deliver a price less than the option's intrinsic value, and an American option can never have a price less than its intrinsic value. So the formula for P_A is the same as that for P_E, except that this constraint is allowed for. Thus the formulae for put options, if there is no volatility, are:

$$P_E = \text{Max}\{0, [E/(1 + r)^T - S^*]\} \tag{7.13}$$

$$P_A = \text{Max}\{0, [E/(1 + r)^T - S^*], [E - S]\} \tag{7.14}$$

To allow also for the time value created by volatility, (7.13) and (7.14) must be rewritten as:

$$P_E \geq \text{Max}\{0, [E/(1 + r)^T - S^*]\} \tag{7.15}$$

$$P_A \geq \text{Max}\{0, [E/(1 + r)^T - S^*], [E - S]\} \tag{7.16}$$

Graphical representations

The formulae derived above do not give precise values for put options in the presence of volatility, but they do allow some useful graphs of option values to be drawn. Consider two equity puts that are identical except that one is European and the other is American. Figure 7.4(a) illustrates the prices that they would have today at different possible spot prices if no dividend was due before expiry, while Figure 7.4(b) illustrates the prices that they would have today if a sizeable dividend was due before expiry. The horizontal axes show possible spot prices and also mark the exercise price, E.

In part (a), line 1 shows the intrinsic value of the European put and the American put at each possible spot price, S, as given by $\text{Max}\{0, [E - S]\}$. The intrinsic value is positive only when S is less than E. Line 1, and the later lines, must be regarded as kinked and running along the horizontal axis to the right of the point where they meet it. At expiry, the options will only have

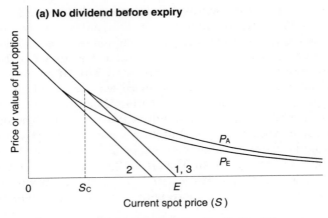

(a) No dividend before expiry

1   Intrinsic value of European and American puts = Max{0, [E − S]}
2   Value of European put allowing for interest = Max{0, [E/(1 + r)^T − S]}
3   Value of American put allowing for interest = Max{0, [E − S]}
P_E Value of European put also allowing for volatility ≥ Max{0, [E/(1 + r)^T − S]}
P_A Value of American put also allowing for volatility ≥ Max{0, [E − S]}

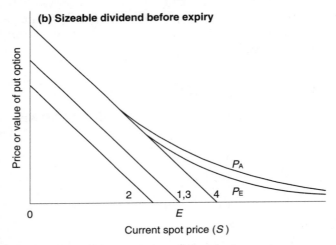

(b) Sizeable dividend before expiry

1   Intrinsic value of European and American puts = Max{0, [E − S]}
2   Value of European put allowing for interest = Max{0, [E/(1 + r)^T − S]}
3   Value of American put allowing for interest = Max{0, [E − S]}
4   Value of European and American puts also allowing for dividend = Max{0, [E/(1 + r)^T − S*]}
P_E Value of European put also allowing for volatility ≥ Max{0, [E/(1 + r)^T − S*]}
P_A Value of American put also allowing for volatility ≥ Max{0, [E/(1 + r)^T − S*]}

Figure 7.4   Prices or values of put options.

the intrinsic value shown by line 1, but before expiry they may also have some time value. If the only source of time value was interest, then the European put would have a negative time value and it would have the price shown by line 2, as given by (7.9). However, the price of the American put cannot be given by line 2, for this would give it a price below its intrinsic value. Instead, its price still equals its intrinsic value, as given by (7.10) and as shown by line 1. This line is also marked as line 3 to show that it is also the price after allowing for interest.

However, both options have some extra positive time value created by volatility. Allowing for this, part (a) takes the final price of the European put from line 2 to the curve P_E and the final price of the American put from line 3 to the curve P_A. The formulae for P_E and P_A are given by (7.11) and (7.12). The gaps between P_E and line 2 and between P_A and line 3 are largest when the spot price makes the options just about at-the-money. As drawn, P_E coincides with line 2 at low spot prices to show that the time value created by volatility is negligible for a put option that is deeply in-the-money. P_E cuts through line 1 to show that, at low spot prices, the European put can have a price below its intrinsic value. That cannot happen with the American put. Its final curve, P_A, ends up touching line 1 but never goes below it. P_A lies above P_E at all values of the spot price. The reason is that no matter how low the spot price may fall, an American put can never have a price below its intrinsic value, whereas a European put can. So the American put is more desirable and hence more valuable.

In part (b), lines 1, 2 and 3 are the same as in part (a). But here there is also a source of positive time value from a sizeable dividend. Ignoring volatility for a moment, the price of the European put would be as shown by line 4, as given by (7.13). This is above line 2 to reflect the upward effect that a dividend has on the price of a European put, and it is above line 1 because the dividend is a sizeable one. Line 4 also applies to the American put when the dividend is large enough to take its price above its intrinsic value, as implied by (7.14).

Allowing in part (b) for the extra positive time value created by volatility takes the final prices of the European and American puts from line 4 to curves P_E and P_A respectively. These curves are based on two similar formulae, (7.15) and (7.16). The only difference is that (7.16) shows that an American put cannot have a price below its intrinsic value, but this is irrelevant in part (b) where the sizeable dividend means that line 4 is above line 1 so that the American put always has a price well over its intrinsic value. So it might seem that P_E and P_A should coincide, yet P_A is above P_E. This is because the American put will have a higher value after the dividend is paid, as implied by part (a), so it will naturally fetch a higher price beforehand as well. Both P_E and P_A have their largest gaps above line 4 when the spot price makes the options just about at-the-money, for this is when volatility generates the highest time value.

Early exercise of American puts

Suppose for a moment that no dividend is due before expiry, as in Figure 7.4(a). Then the curve P_E in part (a) shows that the price of the European put may be *below* its intrinsic value if S falls low enough for the price to lie on that part of the curve that is below line 1. In contrast, the price of the American put can never be below its intrinsic value because American options can always be exercised for their intrinsic values. So, as just noted, American options are more desirable and have higher prices, so P_A is above P_E.

The gap between P_A and P_E reflects the early exercise premium, that is the extra value of the American put that arises because it may be worth exercising before expiry if the spot price falls far enough. At low spot prices, the European put is worth less than its intrinsic value and its holder wishes it could be exercised for its intrinsic value. The only advantage of the American option over the European one is that it can be exercised early for its intrinsic value, but to secure this advantage, it must be exercised early when exercise is advantageous. So, broadly speaking, the American put must be exercised at spot prices which would make the holder of the European put wish it could be exercised. More precisely, the American put should be exercised if the spot price falls to the critical price, S_C, where the option's price ceases to exceed its intrinsic value. But if its holder wished to dispose of it when the spot price was above S_C, then selling it would raise more money than exercising it.

Suppose, next, that a sizeable dividend is due before expiry, as in Fig. 7.4(b). Then P_A shows that the price of the American put always exceeds its intrinsic value, which is given by line 1. Thus any holder of an American put who wished to dispose of it would receive more by selling it than by exercising it early, so no holder would ever exercise the put early for its intrinsic value. However, this result might not apply if the line equivalent to line 4 in part (b) lay below line 1, which could happen if any dividend due before expiry was small. Either way, though, P_A in part (b) would lie above P_E, for, as noted above, the American put will be worth more after the dividend is paid, as shown in part (a), so it must also be worth more beforehand.

7.4 FUTURES CALL OPTIONS

This section explains the factors that affect the price of a futures call option by considering the futures call options on LML shares. To see how these **equity futures options** work, suppose that X holds a futures call option for one LML share. If he exercises it, either at expiry or, perhaps, earlier in the case of an American option, then he will be given a futures contract. This will entitle him to buy one LML share at a futures price equal to the exercise price of the option, E_F. He will be able to buy the share when the futures contract matures, which will be taken to be just after the expiry time of the original option. Of course, X will exercise the option only if the futures price of the contract that he will secure is below the spot futures price, S_F, that is currently being agreed on new futures contracts for LML shares that mature on the same day as the futures contract that underlies his option.

Intrinsic value

Like ordinary call options, futures call options have intrinsic values. For American futures calls, the **intrinsic value** shows the gain that could be secured by immediate exercise, while for all futures calls that are about to expire, it shows the gain that is about to be made. The intrinsic value of a futures call option is defined as $\text{Max}\{0,[S_F - E_F]\}$. So, to work out the intrinsic values of the 150 and the 200 futures call options, where E_F is respectively 150 and 200, it is first necessary to work out the relevant S_F. This will be different for options with different expiry dates. For example, the underlying asset of a futures call option that expires today, on the fourth Wednesday in September, is a futures contract that matures today, whereas the underlying asset for a futures call option that expires in, say, nine months, is a futures contract that matures next June; and the S_F that people will agree today to pay for LML shares in futures contracts that mature today is different from the S_F that they will agree today to pay for LML shares in futures contracts that mature next June.

· Consider, first, futures call options that expire today. Their underlying asset is a futures contract that matures today. With these futures contracts, S_F will equal today's spot price for LML shares of 180. For Section 5.3 explained that the futures price agreed in new futures contracts always converges with the current spot price of the underlying asset as maturity approaches. As S_F is 180, the intrinsic value of a 150 futures call expiring today is 30, so it is-in-the-money by 30. So anyone who holds one is about to gain 30 by exercising it to secure a futures contract to buy an LML share today at a futures price of 150 which is 30 below the futures price being agreed on new futures contracts maturing today. But the intrinsic value of any 200 futures call expiring today is zero, so it is out-of-the-money. So anyone who holds one of these is about to gain nothing at all, for they will not exercise the option to secure a futures contract to buy an LML share today at a futures price of 200 when futures contracts maturing today can instead be agreed at a futures price of 180.

Consider, next, the futures options that expire next June. Their underlying asset is a futures contract that matures in June. In these futures contracts, S_F will equal today's spot price of their underlying asset, which is an LML share, plus the cost of carrying that asset until maturity. The carrying cost of an LML share is the interest lost by buying it, minus any dividend due before maturity. Assume for the moment that no LML dividend is due before maturity. Then the precise relationship between S_F and the spot price of LML shares, S, will actually be given by $S_F = S(1 + r)^T$, where T is the time to maturity. Suppose that the risk-free interest rate, r, is 6%. Then, with S equal to 180 and T equal to nine months or 0.75 years, S_F will be $180(1.06)^{0.75}$ or 188.04.

To see why S_F will be 188.04, suppose first that it was higher at, say, 195. Then many people would buy LML shares today for 180 and agree futures contracts to sell them next June, so pushing the futures price down. By paying 180 for a share, they would, of course, lose the risk-free interest they could have earned on that sum by June, that is 8.04, but they would instead sell the share for 195 to make a capital gain on it of 15. So they would make an overall profit next June of $(15 - 8.04)$ or 6.96. In contrast, if the futures price was below

188.04 at, say, 183, then many people who own LML shares would sell them today for 180 and agree futures contracts to buy LML shares next June, so pushing the futures price up. By selling a share for 180 today, they would raise a sum of 180 which they could lend risk-free at 6% and so have 180 plus 8.04 interest after nine months, that is 188.04. They would use 183 of this next June to buy the share back for 183 and so have 5.04 left over as a profit.

As the S_F for next June is 188.04, the June 150 futures call options have intrinsic values of 38.04 and are in-the-money by 38.04. So, for example, the holder of a American June 150 call could gain 38.04 today by exercising it. For the holder would then secure a futures contract to buy an LML share at a futures price of 150, and could at once close this futures position by making an offsetting futures contract to sell an LML share at a futures price of 188.04. The gain of 38.04 would be received at once through the marking-to-market system used with futures. Conversely, the June 200 options have intrinsic values of zero and are out-of-the-money. So, for example, the holder of an American 200 June call would not exercise it to secure a futures contract to buy an LML share at a futures price of 200, for it is possible to agree such contracts today at a futures price of 188.04.

Time value and its sources

The price of a futures call option with some time before expiry rarely equals its intrinsic value and is usually higher. The gap between its price and its intrinsic value is its **time value**. This gap diminishes as expiry approaches and disappears at expiry. It might be expected that the three sources of time value for an ordinary call would also create time value for a futures call. These three sources will be considered in turn, using the example of a futures call option on LML shares that expires in nine months' time next June.

It will be seen that the first source, which is that people can lend for interest, tends to create negative time value for futures call options. In contrast, the second source, which is that the spot price of the underlying asset is volatile and hence unpredictable, creates positive time value. In the example, the price of the underlying asset is the futures price of LML shares, and, of course, this futures price is volatile only because the spot price of LML shares themselves is also volatile. The third source, which is the cost of storing the underlying asset, does not apply to futures options because the underlying asset is a futures contract which costs nothing to store. Of course, there is an asset underlying the futures contract, in the example LML shares, and these may have a negative storage cost in the form of a dividend before expiry. But it will be seen that a dividend does not affect the relationship between the price of a futures call option and the futures price of the shares.

Interest as a source of time value

Suppose for the moment that the future price of LML shares is predictable, so that the only source of time value for a futures call option is interest. Also, suppose for simplicity that no dividend is due on LML shares before next June.

To see why interest creates time value, consider X who wants to own an LML share in nine months' time. He could decide to buy one then. Normally, the problem with this strategy would be that he would not know how much he would have to spend, because the price of LML shares is unpredictable. So, normally, he might consider other strategies that enable him to determine his outlay today. In fact, X will not have this problem if, as is presently assumed, the price of LML shares is predictable. However, it is worth comparing two of the other strategies in these special circumstances and then seeing the effect of relaxing the assumption that LML share prices are predictable. The two strategies that will be considered are (A) buying an LML share now for 180, and (B) buying a June *European* futures call option with an exercise price of, say, 150.

(A) requires an outlay today of 180, so (B) would be equally attractive if it also required an outlay of 180. In fact, (B) would require such an outlay if the futures call price was 36.41. For in that case, if X laid out 180 today, then he could spend 36.41 buying the option and lend the remaining 143.59 for nine months at the risk-free rate of 6%. When this loan was repaid with interest in June, he would receive 150. So he could exercise the option and use the 150 to pay the futures price for the share. More generally, in the absence of volatility, a European futures call has the same price as an ordinary call, namely $\text{Max}\{0,[S - E_F/(1 + r)^T]\}$, as shown in (7.1). In the example this is $\text{Max}\{0,[180 - 150/1.06^{0.75}]\}$ which is $\text{Max}\{0,36.41\}$, or 36.41.

It was shown above that $S_F = S(1 + r)^T$, so that $S = S_F/(1 + r)^T$. Consequently, $\text{Max}\{0,[S - E_F/(1 + r)^T]\}$ can be re-written as $\text{Max}\{0,[(S_F/(1 + r)^T - E_F/(1 + r)^T]\}$ which simplifies to $\text{Max}\{0,[(S_F - E_F)/(1 + r)^T]\}$. This formula always delivers a price below the option's intrinsic value of $[S_F - E_F]$, which was shown earlier to be 38.04 for a 150 futures call. So interest here creates a negative time value. However, as this formula delivers a price below an option's intrinsic value, it cannot apply to an American futures call. For no holder of an American option would sell it for less than the intrinsic value that could be secured by exercising it. So, in the absence of volatility, the price of an American futures call equals its intrinsic value, and the prices of futures call options are:

$$FC_E = \text{Max}\{0,[(S_F - E_F)/(1 + r)^T]\} \qquad (7.17)$$

$$FC_A = \text{Max}\{0,[S_F - E_F]\} \qquad (7.18)$$

Volatility as a source of time value

The assumption that the price of LML shares has no volatility will now be relaxed. This means that the share price is unpredictable. Recall X who wants to own an LML share in nine months' time and who considers (A) buying a share now for 180, and (B) buying a June European futures call option with an exercise price of, say, 150. In the absence of volatility, X would outlay no more today for (B) than for (A) because (B) would have no advantage over (A). This meant that he would pay only 36.41 for the option. But the presence of volatility gives (B) an advantage over (A). So X will be willing to pay more than 36.41 for the option.

The reason that (B) has an advantage is that the spot price of LML shares, S, could fall below 150 before expiry. If this happened, then on strategy (B) X need not exercise the option and could instead buy LML shares at a sub-150 spot price. In contrast, X could not take advantage of any such fall in the spot price if he adopted strategy (A). Even so, X would not be willing to pay much extra for the option. This is because S could well stay above 150. In that case, X would exercise the option and would buy the share for 150, but by paying more than 36.41 for the option, the cost of the share in terms of the outlay required today would exceed 180. Working out precisely how much extra X would pay for options beyond the amounts given in (7.17) and (7.18) requires exact formulae of the sort discussed in Chapter 8. For this chapter, the extra will be allowed for simply by replacing the '=' by a '≥'. So the formulae are:

$$FC_E \geq \text{Max}\{0,[(S_F - E_F)/(1 + r)^T]\} \qquad (7.19)$$

$$FC_A \geq \text{Max}\{0,[S_F - E_F]\} \qquad (7.20)$$

For an in-the-money option, like the 150 futures call, the time value created by volatility arises because S could fall below 150 before or at expiry. If it was below 150 at expiry, then S_F would also be below 150, for S_F will equal S at expiry. So this time value arises partly because there is a chance of S_F ending up below E_F to make the option end up out-of-the-money. But this time value naturally depends on how big that chance is. So it is higher for options that are just in-the-money than for those which are deeply in-the-money. Indeed, it would be negligible on a 150 futures call if S was, say, 600, for then the chance of S falling below 150 by expiry would seem negligible.

Volatility also creates time value for out-of-the-money options. To see this, consider X's attitude to an out-of-the-money 200 futures call. It might seem unlikely that X would pay anything for an option that allows him to secure a futures contract in which he could buy a share at a futures price of 200 when he could buy a share today for 180. But the attraction of the option is that, if the spot price falls, then X need not exercise it and could instead buy the share for less than 180. In contrast, he could not take advantage of any future fall in the future spot price if he bought the share now. Of course, the spot price might instead rise, but if it does, then the futures option effectively insures X against having to pay more than 200. The time value that volatility creates for an out-of-the-money futures call is higher if it is just out-of-the money than if it is deeply out-of-the-money. Indeed, it would be negligible on a 200 futures call if the spot price was, say, 50, for then the chance of the spot price exceeding 200 by expiry would seem so small that people would pay very little to insure against it.

Dividends and futures call options

The assumption that there are no dividends due on LML shares before the nine-month options expire next June will now be relaxed. It will be supposed that a dividend of 7 is due in six months. This means that the carrying cost of LML shares is lower than before, and that in turn means that the futures price for LML shares in futures contracts maturing next June will be lower than before. It will actually drop to 180.94.

For, if the futures price of LML shares for next June was higher than 180.94, say 184, then many people would buy an LML share today for 180 and agree to sell it next June in a futures contract, so pushing S_F down. By paying 180, they would admittedly lose the risk-free interest they could otherwise have secured, and so lose the 188.04 they would have had in nine months allowing also for the interest on this sum. However, by buying the LML share they will secure a dividend of 7 in six months, which could be lent at 6% and be worth 7.10 in nine months, so in nine months they would have 7.10 from the dividend plus a share they have agreed to sell for 184, making a total of 191.10. This is well above the 188.04 they would have had if the share was not bought.

In contrast, if the futures price was below 180.94, say, 177, then many people with LML shares would sell them today for 180 and agree to buy LML shares next June in futures contracts, so pushing the futures price up. Anyone selling a share today would raise 180, which they could lend risk-free at 6% to secure 188.04 in nine months, although they would lose the 7.10 which they would have been able to get if they had kept the share and lent the dividend of 7 when it came after six months. However, even allowing for this loss, they will secure 180.94, that is $(188.04 - 7.10)$, which will more than cover the 177 needed to buy the share back, so they would make a profit.

In general, the futures price agreed on a futures contract maturing in T years is given by $S_F = S^*(1 + r)^T$. S^* here is $S - D/(1 + r)^t$, that is the spot price, S, minus the present value of the dividend which is due in t years. In the example, t is 0.5 years, so the present value of the dividend is $7/(1.06)^{0.5}$, or 6.80. So S^* is $(180 - 6.80)$, or 173.20. In turn S_F is $173.20(1.06)^{0.75}$, or 180.94.

To see the effect of a dividend before expiry, recall X who wants to own an LML in nine months' time, next June. He is considering (A) buying an LML share now for 180, and (B) buying a June European futures call option with an exercise price of, say, 150.

Suppose for a moment that there is no volatility. In that case, it was argued previously that X would regard (A) and (B) as equally attractive if they required the same outlay today, and this would occur if the option price was 36.41. However, now that a dividend is due before expiry, X would prefer (A) to (B) if they required the same outlay, because with (A) he will secure a dividend in six months, while with (B) he will not. So he would not consider (B) unless the option price was reduced to offset this drawback. The price does not have to be reduced by the full amount of the dividend, that is 7. Instead, it must be reduced by an amount which X could lend today and have repaid with interest in six months to give him 7 then. With an interest rate of 6%, X must today lend 6.80. So the price must be reduced by 6.80 from 36.41 to 29.61. In general, the price must be reduced by the present value of the dividend, that is $D/(1 + r)^t$. In the example, this is $7/(1.06)^{0.5}$ or 6.80.

As a dividend before expiry reduces the option's price, it might seem that the price formulae (7.17) and (7.18) need changing. However, (7.17) gives FC_E as $\text{Max}\{0, [(S_F - E_F)/(1 + r)^T]\}$, and this does not need changing because it refers to S_F which itself allows for the dividend. For, as explained above, S_F equals

$S^*(1+r)^T$ when a dividend is due, and S^* equals $S - D/(1+r)^t$, where D is the dividend. Indeed, in the example, (7.17) gives FC_E correctly as Max$\{0,[(180.94 - 150)/(1.06)^{0.75}]\}$, which is Max$\{0,29.61\}$ or 29.61. However, (7.17) gives a price below the intrinsic value, which is $[S_F - E_F]$, so it still does not apply to an American futures call. So FC_A is still given by (7.18), which shows that it cannot be less than the intrinsic value.

As (7.17) and (7.18) continue to apply in the absence of volatility, so (7.19) and (7.20) continue to apply in the presence of volatility. They repeat (7.17) and (7.18) except that they replace the '=' by a '≥'. However, the fact that the same formulae apply does not mean that a dividend before expiry has absolutely no effect on the option's value for a given S_F. Section 8.5 explains that the volatility of the futures price may be very slightly higher when a dividend is due, so the extent to which volatility creates time value may also be very slightly higher.

Graphical representations

The formulae derived above do not give precise prices for European and American futures call options in the presence of volatility, but they do allow some useful graphs of option prices to be drawn. Consider two futures call options that are identical except that one is European and one is American. Figure 7.5 illustrates the price that each would have today at different possible current futures prices. The horizontal axis shows the possible current futures prices and the exercise price, E_F, and the vertical axis measures the option prices. This graph applies whether or not a dividend is due before expiry, but a dividend before expiry will affect the current futures price.

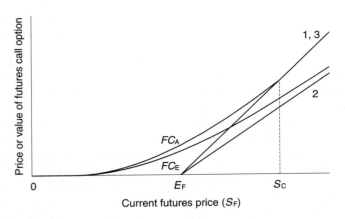

1   Intrinsic value of European and American Futures calls = Max$\{0, [S_F - E_F]\}$
2   Value of European futures call allowing for interest = Max$\{0, [(S_F - E_F)/(1 + r)^T]\}$
3   Value of American futures call allowing for interest = Max$\{0, [S_F - E_F]\}$
FC_E Value of European futures call also allowing for volatility ≥ Max$\{0, [(S_F - E_F)/(1 + r)^T]\}$
FC_A Value of American futures call also allowing for volatility ≥ Max$\{0, [S_F - E_F]\}$

Figure 7.5 Prices or values of futures call options.

Line 1 shows the intrinsic value of the European and American futures calls at each possible spot futures price, as given by $\text{Max}\{0,[S_F - E_F]\}$. This line, and later lines, must be seen as kinked and following the horizontal axis to the left of the point where they meet it. At expiry, the options will have only the intrinsic value shown by line 1, but before expiry they will also have some time value. If the only source of time value was interest, then the European futures call would have a negative time value and its price would be shown by line 2, as given by (7.17). Line 2 shows that the European option has a price below its intrinsic value which is shown by line 1. So line 2 cannot apply to the American option. Instead, the price of an American futures call still equals its intrinsic value, as given by (7.18) and as shown by line 1. This line is also marked as line 3 to show that it is also its price after allowing for interest.

Allowing for the time value created by volatility raises the final price of the European call from line 2 to FC_E and the final price of the American call from line 3 to FC_A. The formulae for FC_E and FC_A are as given by (7.19) and (7.20). The widest gaps between FC_E and line 2 and between FC_A and line 3 occur when the spot price makes the options just about at-the-money, which is when volatility creates the most time value. The curves also show that volatility may create negligible time value at low spot futures prices. The price of an American option call can never be below its intrinsic value, so FC_A ends up touching line 1 but never goes below it.

Early exercise of American futures calls

In Fig. 7.5, the curve FC_E shows that the price of a European futures call may be *below* its intrinsic value if S_F rises high enough for the price to lie on that part of FC_E that is below line 1. In contrast, the price of an American futures call can never be below its intrinsic value, for an American option can always be exercised for its intrinsic value. Because the price of a European option can fall below its intrinsic value, while the value of an American option cannot, an American option is more desirable and has a higher price, so FC_A is above FC_E.

The gap between FC_A and FC_E is the early exercise premium, that is the extra value of the American futures call that arises because it may be worth exercising before expiry if the futures price rises far enough. At high futures prices, the European option is worth less than its intrinsic value and its holder wishes it could be exercised for its intrinsic value. The only advantage of the American option over the European one is that it can be exercised early for its intrinsic value, but to secure this advantage, it must be exercised early when exercise is advantageous. So, broadly speaking, the American option must be exercised at spot futures prices which would make the holder of a European option wish it could be exercised. More precisely, the American option should be exercised if the spot futures price rises to S_C, that is the critical price where the option's price ceases to exceed its intrinsic value. But if its holder wished to dispose of it when the spot futures price was below S_C, then selling it would raise more money than exercising it and at once closing out the futures contract that would be acquired.

7.5 FUTURES PUT OPTIONS

This section explains the factors that affect the price of a futures put option by considering futures put options on LML shares. To see how these options work, suppose that Y holds a futures put option for one LML share. If she exercises it, either at expiry or, perhaps, earlier in the case of an American option, then she will be given a futures contract. This will entitle her to sell one LML share at a futures price equal to the exercise price of the option, E_F. She will be able to sell the share when the futures contract matures, which will be taken to be just after the expiry time of the original option. Of course, Y will exercise the option only if the futures price of the contract that she will secure is above the spot futures price, S_F, that is currently being agreed on new futures contracts for LML shares that mature on the same day as the futures contract that underlies her option.

Intrinsic value

Like ordinary put options, futures put options have **intrinsic values**. For American futures puts, the intrinsic value shows the gain that could be secured by immediate exercise, while for all futures puts that are about to expire, it shows the gain that is about to be made. The intrinsic value of a futures put option is defined as by $Max\{0,[E_F - S_F]\}$. So, to work out the intrinsic value of the 150 and 200 futures put options, where E_F is respectively 150 or 200, it is first necessary to work out the relevant S_F. As explained in Section 7.4, if the current spot price of LML shares is 180 and the risk-free interest rate is 6%, then the S_F agreed today in futures contracts that will mature today will be 180. Also, if there is no dividend due on LML shares over the next nine months, then the S_F that is agreed today for futures contracts that will mature in nine months' time next June will be 188.04.

Consider, first, futures put options that expire today. Their underlying asset is a futures contract that matures today, so the relevant S_F is 180. So the intrinsic value of any 200 futures put expiring today is 20, and it is in-the-money by 20. This means, for example, that anyone who holds one is about to gain 20 by exercising it to secure a futures contract to sell an LML share today at a futures price of 200 which is 20 above the futures price being agreed on new futures contracts maturing today. But the intrinsic value of any 150 futures put expiring today is zero, so it is out-of-the-money. Anyone who holds one of these is about to gain nothing at all, for they will not exercise the option to secure a futures contract to sell an LML share at a futures price of 150 because futures contracts can instead be agreed to sell them today at a futures price of 180.

Consider next, futures put options that expire next June. Their underlying asset is a futures contract that will mature next June, so the relevant S_F is 188.04. So the June 200 futures puts have intrinsic values of 11.96 and are in-the-money by 11.96. So, for example, the holder of a American June 200 futures put could gain 11.96 today by exercising it. For the holder would then secure a futures contract to sell an LML share at a futures price of 200, and could at once close this futures position by making an offsetting futures contract to buy an LML share at a futures price of 188.04. The gain of 11.96 would be received at once through the marking-to-market system used with futures. Conversely, the June 150 futures puts have intrinsic values of zero and are out-of-the-money. So, for example, the holder of an American 150 June futures put would not exercise it to secure a futures contract to sell an LML share at a futures price of 150 as it is possible to agree such contracts today at a futures price of 188.04.

Time value and its sources

The price of a futures put option with some time before expiry rarely equals its intrinsic value and is usually higher. The gap between its price and its intrinsic value is its **time value**. This gap diminishes as expiry approaches and disappears at expiry. It might be expected that the three sources of time value for an ordinary put would also create time value for a futures put. These three sources will be considered in turn, using the example of a futures put option on LML shares that expires in nine months' time next June.

It will be seen that the first source, which is that people can lend for interest, tends to create negative time value for futures put options. In contrast, the second source, which is that the spot price of the underlying asset is volatile and hence unpredictable, creates positive time value. In the example, the price of the underlying asset is the futures price of LML shares, and, of course, this futures price is volatile only because the spot price of LML shares themselves is also volatile. The third source, which is the cost of storing the underlying asset, does not apply to a futures option because the underlying asset is a futures contract which costs nothing to store. Of course, there is an asset underlying the futures contract, in the example of LML shares, and these may have a negative storage cost in the form of a dividend before expiry. But it will be seen that a dividend does not affect the relationship between the price of a futures put option and the futures price of the shares.

Interest as a source of time value

Suppose for the moment that the future price for LML shares is predictable, so that the only source of time value for a futures put option is interest. Also, suppose for simplicity that no dividend is due on LML shares before next June. To see why interest creates time value, consider Y who wants to raise some money in nine months' time by selling an LML share. She could decide to sell one then. Normally, the problem with this strategy would be that she would not know how much money she would secure, because the price of LML shares is unpredictable. So, normally, she might consider other strategies that would enable her to determine today the amount she will secure. In fact, Y will not have this problem if, as is presently assumed, the price of LML shares is predictable. But it is worth comparing two of the other strategies in these special circumstances and then seeing the effect of relaxing the assumption that LML share prices are predictable. The two strategies that will be considered are (A) selling an LML share now for 180 and lending the proceeds risk-free at, say, 6% for nine months, and (B) buying a June European futures put option with an exercise price of, say, 200.

(A) secures 180 today, so it will secure 188.04 by next June when the loan is repaid with nine months' interest. So (B) would be equally attractive if it also resulted in Y securing 188.04 in June. In fact, (B) would secure 188.04 if the option price was 11.45. For in that case, if Y bought the option today for 11.45, then next June she would be worse off by that 11.45 and the interest it would have earned, that is 11.96 in all. However, she could also sell the share for 200. So she could use 11.96 of that to make up her loss and still secure 188.04, as on (A). More generally, in the absence of volatility, a European futures put has the same price as an ordinary call, namely $\text{Max}\{0,[E_F/(1+r)^T - S]\}$, as given by (7.9). In the example, this is $\text{Max}\{0,[200/1.06^{0.75} - 180]\}$ which is $\text{Max}\{0,11.45\}$ or 11.45.

It was shown in Section 7.4 that $S_F = S(1+r)^T$, so that $S = S_F/(1+r)^T$. So $\text{Max}\{0,[E_F/(1+r)^T - S]\}$ can be rewritten as $\text{Max}\{0,[E_F/(1+r)^T - S_F/(1+r)^T]\}$, which simplifies to $\text{Max}\{0,[(E_F - S_F)/(1+r)^T]\}$. This formula always delivers a price below the option's intrinsic value of $[E_F - S_F]$, which was shown earlier to be 11.96 for a 200 futures put. So interest here creates a negative time value. However, as this formula delivers a price below an option's intrinsic value, it cannot apply to American futures call. For no holder of an American option would sell it for less than the intrinsic value that could be secured by exercising it. So, in the absence of volatility, the price of an American futures put equals its intrinsic value, and the prices of futures put options are:

$$FP_E = \text{Max}\{0,[(E_F - S_F)/(1+r)^T]\} \tag{7.21}$$

$$FP_A = \text{Max}\{0,[E_F - S_F]\} \tag{7.22}$$

Volatility as a source of time value

The assumption that the price of LML shares has no volatility will now be relaxed. This means that the share prices is unpredictable. Recall Y who wants to raise some money in nine months' time by selling an LML share. She considers (A) selling a share now for 180 and lending that 180 risk-free at 6% to secure 188.04 in nine months, and (B) buying a European June put option with an exercise price of, say, 200. In the absence of volatility, Y would outlay no more today for (B) than the sum that would leave her with 188.04 in nine months, because (B) would have no advantage over (A). This meant that she would pay only 11.45 for the option. But the presence of volatility gives (B) an advantage over (A). So Y will be willing to pay more than 11.45 for the option.

The reason that (B) has an advantage is that the spot price of LML shares, S, could rise above 200 before expiry. If this happened, then on strategy (B) Y need not exercise the option and could instead sell her LML share at an above-200 spot price. In contrast, Y could not take advantage of any such rise in the spot price if she adopted strategy (A). Even so, Y would not want to pay much extra for the option. This is because S could well stay below 200. In that case, Y would exercise the option and sell her share for 200, but she would then secure less than 188.04. This is because she will have spent more than 11.45 on the option and so, once the lost interest on its premium is allowed for too, she will have lost more than 11.96 by buying it. Working out precisely how much extra Y would pay for options beyond the amounts given in (7.21) and (7.22) requires exact formulae of the sort discussed in Chapter 8. For this chapter, the extra will be allowed for simply by replacing the '=' by a '≥'. So the formulae are:

$$FP_E \geq \text{Max}\{0,[(E_F - S_F)/(1 + r)^T]\} \tag{7.23}$$

$$FP_A \geq \text{Max}\{0,[E_F - S_F]\} \tag{7.24}$$

For an in-the-money option, like the 200 futures put, the time value created by volatility arises because S could rise above 200 before expiry. If it was above 200 at expiry, then S_F would also be above 200, for S_F will equal S at expiry. So this time value arises partly because there is a chance of S_F ending up above E_F to make the option end up out-of-the-money. But this time value naturally depends on how big that chance is. So it is higher for options that are just in-the-money than for those which are deeply in-the-money. Indeed, it would be negligible on a 200 futures put if S was, say, 50, for then the chance of S rising above 200 by expiry would seem negligible.

Volatility also creates time value for out-of-the-money options. To see this, consider Y's attitude to an out-of-the-money 150 futures put. It might seem unlikely that Y would pay anything for an option that allows her to secure a futures contract in which she could sell a share at a futures price of 150 when she could sell a share today for 180. But the attraction of the option is that, if the spot price rises, then Y need not exercise it and could instead sell the share for more than 180. In contrast, she could not take advantage of a high future spot price if she sold the share now. Of course, the spot price might instead fall, but, if it does, then the futures option effectively insures Y against having to receive less than 150. The time value created by volatility is higher for options that are just out-of-the-money than for options which are deeply out-of-the-money. Indeed, it would be negligible on a 150 futures put if the spot futures price was, say, 600, for then the chance of the spot futures price falling below 150 by expiry would seem so small that people would pay a negligible amount to insure against it.

Dividends and futures put options

The assumption that there are no dividends due on LML shares before the nine-month options expire next June will now be relaxed. It will be supposed that a dividend of 7 is due in six months. This means that the carrying cost of LML shares is lower than before. Hence the futures price for futures contracts maturing next June will be lower. As explained in Section 7.4, it will actually drop to 180.94. In general, the futures price for a contract maturing after T years is given by $S_F = S^*(1 + r)^T$. In this expression, $S^* = S - D/(1 + r)^t$, that is the spot value, S, minus the present value of the dividend which is due after t years. In the example, the present value of the dividend is $7/(1.06)^{0.5}$ or 6.80. So S^* is $(180 - 6.80)$, or 173.20. Thus S_F is $173.20(1.06)^{0.75}$, or 180.94.

To see the effect of a dividend before expiry, recall Y who wants to raise some money in nine months' time next June by selling an LML share. She considers (A) selling an LML share now for 180 and lending that 180 risk-free at 6% to secure 188.04 in nine months, and (B) buying a European June futures put option with an exercise price of, say, 200.

Suppose for a moment that there is no volatility. In that case, it was argued previously that Y would regard (A) and (B) as equally attractive if they both secured 188.04 next June from selling her share, and this would occur if the option price was 11.45. However, now that a dividend is due before expiry, Y would prefer (B) to (A) if the price was 11.45. This is because (B) would secure a dividend of 7 after six months, and Y could then lend this 7 at the risk-free rate of 6% for three months and have an extra 7.10 after nine months. So Y might now select (B) even if its price was above 11.45. In fact, she would be willing to pay 6.80 extra for the option. For if its price rose by 6.80, then in nine months she would be worse off by that sum plus the interest that it would have earned, which is 7.10, but this would be exactly offset by the 7.10 that she would secure in nine months by receiving the dividend. So if the price was 6.80 higher than 11.45, that is 18.25, then she would once again find (B) equally as attractive as (A). The extra price, 6.80, is the present value of the dividend, that is $D/(1 + r)^t$. So, more generally, the price will be $D/(1 + r)^t$ higher than before.

As a dividend before expiry raises the option's price, it might seem that the price formulae (7.21) and (7.22) need changing. However (7.21) gives FP_E as $\text{Max}\{0,[(E_F - S_F)/(1 + r)^T]\}$, and this does not need changing because it refers to S_F which itself allows for the dividend. For, as explained in section 7.4, S_F equals $S^*(1 + r)^T$ when a dividend is due, and S^* equals $S - D/(1 + r)^t$, where D is the dividend. Indeed, in the example, (7.21) gives FP_E correctly as equal to $\text{Max}\{0,[(200 - 180.94)/(1.06)^{0.75}]\}$, which is $\text{Max}\{0,18.25\}$, or 18.25. However, (7.21) gives a price below the intrinsic value, which is $[E_F - S_F]$, so it still does not apply to an American futures put. So FP_A is still given by (7.22) which shows that it cannot be less than the intrinsic value.

As (7.21) and (7.22) continue to apply in the absence of volatility, so (7.23) and (7.24) continue to apply in the presence of volatility. They repeat (7.21) and (7.22) except that they replace the '=' by a '≥'. However, the fact that the same formulae apply does not mean that a dividend before expiry has absolutely no effect on the option's value for a given S_F. Section 8.5 explains that the volatility of the futures price may be very slightly higher when a dividend is due, so the extent to which volatility creates time value may also be very slightly higher.

Graphical representations

The formulae derived above do not give precise prices for European and American futures put options in the presence of volatility, but they do allow some useful graphs of option prices to be drawn. Consider two futures puts that are identical except that one is European and one is American. Figure 7.6 illustrates the price that each would have today at different possible current

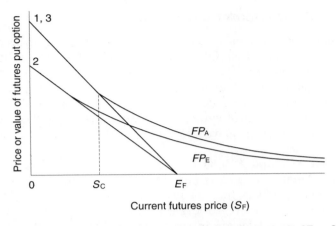

1   Intrinsic value of European and American futures puts = Max{0, [$E_F - S_F$]}
2   Value of European futures put allowing for interest = Max{0, [($E_F - S_F$)/(1 + r)^T]}
3   Value of American futures put allowing for interest = Max{0, [$E_F - S_F$]}
FP_E Value of European futures put also allowing for volatility ≥ Max{0, [($E_F - S_F$)/(1 + r)^T]}
FP_A Value of American futures put also allowing for volatility ≥ Max{0, [$E_F - S_F$]}

Figure 7.6   Prices or values of futures put options.

futures prices. The horizontal axis shows the possible current futures prices and the exercise price, E_F. This graph applies whether or not a dividend is due before expiry, though a dividend will affect the current futures price.

Line 1 shows the intrinsic value of the European and American futures puts at each possible spot futures price, as given by Max{0,[$E_F - S_F$]}. This line, and later lines, must be seen as kinked and following the horizontal axis to the right of the point where they meet it. At expiry, the options will have only the intrinsic value shown by line 1, but before expiry they will also have some time value. If the only source of time value was interest, then the European futures put would have a negative time value and its price would be shown by line 2, as given by (7.21). Line 2 shows that the European option has a price below its intrinsic value which is shown by line 1. So line 2 cannot apply to the American option. Instead, the price of an American futures put still equals its intrinsic value, as given by (7.22) and as shown by line 1. This line is also marked as line 3 to show that it is also its price after allowing for interest.

Allowing for the time value created by volatility raises the final price of the European put from line 2 to FP_E and the final price of the American put from line 3 to FP_A. The formulae for FP_E and FP_A are as given by (7.23) and (7.24). The widest gaps between FP_E and line 2 and between FP_A and line 3 occur when the spot price makes the options just about at-the-money, which is when volatility creates the most time value. The price of an American option call can never be below its intrinsic value, so FC_A ends up touching line 1 but never goes below it.

Early exercise of American futures puts

In Fig. 7.6, the curve FP_E shows that the price of a European futures put may be *below* its intrinsic value if S_F falls low enough for the price to lie on that part of FP_E that is below line 1. In contrast, the price of an American futures put can never be below its intrinsic value because an American option can always be exercised for its intrinsic value. Because the price of a European option can fall below its intrinsic value, while the value of an American option cannot, an American option is more desirable and has a higher price, so FP_A is above FP_E.

The gap between FP_A and FP_E is the early exercise premium, that is the extra value of the American futures put that arises because it may be worth exercising before expiry if the futures price falls far enough. At low futures prices, the European option is worth less than its intrinsic value and its holder wishes it could be exercised for its intrinsic value. The only advantage of the American option over the European one is that it can be exercised early for its intrinsic value, but to secure this advantage, it must be exercised early when exercise is advantageous. So, broadly speaking, the American option must be exercised at spot futures prices which would make the holder of the European option wish it could be exercised. More precisely, the American option should be exercised if the spot futures price falls to the critical price, S_C, where the option's price ceases to exceed its intrinsic value. But if its holder wished to dispose of it when the spot futures price was above S_C, then selling it would raise more money than exercising it and at once closing out the futures contract that would be acquired.

7.6 CHANGES IN OPTION PRICES

The six main factors affecting option prices were listed at the start of the chapter. Their effects are often summarised in a table like Table 7.2. This table shows that storage costs, which apply with commodity options, have the opposite effects of dividends on option prices, for dividends are effectively negative storage costs. Although Table 7.2 gives a useful summary, the effects of the six factors need some amplification and qualification, as indicated in the following paragraphs.

Table 7.2   Reasons why option prices may rise or fall

	Change in option price if there is:					
	(1) a higher exercise price	(2) a rise in the spot price	(3) less time to expiry	(4) a rise in interest rates	(5) a rise in spot price volatility	(6) a higher storage cost or lower dividend
Call option prices:	fall	rise	fall	rise	rise	rise
Put option prices:	rise	fall	fall	fall	rise	fall

1. An option's exercise price is, of course, constant throughout its life. So column (1) of Table 7.2 must be interpreted as showing that, other things being equal, call option prices are lower for calls with higher exercise prices, while put option prices are higher for puts with higher exercise prices. For example, looking back at Fig. 7.1, it will be appreciated that an equivalent call option with a higher exercise price, say 200p, would have a kinked initial intrinsic value line whose sloping part was to the right of *BC*, so it would have a lower premium or price at any given spot price. Likewise, looking back at Fig. 7.3, it will be appreciated that an equivalent put option with a higher exercise price, say 200p, would have an initial intrinsic value line whose sloping part was to the right of *AB*, so it would have a higher premium at any given spot price.

2. For all options, the spot price of the underlying asset is volatile, and changes in it are a major cause of fluctuations in the option's price. The effects shown in column (2) of Table 7.2 are consistent with the upward-sloping final price curves in Figs 7.2 and 7.5, which show that call option price rises when the spot price of the underlying asset rises, and they are also consistent with the downward-sloping final price curves in Figs 7.4 and 7.6, which show that put option prices fall when the spot price of the underlying asset rises. But note that a change in the spot price may have a negligible effect on the price of a call option if the spot price is so low that the value remains negligible.

3. The time to expiry necessarily falls during the life of any option. In turn, an option's time value gets less important as time passes, so the curve showing the option's price at each possible spot price gets closer to the kinked intrinsic value line. With American options, the passing of time generally exerts downward pressure on the price, as implied by column (3) of Table 7.2. The only exceptions arise when an option's price equals its intrinsic value some time before expiry, for on these occasions the passing of time will have no effect on the option price. With European options, the price of a call can be *below* its intrinsic value if the spot price is high enough, as shown in Figs 7.2(b) and 7.5, and the price of a put can be *below* its intrinsic value if the spot price is low enough, as shown in Figs 7.4(a) and 7.6. On these occasions, despite what is implied in Table 7.2, the passing of time tends to *increase* the option prices.

4. Column (4) of Table 7.2 implies that a rise in interest rates will raise all call option prices and reduce all put options prices, but exceptions can arise with some ordinary American puts. The result for ordinary calls is clear from Fig. 7.2 where a rise in interest rates will push each line 2 upwards and so push the final price curves upwards. The results for ordinary puts can be inferred from Fig. 7.4. Here, each line 2 will move down, so that each final P_E curve will also move down, and each P_A will also tend to move down as the gap between P_A and P_E is fixed by the early exercise premium. However, Fig. 7.4(a) shows that at low spot prices, the price of an American put when no dividend is due equals its intrinsic value, so it will *not* be affected by rises in interest rates. For futures calls, it might seem from Fig. 7.5 that a rise in interest rates would reduce the price of European

calls, as it would pivot line 2 down about the point marked E_F and so produce a lower FC_E curve, and it might seem that it would have no effect on the price of American calls as line 3 and the curve FC_A are not affected by interest rates. However, the rise in interest rates *will* raise the prices of futures calls because it will raise the spot futures price. In the case of European calls, this means that the price will be found at a point further to the right on the new FC_E curve, and hence higher up. In the case of American calls, it means that the price will be found at a point further to the right on FC_A, and hence higher up. The results for futures puts can be inferred from Fig. 7.6. In the case of European puts, line 2 will pivot down about the point marked E_F, so pushing the final FP_E curve downwards; moreover, the rise in interest rates will raise the futures price, so that the option price must be read off a point further to the right on the new FP_E curve, and hence lower down. In the case of American puts, line 3 and the final FP_A curve will not move; but the rise in the futures price means that the option price must be read off a point further to the right on FP_A, and hence lower down.

5. The volatility of the price of the underlying asset may not change much during an option's life. However, volatility is always a source of positive time value, so if volatility does increase, then so too will time value. This will be reflected in the figures by an upward shift in all the final price curves, which means that option prices will tend to rise at each possible spot price, as indicated in column (5) of Table 7.2. However, in the case of options which are so deeply in-the-money or so deeply out-of-the-money that they have negligible time value from volatility, a rise in volatility may have no significant effect on the option's price.

6. Column (6) of Table 7.2 implies that dividends before expiry reduce the price of all call options and raise the price of all put options. This applies to all ordinary options, except some deeply out-of-the-money call options where the price may be negligible whether or not there is a dividend before expiry. Dividends scarcely affect the price curves for futures options; instead, they reduce the futures price so that the option prices have to be read off points further to the left along the price curves, which means there will be lower futures call prices and higher futures put prices. It should be noted that if the size of any dividend due before expiry was increased beyond the previously announced value, then no option price would be altered. For ordinary calls and puts, the final price curves would indeed shift downwards and upwards respectively, but this force for the option prices to fall and rise should be offset by the rise in the spot price that would be caused by the announcement, so the prices would be read off points further to the right along the curves. For futures options, there would be no change in any curve or in the futures price, as the attractiveness of the underlying asset at expiry, after the dividend is paid, would be unaltered.

It has been seen that one of the six factors that affects the price of an option is its exercise price. So the price of an option with a given exercise price is affected by the other five factors. It is often useful to measure the sensitivity of the price of any given option to changes in the five other factors. The rest of this section looks at sensitivity measures which concern all of the other five factors except dividends or storage costs. The discussion begins with measures that concern the sensitivity of the option's price to changes in the spot price of the underlying asset.

Delta, lambda and gamma – sensitivity to the spot price

The sensitivity of an option's price to small changes in the spot price of the underlying asset is most usually measured by the option's **delta**. An option's delta is defined as follows:

$$\text{delta} = \frac{\text{change in option price}}{\text{change in the spot price of the underlying asset}} \qquad (7.25)$$

Delta is positive for call options, whose prices rise when the price of the under-lying asset rises, and it is negative for put options, whose prices fall when the price of the underlying asset rises. Deltas are measured by the slopes of the final price curves. Figures 7.2 and 7.5 show that, with call options, the slopes are about zero at low spot prices, when the options are deeply out-of-the-money, and rise to nearly one at high spot prices, when they are deeply in-the-money. Figures 7.4 and 7.6 show that, with put options, the slopes are close to minus one at low spot prices, when the options are deeply in-the-money, and rise to about zero at high spot prices when they are deeply out-of-the-money. For at-the-money call options, deltas are well in between zero and one, say about 0.5, while for at-the-money put options, deltas are well in between minus one and zero, say about -0.5.

There is a measure related to delta called **gamma**. An option's gamma is defined as follows:

$$\text{gamma} = \frac{\text{change in option delta}}{\text{change in the spot price of the underlying asset}} \qquad (7.26)$$

Gammas are always positive. This is because rises in the spot price of the underlying asset increase the deltas of call options, which range from near zero to near one, and they also increase the deltas of put options, which range from near minus one to near zero. Gammas are indicated by the curvature of the final price curves. Gammas are very low for options that are deeply in-the-money or deeply out-of-the-money because the final price curves are then nearly straight, so that changes in the spot price have little effect on the slope and hence have little effect on delta. But gammas are high for options that are at-the-money, especially if there is little time left to expiry, so that the final price curves are close to the kinked intrinsic value lines. This is because the slopes of these kinked lines change markedly at the kink, so any final price curves that are close to them have a marked curvature near that kink. In turn, this means that changes in the spot price near the kink will lead to marked changes in the slope of the curves, and hence lead to marked changes in deltas.

The sensitivity of an option's price to small changes in the spot price of the underlying asset is sometimes measured by its **lambda** rather than its delta. In economic terms, lambda is an elasticity measure. An option's lambda is defined as follows:

$$\text{lambda} = \frac{\%\ \text{change in option price}}{\%\ \text{change in the spot price of the underlying asset}} \qquad (7.27)$$

Lambda is *not* given by the slopes of the option price curves, but it has broadly similar characteristics to delta. So lambda also varies from zero to one for calls and from minus one to zero for puts.

Theta – sensitivity to time

An option's **theta** measures the sensitivity of its price to small changes in the time remaining until it expires. Theta is easy to remember as theta has the same first letter as time. An option's theta is defined as follows:

$$\text{theta} = \frac{\text{change in option price}}{\text{change in the time to expiry}} \qquad (7.28)$$

Theta is usually measured as the change that would occur in an option's price if the option became one day older and if all the other factors that affect its price remained constant. So theta measures the change in time value per day. In broad terms, theta indicates the extent to which an option's price curve moves each day towards the kinked intrinsic value. With most options, time value is positive but diminishes as time passes. So the passing of time reduces the option's price, and hence its theta is negative. However, as shown in Figs 7.2(b), 7.4(a), 7.5 and 7.6, a European option can sometimes have a negative time value, so its price can be below its intrinsic value. In these cases, the passing of time reduces the extent to which the option's time value pulls its price below its intrinsic value. So the passing of time raises the option's price, and hence its theta is positive.

Thetas are subject to two tendencies. First, as expiry approaches, positive thetas tend to get higher, while negative thetas tend to get lower; in other words, the passing of a day tends to have more effect on option prices when there is less time to expiry. Secondly, thetas tend to be highest for at-the-money options. Both of these tendencies arise from the fact that a major source of time value is the volatility of the price of the underlying asset. One day less in the life of an option with 90 days left has little effect on the likely change in the spot price of the underlying asset before expiry, so it has little impact on that aspect of the option's time value. But one day less in the life of an option with 25 hours to go removes almost all chance of a change in the spot price of the underlying asset, so it has a big impact on that aspect of the option's time value. However, volatility creates little time value for options that are deeply in-the-money or deeply out-of-the-money, so the passing of time has less effect on their prices than it has on the prices of at-the-money options.

Rho – sensitivity to the interest rate

An option's **rho** measures the sensitivity of its price to small changes in the rate of interest on risk-free loans. The meaning of rho is easy to remember as rho has the same first letter as rate. An option's rho is defined as follows:

$$\text{rho} = \frac{\text{change in option price}}{\text{change in the risk-free rate of interest}} \qquad (7.29)$$

Rho is usually measured as the change in price for a 1% change in the interest rate. It is positive for call options, where increases in interest rates raise option prices, and it is negative for put options where increases in interest rates generally reduce option prices.

Vega, kappa or sigma – sensitivity to the volatility

An option's **vega** measures the sensitivity of its price to small changes in the volatility of the price of the underlying asset. Vega is the name of a star, not a Greek letter. It is used because its meaning is easy to remember, as vega has the same first letter as volatility. There is no Greek letter beginning with that letter which could be used instead. However, people who prefer Greek letters sometimes call this measure **kappa** or **sigma** or even, confusingly, another sort of lambda. An option's vega is defined as follows:

$$\text{vega} = \frac{\text{change in option price}}{\text{change in the volatility of the price of the underlying asset}} \qquad (7.30)$$

An option's vega can be measured in slightly different ways. Most usually it measures the change that would occur in the option's price if the standard deviation of the price changes in the underlying asset changed by 0.01; Section 8.4 shows how these standard deviations are calculated. Vegas are always positive because increased volatility tends to increase an option's time value and so increase its price. Vegas tend to be highest for options that are about at-the-money. This is because volatility creates little time value for options that are deeply in-the-money or deeply out-of-the-money, so their prices are not very sensitive to small changes in that volatility.

Some uses of sensitivity measures

Some of these sensitivity measures are useful to traders who may simultaneously hold many options on one underlying asset, such as LML shares. Say X is such a trader. X may hold a variety of LML calls and puts with various expiry dates and strike prices. He may also have written a variety of LML call and put options. Unless he is careful, he could find that the total value of his portfolio is very sensitive to changes in the spot price of LML shares. However, he knows that different options have different deltas, so that they will react in different directions and to different extents to changes in that spot price. So he might try to balance his portfolio of LML options so that its overall value would be virtually unaffected by changes in the price of LML shares. If he also owns some LML shares, then he will probably take these into account too. Their delta equals one.

To discover the effect on his portfolio of a small change in the price of LML shares, X must add up the deltas of any LML shares he owns together with the deltas of all his LML options. Some of these deltas will be positive while others will be negative. The total that he arrives at will be the delta for his whole portfolio. To protect his portfolio from changes in the price of LML shares, he will try to ensure that its delta is about zero, so that it is **delta-hedged** or **delta-neutral**. His portfolio will need adjusting whenever the price of LML shares changes, because a change in that price will change the delta of each option and so change the delta of the portfolio. Deltas are closely related to gammas, and some traders aim instead for **gamma-hedged** or **gamma-neutral** portfolios.

Some traders like to have portfolios that are also **theta-neutral**, so that their values will not change as time passes. As all options have negative thetas, a theta-neutral portfolio might seem impossible. However, options fall in value over time because the potential gains to the holders fall. Correspondingly, therefore, the potential losses for the writers also fall. A theta neutral portfolio would combine both written and held options, so that the fall over time in the value of the held options is matched by the fall in the value of the written ones.

SUMMARY

7.1 The main factors that affect an option's price are its exercise price, the spot price of the underlying asset, the time left to expiry, the rate of interest on risk-free loans, the volatility of the price of the underlying asset, and the storage cost of the underlying asset. The storage cost is positive for commodities and negative for assets which earn income.

7.2 Option values comprise intrinsic value and time value. An option with a positive intrinsic value is in-the-money. Other options may be at-the-money or out-of-the-money. The intrinsic value of an ordinary call is $\text{Max}\{0,[S - E]\}$. Its time value arises from interest, volatility, and dividends or storage costs. American equity call options will never be exercised early if there is a sizeable dividend due before expiry. Otherwise they may be exercised early, and this possibility gives them an extra value called an early exercise premium. The prices of ordinary calls can be written as:

$$C_E \geq \text{Max}\{0,[S^* - E/(1 + r)^T]\} \tag{7.7}$$

$$C_A \geq \text{Max}\{0,[S^* - E/(1 + r)^T],[S - E]\} \tag{7.8}$$

7.3 The intrinsic value of an ordinary put is $\text{Max}\{0,[E - S]\}$. Its time value arises from the same sources that apply to call options. An American equity put will not be exercised early if there is a sizeable dividend due before expiry. Otherwise it may be exercised early, so it has an early exercise premium. The prices of ordinary puts can written as:

$$P_E \geq Max\{0,[E/(1 + r)^T - S^*]\} \tag{7.15}$$

$$P_A \geq Max\{0,[E/(1 + r)^T - S^*],[E - S]\} \tag{7.16}$$

7.4 The intrinsic values of futures call options equal $Max\{0,[S_F - E_F]\}$. Their time value depends on interest and volatility. American futures call options may be exercised early, so they have an early exercise premium. The values of futures calls are given by:

$$FC_E \geq Max\{0,[(S_F - E_F)/(1 + r)^T]\} \tag{7.19}$$

$$FC_A \geq Max\{0,[S_F - E_F]\} \tag{7.20}$$

7.5 The intrinsic values of futures put options equals $Max\{0,[E_F - S_F]\}$. Their time value depends on interest and volatility. American futures put options may be exercised early, so they have an early exercise premium. The values of futures puts are given by:

$$FP_E \geq Max\{0,[(E_F - S_F)/(1 + r)^T]\} \tag{7.23}$$

$$FP_A \geq Max\{0,[E_F - S_F]\} \tag{7.24}$$

7.6 The sensitivities of an option's price to changes in the price of the underlying asset, to the time left to expiry, to the risk-free interest rate, and to the volatility of the price of the underlying asset, can be measured respectively by delta or gamma, theta, rho and vega.

QUESTIONS

1. What is meant by time value? What are the three sources of time value on ordinary options? Why may the time value on a European option be negative? Why do American options never have negative time values?

2. What is meant by the terms in-the-money and out-of-the-money? Why are people willing to pay for out-of-the-money options?

3. Look in turn at Figs 7.2(b) and 7.4(b). What, if anything, will happen to each of the various lines and curves as expiry draws nearer?

4. Explain the concepts of an early exercise premium and a critical price. Under what circumstances, if any, would different types of American equity option be exercised early?

5. What is measured by delta, gamma, vega, theta and rho? When, if ever, are they negative?

8 MODELS FOR ESTIMATING OPTION PRICES

8.1 WHY DO INVESTORS WANT MODELS THAT ESTIMATE OPTION PRICES?

Chapter 7 outlined the main factors that affect option prices. One factor is the volatility of the spot price of the underlying asset, but Chapter 7 did not show how much time value is created by this factor, so it could not give any precise option prices. However, people who buy and write options need models that estimate their correct prices or **fair values**. For any option that is priced below its fair value will be attractive to buyers and unattractive to writers, and any that is priced above its fair value will be unattractive to buyers and attractive to writers.

What this chapter covers

It may seem surprising that options can have 'correct' prices, so Section 8.2 explains why they do and how people should react to mispriced options. These fair values depend on the six factors discussed in Chapter 7, but before looking at some models for estimating them, it is necessary to explain how those models measure the risk-free interest rate and the volatility of the spot price of the underlying asset, so this is done in Sections 8.3 and 8.4. Then Section 8.5 looks at the most celebrated option pricing model, which is the **Black–Scholes option** pricing model or formula devised by Black and Scholes (1972 and 1973) for ordinary European equity options. Section 8.6 shows how this formula can be adapted for several other types of European option.

Unfortunately, the Black–Scholes formula rarely applies to American options, especially put options, and it is unlikely that exact formulae for American option prices will ever be found. Of course, any difference in price between an American option and an equivalent European one is accounted for by the early exercise premium which is usually small, so practitioners may sometimes estimate fair values for American options by using the Black–Scholes formula and then making slight adjustments based on experience for the early exercise premium. However, there are several models that give very close approximations to the fair values for American options. The most widely quoted of these is the **binomial model** of Cox, Ross and Rubinstein (1979), as developed in Cox and Rubinstein (1985). This is conceptually simple and yet very flexible and accurate, and it also enables figures to be constructed which show exactly when American options should be exercised early. Section 8.7 explains how this method can be used for ordinary equity options, both European and American, and Section 8.8 shows how it can be used for many other types of option including Asian options.

Several other methods are available for valuing American options. These include the finite difference method of Brennan and Schwartz (1977) and Courtadon (1982), the numerical method of Parkinson (1977), the polynomial approximation method of Geske and Johnson (1984), and the quadratic approximation method of Barone-Adesi and Whaley (1987). All these methods use more advanced mathematics than the binomial method, but they have sometimes been seen as superior because they need less computer time. With modern computers, however, computer time is rarely a relevant issue, and so these methods are not explored in this book.

In practice, options often trade at prices that depart slightly from their fair values. The final section of this chapter, 8.9, looks briefly at some possible reasons for this. All the prices in the chapter are expressed in pence. The notation used is given in Table 8.1.

8.2 THE CONCEPT OF A THEORETICALLY CORRECT PRICE

It may seem surprising that an option has a correct price. After all, options are used by hedgers and speculators, so it might be supposed that option prices would vary whenever the extent to which people wished to hedge or to speculate varied. However, anyone whose portfolio contains an option could, in fact, have an alternative portfolio without the option that would secure equivalent returns. The fair value for the option is the one which makes the portfolio that includes it equally attractive to the equivalent portfolio that excludes it.

This concept will be illustrated using an example of European options on the equities of a hypothetical company, LML. Suppose that call and put options are available on LML equities with an exercise price of 105p, and suppose the options expire after one period. The length of this period is not important and will be taken for simplicity as one year. Suppose, too, that the price of LML shares is today 100 and that it can change only once in that period, specifically at the very end of it, and suppose that when it does change, it can take

Table 8.1   Notation

S	Spot price	L	Sum borrowed or lent
E	Exercise price of (ordinary) option	H	Hedge ratio
S_F	Spot futures price	n	A number (e.g. of shares)
E_F	Exercise price of futures option	N	Number of steps in an option's life
D	Dividend due before expiry	u	Possible spot price growth per step
S^*	S minus present value of D	d	Possible spot price fall per step
δ	Rate of continuous dividend yield	k	A constant $= (R^{T/N} - d)/(u - d)$
T	Time to expiry (in years)	k_F	A constant $= (1 - d)/(u - d)$
t	Time to dividend (in years)	O_U	Option value after step when spot
σ	Standard deviation		price rises
σ^2	Variance	O_D	Option value after step when spot
r_S	Risk-free interest rate (simple)		price falls
r	Risk-free interest rate	$C_1, C_2 \ldots$	Possible call option values at expiry
	(continuously compounded)	C_A	Price of American call option
R	$(1 + r_S)$	C_E	Price of European call option
ρ_S	Foreign risk-free rate (simple)	P_A	Price of American put option
P	Foreign risk-free rate	P_E	Price of European put option
	(continuously compounded)	FC_A	Price of American futures call option
ρ	$(1 + \rho_s)$	FC_E	Price of European futures call option
d_1, d_2	z-values	FP_A	Price of American futures put option
$N(d_1)$	Probability of a z-value being $\leq d_1$	FP_E	Price of European futures put option
$N(d_2)$	Probability of a z-value being $\leq d_2$	C_{ASIAN}	Price of Asian call option

one of only two new values, say 85 and 115. Suppose, finally, that LML shares and options can be bought in fractions, that no LML dividend is due before expiry, and that the risk-free interest rate is equivalent to 6% a year.

Estimating the fair value for a call option

Consider X who owns no LML shares until he buys one today for 100p. If this is all that X does, then he will spend 100 and he will have a wealth next year of either 85 or 115 depending on the spot price of LML shares then. However, suppose X also writes some 105p call options on n LML shares at a premium of C_E. Then X will receive some premiums worth nC_E which will reduce his outlay today to $(100 - nC_E)$. Next year, the value of both his share and the options will depend on the spot price of LML shares. But, if X wishes, he could set n so that his wealth next year would be a guaranteed 85 irrespective of the price of LML shares.

In fact, if the spot price is 85p, then the holders of the 105p call options that X wrote will not exercise them, so his wealth next year will be just the 85 from the share. If, instead, the spot price is 115, then his share will be worth 115, but the holders of the call options that he wrote will exercise them, so he will have to sell n shares to them at a price of 105 when the current price is 115. Although X will only own the one LML share that he bought today, he could still sell n shares at expiry by buying more then at 115 and at once selling them for 105. So X will lose 10 on each of the n shares, or $10n$ in all, so his total wealth from the share and the options will be $(115 - 10n)$. However, if X sets n so that $(115 - 10n) = 85$, then his wealth at expiry will still be 85. This equation can be solved to show that $n = 3.00$.

Suppose that X does buy one share and write three call options. Then his outlay today is $(100 - 3.00C_E)$ and it ensures a wealth next year of 85. Another way of ensuring a wealth of 85 would be to lend some money at the risk-free rate of 6% or 0.06. To get 85 in one year, X would need to lend $85/(1 + 0.06)$ which is 80.19. So buying the share and writing 3.00 calls is equivalent to lending 80.19 risk-free. So investors will be willing to pay exactly 80.19 to buy one share and write 3.00 calls. So $(100 - 3.00C_E)$ will equal 80.19. This equality can be used to show that C_E must equal 6.60. This is the fair value of the option, for it makes the cost of the portfolio that includes it equal to the cost of an equivalent portfolio that excludes it.

Incidentally, this example shows that investors can fix their wealth at expiry by writing 3.00 options for every share they own. Equivalently, they can hold 1/3.00 shares for every option they write and so have a **call hedge ratio**, H, of 1/3.00, or 0.3333. As using this ratio would fix their wealth, it is the ratio for a **hedge portfolio** that is a perfectly hedged portfolio.

Handling a mispriced call option

This example can be used to show how investors should handle a **mispriced call option**. If the actual call price is above 6.60, then the cost to X of buying one share and writing 3.00 call options will be below 80.19. Yet this portfolio ensures a wealth of 85 in one year, so it will secure 85 for less than the 80.19 that it would cost to ensure 85 by lending at the risk-free rate. So combining LML shares and written calls secures a better investment performance than the risk-free asset. Thus investors may enthusiastically buy LML shares and write call options. Of course, this enthusiasm for writing calls will soon drive the call price down to the fair value.

If the price was below 6.60p, then people who own LML shares now could make profits. Suppose Z sells one LML share and buys 3.00 call options. Just as someone who buys one share and writes 3.00 call options will have a wealth next year from them of 85, so Z, who takes the opposite steps, will lose 85. But Z secures 100 now by selling the share. He buys the 3.00 options at a price below 6.60, which means that he has more than 80.19 left over. So Z can afford to lend more than 80.19 at the risk-free rate of 6%, and this means that Z will have more than 85 next year. In other words, selling an LML share and buying 3.00 call options enables Z to secure a guaranteed wealth that exceeds 85, yet the only cost is a loss of 85. So investors like Z should respond by selling shares and buying call options. Of course, their enthusiasm for buying call options would soon drive the call option price up.

Estimating the fair value for a put option

Next, consider Y who owns no LML shares until she buys one today for 100p. If this is all that Y does, then she will spend 100 and she will have a wealth next year of either 85 or 115 depending on the spot price of LML shares.

However, suppose Y also buys some 105p put options on n LML shares at a premium of P_E. Then Y will pay some premiums worth nP_E and will raise her outlay today to $(100 + nP_E)$. Next year, the value of both her share and the options will depend on the spot price of LML shares. But, if Y wishes, she could set n so that her wealth next year would be a guaranteed 115 irrespective of the price of LML shares.

In fact, if the spot price is 115p, then Y's 105p put options will have no value, so her wealth will be just the 115 from the share. If, instead, the spot price is 85, then her share will be worth 85, but she will exercise her put options, so she will sell n shares at a price of 105 when the current price is 85. Although Y will only own the one LML share that she bought today, she could still sell n shares at expiry by buying more then at 85 and at once selling them for 105. So Y will gain 20 on each of the n shares, or $20n$ in all, so her total wealth from the share and the options will be $(85 + 20n)$. However, if Y sets n so that $(85 + 20n) = 115$, then her wealth at expiry will still be 115. This equation can be solved to show that $n = 1.50$.

Suppose that Y does buy one share and 1.50 put options. Then her outlay today is $(100 + 1.50P_E)$ and it ensures a wealth next year of 115. Another way of ensuring a wealth of 115 would be to lend some money at the risk-free rate of, say, 6% or 0.06. To get 115 in one year, Y would need to lend $115/(1 + 0.06)$ which is 108.49. So buying the share and 1.50 puts is equivalent to lending 108.49 risk-free. So investors will be willing to pay exactly 108.49 to buy one share and 1.50 puts. So $(100 + 1.50P_E)$ will equal 108.49. This equality can be used to show that P_E must equal 5.66p. This is the fair value of the option, for it makes the cost of the portfolio that includes it equal to the cost of an equivalent portfolio that excludes it.

Incidentally, this example showed that investors can fix their wealth at expiry, and so have a hedge portfolio, by buying 1.50 put options for every share they own. Equivalently, they can hold 1/1.50 shares for every option they buy and so have a **put hedge ratio**, H, of $-1/1.50$ or -0.6667. The minus sign indicates that they must buy the put options with which they are hedging.

Handling a mispriced put option

This example can be used to show how investors should handle a **mispriced put option**. If the actual put price was below 5.66p, then the cost to Y of buying one share and buying 1.50 put options would be below 108.49. Yet this portfolio ensures a wealth of 115 in one year, so it would secure 115 for less than the 108.49 that it would cost to secure 115 by lending risk-free. So combining LML shares and bought puts secures a better investment performance than the risk-free asset. Thus investors may enthusiastically buy LML shares and buy put options. Of course, this enthusiasm for buying puts will soon drive the put price up to the fair value.

If the price was above 5.66p, then people who own LML shares now could make profits. Suppose Z sells one LML share and writes 1.50 put options. Just as someone who buys one share and buys 1.50 put options will have a wealth next year from them of 115, so Z, who takes the opposite steps, will lose 115.

But Z secures 100 now by selling the share, and he writes the 1.50 options at an option price above 5.66. Altogether, then, he acquires more than 108.49 to lend. So Z can lend more than 108.49 at the risk-free rate of 6%, and this means that Z will have more than 115 next year. In other words, selling a share and writing 1.50 options enables Z to secure a guaranteed wealth that exceeds 115, yet the only cost is a loss of 115. So investors like Z should respond by selling shares and writing put options. Of course, their enthusiasm for writing puts would soon drive the put option price down.

Allowing for more than one step

The above examples showed how fair option values can be found, under certain assumptions. One assumption was that investors could lend at the risk-free rate. The rest of this chapter assumes that they can also borrow at this rate. Even though investors never can borrow at this rate, the assumption that they can does not lead to false option prices; that is because the risk-free rate is the only relevant one, as the examples showed. Another assumption was that the spot price could change only once before expiry. However, more changes or **steps** can be allowed for.

To see this, suppose that X wants to work out today's prices for a European call option and a European put option on LML shares. Suppose that each option has an exercise price of 105p and expires in two years, and suppose that X divides the time until expiry into two steps, so each step lasts one year. Suppose, too, that today's spot price of LML shares is 100p, and that this spot price will change only at the end of each step, when it may either rise by 20% or fall by 20%. X could set out the possible spot prices over time as shown in Fig. 8.1(a). At the end of step 1, the price will either rise by 20% to 120 or fall by 20% to 80. If it is 120, then at the end of step 2 it will either rise by 20% to 144 or fall by 20% to 96; if, instead, it is 80, then after step 2 it will either rise by 20% to 96 or fall by 20% to 64. This spot price is more volatile than the one in the earlier examples which moved only to 115 or 85 after one year. Also, these options have longer to expiry. So they will be worth more than 6.60p and 5.66p

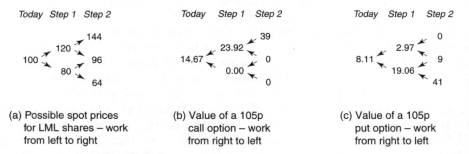

(a) Possible spot prices for LML shares – work from left to right

(b) Value of a 105p call option – work from right to left

(c) Value of a 105p put option – work from right to left

Figure 8.1   Possible price paths and call and put option prices in a two-period model.

To find today's prices for these options, X must work backwards from the values that they could have at expiry, as shown in Fig. 8.1(b) and (c). Sections 7.2 and 7.3 showed that an option's value at expiry equals its intrinsic value, so X needs to find the possible intrinsic values for the options at expiry. Figure 8.1(b) shows that the intrinsic value of the call option at expiry, after step 2, will be 39 if the spot price is then 39 above the 105 strike price at 144, and zero if the spot price then is below the strike price at 96 or 64. Figure 8.1 (c) shows that the intrinsic value of the put option at expiry will be zero if the spot price then is above the 105 strike price at 144, 9 if the spot price then is 9 below the strike price at 96, and 41 if the spot price then is 41 below the strike price at 64.

X must next consider what the options will be worth at the end of step 1. To see how he does this, consider the call option. Its value at the end of step 1 depends on the spot price at that time. If this is 120p, then it could move to 144 or 96 one step later. So X knows that if he bought the option at the end of step 1, then it would be worth either 39 or zero after step 2. To find its fair value, X would work out the cost of an alternative portfolio that would secure equivalent possible returns. He could form such a portfolio by buying H shares and borrowing L at the risk-free rate, provided he chose H and L carefully. The letter H is used for the number of shares as this is, in fact, the call hedge ratio needed for a perfect hedge. After step 2, X's H shares would be worth $144H$ or $96H$, but he would have to repay his loan with interest. The risk-free rate is 6%, or 0.06, and the loan is for one year, so X would have to repay 0.06 more than he borrowed, that is $1.06L$. So, after step 2, X's wealth would be $(144H - 1.06L)$ or $(96H - 1.06L)$. To make this portfolio equivalent to the option, X would have to set H and L so that:

$$144H - 1.06L = 39 \qquad (8.3)$$

$$96H - 1.06L = 0 \qquad (8.4)$$

(8.3) and (8.4) can be solved to give $H = 0.8125$ and $L = 73.58$. The cost of 0.8125 shares at the step 1 spot price of 120 is 97.50. So the alternative portfolio would cost 97.50 minus the borrowed 73.58, that is 23.92. As the option is equivalent to this portfolio, people would also pay 23.92 for the option. So, if the spot price after step 1 is 120, the call will be worth 23.92.

Suppose, instead, that the spot price is 80p at the end of step 1. Then it could move to 96 or 64 one step later. Either way, X knows that if he bought the call at the end of step 1, then it would be worth zero after step 2. So X would not pay one penny for it at the end of step 1, and thus its value then will be zero. Strictly, the returns from the option here would be replicated by buying no shares and lending no money, so H and L would both be zero.

X has now worked out that the call option will be worth 23.92p or 0p in one year from today, after step 1. With this information, he can now calculate today's price by considering the cost of an alternative portfolio that would secure equivalent possible returns after step 1. He could form such a portfolio by buying H shares and borrowing L, provided he chose H and L carefully. His wealth after step 1 would be either $120H - 1.06L$ or $80H - 1.06L$, depending on the share price after step 1. To make this portfolio equivalent to the option, X must set H and L so that:

$$120H - 1.06L = 23.92 \tag{8.5}$$

$$80H - 1.06L = 0 \tag{8.6}$$

(8.5) and (8.6) can be solved to give $H = 0.5980$ and $L = 45.13$. The cost of 0.5980 shares at the initial spot price of 100 is 59.80. So the cost of this alternative portfolio is 59.80 minus the borrowed 45.13, that is 14.67. As the option is equivalent to this portfolio, people would also pay 14.67 for the option. So today's fair value of the call, that is C_E, is 14.67, as shown in Fig. 8.1(b). As expected, this is well over the 6.60p that applied in the earlier example.

A general formula for an option's value at the start of a step

In the example, it was seen that each of the possible step 1 values for the option depended on what it might be worth after step 2, while today's value depended on what it might be worth after step 1. It is possible to derive a general formula for the value of a call option or a put option before a step that lasts T/N years, where T is the life of the option in years and N is the number of steps into which its life is split. In the example, $T = 2$ and $N = 2$, so $T/N = 1$.

Suppose the share price can rise in the step by a factor, u, or fall by a factor d. In the example $u = 1.2$ and $d = 0.8$. The value of an option at the end of the step depends on whether the share price goes up or down. Call these two possible option values O_U and O_D. Finally, suppose that the simple risk-free interest rate is r_S, so that if money is lent for a year, then it will grow at a rate R, where $R = (1 + r_S)$; thus if r_S is 0.06, then R is 1.06, and each 1p lent for a year will grow to 1.06p. In general, the growth in the value of money lent for T/N years will be $R^{T/N}$. For example, if N had been four, so that T/N was six months or 0.5 years, then money lent for six months would grow by a factor of $1.06^{0.5}$ or 1.0296, so 1p would grow to 1.0296p. This is the equivalent to 6% a year, because if the 1.0296p was lent at the end of six months at the same rate for another six months, then it would be worth 1.0296(1.0296) or 1.06p at the end of the year.

In these circumstances, the general formula for the value of a European option is given by:

$$\text{Value of European option} = [kO_U + (1 - k)O_D]/R^{T/N} \tag{8.7}$$

where k is defined as:

$$k = (R^{T/N} - d)/(u - d) \tag{8.8}$$

Consider the value of the call option today. Figure 8.1(b) shows that O_U and O_D are 23.92 and 0.00. With $T/N = 1$, $u = 1.2$ and $d = 0.8$, (8.8) gives the value of k as $(1.06 - 0.8)/(1.2 - 0.8)$ or 0.65, and then (8.7) correctly gives the option value as $[0.65(23.92) + 0.35(0)]/1.06$, for this is 15.55/1.06 or 14.67.

It is also possible to derive a formula for the hedge ratio, H. This is given as:

$$H = (O_U - O_D)/S(u - d) \qquad\qquad (8.9)$$

where S is the current spot price. In the example, S today is 100p, so $S(u - d)$ is $100(1.2 - 0.8)$, which is 40, and thus H is 23.92/40 or 0.5980. So if Y owns some LML shares, she could today secure a perfect hedge by writing a call for one LML share for every 0.5980 shares she owns. H changes between steps and was seen to be 0.8125 or zero after step 1, according to whether S then was 120p or 80p. So if Y wants to maintain a perfect hedge, she must alter the number of shares she has per option, or the number of options per share, whenever S alters. In practice investors rarely seek perfect hedges, because they might as well invest instead in the risk-free asset, but the further their own ratios depart from H, the riskier are their positions.

X could use (8.7) to find today's price of the put option, P_E. He would start with the possible values for the option at expiry, as shown in Fig. 8.1(c), and then work from right to left. He would first work out what the option's value will be after step 1 if the spot price then is 120p. In this case, the spot price could move after step 2 to 144 or 96, when the option's value would be 0 or 9. Using 0 and 9 for O_U and O_D in (8.7) gives the option's step 1 value as [0.65(0) + 0.35(9)]/1.06 or 2.97. X would next work out what the option's value will be after step 1 if the spot price then is 80. In this case, the spot price could move to 96 or 64 after step 2, when the option's value would be 9 or 41. Using 9 and 41 for O_U and O_D in (8.7) gives the option's step 1 value as [0.65(9) + 0.35(41)]/1.06 or 19.06. Finally, X would work out today's value of the option. In one year, its value will be 2.97 or 19.06. Using these figures for O_U and O_D in (8.7) gives today's price, P_E, as [0.65(2.97) + 0.35(19.06)]/1.06 or 8.11p, which, as expected, is over 5.66. X could also use (8.9) to find the put hedge ratios, given that $(u - d) = 0.4$. Today's H is $(2.97 - 19.06)/100(0.4)$, or −0.4023. But H changes whenever S changes. So in step 1, H will be $(0 - 9)/120(0.4)$, or −0.1875, if the spot price is 120, and $(9 - 41)/80(0.4)$, or −1.0000, if it is 80.

Developing the model

The model presented here shows why options have fair values. But it is unrealistic because it allows the price of the underlying asset to change only once or twice before the option expires, and at each change it allows only two alternative new prices. The Black–Scholes model and the binomial model developed later also allow only two alternative new prices each time the price changes, but they are more realistic because they allow for far more changes. The Black–Scholes model allows for an infinite number of infinitely short steps, while the binomial model allows for many steps of a finite length. But before developing these models, it is necessary to see how they refer to the risk-free interest rate and how they measure volatility.

8.3 EXPRESSING THE RISK-FREE RATE AS A CONTINUOUSLY COMPOUNDED RATE

Section 2.2 and 2.3 noted that loans to the government are regarded as risk-free, at least if they are held to maturity when their value is certain. There are different rates on these loans according to their length. When considering risk-free loans as part of alternative portfolios to options, the risk-free rate should be taken as the rate on loans lasting as long as the options. Most options expire in under a year, so the risk-free rates could be taken as the redemption yields on gilts with under a year to run, but for options lasting three months or less, it is usual to use instead the rate of return on Treasury bills with the same time to maturity.

Consider one-year risk-free loans, and suppose the government always pays its interest on these in one instalment at the end of the year. Then its expressed interest rate will be a **simple interest rate,** r_S. Suppose r_S is 100%, well over the 6% assumed earlier. Then people who lend 100p today at this rate, and leave their money on loan for one year, will end up with 200.

Next, suppose that the government decided instead to pay interest at an expressed rate of 100% a year in two half-yearly instalments. Then people who lent 100p today would receive interest of 50 after six months. If they lent that 50 as well as the original 100 at 100% over the remaining six months of the year, then they would be given interest of 75 at the end of the year. So, allowing also for the repayment of their total loan of 150, they would end up with 225. If the government decided to pay interest at 100% per year in even more frequent instalments, say in 365 daily instalments, then it is possible to work out that people who lent 100 today and left their money and all the accumulated interest on loan to the government for a whole year would end up with 271.46, assuming pence can be subdivided. And if the government paid its interest in an infinite number of instalments over the year, then people who lent 100 today would end up with 271.83 at the end of the year. So their 100 would grow by a factor of 2.7183. This figure is important and is called 'e' for exponential.

In this example, a sum of 100p became worth 271.83 when the government paid interest at 100% on what is called a **continuously compounded** basis. More generally, if interest is paid on this basis at a continuously compounded rate r, then a sum of 100 will be worth $100e^r$ after one year. So if $r = 100\%$, or 1.00, then 100 will become worth $100e$, or 271.83, as just noted; but if, say, $r = 0.1$, or 10%, then 100 will become worth $100e^{0.1}$ or 110.52. More generally still, after T years, 100 will become worth $100e^{rT}$, while a sum of, say, 1p, will become worth e^{rT}.

This last expression means that someone who lends 1p now will have e^{rT} in T years' time. So, the present value of e^{rT} in T years' time, that is the sum which must be lent today to secure e^{rT} in T years' time, is 1p. The sum which must be lent today to secure a smaller amount in T years' time, say 1p, is less. For if 1p lent today will be worth e^{rT}, then $1/e^{rT}$ will be worth e^{rT}/e^{rT}, which is 1p. So the present value of 1p in T years' time is $1/e^{rT}$. This is written as e^{-rT}.

The Black–Scholes and binomial models measure the risk-free interest rate as a continuously compounded rate. Suppose the government actually pays its interest on an end-of-the-year basis at a simple rate, r_S, of 6%. Then anyone who today lends, say, 100p will end up with 106 in one year. They could also end up with 106 in one year if the government instead paid interest at a continuously compounded rate of r, where e^r was equal to 1.06. This would arise if r was 5.83%. In short, instead of expressing the risk-free rate as a simple rate, r_S, of 6%, the models would express it as a continuously compounded rate, r, of 5.83%. A quick way of finding the continuously compounded equivalent of any simple rate, such as 6% or 0.06, is to find the natural log of one plus the simple rate, for the natural log of 1.06, that is $\ln(1.06)$, is 0.0583. The models assume that the risk-free rate is constant over the life of any given option.

8.4 ESTIMATING VOLATILITY

When the Black–Scholes and binomial option pricing models are used to give the fair value of any option, they both allow for the volatility of the spot price of its underlying asset. This section explains how people who wish to use the pricing models can estimate that volatility.

Historical volatility and standard deviations

What investors really need to estimate is the future volatility of the price of the underlying asset. Often they assume this will be the same as its past or **historical volatility**, so they try to estimate that. Even if they think the volatility will change, they may start by estimating historical volatility and then adjust that figure to produce an estimate of future volatility.

To estimate historical volatility, they take a sample of past periods and look at the price change in each period. For example, suppose the price of LML shares at the start and end of 10 recent weeks was as shown in columns (1) and (2) of Table 8.2, and suppose for simplicity that no dividend was paid in those weeks. The ratio of the end price to the start price in each week, that is the proportional price change, is shown in column (3). Thus in week 5, the proportional price change was 103:98, which is 1.0510. This means that the price rose by 5.10%, or 0.0510, if the change is expressed as a simple percentage rate, as shown in column (4). However, the models actually measure the price changes at the equivalent continuously compounded rates, here called continuous rates. For week 5, this is 4.98%, or 0.0498, as shown in column (5). This figure is the natural logarithm of the value of one plus the simple rate, that is the logarithm of the proportional change of 1.0510, which is shown in column (3).

The percentage price changes are volatile. For example, the continuously compounded changes given in column (5) range from 0.0498 to –0.0697. The spread of the these percentage price changes can be measured by using their variance and standard deviation.

It was explained in Section 3.3 that calculating the variance of a sample of n observations requires five steps. First, the mean value of the n changes is

Table 8.2 Volatility of LML share prices in a sample of 10 weeks

Week	Start price (p) (1)	End price (p) (2)	End:start ratio (3)	Simple rate (4)	Continuous rate (5)	x (6)	x^2 (7)	$z(= x/\sigma)$ (8)
1	99	102	1.0303	0.0303	0.0299	0.0288	0.0008	0.6923
2	102	105	1.0294	0.0294	0.0290	0.0280	0.0008	0.6715
3	105	101	0.9619	−0.0381	−0.0388	−0.0398	0.0016	−0.9561
4	101	98	0.9703	−0.0297	−0.0302	−0.0312	0.0010	−0.7477
5	98	103	1.0510	0.0510	0.0498	0.0488	0.0024	1.1700
6	103	99	0.9612	−0.0388	−0.0396	−0.0406	0.0016	−0.9746
7	99	103	1.0404	0.0404	0.0396	0.0386	0.0015	0.9264
8	103	104	1.0097	0.0097	0.0097	0.0087	0.0001	0.2077
9	104	97	0.9327	−0.0673	−0.0697	−0.0707	0.0050	−1.6962
10	97	100	1.0309	0.0309	0.0305	0.0295	0.0009	0.7068
Mean					0.0010			
Σx^2							0.0156	

Sample variance $= \Sigma x^2/n = 0.0156/10 = 0.0016.$
Sample standard deviation $= \sqrt{(\Sigma x^2/n)} = \sqrt{0.0016} = 0.0395.$
Estimated $\sigma^2 = \Sigma x^2/(n-1) = 0.0156/9 = 0.0017.$
Estimated $\sigma = \sqrt{0.0017} = 0.0417.$

found. In the example in Table 8.2, where $n = 10$, the figure at the bottom of column (5) shows that the mean percentage change is 0.0010 (or 0.1%). Secondly, the difference is found between each of the n changes and the mean change of 0.0010. These differences, which are called x-values, are shown in column (6). For example, in week 5 the column (5) figure for the weekly change is 0.0498, so the x-value is 0.0498 minus the mean of 0.0010, which is 0.0488. Thirdly, each x-value is squared to get an x^2-value, and these are shown in column (7). Fourthly, all the x^2-values are summed to get Σx^2, and this is shown in column (7) as 0.0156. Finally, as shown at the foot of the table, the variance is worked out as $\Sigma x^2/n$, which is 0.0156/10, that is about 0.0016; and the standard deviation is worked out as the square root of the variance, which is 0.0395.

This variance and standard deviation apply to the price changes in the sample. But investors really want figures for σ^2 and σ which, as noted in Section 3.3, are the symbols used for the variance and the standard deviation of the population. In the example, the population is all the price changes that could occur with LML shares, expressed as continuously compounded rates. So investors may wonder if the sample variance and standard deviation are good estimates of σ^2 and σ.

Section 3.3 noted that the variance of a sample is a biased estimate of the population variance, σ^2. But Section 3.3 also noted that an unbiased estimate of σ^2 can be usually be found from a sample by using the expression $\Sigma x^2/(n-1)$. So the estimate of σ^2 in the example is (0.0156/9) or 0.0017. In turn, the estimate of the population standard deviation, σ, is $\sqrt{0.0017}$ or 0.0417. These estimates are shown in Table 8.2.

Four further points about this example must be made. First, it worked out the weekly variance, whereas the option pricing models require the annual variance; this is 52 times the weekly figure, so here it is 52(0.0017) or 0.0900. The annual standard deviation, σ, is the square root of the annual variance, that is $\sqrt{0.0900}$, which is 0.30, or 30%. Another way of estimating annual variance would be to use a sample of annual price changes over a number of recent years, but this is unsatisfactory as it means going a long way back to get a sizeable sample, and the volatility might have changed significantly over that period.

Secondly, the sample has only 10 observations which is very few. It is possible to get more observations by including more weeks, but going back over, say, 30 weeks, would also mean using quite dated information. A more satisfactory way of getting a sizeable number of observations is to use daily data for, say, 50 recent trading days, and then estimate the daily variance. Over a year, there are about 250 trading days, and this means that an estimate of the daily variance needs to be multiplied by about 250 to give an estimate of the annual variance.

Thirdly, the sample of 10 periods was assumed to avoid any periods where dividends were due. At any moment when a dividend is paid, or more specifically when the share goes ex-dividend so that the new owner will not secure the next dividend, the share price tends to fall by the amount of the dividend. So the share price may well fall during the period concerned. Estimates of σ and σ^2 smooth this out by using an adjusted price for the end of the period concerned. This adjusted price is set as the actual price plus the amount of the dividend. But the actual price at the end of that period is used as the start price for the following period.

Fourthly, the 30% standard deviation in the example is a fairly typical value. For most equities, the figure lies between 20% and 40%.

Z-values and the normal distribution

The Black–Scholes model requires the use of what are called **z-values**. The example in Table 8.2 will be used to show what these are and why they are useful. As a starting point, suppose that someone wanted to draw a frequency distribution graph that would show the frequency with which different percentage price changes occur. This could be done by drawing a graph that showed possible price changes on the horizontal axis and that measured the frequency with which each price change occurred on the vertical axis. But there is another way of representing the distribution of price changes on a graph. Using this approach, a z-value for each week's price change is defined as its (x-value)/σ, and a frequency distribution graph is plotted to show the frequency with which each z-value occurs. The z-values for the 10 LML share price changes are shown in column (8) of Table 8.2. Thus in week 5, the x-value was 0.0488, and dividing this by σ, or 0.0417, gives a z-value of 1.1700. In this example, only 10 z-values arose and none of them occurred more than once, so a frequency distribution graph would be uninteresting. But the graph would take on a more interesting shape with more observations.

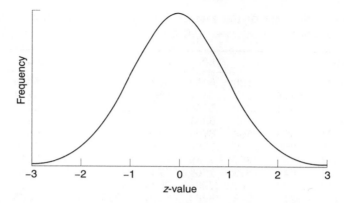

Figure 8.2 The probability distribution of different z-values with a normal distribution.

In the case of many variables, it turns out that the distribution of z-values looks exactly the same, with a bell-shaped curve similar to the one shown in Fig. 8.2. Because this sort of distribution is so common, it is called the **normal distribution**. This distribution is plotted in Fig. 8.2 with z values ranging from −3 to +3. Very few z-values will lie outside this range.

A use of z-values

Suppose that the distribution of price changes – expressed as continuous rates – is normal, and suppose that Y wants to know what percentage of weekly changes lie below or at a given value. This is actually equivalent to wanting to know the probability of the price change in any given week being less than or equal to that given value. Thus Y may want to know the probability of the weekly price change being less than or equal to a rise of 3.5%, that is equal to a change of 0.035 or less. Y may also want to know the probability of the weekly price change being less than or equal to a fall of 1.5%, that is equal to a change of −0.015 or less, or, more simply, to a fall of 1.5% or more.

A price change of 0.035 can be re-expressed as the mean of 0.001 plus 0.034. So this price change has an x-value of 0.034, that is the change minus the mean. So its z-value, that is x/σ, is 0.034/0.0417 or 0.815. A price change of −0.015 can be re-expressed as the mean of 0.001 minus 0.016. So this change has an x-value of −0.016, and it has a z-value of −0.016/0.0417 or −0.384. So Y effectively wants to know the probability of the price change in any given week having a z-value of 0.815 or less, and also the probability of it having a z-value of −0.0384 or less.

These probabilities can be found from widely published tables like Table 8.3. Take, first, the z-value of 0.815. Look down the column headed z to the row marked 0.8. Then look across to the right in the column headed 0.01. The figure there of 0.7910 means that 79.10% of z-values are 0.81 or less, so the probability

Table 8.3 The probability of the z-value for a given observation being less than or equal to any value between 0.0 and 2.99

z	0.00	0.01	0.02	0.03	0.04	0.05	0.06	0.07	0.08	0.09
0.0	.5000	.5040	.5080	.5120	.5160	.5199	.5239	.5279	.5319	.5359
0.1	.5398	.5438	.5478	.5517	.5557	.5596	.5636	.5675	.5714	.5753
0.2	.5793	.5832	.5871	.5910	.5948	.5987	.6026	.6064	.6103	.6141
0.3	.6179	.6217	.6255	.6293	.6331	.6368	.6406	.6443	.6480	.6517
0.4	.6554	.6591	.6628	.6664	.6700	.6736	.6772	.6808	.6844	.6879
0.5	.6915	.6950	.6985	.7019	.7054	.7088	.7123	.7157	.7190	.7224
0.6	.7257	.7291	.7324	.7357	.7389	.7422	.7454	.7486	.7517	.7549
0.7	.7580	.7611	.7642	.7673	.7704	.7734	.7764	.7794	.7823	.7852
0.8	.7881	.7910	.7939	.7967	.7995	.8023	.8051	.8078	.8106	.8133
0.9	.8159	.8186	.8212	.8238	.8264	.8289	.8315	.8340	.8365	.8389
1.0	.8413	.8438	.8461	.8485	.8508	.8531	.8554	.8577	.8599	.8621
1.1	.8643	.8665	.8686	.8708	.8729	.8749	.8770	.8790	.8810	.8830
1.2	.8849	.8869	.8888	.8907	.8925	.8944	.8962	.8980	.8997	.9015
1.3	.9032	.9049	.9066	.9082	.9099	.9115	.9131	.9147	.9162	.9177
1.4	.9192	.9207	.9222	.9236	.9251	.9265	.9279	.9292	.9306	.9319
1.5	.9332	.9345	.9357	.9370	.9382	.9394	.9406	.9418	.9429	.9441
1.6	.9452	.9463	.9474	.9484	.9495	.9505	.9515	.9525	.9535	.9545
1.7	.9554	.9564	.9573	.9582	.9591	.9599	.9608	.9616	.9625	.9633
1.8	.9641	.9649	.9656	.9664	.9671	.9678	.9686	.9693	.9699	.9706
1.9	.9713	.9719	.9726	.9732	.9738	.9744	.9750	.9756	.9761	.9767
2.0	.9772	.9778	.9783	.9788	.9793	.9798	.9803	.9808	.9812	.9817
2.1	.9821	.9826	.9830	.9834	.9838	.9842	.9846	.9850	.9854	.9857
2.2	.9861	.9864	.9868	.9871	.9875	.9878	.9881	.9884	.9887	.9890
2.3	.9893	.9896	.9898	.9901	.9904	.9906	.9909	.9911	.9913	.9916
2.4	.9918	.9920	.9922	.9925	.9927	.9929	.9931	.9932	.9934	.9936
2.5	.9938	.9940	.9941	.9943	.9945	.9946	.9948	.9949	.9951	.9952
2.6	.9953	.9955	.9956	.9957	.9959	.9960	.9961	.9962	.9963	.9964
2.7	.9965	.9966	.9967	.9968	.9969	.9970	.9971	.9972	.9973	.9974
2.8	.9974	.9975	.9976	.9977	.9977	.9978	.9979	.9979	.9980	.9981
2.9	.9981	.9982	.9982	.9983	.9984	.9984	.9985	.9985	.9986	.9986

of any given week's z-value being 0.81 or less is 0.7910. The adjacent figure, in the column headed 0.02, shows that the probability of a given week's z-value being 0.82 or less is 0.7939. The probability of a given week's z-value being 0.815 or less is in between 0.7910 and 0.7939, say 0.7920. So 79.20% of weekly price changes will be less than or equal to a rise of 3.5%. Take next the z-value of −0.384. The table does not cover negative z-values as they can readily be found from the equivalent positive z-values. So consider, first, a z-value of 0.384. Look down the column headed z to the row marked 0.3. Then look across to the right in the column headed 0.08. The figure there of 0.6480 means that the probability of any given week's z-value being 0.38 or less is 0.6480. The adjacent figure, in the column headed 0.09, shows that the probability of it being 0.39 or less is 0.6517. The probability of it being 0.384 or less is in between 0.6480 and 0.6517, say 0.6495. To find the probability of the z-value being −0.384 or less, the figure found for a z-value of 0.384 is subtracted from one, so the probability is $(1 - 0.6495)$ or 0.3505. So 35.05% of weekly price changes will be less than or equal to a fall of 1.5%.

This example shows that in a normal distribution, there is a 0.3505 probability of any given observation, such as the price change in any given week, having a z-value of -0.384 or less. This is expressed more formally as $N(-0.384)$ $= 0.3505$ where $N(-0.384)$ means the probability of any given observation having a z-value of -0.384 or less. The Black–Scholes formula actually includes the probabilities of two z-values. These are not, in fact, the z-values for price changes, but they are the z-values for related variables.

Implicit volatility

So far, it has been assumed that investors always estimate future volatility by using historical volatility, making suitable adjustments if they think that the volatility will change. However, there is another method, which is to look at the actual prices of options and work out what figures for volatility would have to be slotted into the Black–Scholes formula or the binomial method to obtain those prices. The result is known as the **implied volatility** or **implicit volatility**. This method is quite often used, but it is not used by people who are looking for mispriced options. For they think that actual option prices may be incorrect, and actual prices are most likely to be incorrect if they are based on unsound estimates of future volatility.

One problem with this method is that if each available option on a given asset, such as LML shares, is taken in turn, it may produce a different implied volatility. This will happen if people think the volatility will change. Suppose, for example, that investors think the volatility of LML's share price will rise. Then the average volatility they expect over the next month will be less than the average they expect over the next four months, and in turn the prices they will offer for one-month options will be based on different volatilities from the prices they will offer for four-month options. So estimates of implied volatility will be lower if the one-month options are used than if the four-month ones are used. Moreover, even for those options that expire in, say, four months, investors may expect those that will not be exercised early, say calls if no dividend is due before expiry, to have longer lives than those which may be exercised early, say American puts, so using these puts may lead to lower implied volatilities.

There are other possible reasons for different implicit volatilities. For example, option prices have to change by minimum ticks, so their prices rarely reflect precisely the volatilities that investors think is appropriate. Also, many people calculate implicit volatilities by using the published closing prices on a given day for the various options on, say, LML shares, along with the closing spot price of the shares. However, the published option prices actually show the prices agreed in the last option contracts made that day. These options might have been made some time before trading ended, and the price of LML shares then might have differed from its closing price. So the volatility estimates may use a slightly incorrect spot price.

Faced with an array of implicit volatilities, investors can use various methods to get a get a single overall market view of volatility. For example, they might use means of all the different implicit volatilities. Alternatively, they might use means that are weighted to give more weight to those options that are almost at-the-money, for, as shown in Section 7.6, their prices are more sensitive to volatility. Another approach is to work out what the prices of all the available options would have been on the basis of a wide range of possible volatilities, and then select the volatility figure whose forecasts seem, overall, most correct. Yet another procedure is to make estimates that incorporate both historical and implicit volatilities.

8.5 THE BLACK–SCHOLES MODEL AND ORDINARY EQUITY OPTIONS

The Black–Scholes formula was a major breakthrough in option pricing theory. Black and Scholes actually derived their formula by adapting the solution to a problem which had arisen in physics. However, their formula can be derived mathematically from the simple option pricing model given in Section 8.2 by allowing the price of the underlying asset to change in each of an infinite number of small steps over the option's life, rather than in just one or two big steps. This section explains and uses the formula, but it does not give a mathematical derivation.

The assumptions of the Black–Scholes model

It is helpful to see the Black–Scholes as derived from the simple model used in Section 8.2 because it incorporates the same assumptions. These were not all fully specified in Section 8.2 but are:

1. There are no transactions costs involved in buying or selling equities or options; for example, there are no commissions and no bid–offer spreads.
2. There is no dividend before expiry.
3. The option is European.
4. The risk-free rate and the volatility of the price of the underlying asset are constant during the life of the option.
5. The spot price of the underlying asset follows a random walk.

Assumption 1 is needed to ensure that options end up with their fair values. For example, Section 8.2 argued that if call options are overpriced, then investors will buy the underlying asset and write calls on it, so sending the option price down, while if call options are underpriced, then investors will sell the underlying asset and buy calls on it, so driving the option price up. But these actions and the resulting option price changes might not occur if there were large transactions costs.

Assumptions 2, 3 and 4 were made explicitly in Section 8.2. The Black–Scholes model can actually be adapted to allow satisfactorily for dividends before expiry, although the binomial model outlined in Section 8.7 handles them even more precisely. The Black–Scholes model cannot be adapted for American options, except when they have the same prices as European options, but the binomial model can handle American options. The Black–Scholes model can be developed to handle expected changes in the interest rate or volatility, but it is often easier to adapt the binomial model.

Assumption 5 means, strictly, that future changes in the spot price cannot be forecast on the basis of past price changes. However, it can be shown that it is equivalent to assuming that the lifetime of the option can be divided into a large number of short time periods or steps, in each of which the spot price of the underlying asset can change either up or down by constant specified percentages. This assumption was made in Section 8.2, albeit with only one or two steps. If the spot price does not follow a random walk, then the option can best be priced by suitably adapting the binomial model; an example of this situation is given in Fig. 8.7 in Section 8.8. The Black–Scholes assumption that the spot price does follow a random walk has three important implications:

1. It means that the price cannot leap about. Instead, it has to move or 'walk' in a continuous path. However, the Black–Scholes model assumes that the option's life is split into an infinite number of infinitely short time periods, so large price changes can occur over a very short time.
2. It means that the price can never fall to zero. To see why, suppose the price starts at 100p and that in any period it can rise or fall by 20%. Even if it falls by 20% in an infinite number of periods, it will only fall to 80 in the first, 64 in the second, 51.2 in the third, and so on. It would take 10 periods to fall to about 10p, 20 periods to fall to 1p, 30 to fall to 0.1p, and so on, but it would never fall to zero. Consequently, it would never fall by 100p. In contrast, if the price rose by 20% in every period, then it would rise by 100p in just four periods.
3. It means that the probability distribution of the natural logarithms of the possible spot prices at expiry is normal. It is hard to demonstrate this when there are an infinite number of steps, but it is demonstrated in Fig. 8.3(c) in Section 8.7 for a situation where there are just 10 steps.

A price formula when there is no volatility

The Black–Scholes formula relates the price of a European call option on an equity on which no dividend is due before expiry to the five relevant factors. These factors are as follows: the current spot price of the underlying asset, S; the exercise price, E; the time to expiry in years, T, where T is usually less than one; the risk-free interest rate, which is expressed as a continuously compounded rate, r; and the volatility of the price of the underlying asset, as given by σ, which is the estimated standard deviation of the natural logarithms of all the proportional price changes there could be.

Before giving the Black–Scholes formula, it is useful to derive a simple formula which would apply if the price of the underlying asset was completely stable, and then to see in general terms how this simple formula must be modified to allow for volatility. It will be recalled from equation (7.1) in Section 7.2 that, in the absence of volatility and dividends, the price of a European call option is given by $\text{Max}\{0,[S - E/(1 + r)^T]\}$, where r in Chapter 7 was the risk-free rate expressed as a simple rate. So, in terms of the notation used in this chapter, that formula becomes $\text{Max}\{0,[S - E/(1 + r_S)^T]\}$.

In this formula, $E/(1 + r_S)^T$ is simply the present value of the exercise price. So it is the sum that would have to be lent today at the simple risk-free rate, r_S, to secure a sum equal to the exercise price, E, ready to exercise the option when it expires in T years. Suppose that $r_S = 0.06$ or 6%, that $E = 110$, and that $T = 0.6667$ or eight months. Then $E/(1 + r_S)^T$ is $110/(1.06)^{0.6667}$ or 105.81. For the present chapter, however, the risk-free rate is expressed as the equivalent continuously compounded rate which is 5.83%, or 0.0583. To work out present values using this rate, which is here referred to as r, it is necessary to use the method given in Section 8.3 and express the present value as Ee^{-rT}. This gives a value of $110e^{-(0.0583)(0.6667)}$ which is also 105.81. Using this approach means that (7.1) can be modified, by replacing $E/(1 + r_S)^T$ with Ee^{-rT}, to become:

$$C_E = \text{Max}\{0,[S - Ee^{-rT}]\} \tag{8.10}$$

The Black–Scholes formula for European equity call options

The Black–Scholes formula is a modified version of (8.10) which allows the spot price of the underlying asset to be volatile. It can be thought of as including two modifications to (8.10). First, the constraint that the option price cannot be negative is removed, so that (8.10) would simply give $C_E = S - Ee^{-rT}$. Secondly, each of the terms on the right-hand side is adjusted. To see this, it is helpful to present the Black–Scholes formula in a simplified form as follows:

$$C_E = (S \times \text{probability of event 1}) - (Ee^{-rT} \times \text{probability of event 2}) \tag{8.11}$$

It can be seen that the Black–Scholes formula incorporates two probabilities. Unless it is solved by a computer, these probabilities have to be derived from a table of z-values like Table 8.3. The full Black–Scholes formula is:

$$C_E = SN(d_1) - Ee^{-rT}N(d_2) \tag{8.12}$$

where $N(d_1)$ is the probability of any individual observation in a normal distribution having a z-value of d_1 or less, and $N(d_2)$ is the probability of any individual observation in a normal distribution having a z-value of d_2 or less. $N(d_2)$ is actually the probability of the option ending up in-the-money. $N(d_1)$ is a related probability, and it also has another meaning, as explained later. The values of d_1 and d_2 have to be worked out from the following expressions:

$$d_1 = [\ln(S/E) + T(r + \sigma^2/2)]/\sigma\sqrt{T} \tag{8.13}$$

$$d_2 = d_1 - \sigma\sqrt{T} \tag{8.14}$$

where $\ln(S/E)$ is the natural logarithm of (S/E). It can be worked out on most scientific calculators.

The simple derivation of the Black–Scholes model given here removed the constraint in (8.10) which ensured that it could not deliver a negative price. So it might seem that the Black–Scholes model itself could. In fact, though, the way in which it incorporates the two related probabilities ensures that it never does.

Using the Black–Scholes model for a European equity call option

The Black–Scholes formula may look complex but it is relatively easy to use. Consider a call option on LML shares with the following parameters:

$T = 0.6667$, or eight months
$E = 110p$
$S = 100p$
$r = 0.0583$, or 5.83% (expressed as a continuously compounded rate)
$\sigma = 0.30$, or 30%
No dividend before expiry.

Four steps are needed to estimate the price of this call option, C_E:

1. Calculate σ^2 as 0.09 and hence calculate $\sigma^2/2$ as 0.045.
2. Estimate d_1 and d_2. Take d_1 first. This is given by $[\ln(S/E) + T(r + \sigma^2/2)]/\sigma\sqrt{T}$ which is $[\ln(100/110) + 0.6667(0.0583 + 0.0450)]/(0.3\sqrt{0.6667})$; this is $[-0.0953 + 0.0689]/0.2450$ or -0.108. Then take d_2. This is given by $(d_1 - \sigma\sqrt{T})$ which is $(-0.108 - 0.245)$ or -0.353.
3. Work out the probabilities $N(d_1)$ and $N(d_2)$, that is $N(-0.108)$ and $N(-0.353)$. This can be done from Table 8.3. The probability of a z-value below 0.108 is between the 0.5398 for 0.10 and the 0.5438 for 0.11. Say it is 0.543. Then the probability of a z-value below -0.108 is $(1 - 0.543)$, or 0.457. The probability of a z-value below 0.353 is between the 0.6368 for 0.35 and the 0.6406 for 0.36. Say it is 0.638. Then the probability of a z-value below -0.353 is $(1 - 0.638)$, or 0.362.
4. Solve the Black–Scholes equation $C_E = SN(d_1) - Ee^{-rT}N(d_2)$. Ee^{-rT} is $110e^{-0.0583(0.6667)}$ which is 105.81p. So $C_E = 100(0.457) - 105.81(0.362)$. This is $45.70 - 38.30$ or 7.40p.

Put-call parity and the Black–Scholes formula for put options

The Black–Scholes model presented above gives the price of a European call option. It can be readily used also to give the price of a European put option, P_E. To see how, it is necessary to explore the relationship between the prices of European calls and European puts.

Suppose Y owns one share in LML which is today worth 100p. Suppose she also writes a call option on one LML share, expiring in eight months, with a strike price of 110. And suppose she also buys a put option on one LML share, expiring in eight months, with a strike price of 110. So Y has three assets. The value of these three assets when the options expire in eight months will depend on the spot price of LML shares that day. Table 8.4 shows their values for five possible spot prices. Consider two of these: 90 and 130.

If the spot price of LML shares at expiry is 90p, then the value of Y's share will be 90. However, the value of the call option which Y has written will be zero, for no-one will exercise an option allowing them to buy an LML share from Y for 110 when the spot price is 90. On the other hand, the value of Y's

Table 8.4 Value of Y's portfolio in eight months' time

Spot price of LML shares (p)	Value of Y's share (p)	Value of Y's written 110p call option (p)	Value of Y's bought 110p put option (p)	Total value of Y's portfolio (p)
90	90	0	20	110
100	100	0	10	110
110	110	0	0	110
120	120	−10	0	110
130	130	−20	0	110

held put option will be 20, for Y has the right to sell at 110 an LML share which is worth 90. So the total value of Y's portfolio will be 110.

If, instead, the spot price of LML shares at expiry is 130p, then the value of Y's share will be 130. This time, however, the value of the call option which Y has written will be −20, for its holder will exercise it and will buy an LML share from Y at 110 when the share price is 130. But the value of Y's held put option will be zero, for the right to sell an LML at 110 when the spot price is 130 is worth nothing. So, again, the total value of Y's portfolio will be 110.

In fact, as Table 8.4 shows, the total value of Y's portfolio will be 110 at expiry, no matter what the spot price of LML shares is then. This means that the present value of her portfolio is 105.81, for this is $110e^{-rT}$, where r is the risk-free rate expressed as a continuously compounded rate of 0.0583, and T is the period being considered, here eight months or 0.6667 years. More generally, the present value of a portfolio comprising one share, one written call option and one held put option is Ee^{-rT} if each exercise price is E. So Ee^{-rT} is the amount that people will at present pay for that portfolio. In other words, Ee^{-rT} is the current spot price of an LML share, S, minus the premium received from writing a call option, C_E, plus the premium paid on the put option, P_E. In short, Ee^{-rT} equals $S - C_E + P_E$. This relationship can be rearranged to give the **put–call parity** for European options which is:

$$P_E = Ee^{-rT} - S + C_E \qquad (8.15)$$

Substituting the expression for C_E from (8.12) into this gives a formula for P_E which is:

$$P_E = Ee^{-rT}[1 - N(d_2)] - S[1 - N(d_1)] \qquad (8.16)$$

Using the Black–Scholes model for a European equity put option

There are two ways of using the Black–Scholes model to calculate the price of a European put option. One is to solve equation (8.16) for put options in the same way that equation (8.12) for call options was solved above. Another simpler way is to use (8.15), though this is possible only if the price of an equivalent call option, that is a call option with the same exercise price and expiry date, has already been calculated. This simpler way will be used to calculate the price of a European put option with the following parameters:

$T = 0.6667$, or eight months
$E = 110\text{p}$
$S = 100\text{p}$
$r = 0.0583$, or 5.83% (expressed as a continuously compounded rate)
$\sigma = 0.30$, or 30%
No dividend before expiry

It was shown above that the price of the equivalent call option, C_E, equalled 7.40p. Using the put-call parity relationship in (8.15), $P_\text{E} = Ee^{-rT} - S + C_\text{E}$, the price of the equivalent put option is $(105.81 - 100 + 7.40)$, that is 13.21p.

The Black–Scholes model and hedge ratios

Section 8.2 showed how an investor who buys some asset, such as LML shares, can secure a hedge portfolio, that is a perfectly hedged position by writing an appropriate number of call options on LML shares. Section 8.2 also showed that the hedge ratio of shares to options that is required for a perfect hedge depends on the current spot price of the underlying asset. So the investor must adopt a new ratio each time that price changes. The Black–Scholes model actually gives the hedge ratio by the term $N(d_1)$. This can be shown using the call option considered earlier. It had the following parameters:

$T = 0.6667$, or eight months
$E = 110\text{p}$
$S = 100\text{p}$
$r = 0.0583$, or 5.83% (expressed as a continuously compounded rate)
$\sigma = 0.30$, or 30%
No dividend before expiry

It was shown that the price of the option was 7.40p and that $N(d_1)$ was 0.457.

Suppose that X decides to have a portfolio with a hedge ratio given by the of $N(d_1)$. He does this by buying 457 LML shares and by also writing 1,000 call options. With the spot price of shares at 100p and the option price at 7.40p, the total cost of his portfolio is (£457 – £74), which is £383.

Next, suppose that the spot price of LML shares rises by 1p to 101p. This increases the total value of X's 457 LML shares by £4.57. It also increases the price of his written call options. An increase in the price of a call option is good for its holder who could, for example, receive more money by selling it; but it is bad for its writer who would, for example, have to pay more to another writer to persuade that writer to take it over. So the rise the price of call options on LML shares makes X worse off. The Black–Scholes formula can be solved to show that if S rises to 101, then the option price will rise by 0.46p to 7.86p. So the value of the 1,000 options held against X rises by 1,000(0.46p), which is £4.60. Combined with the £4.57 rise in the value of his shares, this means that X's wealth is virtually unchanged.

Suppose, instead, that the spot price of LML shares falls by 1p to 99p. This reduces the value of X's 457 LML shares by a total of £4.57. But it also reduces the price of his written call options which makes X better off. The Black–Scholes formula can be solved to show if S falls to 99, then the option price will fall by 0.46p to 6.94p. So the value of the 1,000 options held against X falls by 1,000(0.46p) which is £4.60. Again, X's wealth is virtually unchanged.

Thus the value of $N(d_1)$ in the Black–Scholes formula does give the hedge ratio required for a perfect hedge with call options. Admittedly, the value of X's portfolio altered very slightly when S changed, so it may seem that $N(d_1)$ gives only an approximate value of the perfect hedge ratio. However, d_1 is given by $[\ln(S/E) + T(r + \sigma^2/2)]/\sigma\sqrt{T}$ which changes when S changes. So $N(d_1)$ changes when S changes. In fact, it rises to 0.473 if S rises to 101, and it falls to 0.441 if S falls to 99. Thus using a hedge ratio of $N(d_1)$ secures a hedge portfolio only for infinitely small changes in S. This means that an investor who wants a hedge portfolio must alter the hedge ratio, and hence the number of shares held for each call option written, or vice versa, every time S alters by the slightest amount. Such an activity is called **dynamic hedging**. In practice, hedgers may not seek fully hedged portfolios. But the concept that a change in S changes the riskiness or exposure to risk of a portfolio is clearly important.

When the spot price was 100p and the hedge ratio was exactly 0.457, X's wealth would be unaffected by infinitely small changes in S from 100. This means that a small change in S of, say, ΔS, must cause the option price to change by $0.457\Delta S$, for then the change in the total value of X's 457 shares, that is $457\Delta S$, will just balance the change in the total value of his 1,000 options, that is $1,000(0.457\Delta S)$. As the change in the option price equals 0.457 times the change in the share price, the call option's delta is also 0.457.

This example shows that a call option's delta, that is the **call delta**, is given by $N(d_1)$. And it shows that the hedge ratio required to form a perfect hedge for a holding of shares by writing calls is also given by $N(d_1)$. Section 8.2 showed that people could instead hedge a holding of shares by buying puts. The hedge ratio they require for a perfect hedge, and also the delta for a put option, or the **put delta**, are both given by $[N(d_1) - 1]$, which is –0.543 when S is 100. So anyone wanting a perfect hedge with put options must buy 1,000 puts for every 543 shares that they own. The minus sign indicates that they must buy options rather than write them.

Adapting the Black–Scholes model to allow for dividends on European equity options

Since it was published in 1973, the Black–Scholes formula has been developed to cover European options on equities where dividends are due before expiry. This is easily done. Recall from Sections 7.2 and 7.3 that a dividend before expiry depresses the price of a call option and increases the price of a put option. In the absence of volatility, the option prices change by the present value of the dividend. Consequently, the simple formulae used in Chapter 7 were modified by replacing S, the current spot price, by S^*, that is S minus the present value of the dividend, D. The present value of D was defined using a simple risk-free interest rate as $D/(1 + r_S)^t$, where t is the time elapsing before the dividend is due.

A similar approach is used in modifying the Black–Scholes formula for call options except that a continuously compounded risk-free rate is used. Thus the present value of the dividend is given by De^{-rt}, so S^* is given by $S - De^{-rt}$. Then S^* is used in the equations in place of S. So the equations for call and put option prices are modified from (8.12) and (8.16) to become:

$$C_E = S^*N(d_1) - Ee^{-rT}N(d_2) \tag{8.17}$$

$$P_E = Ee^{-rT}[1 - N(d_2)] - S^*[1 - N(d_1)] \tag{8.18}$$

where:

$$d_1 = [\ln(S^*/E) + T(r + \sigma^2/2)]/\sigma\sqrt{T} \tag{8.19}$$

$$d_2 = d_1 - \sigma\sqrt{T} \tag{8.20}$$

The price of a put may also be found by finding the price of a corresponding call and then using the put–call parity relationship. But the relationship given in (8.15) must be modified to:

$$P_E = Ee^{-rT} - S^* + C_E \tag{8.21}$$

In effect, this approach regards the spot price, S, as having two parts. It argues, correctly, that one part, the present value of the dividend due before expiry, is irrelevant for the holder of a European call option, so that the other part, S^*, is all that matters. This approach would give exact call option prices if the volatility of the S^* part precisely equalled the volatility of the whole price, S, for the same value of σ is used when S^* is substituted for S. In practice, S^* is relatively more volatile than S. This is because the present value of the dividend simply rises steadily as the dividend approaches, so that all the fluctuations in S arise from the fluctuations in the smaller S^*. Admittedly the difference in volatility between S and S^* is so tiny that the modified Black–Scholes formulae give excellent estimates of the exact option price. But the binomial method discussed in section 8.7 has the advantage of avoiding this assumption.

Using the Black–Scholes model for European equity options when a dividend is due

The effects of replacing S by S^* in the Black–Scholes formula may be illustrated by modifying the call and put option examples used earlier to allow for a dividend of 4p after five months, so that t is five-twelfths of a year or 0.4167. The examples have the following parameters:

> $T = 0.6667$, or eight months
> $E = 110$p
> $S = 100$p
> $r = 0.0583$, or 5.83% (expressed as a continuously compounded rate)
> $\sigma = 0.30$, or 30%
> $D = 4$
> $t = 0.4167$, or five months

282 Financial Claims and Derivatives

Estimating the price of a call option, C_E, now requires five steps.

1. Calculate σ^2 as 0.09 and hence calculate $\sigma^2/2$ as 0.045.
2. Calculate S^* as $S - De^{-rt}$. So $S^* = 100 - 4e^{-(0.0583)(0.4167)}$, or $(100 - 3.904)$, which is 96.10.
3. Estimate d_1 and d_2. Take d_1 first. This is given by $[\ln(S^*/E) + T(r + \sigma^2/2)]/\sigma\sqrt{T}$ which is $[\ln(96.10/110) + 0.6667(0.0583 + 0.0450)]/(0.3\sqrt{0.6667})$; this is $[-0.1351 + 0.0689]/0.2450$ or -0.271. Then take d_2. This is given by $(d_1 - \sigma\sqrt{T})$ which is $(-0.271 - 0.245)$ or -0.516.
4. Work out the probabilities $N(d_1)$ and $N(d_2)$, that is $N(-0.271)$ and $N(-0.516)$. This can be done from Table 8.3. The probability of a z-value below 0.271 is between the 0.6064 for 0.27 and the 0.6103 for 0.28. Say it is 0.607. Then the probability of a z-value below -0.271 is $(1 - 0.607)$ or 0.393. The probability of a z-value below 0.516 is between the 0.6950 for 0.51 and the 0.6985 for 0.52. Say it is 0.697. Then the probability of a z-value below -0.516 is $(1 - 0.697)$ or 0.303.
5. Solve the equation $C_E = S^*N(d_1) - Ee^{-rT}N(d_2)$. Ee^{-rT} is $110e^{-0.0583(0.6667)}$ which equals 105.81p. So $C_E = 96.10(0.393) - 105.81(0.303)$. This is $(37.77 - 32.06)$ or 5.71p.

The price of a corresponding put option can be found in a similar way from (8.18) or by using the put–call parity relationship in (8.21). The latter gives $P_E = Ee^{-rT} - S^* + C_E$ which is $(105.81 - 96.10 + 5.71)$ or 15.42p. It will be noticed that allowing for a dividend reduced the call option price from 7.40p to 5.71, and raised the put option price from 13.21p to 15.42.

The Black–Scholes model and American equity options

The Black–Scholes model applies to European equity options. Thus it typically underestimates the prices of American equity options as they are typically worth more than European ones by the amount of any early exercise premium. But there are occasions when an American option has no early exercise premium so that the Black–Scholes model can be used. This arises on equity call options if no dividend is due before expiry, or if only a small dividend is due, for Section 7.2 showed that American calls would then have the same prices as European calls.

In practice, the model is occasionally used to estimate the price of an American call option on an equity even when one or more sizeable dividends are due, so that the option does have an early exercise premium. Section 7.2 also showed that the only time when an American call like this would be exercised is just before an ex-dividend date. Using the Black–Scholes model for such an option involves working out several different prices. One price is the one that it would have if it was a European call that could be exercised only at expiry. Another price is the one that it would have if it was a European call that expired just before the final ex-dividend date. Further prices are worked out assuming that it is a European call which expires just before any other earlier ex-dividend dates. Each time the Black–Scholes formula is used, S is replaced by a different S^*, which is S minus the present values of any dividends due before the assumed expiry date; the highest S^* is used for the first ex-dividend date because there will be the least value of dividends due before that date. The highest of the several option prices that are worked out is taken as an estimate of the option's current fair value, but it is a slight underestimate because the early exercise premium is not fully reflected in this approach. For this reason, the approach is said to give the price of a **pseudo-American** option.

For American puts, the Black–Scholes model can do little except to indicate the equivalent European option prices which the American option prices should exceed. In this respect, the model is most helpful for American puts which are deeply out-of-the-money and thus have little prospect of being exercised, for they may have small early exercise premiums and so be worth little more than their European equivalents. With most American puts, however, it is usually sounder to use the binomial model or one of the other models noted in Section 8.1.

8.6 THE BLACK–SCHOLES MODEL AND OTHER OPTIONS

Section 8.5 showed how the Black–Scholes model could be used to price European equity options. This section shows how it can be modified to price other types of European options.

The Black–Scholes model and European stock index options

A stock index option is effectively an option on a basket of shares which matches the shares covered by the index. To see this, consider a call option on a 100 share index. Suppose the current value of the index is 4,000, and suppose the option has an exercise price of 4,400, so that its holder will be given 1p at expiry for each point by which the index is then over 4,400. Suppose, too, that Y wants to buy at expiry a basket of shares which matches those in the index and which is now worth 4,000p. Suppose Y buys a 4,400 call. If, at expiry, the price of the basket of shares that she wants is over 4,400p, then Y will be compensated for the excess, so she need not use more than 4,400p of her own funds. So she effectively has an option with an exercise price, E, of 4,400p, on a basket of shares whose current spot price, S, is 4,000p.

The Black–Scholes formulae (8.17) to (8.20) can be used for such a stock index option provided that care is taken in calculating S^*, that is the spot price minus the present value of any dividends due before expiry. There may be many dividends due before expiry, and the present value of each one must be deducted. One way of doing this is to work out how many of each of the 100 companies' shares would be included in a basket that is today worth 4,000p; as, on average, each company contributes only 40p worth of shares, each will have only a fraction of a share in the basket. Then the present value of each dividend due on these fractions of shares is calculated, and the total of these values is deducted from S to obtain S^*.

Merton (1973) proposed a simpler approach to estimating S^* which is satisfactory for stock-index options where the relevant stock index includes many equities whose dividends are paid at different times spread out over the year. This approach assumes that the amount of dividend that is paid at any moment in time depends on the value of the shares at that moment. In effect, dividends are held to be paid at a continuously compounded rate, which is termed δ.

To see what this means, suppose first that share prices are constant and that δ is 0.04. Then a sum of S invested in a portfolio of shares for T years would grow to $Se^{\delta T}$. For example, after one year it would be worth $Se^{0.04}$, or 1.041S; this is a shade above 1.04S, even though $\delta = 0.04$, because δ is a continuously compounded rate of 4% rather than a simple rate of 4%. So after a period of T years, the value of the portfolio that is then attributable to the dividends paid during that period would equal the final value of the portfolio minus its original value, that is $(Se^{\delta T} - S)$, or $S(e^{\delta T} - 1)$. However, S^* in the Black–Scholes formula equals S minus the *present* value of the dividends. The present value of $S(e^{\delta T} - 1)$ is the sum which could be invested today to secure $S(e^{\delta T} - 1)$ after T years. One way of securing that $S(e^{\delta T} - 1)$ would be to lend $S(e^{\delta T} - 1)e^{-rT}$ at the risk-free rate, r, for it has been seen that e^{-rT} lent at this rate grows to 1p, so $S(e^{\delta T} - 1)e^{-rT}$ lent at this rate will grow to $S(e^{\delta T} - 1)$. Another way of securing $S(e^{\delta T} - 1)$ would actually be to invest $S(e^{\delta T} - 1)e^{-\delta T}$ in shares at a rate of δ; this sum simplifies to $S(1 - e^{-\delta T})$, as $e^{\delta T}e^{-\delta T}$ equals one. So if share prices were constant, S^* could be set either as S minus $S(e^{\delta T} - 1)e^{-rT}$, or as S minus $S(1 - e^{-\delta T})$.

The reason for making either deduction is to reduce the premium on a call option by the present value of any dividends that an option buyer forgoes by buying options instead of buying shares right away. The buyer can then invest the saving on the premium to get a return that offsets the forgone dividends. In practice, of course, share prices are not constant. So, assuming that dividend payments depend on the current value of the shares, the present value of any forgone dividends depends on what happens to share prices after the option is bought. To get an appropriate offset, the buyer cannot invest the saving by lending it risk-free, for then the return will not depend on share prices. Instead, the saving must be invested in shares, for then the return will depend on share prices. So S^* must be set as S minus $S(1 - e^{-\delta T})$, which is $Se^{-\delta T}$. For example, if $S = 4,000$, $\delta = 0.04$, and $T = 0.6667$, then S^* is $4,000e^{-0.04(0.6667)}$, or 3,894.7p. This is a simple method of obtaining S^* because it involves only one calculation.

The Garman–Kohlhagen formula and European currency options

The basic Black–Scholes model cannot be used for currency options. This is because the assumption of no dividends, or in effect, no negative storage costs, is inappropriate with currencies, for any currency can earn interest by being lent at the risk-free rate applying in its home country. This interest can readily be allowed for in the Black–Scholes formulae if the interest rate concerned is expressed as a continuously compounded rate. For then options on currencies can be seen as very similar to stock index options where the underlying equities are assumed to earn dividends at a continuously compounded rate.

It has been seen that the Black–Scholes equations can be used for stock index options if each S is replaced by an S^* which equals $Se^{-\delta T}$, where δ is the continuously compounded rate of return that can currently be earned by buying shares. Likewise for currency options, the equations can be used if each S is replaced by an S^* which equals $Se^{-\rho t}$, where ρ is the current risk-free rate of interest in the country using the currency underlying the option, expressed as a continuously compounded rate. This adjustment was put forward by Garman and Kohlhagen (1983), and the resulting modified formulae are called the **Garman–Kohlhagen currency option pricing formulae.**

The Black formulae for European futures options on commodities and equities

Black (1976) developed the Black–Scholes model to give the **Black futures option pricing model** for the prices of European futures call and put options, FC_E and FP_E. His formulae apply to commodity futures options and also to equity futures options. They assume that the underlying futures contracts mature when the options expire. Taking S_F as the spot futures price and E_F as the exercise price of the futures option, the formulae are:

$$FC_E = e^{-rT}\{S_F N(d_1) - E_F N(d_2)\} \tag{8.22}$$

$$FP_E = e^{-rT}\{E_F[1 - N(d_2)] - S_F[1 - N(d_1)]\} \tag{8.23}$$

where:

$$d_1 = [\ln(S_F/E_F) + T(\sigma^2/2)]/\sigma\sqrt{T} \tag{8.24}$$

$$d_2 = d_1 - \sigma\sqrt{T} \tag{8.25}$$

(8.22) and (8.23) are related by the **put–call parity** relationship which, for futures options, is:

$$FP_E = FC_E - (S_F - E_F)e^{-rT} \tag{8.26}$$

These formulae do not refer to carrying costs such as storage costs or dividends before expiry. This is because the underlying asset for a futures option is a futures contract, which has no carrying costs. However, when using the formulae, it is necessary to use the current futures price, S_F. Section 7.4 showed that, for equity options, this is related to the current spot price, S, by $S_F = S(1 + r_S)^T$ if no dividend is due before expiry, and by $S_F = S^*(1 + r_S)^T$ if a dividend is due before expiry. So, for any given S, a dividend before expiry leads to a lower S_F, and hence, in turn, to a lower FC_E and to a higher FP_E.

When (8.22) to (8.26) are used, the σ that is used should, strictly, measure the volatility of the spot futures price, S_F, but typically it instead measures the volatility of the price of the asset underlying the futures contract, S. As the two volatilities may be very slightly different, so the formulae may not produce exact results. However, the results should be exact in the case of a futures equity option when no dividend is due before expiry. For then, as just noted, $S_F = S(1 + r_S)^T$ so that S_F is proportional to S. Consequently, their volatilities should be the same.

Using the Black model for a European futures equity option when no dividend is due

To illustrate the Black formulae, an example will be used for a futures call option on LML shares when no dividend is due before expiry. The example will have similar parameters to the ordinary call option on LML shares used earlier. But to use (8.22), it is also necessary to have the current futures price, S_F, for LML shares, which, as just noted equals $S(1 + r_S)^T$. In the example, the spot price of LML shares is 100p, the simple risk-free rate is 6%, and the time to expiry is 0.6667. So here S_F is $100(1.06)^{0.6667}$, or 103.96. The full parameters are:

$T = 0.6667$, or eight months
$E_F = 110p$
$S_F = 103.96p$
$r = 0.0583$, or 5.83% (expressed as a continuously compounded rate)
$\sigma = 0.30$, or 30%
No dividend before expiry

Four steps are needed to calculate the price of the futures call option, FC_E:

1. Calculate σ^2 as 0.09 and hence calculate $\sigma^2/2$ as 0.045.
2. Estimate d_1 and d_2. Take d_1 first. This is given by $[\ln(S_F/E_F) + T(\sigma^2/2)]/\sigma\sqrt{T}$, which is $[\ln(103.96/110) + 0.6667(0.0450)]/(0.3\sqrt{0.6667})$; this is $[-0.0565 + 0.0300]/0.2450$, or -0.108. Then take d_2. This is given by $(d_1 - \sigma\sqrt{T})$, which is $(-0.108 - 0.245)$, or -0.353.
3. Work out the probabilities $N(d_1)$ and $N(d_2)$, that is $N(-0.108)$ and $N(-0.353)$. This can be done from Table 8.3. The probability of a z-value below 0.108 is between the 0.5398 for 0.10 and the 0.5438 for 0.11. Say it is 0.543. Then the probability of a z-value below -0.108 is $(1 - 0.543)$ or 0.457. The probability of a z-value below 0.353 is between the 0.6368 for 0.35 and the 0.6406 for 0.36. Say it is 0.638. Then the probability of a z-value below -0.353 is $(1 - 0.638)$, or 0.362.
4. Solve the Black equation $FC_E = e^{-rT}\{S_F N(d_1) - E_F N(d_2)\}$, where e^{-rT} is $e^{-0.0583(0.6667)}$, or 0.962. So $FC_E = 0.962\{103.96(0.457) - 110(0.362)\}$, which is $0.962\{47.51 - 39.82\}$, or 7.40p.

It is not surprising that this price of 7.40p is the same as that obtained earlier for the ordinary call, for both the futures call and the ordinary call considered in these examples enable the holder to obtain an LML share in eight months for 110. The ordinary option entitles the holder to buy a share from the writer at expiry for 110, whereas the futures option entitles the holder to obtain a futures contract under which a share may be bought at its maturity for 110.

Using the Black model for a European futures equity option when a dividend is due

The Black model works in the same way if a dividend is due before expiry. Say the parameters of the example just considered are adjusted so that there is a dividend of 4 due after time t of 0.4167, that is five months. Then, as noted in an earlier example, $S*$ would be 96.10. So S_F would be given by $S*(1 + r_S)^T$, which would be 99.91. If this figure was slotted into the Black formulae, it would give FC_E as 5.73p.

The Black formulae for European interest rate futures options

Black's formulae (8.22) to (8.26) assume that the premiums are paid when the options are agreed. If, instead, the premiums are not due until expiry, then buyers will pay slightly more, because they can lend the money which they would have spent on the premiums when the options were agreed, and so have more money at expiry. In this case, the formulae must be adjusted by dropping the e^{-rT} terms in (8.22) and (8.23), for these terms produce the present value of the expressions inside the following square brackets. So the formulae become:

$$FC_E = S_F N(d_1) - E_F N(d_2) \tag{8.27}$$

$$FP_E = E_F[1 - N(d_2)] - S_F[1 - N(d_1)] \tag{8.28}$$

where d_1 and d_2 are given by (8.24) and (8.25). (8.27) and (8.28) are often used for LIFFE's long-term interest rate futures options as their premiums are payable on exercise or at expiry.

Further adjustments are needed to the formulae for LIFFE's short-term interest rate futures because here the quoted 'prices' are really interest rates. For example, a futures spot 'price', S_F, of 9350 means an interest rate of 6.50%, while a futures exercise 'price', E_F, of 9425 means an interest rate of 5.75%. Thus these 'prices', which get slotted into the formulae, are percentages and not true monetary prices at all. The modified formulae assume that the 'prices' are quoted as, for example, 93.50 rather than 9350. These formulae are:

$$FC_E = -(100 - S_F)[1 - N(d_1)] + (100 - E_F)[1 - N(d_2)] \tag{8.29}$$

$$FP_E = -(100 - E_F)N(d_2) + (100 - S_F)N(d_1) \tag{8.30}$$

where:

$$d_1 = \{\ln[(100 - S_F)/(100 - E_F)] + T(\sigma^2/2)\}/\sigma\sqrt{T} \tag{8.31}$$

$$d_2 = d_1 - \sigma\sqrt{T} \tag{8.32}$$

However, all LIFFE's futures options are American rather than European, and for American futures options it may often be sounder to use another model such as the binomial model.

8.7 THE BINOMIAL MODEL AND ORDINARY EQUITY OPTIONS

The basic concept

Like the Black–Scholes model, the binomial option pricing model is an extension of the simple model given in Section 8.2. In that model, the time to the option's expiry was divided into one or two steps. The spot price of the underlying asset was allowed to change only at the end of each step, and when it did change it was allowed to take only one of two alternative values. The Black–Scholes model extended that simple model by allowing for an infinite number of steps, whereas the binomial model merely allows for many steps. A further difference between the Black–Scholes model and the binomial model is that the former produces some reasonably neat formulae, whereas the latter essentially requires the user – or the user's computer – to do a large number of calculations of the sort done in Section 8.2, using (8.7) and (8.8).

To illustrate the principles of the binomial model, the call option for an LML share that was used to illustrate the Black–Scholes model will be used again. It will be recalled that the current spot price of LML shares was taken to be 100p, and that the option expires in eight months or about 243 days. The binomial model divides the option's remaining life into steps and assumes that the spot price can change only at the end of each step. In the present example, the option's life will be divided into 10 steps, so each lasts about 24.3 days. Allowing for only 10 changes in the spot price is very crude compared with the infinite number allowed for in the Black–Scholes model, but the results are very good. They would be even better if the step length was reduced to one day, as is often done in practice, but it is hard to illustrate the principles with more than 10 steps. Like the Black–Scholes model, the binomial model restricts the price changes that can occur in each step. For reasons that are explained later, it is assumed in the present example that, in each step, the price may either rise by a factor of about 1.0805, that is by 8.05%, or fall by a factor of about 0.9255, that is by 7.45%. These upward and downward changes per step are referred to as u and d, so $u = 1.0805$ and $d = 0.9255$.

It is possible to work out the various possible spot prices for LML shares that could arise after each step. They are shown in Fig. 8.3(a). The price today is 100p. At the end of step 1, the price can either rise by 8.05% to 108.05 or fall by 7.45% to 92.55. If it rises to 108.05, then at the end of step 2 it could either rise again by 8.05% to 116.76, or fall by 7.45% to 100.00. If, instead, the price falls at the end of step 1 to 92.55, then at the end of step 2 it could either rise by 8.05% to 100.00, or fall again by 7.45% to 85.65. The triangular shape formed by the numbers given in the figure shows how the possible prices become more spread out after each step. This shape is called a **binomial tree** and each number in it is called a **node**. If the spot price rises in every step, then it will eventually rise to 216.97, and if it falls in every step, then it will eventually fall to 46.09. Most likely it will rise in some steps and fall in others and so reach one of the few other possible final values shown, such as 185.83, 159.16, and so on.

The binomial distribution

Between the start and expiry, the share price changes just 10 times. There is only one set of price changes which will take the price to 216.97 at expiry, and this is if the price goes up in each step. So there is only one path along the tree which will take the price to 216.97, which is if the price moves along

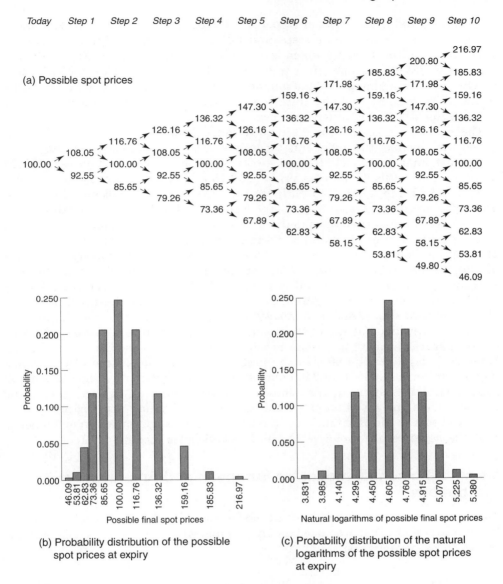

Figure 8.3 Possible future spot prices for LML shares and the probability distribution of possible expiry day spot prices.

the top edge of the tree. Likewise, there is only one path to the lowest expiry day price, 46.09, and this is if the price falls in each step.

There are 10 possible paths which would take the share price to the second highest final price, 185.83. One path would involve the price rising in the first nine steps to 200.80 and then falling in step 10. Another slightly different path would involve a rise in the first eight steps to reach 185.83, then a fall in step

9 to 171.98, and then a rise in step 10 to 185.83. In fact, to end up at 185.83, the price has to rise in nine steps and fall in one step, but the fall can take place in any of the 10 steps which is why there are 10 possible paths to 185.83. There are also 10 possible paths to the second lowest final price of 53.81, each of which involves nine price falls and one price rise. There are even more paths to the third highest and the third lowest final prices, 159.16 and 62.83, and more paths still to the other final prices.

The numbers of paths can be readily found from a mathematical theorem called the binomial theorem. This theorem shows that there is one route to the outermost final prices, 216.97 and 46.09, 10 paths to the next prices, 185.83 and 53.81, 45 paths to the next prices, 159.16 and 62.83, 120 paths to the next prices, 136.32 and 73.36, 210 paths to the next prices, 116.76 and 85.65, and 252 paths to the central price, 100.00. There are 1,024 paths altogether.

It is never necessary to refer to the numbers of paths when using the binomial model, but it is interesting to use them to work out the probability of arriving at each possible final spot price. As 252 of the 1,024 paths end up at a price of 100.00, the probability of arriving at that price is 252/1,024 or 0.246. The probability of arriving at an adjacent price of 85.65 or 116.76 is 210/1,024, or 0.205, and so on. Figure 8.3(b) shows the distribution of these probabilities. This **binomial distribution** is not symmetrical, so it is not a normal distribution. But consider Fig. 8.3(c) which shows the distribution of the probabilities of the natural logarithms of the possible final spot prices. For example, the logarithm of 100.00 is 4.605, so the probability of the logarithm of the expiry day price being 4.605 is 0.246, and so on. This distribution has a similar symmetrical bell-shape to that shown in Fig. 8.2 and is, in fact, just about normal. Thus the distribution of the possible expiry day spot prices is **lognormal** because the distribution of their logarithms is normal. Section 8.5 noted that the same result applies with the Black–Scholes model.

Using the binomial model for European and American equity call options

To illustrate the use of the binomial model, consider the European call option for an LML share that was used as an example with the Black–Scholes model. It has these parameters:

$T = 0.6667$, or eight months
$E = 110\text{p}$
$S = 100\text{p}$
$r = 0.0583$, or 5.83%, so $r_S = 0.06$, or 6%
$\sigma = 0.30$, or 30%
No dividend before expiry

Figures 8.4(a) and (b) show all the calculations that must be done to find today's price for the option, C_E, which appears at the left hand end of part (b) as 7.59p. In practice there would be far more calculations, because there would be more than 10 steps, but a computer would do all the calculations without showing any of them. It would just give the final figure for C_E.

Figure 8.4(a) repeats the possible spot prices for LML shares from Fig. 8.3(a). To find C_E, it is necessary to start at step 10 of Fig. 8.4(b) and then work right to left. The step 10 figures show what the value of the option would be at expiry for each of the corresponding possible spot prices at expiry given in part (a). These step 10 option values show the possible intrinsic values of the option at expiry, so they are positive if the spot price then exceeds the 110p exercise price, and zero otherwise. Say the expiry-day spot price is 216.97: then the option will be worth 106.97, for its holder could buy a share worth 216.97 at the exercise price of 110. But if the expiry-day spot price is under 110, then the option will be worth nothing.

Having worked out the possible values for the option after step 10, it is necessary to work out the values that it could have after step 9. Suppose that after step 9 the spot price is 200.80, so it can either rise to 216.97 or fall to 185.83. Part (b) shows that, after the next step, the option will be worth either 106.97 or 75.83, so that $O_U = 106.97$ and $O_D = 75.83$. Given these two possibilities, it is possible to find the option's value after step 9. This is done by using (8.7) which gives the value as $[kO_U + (1-k)O_D]/R^{T/N}$, with k given by (8.8) as $k = (R^{T/N} - d)/(u - d)$.

In the example, $u = 1.0805$ and $d = 0.9255$. $R^{T/N}$ is the growth of money over one step. With $T = 0.6667$ and the number of steps, N, equal to 10, (T/N) is 0.6667/10 or 0.0667; and with $r_S = 0.06$, $R = 1.06$, so $R^{T/N}$ equals $1.06^{0.6667/10}$, which is 1.0039. Slotting this figure into (8.8) gives k as $(1.0039 - 0.9255)/(1.0805 - 0.9255)$, or 0.5057, so $(1-k)$ is 0.4943. So with $O_U = 106.97$ and $O_D = 75.83$, (8.7) gives the value as $[0.5057(106.97) + 0.4943(75.83)]/1.0039$, which is 91.23. This value is shown at the appropriate step 9 node in Fig. 8.4(b).

It is possible to work out all the other possible values for the option after step 9 in the same way, each one corresponding to a different step 9 spot price. For example, if the spot price after step 9 was the second highest it could be at 171.98, then the option value would be 62.41. Next, all the step 8 values for the option are worked out. For example, the highest value after step 8 shown in Fig. 8.4(b), that is 76.68, was found using (8.7) and (8.8) with $O_U = 91.23$ and $O_D = 62.41$. All the values for earlier steps are worked out likewise until finally today's price for the option, C_E, is found. This figure is shown as 7.59p which compares with the 7.40p found earlier using the Black–Scholes model. The difference would be even smaller if many more steps were used, as is usual with the binomial model in practice. For example, if 20 steps had been used, the price obtained would be within 0.02p of the correct price.

It remains to explain the values used for u and d. These affected all the spot prices in part (a). So in part (b) they affected the step 10 values and then, in turn, the earlier values. The values of u and d have to reflect the volatility of the spot price, σ. They are usually set as follows:

$$u = e^{\sigma\sqrt{(T/N)}} \tag{8.33}$$

$$d = e^{-\sigma\sqrt{(T/N)}} \tag{8.34}$$

In the present example, $u = e^{0.3\sqrt{(0.6667/10)}}$, which is about 1.0805, and $d = e^{-0.3\sqrt{(0.6667/10)}}$, which is about 0.9255.

This example was for a European call option for an equity where no dividend is due before expiry. Section 7.2 explained that, under these circumstances,

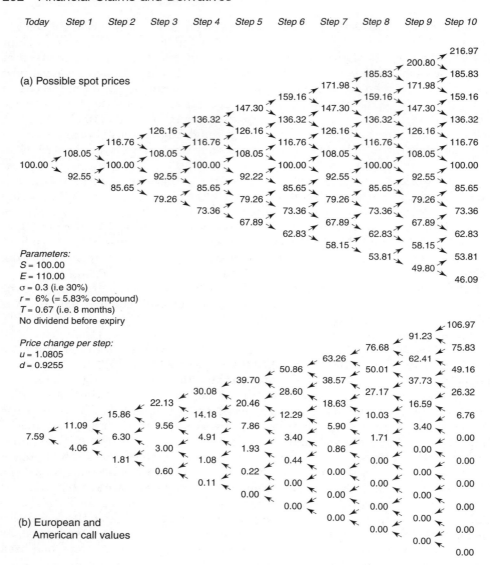

Today Step 1 Step 2 Step 3 Step 4 Step 5 Step 6 Step 7 Step 8 Step 9 Step 10

(a) Possible spot prices

Parameters:
S = 100.00
E = 110.00
σ = 0.3 (i.e 30%)
r = 6% (= 5.83% compound)
T = 0.67 (i.e. 8 months)
No dividend before expiry

Price change per step:
u = 1.0805
d = 0.9255

(b) European and
American call values

Figure 8.4 Possible future spot prices for LML shares and ordinary option values when no dividends are due.

American calls have the same price, so the example gives C_A as well as C_E, as noted in the caption for Fig. 8.4(b).

Using the binomial model for European and American equity put options

Suppose it is desired to find the price of a European put option with the following parameters:

Today Step 1 Step 2 Step 3 Step 4 Step 5 Step 6 Step 7 Step 8 Step 9 Step 10

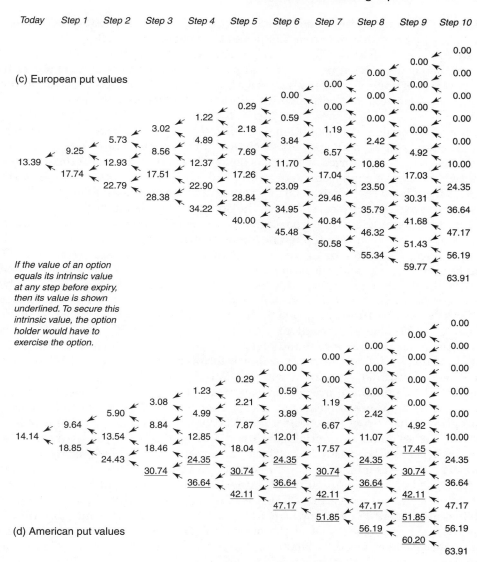

(c) European put values

If the value of an option equals its intrinsic value at any step before expiry, then its value is shown underlined. To secure this intrinsic value, the option holder would have to exercise the option.

(d) American put values

Figure 8.4 continued

$T = 0.6667$, or eight months
$E = 110\text{p}$
$S = 100\text{p}$
$r = 0.0583$ or 5.83%, so $r_S = 0.06$, or 6%
$\sigma = 0.30$, or 30%
No dividend before expiry

One way of finding P_E would be to find the price of the corresponding call option, which has just been estimated as 7.59p, and then use the put–call parity in (8.15), where $P_E = Ee^{-rT} - S + C_E$. This gives $P_E = 105.81 - 100 + 7.59 = 13.40$p. However, P_E can also be estimated in the same way that C_E was estimated. It is useful to see how this is done, because this approach can then be modified to estimate the price of an American put option which will normally be a little higher.

P_E is found on this approach in Fig. 8.4(c). The process begins in step 10 by working out the value of the option at expiry, that is its intrinsic value, for each of the possible expiry day spot prices shown in Fig. 8.4(a). These step 10 values are positive if the spot price at expiry is below the exercise price of 110p and zero otherwise. Say the expiry-day spot price is 46.09: then the option will be worth 63.91, for its holder will gain 63.91 by selling a share worth 46.09 for 110. But if the expiry-day spot price exceeds 110, the option will be worth nothing.

It is then possible to work from right to left in Fig. 8.4(c) to find the possible values of the option after step 9, and then in turn after each earlier step, until today's price, P_E, is found. In this process, every value is found by using (8.7). The figures for $R^{T/N}$ and k used for (8.7) in part (c) are the same as those used in part (b) for the call option, that is 1.0039 and 0.5057, k being as given by (8.8). For example, the lowest step 9 value shown in part (c) was found using (8.7) with $O_U = 56.19$ and $O_D = 63.91$ as $[0.5057(56.19) + 0.4943(63.91)]/1.0039$, which is 59.77. The end result in part (c) is a figure for P_E, of 13.39. This is about the same as the price found using put–call parity. It is close to the 13.21 found earlier by using the Black–Scholes formula. If 20 steps had been used, the binomial estimate would be within 0.02p of that price.

Figure 8.4(d) finds the price of an American put, P_A. The process is identical to that used for the European put except that at any step where (8.7) gives a put option value below the option's intrinsic value, the intrinsic value is shown instead, for an American option can always be exercised for its intrinsic value and so it cannot be worth less. The option values are underlined when this happens. For example, suppose the spot price falls in all the first nine steps to 49.80p. Then after step 10 it will either rise to 53.81 or fall to 46.09, so the option will end up worth either 56.19 or 63.91. In turn, (8.7) gives its value after step 9 as 59.77, as shown in part (c) for the European put. But this is less than the intrinsic value of the option which, given its strike price of 110 and a spot price of 49.80, is 60.20. As the holder of this American option could exercise it for 60.20, it is given this value in part (d), not 59.77. This value is then used in (8.7) to help calculate one of the step 8 values, but that too turned out to be less than the corresponding step 8 intrinsic value of 56.19. In fact, the underlining in part (d) shows that the option could be exercised as early as the end of step 3 if the price falls in all the first three steps. The end result in part (d) is a price for the American put, P_A, of 14.14p. As expected, this exceeds the price of the European put which part (c) gives as 13.39p.

The binomial model, hedge ratios, and deltas

It was noted in Section 8.2 that the hedge ratio, H, for perfect hedges with European options changes whenever S changes, so investors who want to maintain hedge portfolios must use dynamic hedging. In the binomial model, the ratios in any step are given by (8.9) as $(O_U - O_D)/S(u - d)$. Suppose that today in Fig. 8.4(b), X hedges some LML shares by writing some call options. Then H is $(11.09 - 4.06)/100(1.0805 - 0.9255)$, or 0.454. If X instead hedges by buying European put options, then H today is $(9.25 - 17.74)/100(1.0805 - 0.9255)$, or −0.548. These figures are close to the true figures of 0.457 and −0.543 that were given by the Black–Scholes model in section 8.4. As noted there, the two H values also show respectively the call delta and the put delta.

Using the binomial model when dividends are due

Section 8.5 showed that for European options on shares where a dividend is due before expiry, the Black–Scholes model is modified by replacing S by S^*, that is the spot price minus the present value of the dividend. This approach can also be used with the binomial model, so that the binomial tree of possible spot prices would start with S^* instead of S. However, this approach is not wholly satisfactory because it assumes that the volatility of S^* equals that of S.

The binomial model also allows an alternative approach which gives a closer approximation of the fair values of all options when dividends are due and which shows when American options should be exercised early. This approach needs a binomial tree which starts with S, not S^*. So this tree shows the true spot price, and thus it shows the price falling when the share goes ex-dividend. Trees like this can become very big, but the examples given here keep the tree to a modest size by dividing the options' lives into only eight steps. These examples use the same LML options as those used in Section 8.5. These options have the following parameters:

$T = 0.6667$, or eight months
$E = 110$p
$S = 100$p
$r = 0.0583$, or 5.83%, so $r_S = 0.06$, or 6%
$\sigma = 0.30$, or 30%
$D = 4$
$t = 0.4167$, or five months

As there are here eight steps for an option with an eight-month life, so each step lasts one month. And the share goes ex-dividend after five months, just after step 5. With eight steps, N equals 8, whereas previously N equalled 10. So new u and d values are needed. These are given by (8.33) and (8.34) as $u = e^{0.3\sqrt{(0.6667/8)}}$, or about 1.0905, and $d = e^{-0.3\sqrt{(0.6667/8)}}$, or about 0.9170.

Figure 8.5(a) shows the binomial tree of possible spot prices. The first five steps correspond exactly to those on Fig. 8.4(a), except that the higher value for u and the lower value for d produce slightly more marked price changes. Also, the prices are printed in a more spread out way to leave room for what happens later. At the end of step 5, two things happen. First, the spot price makes its usual end of step rise or fall. Then the share goes ex-dividend, so that the spot price immediately falls by the amount of the dividend which is 4p. Thereafter, the spot price rises or falls at the end of each step as before.

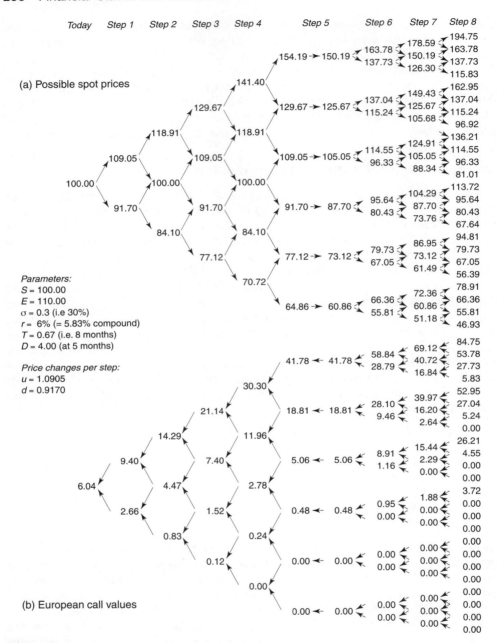

Figure 8.5   Possible future spot prices for LML shares and ordinary option values when a dividend is due.

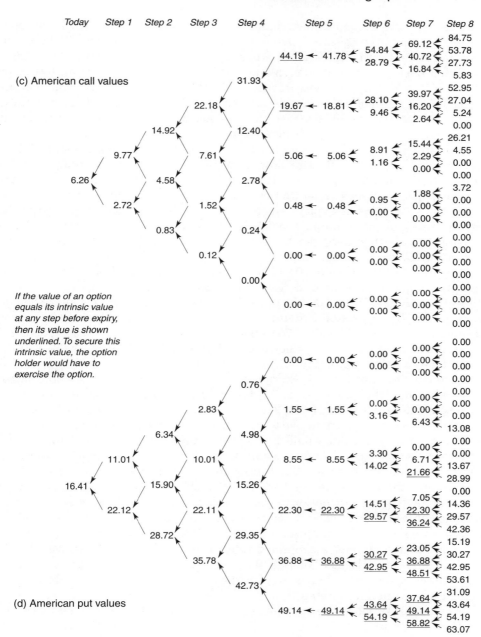

(c) American call values

If the value of an option equals its intrinsic value at any step before expiry, then its value is shown underlined. To secure this intrinsic value, the option holder would have to exercise the option.

(d) American put values

Figure 8.5 continued

However, the tree becomes more complex for a reason that can readily be seen. Just before the share goes ex-dividend, the spot price would be 154.19 if the price had risen in all the first five steps, and 129.67 if it had risen four times and fallen once. After it goes ex-dividend, the price will be 4 less at 150.19 or 125.67. If it is 150.19 and subsequently falls, then it will go to 137.73, whereas if it is 125.67 and subsequently rises, then it will go to 137.04. Unfortunately, 137.73 and 137.04 are different, so the tree needs separate nodes for them. In turn, it requires more nodes in later steps.

Once the tree is complete, option valuation proceeds as before. Figure 8.5(b) considers a European call. The process begins in step 8 by working out the value of the option at expiry for each of the possible spot prices shown in part (a). These option values show its possible intrinsic values at expiry. They are zero if the spot price at expiry is below the exercise price of 110p. Otherwise they are the spot price minus 110. Then all the step 7 option values are found by using (8.7) with k as given by (8.8). Here $u = 1.0905$ and $d = 0.9170$; also, as r_S is 0.06, so $R = 1.06$, and thus $R^{T/N} = (1.06)^{0.0667/8}$ which is 1.0049. So $k = (1.0049 - 0.9170)/(1.0905 - 0.9170)$, or 0.5066, and $(1 - k) = 0.4934$. As an example, suppose the spot price rises in all the first seven steps to 178.59. It will be either 194.75 or 163.78 at expiry, giving the option a value then of 84.75, or 53.78. So in step 7 here, $O_U = 84.75$ and $O_D = 53.78$, and (8.7) gives the option value as $[0.5066(84.75) + 0.4934(53.78)]/1.0049$, or 69.12. Next, all the step 6 values are found likewise, and then all the earlier values, until finally today's price, C_E, is found. This is 6.04p.

Figure 8.5 does not cover a European put, but the calculations would begin by working out the possible expiry-day values of the put option, and then working right to left using (8.7). The expiry-day spot values would be exactly the same as those shown in part (d) which concerns an American put. The result for a European put would be to give today's price, P_E as 15.76p.

Figure 8.5(c) covers an American call. Its possible values at expiry, after step 8, are the same as those for the European call in part (a). For earlier steps there is one change to the method used for the European call. This is that whenever (8.7) gives an option value below the option's intrinsic value, the intrinsic value is shown instead, for an American option can always be exercised for that value and so it cannot be worth less. The two option values concerned are underlined. Section 7.2 explained that an American equity call would only ever be exercised early just before a share goes ex-dividend, and the two underlined values show that this is so, for they occur just before the share goes ex-dividend at the end of step 5.

For example, suppose the spot price rises in all the first five steps to 154.19 and then drops to 150.19 when the share goes ex-dividend. The value of the American call after the share goes ex-dividend is 41.78, which is the same as the European call in step 5. But just before the share goes ex-dividend, when the share price is 154.19, the option has an intrinsic value of 44.19. This exceeds 41.78, so at that moment the American call would be exercised for its intrinsic value, and thus it has a value of 44.19. In the end, part (c) shows that today's price for the American call, C_A, is 6.26p. As expected, this exceeds the 6.04p price of the European call.

Figure 8.5(d) covers the American put. Step 8 shows its possible expiry day values. These are zero if the spot price is above 110. Otherwise they equal 110 minus the spot price. Then the calculations are made from right to left working out the option's value in earlier steps by using (8.7), except that whenever this gives an option value below the option's intrinsic value, the intrinsic value is shown instead. This is because an American option can always be exercised for that value, so it cannot be worth less. The option values concerned are underlined. On most price paths, there is either no early exercise, or else early exercise occurs just after the share goes ex-dividend after step 5. But there is one step 7 option value of 21.66 which would be realised by exercising the option then, even though it would not have been worth exercising after step 5 on the path concerned. In the end, part (d) shows today's price for the American put, P_A, as 16.41p. As expected, this exceeds the 15.76p price of the European put.

8.8 THE BINOMIAL MODEL AND OTHER OPTIONS

The binomial model and futures options when no dividends are due

The binomial model can be used for futures options. Consider the futures call option on LML shares that was used earlier for the Black model. In this option, the futures contract underlying the option is taken to mature on the same day that the option expires. The parameters are:

$T = 0.6667$, or eight months
$E_F = 110$p
$S_F = 103.96$p
$r = 0.0583$ or 5.83%, so $r_S = 0.06$, or 6%
$\sigma = 0.30$, or 30% (for LML share prices, not for S_F)
No dividend before expiry

Suppose the time to expiry is split into 10 steps. The first task is to build the binomial tree in Fig. 8.6(a) showing the possible futures prices for LML shares in each step. The initial futures price, that is today's futures price, is 103.96. This figure was found in Section 8.6. The possible futures prices at expiry after step 10 are the same as the possible spot prices for LML shares at that time, as shown in step 10 of Fig. 8.4(a). This is because spot prices and futures prices converge when futures contracts mature, and the futures contract here matures after step 10 when the option expires. To get to these step 10 prices from today's futures price of 103.96, the values for u and d cannot be set as in (8.33) and (8.34). Instead, they are set as:

$$u = e^{\sigma\sqrt{(T/N)} - r(T/N)} \tag{8.35}$$

$$d = e^{-\sigma\sqrt{(T/N)} - r(T/N)} \tag{8.36}$$

So $u = e^{0.3\sqrt{(0.6667/10)} - 0.0583(0.6667/10)}$, or 1.0763, and $d = e^{-0.3\sqrt{(0.6667/10)} - 0.0583(0.6667/10)}$, or 0.9219. These values for u and d can then be used with today's futures price

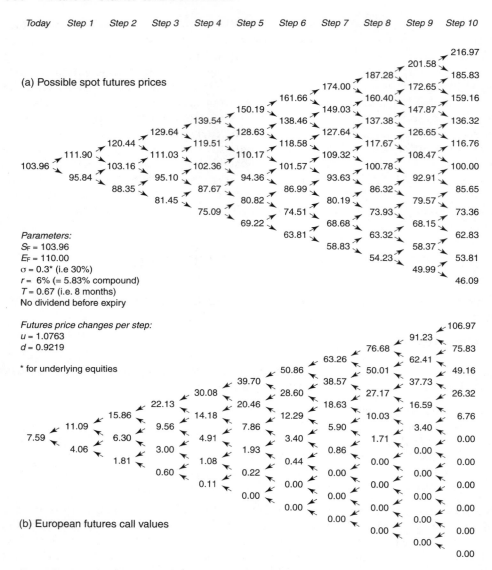

Figure 8.6 Possible future spot futures prices for LML shares and futures option values when no dividend is due.

of 103.96 to work out the possible futures prices in step 2 and, in turn, in all the later steps.

Figure 8.6(b) finds today's price of the European futures call, FC_E. It starts at step 10 by working out the expiry day value of the option for all the possible expiry day futures prices. If the spot futures price is above the exercise price of 110, then this value equals the difference between the spot futures price and 110. Otherwise it is zero. Then part (b) works from right to left to find FC_E

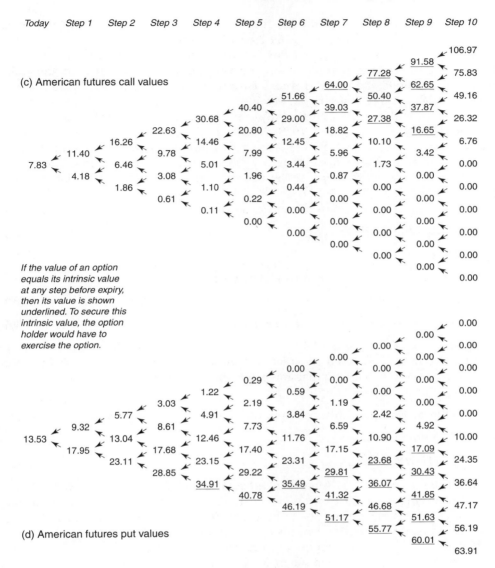

Today   Step 1   Step 2   Step 3   Step 4   Step 5   Step 6   Step 7   Step 8   Step 9   Step 10

(c) American futures call values

If the value of an option equals its intrinsic value at any step before expiry, then its value is shown underlined. To secure this intrinsic value, the option holder would have to exercise the option.

(d) American futures put values

Figure 8.6   continued

as 7.59p. This is the same as the price found in Fig. 8.4(b) for a comparable ordinary call. Also, it is close to the Black figure of 7.40 found earlier, and it would be even closer if more steps were used. An important point to note about Fig. 8.4(b) is that each value of the futures option in step 9 and the earlier steps is given by a modified version of (8.7).

To see why, consider Y. She works out what would happen if she bought the futures option in step 9. Depending on the current futures price, S_F, she can discover from Fig. 8.6(b) what the option would be worth at expiry. For example, if the futures price rises in all the first nine steps, so that S_F is 201.58, then the option will be worth either 106.97 or 75.83 after step 10. Call these values O_U and O_D. Y could get similar returns if she instead agreed a futures contract to buy H LML shares at the current futures price, S_F, and lent L at the risk-free rate, provided she chose H and L carefully. On this strategy, if the futures price of LML shares rises by a factor of u to $S_F u$, then her futures contract after step 10 will be worth $H(S_F u - S_F)$. In contrast, if the futures price of LML shares falls by a factor of d, to $S_F d$, then her futures contract after step 10 will be worth $H(S_F d - S_F)$. Either way, the value of her loan after step 10 will be $LR^{T/N}$, where R shows its growth by being lent at the risk-free rate for a step that is T/N years long. In the example, the step length is 0.0667 years, for T is 0.6667 and N is 10.

So Y would need to choose H and L so that:

$$H(S_F u - S_F) + LR^{T/N} = O_U \qquad (8.37)$$

$$H(S_F d - S_F) + LR^{T/N} = O_D \qquad (8.38)$$

(8.37) and (8.38) can be solved to show that:

$$H = (O_U - O_D)/S_F(u - d) \qquad (8.39)$$

$$L = [O_U(1 - d)/(u - d) + O_D(u - 1)/(u - d)]/R^{T/N} \qquad (8.40)$$

The only cost of this equivalent strategy is the sum lent, L, because it costs nothing to agree a futures contract. So the expression for L in (8.40) is also the value that the option must have for the two strategies to be equivalent. This expression can be simplified to:

$$\text{Value of European futures option} = [k_F O_U + (1 - k_F)O_D]/R^{T/N} \qquad (8.41)$$

where k_F is defined as:

$$k_F = (1 - d)/(u - d) \qquad (8.42)$$

Figure 8.6(c) covers an American futures call option. It exactly follows the methods of Figure 8.6(b) except that if (8.41) gives an option value below the option's intrinsic value, then the intrinsic value is shown instead. This is because an American option can always be exercised for that value, so it cannot be worth less. The option values are underlined when this happens. Unlike an ordinary American call option when no dividends are due, an American futures call option may be exercised early. Figure 8.6(c) shows that today's price for the American futures call, FC_A, is 7.83p, which is slightly above the FC_E figure of 7.59p.

It may be noted that the whole of Figure 8.6(b), which covers a European futures call option, exactly corresponds to Figure 8.4(b). Figure 8.6 does not cover a European futures put option, but if it did, then it would exactly correspond to Fig. 8.4(c) and would give its price today, FP_E, as 13.39p. The procedure would be identical to that followed in Fig. 8.6(b).

Figure 8.6(d) covers an American futures put option. It exactly follows the methods of Fig. 8.6(b) except that if (8.41) gives an option value below the option's intrinsic value, then the intrinsic value is shown instead. This is because an American option can always be exercised for that value, so it cannot be worth less. The option values are underlined when this happens. The figure shows that FP_A is 13.53p, slightly above the FP_E figure of 13.39p. This option would be exercised as early as step 4 if the futures price fell in each of the first four steps.

The binomial model and futures options when a dividend is due

Figure 8.7 shows the sharpest way of using the binomial model for futures options when a dividend is due before expiry. It concerns futures options on LML shares and divides the time to expiry into eight steps. The examples have the following parameters:

$T = 0.6667$, or eight months
$E_F = 110$p
$S_F = 99.90$p
$r = 0.0583$, or 5.83%, so $r_S = 0.06$ or 6%
$\sigma = 0.30$, or 30% (for LML share prices, not S_F)
$D = 4$
$t = 0.4167$, or five months

The initial S_F here is derived from the figure of 100.00 for S used previously by making two adjustments. First, S^* was found, that is the present value of the share ignoring the dividend which will be paid before the futures contract matures. Section 8.5 showed that $S^* = S\text{-}De^{-rt}$, which is 96.10. Then S_F was found. Section 8.6 showed that $S_F = S^*(1 + r_S)^T$, which is 99.90p.

Figure 8.7(a) shows the binomial tree of possible futures prices, ignoring the present value of the dividend. These prices are *not* calculated by using constant up and down changes. Instead, they are each calculated from the spot prices for LML shares shown in Fig. 8.5(a) by making the same two adjustments that had to be made to the starting price shown there of 100.00; that is, the present value of the dividend has to be deducted, and then the value has to be raised by $(1 + r_S)^T$. Regarding the first adjustment, the present value of the dividend rose as step 5 came closer, but after step 5 no adjustment was needed because the dividend had then been paid. Regarding the second adjustment, the figure used for T fell as the time to expiry diminished.

The remaining parts of the figure show the calculations used for European futures calls, American futures calls and American futures puts. These parts follow the procedures used in Fig. 8.5 with one exception. In Fig. 8.7, there are no constant figures for u and d. Instead, different individual figures are used for u and d at each node. These figures were deduced from the numbers in part (a). For example, suppose that the futures price rises in the first seven steps to 179.46. It may then rise to 194.75 or fall to 165.28, and this means that at that step 7 node, $u = 194.75/179.46$, or 1.0852, and $d = 165.28/179.46$ or 0.9210. These figures for u and d were then slotted into (8.42) to calculate k_F and then the option values at that step 7 node in parts (b), (c) and (d).

It can be seen from part (b) of Fig. 8.7 that today's price for a European futures call, FC_E, is 5.72p. As would be expected, this is less than the price of

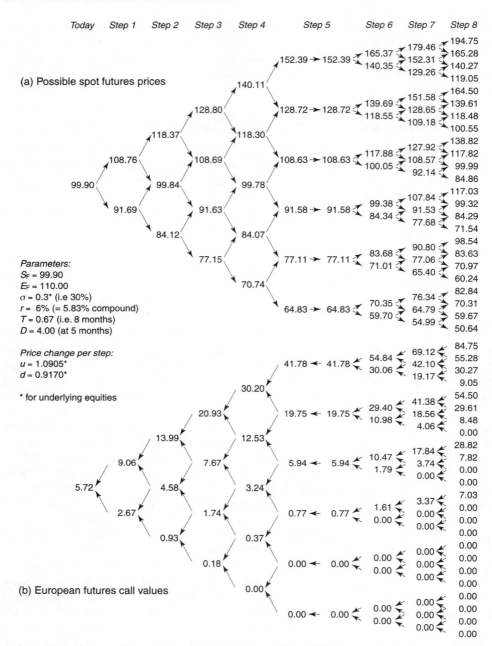

Figure 8.7 Possible future spot futures prices for LML shares and futures option values when a dividend is due.

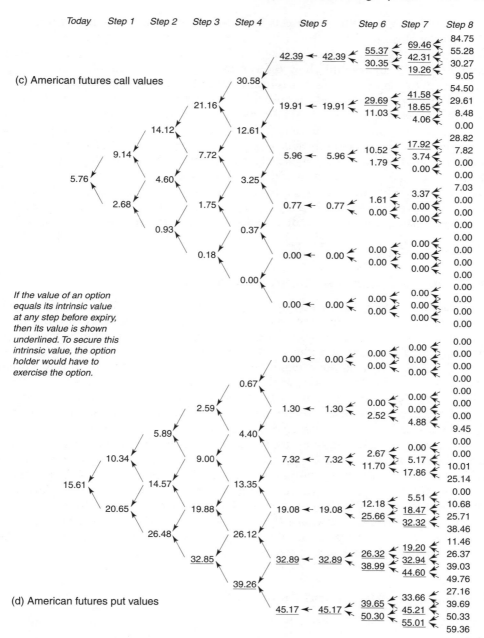

Today   Step 1   Step 2   Step 3   Step 4   Step 5   Step 6   Step 7   Step 8

(c) American futures call values

If the value of an option
equals its intrinsic value
at any step before expiry,
then its value is shown
underlined. To secure this
intrinsic value, the option
holder would have to
exercise the option.

(d) American futures put values

Figure 8.7   continued

7.59p found in Fig. 8.6(b) for a comparable call when no dividend is due. The 5.72 is very close to the 5.73 which Section 8.6 noted is the price given by the Black model. Figure 8.7 does not cover a European futures put, but this could readily be done and would show today's price, FP_E, to be 15.43p.

Figure 8.7(c) gives today's price of an American futures call, FC_A, as 5.76p, while Fig. 8.7(d) gives today's price of an American futures put, FP_A, as 15.61p. Both these options could be exercised early at various times, and in each case the underlined option values show occasions when these values were given by the option's intrinsic value rather than by (8.41). At 5.76, FC_A is slightly higher than FC_E, as would be expected. Also, FC_A is less than the price of a comparable American futures call when no dividend is due, for FC_A was shown in Fig. 8.6(c) as 7.83p. At 15.61, FP_A, is slightly higher than FP_E, as would be expected. Also, FP_A is higher than the price of a comparable American futures put when no dividend is due, for FP_A was shown in Fig. 8.6(d) as 13.53p.

Stock index options and currency options

The binomial model can be adapted to price any sort of option including stock index options and currency options. With these, the first task is to build a binomial tree showing the possible future spot prices for a foreign currency, or the possible future stock indices. Then the value of the option at expiry is worked out for each possible expiry day spot price. Finally, the initial option price is worked out by working right to left through successively earlier steps.

In this process, allowance must be made for the negative storage cost of the underlying asset, that is the dividends earned by the basket of securities covered by the stock index, or the risk-free interest which a foreign currency can earn. This allowance can be made by modifying (8.8) which gives the k used in (8.7). (8.8) gives k as $(R^{T/N} - d)/(u - d)$. This assumes that the only carrying cost is the interest lost on buying the underlying asset, as reflected by R. When there is a negative storage cost, the carrying cost falls. So R must be replaced by something smaller. With a currency option, it can be replaced by R/ρ, where $R = (1 + r_S)$ as before, and where $P = (1 + \rho_S)$, ρ_S being the relevant foreign risk-free interest rate expressed as a simple rate. An analogous approach can be used to handle dividends in the case of stock index options.

The binomial model and Asian options

The binomial model can even be adapted to price Asian options, though the procedure with these is rather cumbersome. It is helpful to have an example with few steps and hence few price paths. Consider an Asian call option for LML shares which expires in 40 days and which can be exercised only at expiry, and suppose that the value of the option at expiry is set at the average spot price of the underlying asset over the previous 30 days minus the exercise price, provided that gives a positive figure. Suppose that the following parameters apply:

$T = 0.1096$, or 40 days
$E = 90$
$S = 100$
$r = 0.0583$, or 5.83%, so $r_S = 0.06$, or 6%
$\sigma = 0.30$, or 30%
No dividend before expiry

Suppose there are four steps to expiry, each lasting 10 days. Then Fig. 8.8(a) shows the binomial spot price tree, which is worked out in the normal way. It uses (8.33) and (8.34) to get $u = e^{\sigma\sqrt{(T/N)}}$ and $d = {}^{-\sigma\sqrt{(T/N)}}$. So $u = e^{0.30((0.1096/4)}$, or 1.0509, and $d = e^{-0.30\sqrt{(0.1096/4)}}$, or 0.9516.

As there are only four steps, there are only five possible prices at expiry. With European and American options, it would be necessary to work out only five possible option values at expiry, and then work from right to left to find the option's current price. But with an Asian option, the expiry value depends on the price over a period before expiry. In this case, the value depends on the average price over the 30 days before expiry, which will be taken to be the average price in steps one, two, three and four. As the value at expiry depends on the path followed by the spot price over those steps, it is necessary to look separately at all the paths that the spot price could have taken over those steps. There are 16 possible paths and they are explored in Fig. 8.8(b).

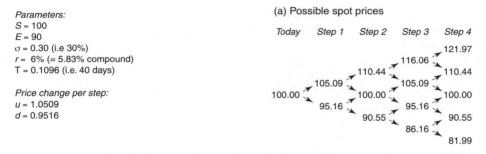

Parameters:
$S = 100$
$E = 90$
$\sigma = 0.30$ (i.e 30%)
$r = 6\%$ (= 5.83% compound)
$T = 0.1096$ (i.e. 40 days)

Price change per step:
$u = 1.0509$
$d = 0.9516$

(a) Possible spot prices

(b) Calculating the two possible option values at step one

| Path | Finding the step 1 value if the spot price is 105.09 | | | | | | Finding the step 1 value if the spot price is 95.16 | | | | | |
	Step 2 price	Step 3 price	Step 4 price	Average price*	Expiry value	Step 1 value	Step 2 price	Step 3 price	Step 4 price	Average price*	Expiry value	Step 1 value
Up Up Up	110.44	116.06	121.97	113.39	23.39	2.97	100.00	105.09	110.44	102.67	12.67	1.61
Up Up Dn	110.44	116.06	110.44	110.51	20.51	2.57	100.00	105.09	100.00	100.06	10.06	1.26
Up Dn Up	110.44	105.09	110.44	107.77	17.77	2.23	100.00	95.16	100.00	97.58	7.58	0.95
Up Dn Dn	110.44	105.09	100.00	105.16	15.16	1.87	100.00	95.16	90.55	95.21	5.21	0.64
Dn Up Up	100.00	105.09	110.44	105.16	15.16	1.90	90.55	95.16	100.00	95.21	5.21	0.65
Dn Up Dn	100.00	105.09	100.00	102.55	12.55	1.55	90.55	95.16	90.55	92.85	2.85	0.35
Dn Dn Up	100.00	95.16	100.00	100.06	10.06	1.24	90.55	86.16	90.55	90.60	0.60	0.07
Dn Dn Dn	100.00	95.16	90.55	97.70	7.70	0.94	90.55	86.16	81.99	88.46	0.00	0.00
Total						15.27						5.55

*Average of step 1, step 2, step 3 and step 4 prices.   At the start, $C_U = 15.27$ and $C_D = 5.55$, in turn, $C_{ASIAN} = 10.43$

Figure 8.8   Possible future spot prices for LML shares and the value of an Asian call option.

Eight of these paths could occur if the spot price rises in step 1 to 105.09, and eight could occur if it falls in step 1 to 95.16. Figure 8.8(b) shows, for instance, that if the price falls to 95.16 and subsequently goes successively up, down and up, then it will end up at 100.00 at expiry in step 4. The four prices that it would have over the last 30 days are 95.16, 100.00, 95.16 and 100.00. The average of these is 97.58, so the option's value at expiry would be that amount less the exercise price of 90, that is 7.58.

To find today's price for an Asian option, it is first necessary to estimate all the possible values that it could have at the first step whose spot price will be relevant in calculating the average price at expiry. So, in the example, it is necessary to begin by working out the values which the option could have at each of the two step 1 nodes. In each case, the option's value depends on what could happen to the spot price over the next three steps. There is a formula for working it out which is derived from (8.7). (8.7) looked just one step ahead and assumed there were two possible option values that could arise after that step, and it worked out an option's value on the basis of those two possible future values. The new formula given here allows the option value at any node to be calculated from all the possible option values that could arise after n steps. These values are termed C_1, C_2 and so on. The formula is:

$$C_{\text{ASIAN}} = C_1[k^{\text{no. of rises}}(1-k)^{\text{no. of falls}}]/R^{Tn/N}$$
$$+ C_2[k^{\text{no. of rises}}(1-k)^{\text{no. of falls}}]/R^{Tn/N} + \ldots \qquad (8.43)$$

where the numbers of rises and falls are the numbers of subsequent rises and falls in the price of the underlying asset needed to get to C_1, C_2 and so on. k is still given by (8.8).

In the example, this formula is applied in turn to each of the two step 1 nodes. In each case, (8.43) has to refer to the *eight* subsequent option values that could arise at expiry from the eight possible paths that the spot price might subsequently follow. As $R^{T/N}$ equals $(1.06)^{0.1096/4}$, which is 1.0016, so k can be found from (8.8) as $(1.0016 - 0.9516)/(1.0509/0.9516)$, or 0.5035, and thus $(1-k)$ is 0.4965. (8.43) also needs $R^{Tn/N}$. As expiry is three steps ahead, in step 4, so $n = 3$. So $R^{Tn/N}$ is $(1.06)^{3(0.1096)/4}$, or 1.0048.

To see how (8.43) is applied, suppose the spot price rises in step 1 to 105.09. To work out the value of the option at that node, it is necessary to consider in turn the eight paths that the spot price could subsequently follow, and to find out in each case what the expiry day value of the option would be. The first one of these paths is described in Fig. 8.8(b) as 'Up, Up, Up' and it arises if the spot price rises in each of the remaining three steps and falls in none. If the spot price follows this path, then Fig. 8.8(b) shows that the value of the option at expiry will be 23.39. Call this value C_1. The next value, C_2, is shown as 20.51, and it arises if the spot price subsequently rises twice and falls once. It can be seen that the eight possible paths lead to expiry day option values that range from 23.39 to 7.70. Consider, as an example, the second path which leads to a final value, C_2, of 20.51. The contribution of C_2 to the option value at step 1 is given by the second term in (8.43) as $C_2[k^{\text{no. of rises}}(1-k)^{\text{no. of falls}}]/R^{Tn/N}$, which is $20.51[(0.5035)^2(0.4965)]/1.0048$, or 2.57. The corresponding values for the seven other possible expiry-day option values are derived similarly and are shown in Fig. 8.8(b). They add up to 15.27, so this is the value of the option in step 1 if the spot price is then 105.09.

Figure 8.8(b) then uses (8.43) to find the value of the option in step 1 if the spot price falls then to 95.16. In this case, (8.43) gives the step 1 value of the option as 5.55. With these two possible values of the option in step 1, 15.27 and 5.55, today's option price, C_{ASIAN} can be found by using (8.7). So C_{ASIAN} is $[0.5035(15.27) + 0.4965(5.55)]/1.0016$ or 10.43. This is a little less than the price of an analogous 90p European call, which could be found from a four-step binomial model as 11.06. This is not surprising. Figure 8.8(b) shows that the range of possible values at expiry for the Asian option run from 23.39 to zero. With a European call, it can readily be seen from Fig. 8.8(a) that the possible values at expiry would run from 31.97 to zero, being 31.97 if the spot price at expiry was the highest figure shown there of 121.97.

It may be noted that (8.43) is consistent with (8.7). To see this, imagine there was only one step left after step 1. Then n would equal one, and there would be only two possible paths left for the spot price. One path would involve one price rise and no falls, while the other would involve no price rises and one fall. In turn, there would be only two possible expiry values for the option. In terms of (8.43), these values would be called C_1 and C_2, but they could instead be called O_U and O_D. Thus (8.43) would give the option value as $O_U k(1-k)^0/R^{T/N} + O_D k^0 (1-k)/R^{T/N}$. This simplifies to $[O_U k + O_D(1-k)]/R^{T/N}$, which is identical to (8.7).

The only problem with using the binomial model in this way for Asian options is that the number of steps has to be strictly limited. In the example, the last 30 days were split into three steps and there were eight paths, or 2^3 paths, from each step 1 node. If those 30 days were split into 30 steps, there would be 2^{30} paths. This could just be handled on the fastest computers, but using any more paths, say 50, would use a great deal of computer time. As an alternative to the binomial method, it is possible to use a more approximate method such as a Monte Carlo simulation, as discussed by Boyle (1977).

8.9 COMPARING FAIR VALUES AND ACTUAL OPTION PRICES

In practice, the prices at which options trade do not always equal the fair values predicted by the Black–Scholes model, or by the binomial model, or even by any other model. Before mentioning why fair values and actual prices may differ, it is worth noting that comparing them is not quite as easy as it sounds.

Some difficulties in comparing fair values and actual prices

A major difficulty in comparing a fair value with an actual option price is that the fair value depends, among other factors, on the current price of the underlying asset. Thus the fair value for an option on LML shares at, say, 1530 on 12 December depends on the price of LML shares at that moment. If a researcher wanted to discover whether the actual price equalled the theoretical price, she would have to contact both the stock exchange and the options exchange at 1530 to discover the two prices, and even then the information she secured might not be wholly satisfactory. There might have been no trade in LML options for the last 30 minutes, so that the option price quoted could be that on the most recent trade made at 1500, and there might have been no LML shares dealings for the last 10 minutes, so that the share price quoted might have been that on the most recent trade at 1520. So neither of the prices given to her could be said with certainty to be the price that would have applied at 1530 had a trade in either an option or a share occurred then.

Researchers often ignore this problem and make their comparisons on the basis of the closing prices quoted in the press, assuming that these relate to trades made just before closing time. Even if this assumption is correct, it is important to note that the quoted stock exchange prices will be the middle of the bid and ask prices for the shares, while the price quoted for the option will be on the most recent trade which may have been made by a trader buying an option at a bid price or writing one at an ask price, or by a broker with an intermediate price.

Some reasons why fair values may differ from actual prices

Despite these difficulties, fair values and actual prices are frequently compared, and some discrepancies arise. Some of the reasons why this could happen are given below.

1. The option pricing models may be deficient and produce poor estimates of the fair values or correct prices. In contrast, market forces might manage to produce the correct prices.
2. Some options may indeed be overvalued or undervalued.
3. When people use the pricing models to produce fair values, they incorporate an estimate of the volatility of the price of the underlying asset, and they usually base this on historical volatility in a recent period. But different investors may look at different periods. Also, some may believe that the volatility will change, so their volatility estimates might reflect adjusted historical values. So different people may get different fair values and so they will be willing to offer or accept different option prices. In turn, the observed actual prices could be seen as reflecting the average view of volatility taken by different investors. The only investors who believe that the actual prices are correct will be those who take the average view.
4. The models use a single risk-free interest rate, but some investors may believe that this rate will change over the life of an option, and they may adapt their fair values to take this into account. Different investors may take different views and so reach different fair values. So, again, the actual prices could be seen as reflecting the average view taken of interest rates, and the only investors who believe that the actual prices are correct will be those who take the average view.
5. The idea that the prices of options should equal their fair values rests on the assumption that, if the actual prices are higher, then the options are overvalued and should be sold or written, so that their prices will

fall, while if the actual prices are lower, then the options are undervalued and should be bought but not written, so that their prices will rise. But these responses will occur only if the gap between the actual price and the fair value is large enough to cover transaction costs such as commissions. So small gaps could persist.

6. There may be significant gaps between actual prices and fair values in the case of stock index options. To see why, compare X, who is the writer of a call option on LML shares, and Y, who is the writer of a call option on a stock index. Each writer may wish to cover the option. X does so by buying some LML shares. In principle, Y can do so by buying a portfolio that matches the shares in the index, but the high transactions costs may deter her from buying more than a selection of shares, so that her cover is not perfect. Moreover, suppose the options are American ones and are exercised early. X can deliver his LML shares, but Y has to pay a money compensation which she secures by selling her portfolio. Y runs the risk that share prices may fall between the time when the option is exercised and the time when she can sell her portfolio. It is clear that writers of call stock index options face special risks, so they may want premiums that slightly exceed the fair values.

SUMMARY

8.1   Investors need to be able to ascertain the fair or theoretically correct values for options to ensure that they do not buy them for more than they are worth or write them for less.

8.2   Fair values for options are found by comparing portfolios which contain them with equivalent portfolios that lack them. If the time to expiry, T, is divided into N steps, and if the spot price of the underlying asset can change in the next step by either a given proportion u up or d down, then the value of the option at the end of the step will be either O_U or O_D. The value of a European option at the start of a step is given by:

$$\text{Value of European option} = [kO_U + (1 - k)O_D]/R^{T/N} \qquad (8.7)$$

where k is given by:

$$(R^{T/N} - d)/(u - d) \qquad (8.8)$$

The hedge ratio, H, is given by (8.9) as $(O_U - O_D)/S(u - d)$.

8.3   Money grows more rapidly if it is lent on a continuously compounded interest basis than on a simple interest basis at the same rate. For any given simple rate, r_S, there is a lower continuously compounded rate, r, that yields an equal return. This rate, r, equals $\ln(1 + r_S)$. A sum of 1p lent at a continuously compounded rate, r, for T years becomes worth e^{rT} when that time has elapsed. The present value of 1p after a period of T is e^{-rT}.

8.4 The volatility of share prices is measured by using samples of past periods, often a large number of short periods. The Black–Scholes and binomial models assume that the price of the underlying asset changes over time in such a way that the distribution of the natural logarithms of the possible spot prices for the asset at expiry is normal.

8.5 The Black–Scholes formulae for C_E and P_E when no dividend is due before expiry are:

$$C_E = SN(d_1) - Ee^{-rT}N(d_2) \tag{8.12}$$

$$P_E = Ee^{-rT}[1 - N(d_2)] - S[1 - N(d_1)] \tag{8.16}$$

Here $N(d_1)$ and $N(d_2)$ are respectively the probabilities of any individual observation in a normal distribution having a z-value of d_1 or less or d_2 or less. $N(d_1)$ is also the call delta while $[N(d_1) - 1]$ is the put delta. The values of d_1 and d_2 are given by:

$$d_1 = [\ln(S/E) + T(r + \sigma^2/2)]/\sigma\sqrt{T} \tag{8.13}$$

$$d_2 = d_1 - \sigma\sqrt{T} \tag{8.14}$$

C_E and P_E are linked by the put–call parity equation $P_E = Ee^{-rT} - S + C_E$, as given in (8.15).

If a dividend is due before expiry, the formulae give good results if the spot price, S, is replaced by S^*, that is $S - De^{-rT}$ where De^{-rT} is the present value of the dividend.

8.6 For European futures options, the following formulae are used, though the e^{-rt} terms are omitted if the premium is not due until expiry.

$$FC_E = e^{-rT}[S_FN(d_1) - E_FN(d_2)] \tag{8.22}$$

$$FP_E = e^{-rT}\{E_F[1 - N(d_2)] - S_F[1 - N(d_1)]\} \tag{8.23}$$

$$d_1 = [\ln(S_F/E_F) + T(\sigma^2/2)]/\sigma\sqrt{T} \tag{8.24}$$

$$d_2 = d_1 - \sigma\sqrt{T} \tag{8.25}$$

The Black–Scholes model can also be adapted for stock index options, currency options and interest rate futures options. It rarely gives exact prices for American options, but it will do so for equity call options if no dividend is due before expiry.

8.7 The binomial model divides the remaining life of an option into steps. The possible future spot prices of the underlying asset are worked out for each of those steps to build a binomial tree. The tree gets complex if there is a dividend due before expiry. Usually the spot price is allowed to move in each step in proportions u or d given by:

$$u = e^{\sigma\sqrt{(T/N)}} \tag{8.33}$$

$$d = e^{-\sigma\sqrt{(T/N)}} \tag{8.34}$$

To find an option's price, it is necessary to find first its possible values at expiry, and then to find its possible values in successively earlier steps. The value of a European option at the start of any step is found from (8.7) and (8.8) noted above. The same method is used for an American option, but the model allows that it may be exercised for its intrinsic values in any step where that exceeds the value given by (8.7).

8.8 The binomial model can be adapted for most types of option including Asian options. When the binomial model is used for futures options, u and d may be given by:

$$u = e^{\sigma \sqrt{(T/N)} - r(T/N)} \tag{8.35}$$

$$d = e^{-\sigma \sqrt{(T/N)} - r(T/N)} \tag{8.36}$$

while k in (8.7) and (8.8) must be replaced by k_F, which is given by (8.42) as $(1 - d)/(u - d)$.

8.9 It is hard to make exact comparisons of fair values and observed option prices. In practice there are a number of reasons why they may differ slightly.

QUESTIONS

1. Explain what is meant by a hedge ratio in the context of both call and put options.

2. Suppose that the spot price of LML shares is 100p and that it will either rise to 125p or fall to 75p at the end of the next year. The simple risk-free interest rate is 6%. Show that k in (8.8) is 0.62 if both T and N are 1.0. Use (8.7) to show that the prices of a 105p call option and a 105p put option which each expire in one year are 11.70p and 10.75p.

3. Suppose that the call options discussed in question 2 are mispriced and have a price of 13p. How could investors take advantage of this? Suppose instead that the put options are mispriced at 12p. How could investors take advantage of this?

4. Use the Black–Scholes model to compute the price of a call option on Aco shares. The option expires in six months and no dividend is due before expiry. The risk free interest rate is 5.83% expressed as a continuously compounded rate. The spot price of Aco shares is 220, the exercise price is 200, and the estimated annual σ is 35%. What is the call delta? What is the value of an equivalent 200 put option, and what is the put delta?

5. Use the Black model to estimate the price of a six-month European futures call option on Bco shares with an exercise price of 200. The option is for a futures contract maturing on the same day that the option expires. The risk-free interest rate is 5.83% at a continuously compounded rate, the spot price for futures contracts expiring in six months is 235, and the estimated annual σ is 20%.

6. An investor uses the binomial model to estimate the price of the Aco call
    option in question 4. Assume she divides the time to expiry into four steps.
    (a) Use (8.33) and (8.34) to work out the values she should use for u and d.
    (b) Work out k from (8.8), noting that $R = (1 + r_s)$ and that $r_s = 0.06$. (c) Draw
    up a binomial tree of possible spot prices in each step to expiry. (d) Work
    out the possible values of the option at expiry. (e) Work from right to left to
    find the initial price of the option.

REFERENCES

Barone-Adesi, G. and Whaley, R. E. (1987) 'Efficient analytic approximation of American
    option values', *Journal of Finance*, **42** (June), 301–20.
Black, F. (1976) 'The pricing of commodity contracts,' *Journal of Financial Economics*,
    3 (January–March), 167–79.
Black, F. and Scholes, M. (1972) 'The valuation of option contracts and a test of market
    efficiency', *Journal of Finance*, **27** (May), 399–418.
Black, F. and Scholes, M. (1973) 'The pricing of options and corporate liabilities', *Journal
    of Political Economy*, **81** (May–June), 637–59.
Boyle, P. (1977) 'Options: a Monte Carlo approach' *Journal of Financial Economics*, **4**
    (May), 323–38.
Brennan, M. and Schwartz, E. (1977) 'The valuation of American put options', *Journal
    of Finance*, **32** (May), 449–62.
Courtadon, G. (1982) 'A more accurate finite difference approximation for the valuation
    of options', *Journal of Financial and Quantitative Analysis*, **17** (December) 697–703.
Cox, J. and Rubinstein, M. (1985) *Options Markets* (New Jersey: Prentice-Hall).
Cox, J., Ross, S. A. and Rubinstein, M. (1979) 'Option pricing: a simplified approach',
    Journal of Financial Economics, **7** (September), 229–63.
Garman, M. B. and Kohlhagen, S. W. (1983) 'Foreign currency option values', *Journal
    of International Money and Finance*, **2** (December), 231–7.
Geske, R. and Johnson, H. E. (1984) 'The American put valued analytically', *Journal of
    Finance*, **39** (December), 1511–24.
Merton, R. C. (1973) 'Theory of rational option pricing', *Bell Journal of Economics and
    Management Science*, **4** (Spring), 141–83.
Parkinson, M. (1977) 'Option pricing: the American put', *Journal of Business*, **50**
    (January), 21–36.

9 SWAPS

9.1 WHAT ARE SWAPS?

Swaps are contracts where two parties agree to swap streams of future periodic payments. The parties are often called **counterparties**. Each contract specifies the terms of the swap, including the **effective date** when it will start and the **maturity date** when it will stop. In some contracts the parties agree to swap streams of future payments that they will receive, while in others they agree to swap streams of future payments that they will make. Swaps are not arranged on exchanges. People who want to make swaps often agree them with banks. Alternatively, they may contact swap dealers who will either find willing counterparties or act as counterparties themselves.

Topics covered in this chapter

This chapter considers the main types of swap and explains why people make them. Many swaps are **interest rate swaps** where the counterparties swap two streams of future interest payments. Section 9.2 looks at straightforward interest rate swaps while Section 9.3 looks at some less straightforward interest rate swaps. Section 9.4 looks briefly at three other types of swap: currency swaps, equity swaps and commodity swaps.

9.2 VANILLA INTEREST RATE SWAPS

Interest rate swaps involve two counterparties who swap streams of interest payments. With **asset interest rate swaps**, the counterparties are lenders who swap future interest receipts, whereas with **liability interest rate swaps** the counterparties are borrowers who swap future interest payments. Most interest rate swaps are **vanilla swaps** or **generic swaps** where one counterparty has a fixed rate stream and the other has a floating rate stream, and where each counterparty would prefer the other sort of stream. This section looks at vanilla swaps and begins with two examples to show why they are made.

An example where one counterparty has an absolute advantage in both streams

To see why two counterparties may agree interest rate swaps, take first a liability interest rate swap between two companies, Aco and Bco, that wish to borrow identical sums for five years. Aco is regarded as a less risky company and can thus borrow at more favourable rates. For example, if each borrows at fixed rates, perhaps by issuing five-year bonds, then Aco can borrow at 7% and Bco at 9%. And if they borrow at floating rates, perhaps by borrowing from their banks, then Aco can borrow at 2% above the six-month LIBOR, that is at (LIBOR + 2%), while Bco can borrow at (LIBOR + 3%). These available rates are shown in Table 9.1. The fact that Aco has access to more favourable rates with each type of stream means that Aco has an **absolute advantage** with each type while Bco, correspondingly, has an **absolute disadvantage** with each type.

Suppose Aco wants to borrow at a floating rate. Then it seems it must borrow at (LIBOR + 2%). And suppose Bco wants to borrow at a fixed rate. Then it seems it must borrow at 9%. However, they can improve on these rates of (LIBOR + 2%) and 9% if they make a swap. To see this, suppose Aco borrows at a fixed rate of 7%, while Bco borrows at a floating rate of (LIBOR + 3%). Suppose, also, that they agree a swap. In this swap, Aco will pay each year to Bco a floating amount equal to the amount that it has borrowed times LIBOR; this will add to Aco's costs but reduce Bco's costs. In return, Bco will pay each year to Aco a fixed amount equal to 5½% of the identical amount that it has borrowed; this will reduce Aco's costs but raise Bco's costs.

Table 9.1 shows their actual borrowing rates and the effects of the swap on their costs. It also shows their final effective borrowing rates. For example, Aco borrowed at 7% and also pays LIBOR to Bco, but it receives 5½% from Bco, so it is effectively borrowing at (LIBOR + 1½%). Bco borrowed at (LIBOR + 3%) and also pays 5½% to Aco, but it receives LIBOR from Aco, so it is effectively borrowing at 8½%. Each counterparty ends up effectively borrowing at a ½% lower rate than initially appeared possible, for Aco ends up effectively borrowing at a floating rate of (LIBOR + 1½%), while Bco ends up effectively borrowing at a fixed rate of 8½%.

Swaps always benefit both counterparties if the gaps in the interest rates they face are different on each type of stream. Here, the gaps in Aco's favour were 2% for the fixed rate stream and 1% for the floating rate stream, and it made sense for Aco to borrow at the fixed rate and for Bco to borrow at the floating rate. A counterparty should always use the stream where it has a **comparative advantage**, for it should either act like Aco and use the stream where it can borrow at a comparatively more favourable rate, or else act like

Table 9.1   The effects of a liability interest rate swap on borrowing rates

Company	Available rates	Actual rates	Effects of swap	Effective rates
Aco	7% and (LIBOR + 2%)	7%	+LIBOR − 5½%	(LIBOR + 1½%)
Bco	9% and (LIBOR + 3%)	(LIBOR + 3%)	−LIBOR + 5½%	8½%

Bco and use the stream where it can borrow at a comparatively less unfavourable rate. Having borrowed at the rates where they have a comparative advantage, they should then arrange a swap.

In the example, Aco was regarded as the better-quality borrower, and its lower rates reflected this superior quality. The case for the swap arose only because Aco had a different interest rate advantage on each stream. In effect, its better quality was perceived differently by bond buyers and the banks. This situation, where different quality borrowers face unequal gaps or spreads in the interest rates available to them on the two types of loan, is defined as one where there is a **quality spread differential**. In the example, there is a 2% spread on one stream and a 1% spread on the other. Quality spread differentials often arise and are often cited as reasons for swaps.

In practice, however, some care should be taken before the counterparties undertake swaps, despite the arguments for swaps presented above. In particular, Aco should consider why Bco is being asked to pay 2% more on fixed rate loans and only 1% more on floating rate loans. It could be that Bco has made a series of floating rate loans itself in the past, so that it is felt well able to maintain the interest payments on any floating rate loan made to it; but there may be a question mark over whether Bco could meet the interest payments on any fixed rate loans made to it, for if interest rates fell, then its income from any floating rate loans that it has made will drop. Thus the 2% addition for the fixed rate loan to Bco could be a result of it being perceived as a very risky loan to make to Bco. In turn, there must be a question mark over whether Bco really could honour its obligations under the swap to pay a constant 5½% to Aco. If Bco ever defaulted, then Aco would quickly decide that the swap had been a mistake.

However, it is sometimes argued that the quality spread differential does not reflect real differences in credit-worthiness for different types of loan. Typically, fixed interest loans are obtained by selling bonds, while floating interest loans are obtained from banks. If Bco is a little known company, or if it is a company with an unflattering history, then investors may well seek a 2% higher coupon, but Bco's bank may be better informed about its future prospects and may feel that a 1% extra is all that is needed. This argument is presumably accepted by the banks and dealers who act as one counterparty to most swaps, for they typically offer similar terms to all other counterparties and so do not seem troubled about the causes of quality spread differentials.

An example where one counterparty has an absolute advantage in only one stream

In the last example, one counterparty, Aco, had an absolute advantage in both streams. Sometimes a counterparty has an absolute advantage in only one stream. Even so, an interest rate swap will still be beneficial provided there are comparative advantages to exploit.

To see why, take an asset interest rate swap between two companies, a building society and a pension fund, that wish to lend identical sums for 10 years. If they lend at fixed rates, then maybe the best each can do is to buy bonds with

Table 9.2 The effects of an asset interest rate swap on lending rates

Company	Available rates	Actual rates	Effects of swap	Effective rates
Building society	6% and (LIBOR + 2%)	(LIBOR + 2%)	–LIBOR + 4½%	6½%
Pension fund	6% and (LIBOR + 1%)	6%	+LIBOR – 4½%	(LIBOR + 1½%)

a fixed 6% rate. If they lend at floating rates, then the pension fund may be limited to buying FRNs with a rate of 1% above the six-month LIBOR rate, that is (LIBOR + 1%), while the building society may be able to lend a mortgage at a rate of (LIBOR + 2%). These available rates are shown in Table 9.2.

Suppose the building society wants to lend at a fixed rate. Then it seems the highest rate it can get is 6%. Suppose the pension fund wants to lend at a floating rate. Then it seems the highest rate it can get is (LIBOR + 1%). However, they can improve on these rates of 6% and (LIBOR + 1%) if they make a swap. To see this, suppose that the building society lends at a floating rate of (LIBOR + 2%), while the pension fund lends at a fixed rate of 6%. Suppose, also, that they agree a swap. In this swap, the building society will pay each year to the pension fund a floating amount equal to the amount that it has lent times LIBOR; this will effectively reduce the building society's income but add to the pension fund's income. In return, the pension fund will pay each year to the building society a fixed amount equal to 4½% of the identical amount that it has lent; this will add to the building society's income but effectively reduce the pension fund's income.

Table 9.2 shows their actual lending rates and the effects of the swap on their incomes. It also shows their final effective lending rates. For example, Aco lent at (LIBOR + 2%) and also receives 4½% from Bco, but it pays LIBOR to Bco, so it is effectively earning a return of 6½%. Bco lent at 6% and also receives LIBOR from Aco, but it pays 4½% to Aco, so it is effectively earning (LIBOR + 1½%). Each counterparty will effectively end up earning at a ½% higher rate than initially appeared possible, for the building society ends up effectively earning at a fixed rate of 6½%, while the pension fund ends up effectively earning a floating rate of (LIBOR + 1½%).

In this example, the building society had an absolute advantage with the floating rate loan as it had access to a more favourable floating rate; the pension fund had a corresponding absolute disadvantage with floating rate loans. Neither counterparty had an absolute advantage or disadvantage with fixed rate loans. But, as always, what is required for swaps to benefit both counterparties is that the gaps in the interest rates they face are different on each type of stream. Here, the gap in the building society's favour for the fixed rate stream was 0%, but the gap in its favour for the floating rate stream was 1%, and it made sense for the building society to lend at the floating rate and for the pension fund to lend at the fixed rate. A counterparty should always use the stream where it has a comparative advantage, that is the stream where the gap is either more favourable or less unfavourable. Having borrowed at the rates where they have a comparative advantage, the counterparties should arrange a swap.

The terms agreed in swaps

The two examples considered above have shown that the counterparties stand to gain by making a swap. But they have not shown how the counterparties decide precisely how much interest to swap. To understand the basic principle, take a simple example where a swap is made between two companies, Cco and Dco.

Suppose, here, that Cco and Dco are companies of identical credit quality. Suppose, also, that they have each previously borrowed £100m, and suppose their loans have five years to run. Suppose, finally, that Cco is making floating interest payments on its loan, while Dco is making fixed interest payments on its. However, Cco wishes in future to pay fixed interest payments and Dco wishes in future to make floating interest payments. So they make a swap in which Cco will each year make a fixed interest payment to Dco, while Dco will make a floating interest payment to Cco. The question arises as to what is a fair interest rate swap between the two counterparties.

To answer this question, consider what rates Cco and Dco would have to pay if they today issued some five-year securities. If they issued five-year floating rate FRNs, then they might each find that they had to offer coupons of (LIBOR + 2%). If they issued five-year corporate fixed coupon bonds, then they might each find that they had to offer coupons of 7%. In these circumstances, they could fairly agree a swap in which Cco would pay Dco a rate of 7% in return for (LIBOR + 2%).

In practice, the swap of 7% for (LIBOR + 2%) would be simplified in two ways. First, it would be replaced by an equivalent swap, whereby Cco would give Dco 5% and Dco would give Cco LIBOR. This simply reduces by equal amounts of 2% the payments by each counterparty to the other. Secondly, instead of the counterparties paying each other large sums, they would agree that there would simply be a net flow in one direction or the other whenever interest payments were due. Thus if LIBOR was under 5%, Cco would pay the difference to Dco, and vice versa.

This example assumed that Cco and Dco have equal credit rating. Very often the counterparties are of different credit rating. Maybe Cco could issue bonds with a rate of 7% and FRNs with a rate of (LIBOR + 2%), while Dco would have to offer rates of 9% and (LIBOR + 4%). In this case, Dco will always pay 2% more than Cco. It would be fair either to do a swap using the rates faced by Cco, that is 7% in return for (LIBOR + 2%), or to do a swap using the rates faced by Dco, that is 9% in return for (LIBOR + 4%). But both of these would be equivalent to a simpler swap whose terms were 5% in return for LIBOR, and these are doubtless the terms that would be agreed.

In practice, many swaps are made with banks or other dealers, and it is the dealers who set the terms. They quote terms which apply to all the counterparties who make agreements with them. They set these terms to ensure that the total amount of fixed stream payments which they end up paying out just balances the total amount of fixed stream payments which they end up receiving, and also so that the total amount of floating stream payments which they end up paying out just balances the total amount of floating stream payments which they end up receiving. This is because it would be risky to have, say, a large net inflow of fixed stream payments and a large net outflow of floating stream payments, for then a rise in interest rates could cause them to make huge losses.

If, today, terms equivalent to 5% in return for LIBOR were fair for *all* companies of any credit standing, then the dealers would certainly quote those rates or terms. For if they quoted any other terms, they would find themselves committed to receiving large net inflows in one sort of stream and making large outflows in the other. To see why, suppose, for example, that they quoted 6% in return for LIBOR, and consider other counterparties who might want to borrow or lend.

For example, a counterparty which wanted to borrow might find that it could borrow at 9% or (LIBOR + 4%). If it wanted to borrow at a floating rate, then it would actually borrow at 9% and then do a swap where it received 6% from a dealer and paid LIBOR to the dealer. Thus it would effectively borrow at (LIBOR + 3%). Conversely, a counterparty which wanted to lend might find that it could lend at 6% or (LIBOR + 1%). If it wanted to lend at a fixed rate, then it would actually lend at (LIBOR + 1%) and then do a swap where it paid LIBOR to a dealer and received 6% from the dealer. Thus it would effectively lend at 7%. In each case, the dealers would end up receiving LIBOR and paying out 6%. So they would have an unbalanced position with a huge net inflow of floating stream payments and a huge net outflow of fixed stream payments.

In practice, the rates for fixed and floating rate streams which confront different companies are not all equivalent to an identical swap rate of, say, 5% in return for LIBOR. Indeed, it is only because companies face different relative rates that they are interested in making swaps at all. In practice, then, the terms quoted by dealers reflect the *average* differential faced by companies. For these are the terms that tempt as many counterparties to swap fixed streams for floating streams as they tempt to swap floating streams for fixed streams, and thus they are also the terms which will ensure that the dealers end up with balanced positions. When dealers quote these terms, they find that many companies agree swaps with them precisely because these average terms differ from those which the companies themselves face. This, in turn, means that the companies who make swaps have a comparative advantage in one stream and a comparative disadvantage in the other.

One further point to note is that dealers who put counterparties in contact make profits by charging commissions, whereas banks and dealers who act as counterparties make profits by having bid–ask spreads. Thus a bank might offer to pay, or bid, 4¾% in return for being paid LIBOR, and yet want, or ask for, 5¼% in return for paying LIBOR. The rates quoted by banks and dealers usually refer to the six-month LIBOR.

Closing out an interest rate swap

Parties to a swap sometimes wish to close out their swaps before the agreed maturity date. They can try to do this in three ways, though each will prove costly if swap terms have moved adversely between the effective date and the closing date. To illustrate these three ways, suppose a hypothetical company, LML, agrees a five-year swap in which it will pay to a dealer a fixed rate of 5% on £100m, that is £5m a year. In return, the dealer will pay to LML a sum equal to LIBOR on £100m. Suppose that three years after the effective date, LML wishes to close out.

First, LML could make a **swap reversal**. This would mean making an off-setting swap to pay LIBOR and receiving a fixed rate of interest. But when LML does this, the rate being offered against LIBOR might have fallen to, say, 4½%, so that LML would get only £4½m a year in return for paying LIBOR on £100m. So LML would end up receiving LIBOR on its first swap and paying LIBOR on the second, but also paying £5m on the first and receiving only £4½m on the second. So LML would lose £½m a year. Of course, if the rate being offered against LIBOR had risen to, say, 5½%, then LML would receive £5½m a year in return for LIBOR and so gain £½m a year.

Secondly, LML could try to arrange a **swap sale** or **assignment** which means finding someone to take over the swap. If the rate was still 5% against LIBOR, then LML might find someone who would take it over free of charge. But if the rate had fallen to 4½% against LIBOR, then LML would have to pay someone £½m a year to take it over. Of course, if the rate had risen to 5½% against LIBOR, then LML might find someone who would pay £½m a year to take it over.

Thirdly, LML might try to make a **cancellation**, **close-out** or **buy-back** in which it would seek to terminate the agreement with the original dealer. If the rate had fallen to 4½% against LIBOR, then LML would have to pay the dealer £½m a year to agree to this. Of course, if the rate had risen to 5½% against LIBOR, then the dealer might pay LML £½m a year in return for the cancellation.

9.3 VARIANT TYPES OF INTEREST RATE SWAP

As swaps are agreed over-the-counter, rather than on exchanges, their terms are often tailor-made. This section looks at some of the most common variants of interest rate swaps.

Forward swaps

Forward swaps have some characteristics of forwards. A forward swap resembles a vanilla swap except that the effective date when it will start is set some way off. When the effective date for a forward swap arrives, the terms agreed on new swaps may be different from those in the forward swap, so one counterparty will gain from having made a forward swap, while the other will lose.

Callable and putable swaps

Some interest rate swap contracts include clauses that allow one or other counterparty to terminate the agreement. With a **callable swap**, the counterparty gaining the fixed rate stream has the right to end it, and with a **putable swap**, the counterparty gaining the floating rate stream has the right to end it. The right to terminate the agreement can be important.

For example, suppose Bco borrows at a floating rate and then swaps a floating payment stream for a fixed payment stream, using a callable swap. If interest rates fall, Bco will terminate the swap and resume paying a floating rate stream on current low interest rates. Conversely, suppose a pension fund lends at a fixed rate and then swaps a fixed income stream for a floating income stream, using a putable swap. If interest rates fall, the pension fund will terminate the swap and resume receiving a fixed income stream, rather than persist with a floating stream on current low interest rates.

Swaptions

Swaptions are a type of option where the underlying asset is a swap. Each swaption contract specifies the expiry date of the swaption and the terms of the underlying swap. These terms include the strike price or **strike rate** of the swap, say 6% for LIBOR, and also the maturity date of the swap, say three years after expiry. Swaptions may be divided into European swaptions, which may be exercised only on the expiry date, and American swaptions, which may be exercised at any time up to it. Swaptions can also be divided into call swaptions and put swaptions.

Suppose X buys a **call swaption,** or **payer swaption**, at a strike rate of 6% for LIBOR. Then he has the right to exercise it and pay a fixed stream of 6% to the writer and receive LIBOR from the writer. This swaption would appeal to X if he has borrowed at a floating rate and fears that floating rates may rise, for, if they do, he can exercise the swaption and pay 6% in return for a high LIBOR which will help meet the high rate on his loan. The swaption would also appeal to X if he has lent at a fixed rate but thinks floating rates may soon rise and become more attractive, for, if they do, he can exercise the swaption and pay 6% in return for a high LIBOR and so, no doubt, increase his income.

In contrast, suppose Y buys a **put swaption**, or **receiver swaption,** at the same strike rate. Then she has the right to exercise it and pay LIBOR to the writer and receive a fixed stream of 6% from the writer. This swaption would appeal to Y if she has lent at a floating rate and fears that floating rates may fall, for, if they do, she can exercise the swaption and pay a low LIBOR in return for 6% which will prevent her income from falling. The swaption would also appeal to Y if she has borrowed at a fixed rate but thinks floating rates may soon fall and become more attractive, for, if they do, she can exercise the swaption and pay a low LIBOR in return for 6% and so benefit from the falling floating rates.

The binomial option pricing method outlined in Section 8.7 can be used to find the fair price of a swaption. To take a simple example, suppose X borrows £10m at a floating rate and makes an interest payment every six months. Each payment is set at £10m times a rate that is 2% above the six-month LIBOR that applied six months previously. X fears that LIBOR could rise briefly in 12 months, so he is worried about the LIBOR which will determine the interest payment which he will make in 18 months. To hedge against a high LIBOR, X buys a European call swaption which he can exercise in 12 months and which will allow him to pay 6% on £10m in return for LIBOR on £10m over a six-month period. If the six-month LIBOR in 12 months exceeds 6%, then X will exercise the swaption. Say LIBOR is 7%, so he does exercise it. Then, six months later, the writer will pay him the difference between LIBOR and 6% on £10m over 6 months, that is £50,000.

To estimate the fair price of this swaption, X can divide the period until expiry into steps. He can then estimate the volatility of LIBOR and so construct a binomial tree that gives him a range of possible LIBOR values in 12 months. Next, he can work out the value of the swaption at expiry at each of these possible rates. For example, he knows that if LIBOR is 7% at expiry, then he will receive £50,000 in 18 months, and he can work out the value of that sum in 12 months by adapting the standard present value techniques. Armed with these possible monetary gains in 12 months, X can use the normal right-to-left binomial process to estimate the current value of the swaption.

Amortising and accreting swaps

Amortising swaps occur when the sum on which the swapped interest rates apply diminishes over time and reaches zero by the maturity date. These swaps appeal to counterparties who have to pay interest on loans which they have borrowed and which they intend to repay gradually over the life of the swap. They also appeal to counterparties who have lent loans which will be gradually repaid over the life of the swap.

Accreting swaps are the opposite of amortising swaps. With accreting swaps, the sum on which the swapped interest rates apply increases at an agreed rate over time. These swaps appeal to counterparties who borrow increasing sums over the life of the swap. For example, a company might borrow extra sums over a period of three years while a new factory is built, thereby building up an increased debt with increasing interest obligations.

Basis swaps

Basis swaps arise when both the swapped streams are floating rate streams. These will only be made between two counterparties whose streams are based on different floating rates. For example, one stream might be based on LIBOR and the other on banks' base rates. Base rates change less often than LIBOR, so streams based on these two rates can move differently over time.

9.4 OTHER TYPES OF SWAP

Currency swaps

Currency swaps resemble interest rate swaps but there are two differences between them. First, the interest streams are in different currencies. Secondly, the counterparties swap the sums borrowed as well as the interest streams. Currency swaps can involve swapping a fixed rate stream for a floating rate one or swapping two streams of one type.

To see why currency swaps occur, and why the loans are swapped as well as the interest streams, consider a United Kingdom company UKco and a French company Fco. Suppose the current exchange rate is £1 = FFr7, and suppose that each company wants a fixed interest rate loan worth £10m or, equivalently, FFr70m. UKco finds that it can sell sterling bonds in the United Kingdom at 10% or franc bonds in France at 11%; French lenders want a higher coupon as UKco is little known there. Fco can sell sterling bonds in the United Kingdom at 11% and franc bonds in France at 10%; United Kingdom lenders want a higher coupon as Fco is little known here. It seems that each will borrow its own domestic currency in its own country at 10%. Certainly this will happen if UKco wants sterling to spend in the United Kingdom and Fco wants francs to spend in France.

But suppose UKco actually wants FFr70m to set up a French branch while Fco actually wants £10m to set up a United Kingdom branch. It may seem that each should sell 10% bonds in its own country and then convert the borrowed money into foreign currency, but doing so would be risky. To see why, consider UKco. At £1 = FFr7, it could borrow £10m and pay 10% interest, that is £1m a year, and it could convert the £10m into FFr70m. Moreover, its new French branch may well earn FFr7m a year profit which can be converted into £1m to meet the interest. However, there is a risk that the franc could fall in value. Thus the exchange rate might soon be, say, £1 = FFr10, in which case FFr7m would not cover the interest. To avoid the risks associated with exchange rate changes, UKco may feel it should borrow francs in France and pay the 11% interest required there.

For similar reasons, Fco may feel that it should borrow sterling in the United Kingdom and pay the 11% interest required here. However, both UKco and Fco could save 1% by doing a currency swap. UKco should borrow £10m in the UK at 10%, while Fco should borrow FFr70m in France at 10%. They can then swap the sums they have borrowed, and they can also swap their interest obligations. In this way, UKco has effectively borrowed FFr70m at 10% while Fco has effectively borrowed £10m at 10%, and each largely eliminates exchange rate risks.

In fact, the only remaining exchange rate risk concerns the repayment. In the example, UKco initially gives Fco £10m and is given FFr70m by Fco. When the swaps terminate, UKco will have to repay FFr70m to Fco and Fco will have to repay £10m to UKco. These sums will stand, no matter what the spot exchange rate is at maturity. Suppose, for example, that the spot rate is then £1 = FFr10. In that case, UKco need only spend £7m buying FFr70m to give to Fco, but it will be given £10m by Fco. So UKco will make a profit of £3m. Conversely, Fco will receive FFr70m from UKco, but it will also have to pay FFr100m to buy the £10m it must give to UKco. So Fco will make a loss of FFr30m. The gains and losses would work the other way if the franc had risen. If the repayment date is within about five years, then each counterparty might also be able to make a quite separate currency forward agreement to convert sterling and francs at an agreed forward rate when the repayments are due, and so hedge against the risk of making a loss at that time.

Equity swaps

Equity swaps are similar to interest rate swaps, but instead of two interest streams being swapped, at least one of the streams concerns the returns from some equities. The returns from equities accrue both through dividends and changes in the value of the shares. So equity swaps usually involve swapping an interest stream for a stream that is based on a FTSE total return index which covers both dividends and capital gains or losses. In effect, while two counterparties to an interest rate swap might agree to swap a fixed rate stream and a floating rate stream on a sum of, say, £1m, the counterparties to an equity swap might agree to swap the interest rate stream on, say, £1m, for the returns on £1m invested in equities. But they work out the value of the returns from the equities by using a FTSE total return index. Some equity swaps involve two streams of payments on total return indices. They could involve payments on two different indices for one country, but more usually they involve payments on indices for two different countries.

Table 9.3 gives an example of the payments that would arise in an equity swap agreed between X and Y. With this swap, X and Y will pay sums to each other at the end of each quarter. The table covers the first four quarters. X agrees to pay Y a sum at the end of each quarter which equals the interest that would have been earned by lending £1m over that quarter at the three-month LIBOR that applied at the start of the quarter. The table shows the LIBOR at the start of each quarter. At the start of the first quarter LIBOR is 6.00%. So, at the end of the first quarter, X owes Y one-quarter of 6% of £1m which is £15,000.

In return, Y agrees to pay X a sum at the end of each quarter that is based on the returns that would have been earned by investing £1m in equities at the start of the quarter. These returns are measured by the change in the FTSE 100 total return index over the quarter. Suppose this FTSE index is 2,000 at the start of the first quarter, as noted in the caption for Table 9.3. The first line of the table shows that the index rose to 2,150 over the first quarter, that is a rise of 7.50%. It is possible that Y agreed to pay this percentage of £1m to X, which would be £75,000. However, the counterparties to equity swaps whose payments, like Y's, are based on the FTSE index, usually agree instead to make base their payments on a slightly lower percentage than the change in that index. The reduction, or **equity swap spread**, is whatever is needed to make the same number of people willing to take each side of the swaps. In this example the spread is –0.5%. So Y's payment is 7.0% of £1m, rather than 7.5%, and that is £70,000.

In practice, there would be a single net payment each quarter. The net payment in the first quarter would be £55,000 from Y to X. This is shown in the last column of the table as a net payment from X to Y of –£55,000. In the second quarter, the FTSE 100 total return index *fell*, which means that shares had negative returns as a result of falling share prices. The fall was –4.5%, so

Table 9.3 An equity swap with a -0.5% spread and a starting FTSE index of 2000

Quarter	Three-month LIBOR at start of quarter (%)	X's LIBOR-based payments to Y (£)	FTSE 100 total return index at end of quarter	Change in FTSE index over quarter (%)	Y's FTSE-based payments to X (£)	Net payments from X to Y (£)
First	6.00	15,000	2,150.00	7.50	70,000	–55,000
Second	6.50	16,250	2,053.25	–4.50	–50,000	66,250
Third	6.25	15,625	2,114.80	3.00	25,000	–9,375
Fourth	5.75	14,375	2,135.95	1.00	5,000	9,375

Y owes X –5% of £1m, or –£50,000. This contributes to a large net payment of £66,250 from X to Y. There are smaller net payments in the last two quarters, and by chance these last two payments happen to offset each other exactly.

Commodity swaps

With **commodity swaps**, at least one counterparty swaps an income flow that is based on a commodity price. For example, X may each year give a dealer a stream equal to (LIBOR + 2%) on £6m, provided that each year the dealer gives X enough money to buy 100 tonnes of tin. This swap would appeal to X if X needs tin in his business and is worried that tin prices will fluctuate. It would especially appeal if X has made some floating rate loans at a rate tied to LIBOR, and so has an assured income related to LIBOR. The dealer would hope to make an offsetting swap.

Maybe the dealer makes an offsetting swap with Y, who is a tin producer. Y might agree to give the dealer each year a sum equal to the current value of 100 tonnes of tin in return for a receipt equal to (LIBOR + 2%) on £6m. This swap would appeal to Y if she is worried that tin prices might fluctuate, and yet she has borrowed a large sum at a floating rate tied to LIBOR, for the swap ensures that she can service her loan, no matter what happens to the price of tin.

SUMMARY

9.1   Swaps are contracts where two counterparties agree to swap future streams of periodic payments. They may swap future streams of payments that they will receive or swap future streams of payments that they will make.

9.2   Interest rate swaps involve two counterparties who swap interest streams. Most interest rate swaps are vanilla swaps or generic swaps where one counterparty has a fixed rate stream and the other has a floating rate stream, and where each counterparty would prefer the other sort of stream. These swaps are beneficial to each counterparty whenever one has a comparative advantage in one type of stream and the other has a comparative advantage in the other. Swaps are usually based on the average fixed and floating rates that different borrowers face.

9.3   There are several variant types of interest rate swap. These include forward swaps which start on an agreed future date, callable and putable swaps where one counterparty has the right to terminate the swap, and swaptions which one counterparty pays a premium for the right to initiate the swap. With basis swaps, both streams may be floating.

9.4   Currency swaps resemble interest rate swaps except that the streams are in different currencies and the sums initially borrowed or lent are swapped as well as the income streams attached to them. With equity swaps, at least one stream is related to the returns from equities; this stream is usually based on the performance of a total return equity index. With commodity swaps, at least one stream is based on the price of a commodity.

QUESTIONS

1. Explain what is meant by the following terms: (a) vanilla swap; (b) absolute advantage; (c) comparative advantage; and (d) quality spread differential.

2. LML wishes to borrow £10m in six months' time for six months at a fixed rate. The managing director thinks they should to hedge against a rise in interest rates before then. He asks for a memo explaining whether any of the following would be of any help, and, if so, their advantages and disadvantages: (a) an FRA; (b) an interest rate futures contract; (c) an interest rate futures option; (d) a vanilla swap; (e) a forward swap; (f) a putable swap; and (g) a swaption. Write such a memo.

3. X and Y agree to a swap over the next four years whereby X will pay to Y 5½% of £2m at the end of each year, while Y will pay to X the sum of LIBOR on £2m at the end of each year, each LIBOR being the published twelve-month LIBOR at the beginning of the year. What net cash flows will take place at the end of each of the next four years if the twelve-month LIBOR at the start of each year is successively 4%, 5%, 6% and 7%? At the end of the four years, would either counterparty feel it had made a net gain from the swap?

4. X and Y agree to a swap over the next two years, whereby at the end of each six-month period X will pay Y the interest due on £5m at the six-month LIBOR published at the beginning of the period. In return, Y will pay X the returns on £5m invested in equities as measured by the FTSE 100 total return index, allowing for a spread of –0.2%. LIBOR at the beginning of each of the four six-month periods is successively 6%, 6¼%, 6½% and 6¾. The initial value of the index is 2,000, while at the end of the four six-month periods its value is successively 2,200, 2,100, 2,150 and 2,250. What net cash flows will take place at the end of each six-month period?

INDEX

Note: references in **bold** show pages where the terms are printed in bold type and explained.